THE COMPLETE
Do It Yourself
BIKE BOOK

First published in 2006

This edition first published in 2009

10 9 8 7 6 5 4 3 2 1

Text and design © Carlton Books Limited 2009

A CIP catalogue record for this book is available from the British Library.

ISBN 13: 978-1-84732-416-0

Editor: Nigel Matheson
Design & art direction: Darren Jordan
Production: Lisa French
Layout photography: Karl Adamson
Picture research: Tom Wright
Author photograph: Julia Parry

Printed in China

THE COMPLETE
Do It Yourself
BIKE BOOK

MEL ALLWOOD

CARLTON
BOOKS

Contents

Contents

Introduction

There are plenty of really good reasons for using a bicycle to get around. It's good for you, it helps keep the air clean and it's good for the planet. All of these notions are very worthy and, no doubt, provide the impetus for many people to get out of their cars and back onto two wheels. But I'm sure there are plenty of others like me carrying around a guilty secret. We don't cycle because we're virtuous. We do it because it makes us smile.

I became a cyclist originally because I live in a big crowded city, and I'm an impatient traveller. Bikes are the quickest way to get around and mean you're travelling under your own steam. I can't be doing with sitting in a tin box in traffic, or waiting for another piece of non-existent public transport to arrive. I love being out and about, able to stop and start whenever I fancy as well as being close to the way the city changes with the seasons.

Even wet, miserable days are worth it because I know they'll be balanced by that great feeling of riding around when spring's just arrived, or when you get pushed all the way home after a long day by a miraculous autumn tailwind. Sitting in a car, with the heating on and the windows sealed, you're divorced from the weather and every journey is much like any other.

But once you own a bicycle, it doesn't take long to find that you'll enjoy it more if you've got an idea how it works. A little bit of knowledge means you're more self-sufficient, so that if something goes wrong by the side of the road or when you're just about to set off on a journey, you can sort it out and get on with your life. It's not all about emergencies though: if you've got a few tools and a bit of time to tinker, you can set your bike up so that it's comfortable to ride. And finally it's not just about fixing things that don't work. If you spend time keeping your bike clean and in good working order, the parts will last longer, saving you time and money. Regular, mild care and attention is much more effective, and cheap, than occasional guilty servicing frenzies.

None of the procedures listed in the mechanics section of the book are difficult, but that's not to say they're easy if you haven't done them before. However carefully you follow the instructions, they always take longer the first time than you expect. But each time you return to the same job – and some will become quite familiar, as city roads give you plenty of practice at punctures – it will get a little bit quicker and easier. You'll find yourself having to collect tools quite rapidly at first; each new job you tackle will require another gadget or two. Don't panic about this. The rate of acquisition tails off after a while and you'll find you can rely on a relatively small toolkit to cover most eventualities.

Part of what I love about bicycles is their simplicity. Bicycles rely on your energy to keep them moving, so there's a big incentive to make them as light as possible. This leads to almost zero tolerance for anything that's not essential to rolling you along – the bicycle is no 'kitchen sink' means of transport. Although appealing from an aesthetic perspective, this has its disadvantages. If everything's essential, then anything that goes wrong by the side of the road will stop you getting where you're going. This is why you should learn to tackle problems in an emergency. As a side benefit, since most bicycles work in similar ways, if you've learned to fix your own steed, chances are you can make yourself useful if somebody else has a problem, too.

Like so many bike mechanics, most of what I've learned about how to make bikes feel nice and work efficiently comes from just taking things apart and putting them back together. Bikes seldom need complex or expensive tools, but respond magically to a bit of care and attention – a nurtured bicycle feels better than a neglected one that cost twice as much. I've been very lucky to have had a job that I really loved, working for 18 years at Brixton Cycles Co-op in south London. Everything in this book comes from having spent that time trying to keep a startling range of different kinds of bicycle on the road for a sensible amount of money.

This book is particularly useful for people new to cycling, or new to using their bicycle to get about town. There's plenty of mechanics, starting with how to fix a puncture, but also advice for looking after the most important part of your cycling machine – you. Your body is the engine and needs to be allowed to work as efficiently as possible so that your journey can be made with a minimum of effort. This means you need to be warm, dry and comfortable – nobody ever gives their best effort when they're wet and cold. Hopefully, there are also some useful tips for the people who've had experience of tinkering with their bicycles, but want to expand into more involved procedures. Either way, what I hope you'll learn from it is how to understand your bicycle better and to feel more confident about working on it.

Whether you're completely new to cycling or have been riding for ages and want some tips to fix and maintain your machine, this book should help you get out there and enjoy riding your bike. I like the way cycling helps you see the world in a different way. Slightly more slowly, perhaps, but much more clearly.

Mel Allwood

Careful preparation saves trouble later

Cycling and mechanics

Most of this book is concerned with practical transport cycling, the type that gets you from where you are to where you want to be with the minimum of fuss. But there's nothing about this that means you have to buy a bicycle that's been specially made for riding around town. Don't be discouraged by the way catalogues from manufacturers divide their range into myriad different and distinct kinds of cycling, each of which has to be done on a specific type of machine designed for that exact task. This is convenient for them, but in reality you have to get pretty specialized before you actually need one kind of bike over another.

This becomes apparent whenever you check out the bikes that you stop beside at traffic lights. One minute you'll get some lean mean tri-bike, festooned with gadgets and widgets, then a folding shopper, then a fully suspended freeride monster that would look most at home hurtling off the back of an Alp. The great thing is that all of them do the job just fine.

When it comes to fixing them, bicycles are easier to work on than most of the other equipment you come across. They're made to be taken to pieces and put back together again, and all the spares are readily available in shops and online, which is something of a relief in what seems to have become a disposable world. They're light enough to turn over if you need to get a look at the other side, and to hang from a hook if you need to get them off the ground. All the mechanisms are visible without having to dig around under panels or shine a light into poky compartments. There's a surprising amount of compatability, too, which allows you to take a vital organ off one bike and put it on another made by a completely different manufacturer. And if you have a disaster and end up not being able to reassemble it in the right order, you can put the whole lot in a bag and take it to the bike shop on the bus to ask for help. If that's embarrassing, you can always lie and tell them that someone else took it to pieces.

Instructions that you find in books like these – and in the bumf you get with new parts – always seem to suggest that there's only one way of doing things. Once you've had a few goes at fixing your bicycle, you'll realise this isn't the whole story. Every repair is different and the instructions can only ever give you pointers towards guessing what the problem and the solution might be. I've tried as much as possible when explaining what you have to do to explain why as well. This should give you a chance to explore the possibilities if you come across something unusual.

Whenever you decide to fix your bike, the single best piece of advice has to be to make sure you have enough time to do it calmly. If you're trying out something you've never tackled before, do it when you know the bike shop is open, in case you

have to nip out for spares halfway through the job. Make time to clean your bike before you start fixing it. It's much quicker to do it this way than to have to wash your hands every five minutes all the way through a job on a dirty bicycle. It usually makes sense to take everything apart, work out what's wrong, get all the dirt off, then wash your hands before you start putting all the clean stuff back together.

There's a fair question about why you would want to fix your own bike when you can take it to the shop and pay a mechanic to do it for you. Any good mechanic will be able to make your bicycle work well. But only you will be able to make it work exactly how you like it. It'll take you longer to get it on the road than the pro would, but you'll be able to tinker away until your brakes feel just like you like them to and your gears change just when you expect them to.

If your bike does let you down by the side of the road, you're in a much better position to sort it out if the broken part is something you've worked on, or even just cleaned, recently. At least you knew what it looked like before it was broken, so you have an idea what you're supposed to be working towards.

And this brings us to what I think is the most important bit. Working on your bike means you're familiar with it, so you're much more likely to know that something on it is not quite how it should be – maybe the tyres are a little soft, indicating the onset of a slow puncture, or the brakes aren't biting as crisply as usual, suggesting that the brake blocks may be wearing out. This gives you a chance to sort whatever it is out before it lets you down.

I've got a strong bias towards real bike shops. There's a lot to be said for being able to go somewhere where somebody can actually look at your bike and help you work out where you've gone wrong with your repair. You'll generally find that, if you bought the bits off them in the first place, the person in the bike shop will be happy to give you advice about how to fit it so that it works. And if that helps you out, it can do you no harm to let them know by giving them biscuits or beer occasionally as well.

Regular commuting

For me, the best thing about using my bicycle to get about is that I arrive at places alert and full of beans. Travelling by public transport can be fine, and you can read the paper as you go, but you can never really tell how long it's going to take. Driving in cities generally leaves me annoyed and distracted, as well as confused as to why it always takes so much longer to get places in the car than the bicycle would have taken. Having said that, cars are great for some things, like transporting flat-pack furniture, getting to places on the other side of the country or climbing into to eat your picnic in comfort on really rubbish days.

Commuting to work on a bicycle doesn't raise many eyebrows any more. So many people are doing it that it's normal, rather than a sign of being slightly strange and probably unreliable. More enlightened offices and workplaces are coming round to the idea that employees who arrive by bicycle are healthier and more punctual than those who don't, and so are beginning to install showers, lockers, and secure bike parking – although it may well be that the motivation behind this is more cynical, having more to do with somebody in the accounts department realising how much it costs to build and maintain company car parks. But whatever the underlying reason, these kinds of facilities are becoming more common and they make it easier to cycle to work if you have the kind of job where you have to look smart.

There's no need to be fanatical about cycle commuting. You don't need to do it every day, especially when you're just starting out. It's a perfectly normal thing to combine cycling to work with driving, walking or using public transport. Unlike a car or a season ticket, it doesn't cost you anything to leave your bike in the garage for a few days. There's no reason not to cycle to work, then leave your bike there and catch the train home. You can take the train if it starts snowing, or drive in on days when you need to be particularly smart, or have a day off the bike if you're feeling under the weather.

Lots of people using their bikes regularly has the same effect on reducing traffic levels as a few people using them obsessively in all conceivable circumstances.

Commuting by bike isn't just the usual A-to-B, home-work-home journey either. It's going to bits of your city you've never discovered before, travelling slowly enough to actually see where you are. And generally you're going so slowly that, if you spot something interesting, you can stop and take a proper look.

This just doesn't happen in cars, where you whizz along concentrating on the traffic lights and missing all the good stuff. Getting about by bicycle allows you to enjoy the bits of your city that you normally sail through, oblivious to all the interesting things happening around you.

On a bicycle you get to see interesting parts of the city that you would normally miss out on in a car

New cyclists

Cycling seems to have reaped the benefits of two big changes in attitude in the last few years. More people have become concerned about the environmental damage that cars do to urban environments, and more people are becoming worried about the effects on their health of a sedentary lifestyle, while at the same time being too busy to find enough time to get themselves regularly to the gym to get some exercise in.

Cycling to work provides a neat solution to both these problems in one go, by getting you out of your car and letting you pedal your way to the office under your own steam. It's a lot less pointless than pounding away on the running machine without getting anywhere, or churning backwards and forwards across the pool. On top of that, the constantly changing view makes it impossible to be bored.

The result has been that, where it used to be possible to cycle home on a wet winter evening and not see another cyclist, now you'll often find yourself just one of a great flock of riders. This makes you more visible – and so safer – not just because of the industrial quantities of eyewatering yellow fabric, but through sheer weight of numbers.

Most people are persuaded to start cycling for practical, rational, sensible reasons. But one of the things I like most about talking to recent converts to cycling is their shocked discovery that they actually enjoy it. Instead of being a chore that they

New cyclists should remember that, if their equipment looks too new and shiny, they could become the victim of thieves

have to talk themselves into for the purposes of reducing their carbon footprint or their waistline, they find that the bicycle gets them about quicker than before and is more reliable than they'd ever expected.

Of course, there exists a reasonable element of danger to cycling on the roads. Nipping about in the traffic can be exhilarating, but you cannot rely on car drivers to be concentrating, to behave in a predictable manner or to be looking where they're going.

And the consequences of their inattention could be much more serious for you than they would be for them. They're swaddled in their tin boxes with airbags and seatbelts to cushion them from the effects of their actions. If you've been commuting for a while, you get a sixth sense for when somebody's about to do something daft. But when you've just started, you may not yet have the full radar, so busy streets can be daunting.

There are two bits of good news. The first is that the benefits to your health of

Nipping in and out of traffic can be exhilarating, but don't rely on drivers to look where they are going

the vigorous exercise that cycling gives you far outweigh your chances of injury. The second is that a bit of preparation goes a long way towards keeping you out of trouble. A helmet will protect your head and remind drivers that it needs protecting. Keeping your bike in good working order also means you can react quickly to events around you, braking or sprinting out of trouble at short notice. Making sure you're always alert means that you have plenty of time to respond to the unexpected. Staying well away from lorries is essential. They're too big to argue with and seldom have any idea that you're there.

Finally, just take things at your own pace, making the journeys you feel comfortable with and confident about and leaving the trickier ones for a later date.

One of the problems with starting off as a new cyclist is that suddenly it seems like you need a whole bunch of expensive gear to cope with every eventuality. Bike shops are full of Shiny Appealing Gadgets and, if you're anything like me, it's easy to persuade yourself that they're all essential. The only way around it is to build up your kit store gradually, buying as and when you need items rather than trying to kit yourself out all at once. Some things have to be bought to cope with seasons, others to deal with specific tasks. Eventually, though, there does come a time when you've got enough of everything to cope and you only have to get new kit to replace items you've worn out.

The other problem suffered by shiny new cyclists is that shiny new bicycles are appealing to the light-fingered. They glint in the sunlight and act as magnets for opportunist thieves. Sadly, new cyclists are often not as thorough in their locking-up ritual as they'll be when they become more seasoned and this can lead to a spate of losses near the beginning of your cycling career. The key message is always to be thinking about how and where to lock, as well as what with.

Making your bike look less appealing to the casual observer helps too. Personalisation always makes it more readily identifiable and therefore less saleable. Camouflage is also good. Anything you can paint or stick on will make it look less like a new bike. It's a lot easier to make a new bike look dishevelled than to make an old bike work like new.

If you feel nervous about the traffic, get some lessons in how to ride safely. Going out in your local area with an instructor will give you invaluable tips on how to ride in a way that means that other road-users can see you, predict what you're going to do next and thus avoid you.

Help can often be forthcoming from your cycling mates, a local cycling club or one of the national cycling organisations. Your local bike shop is likely to have access to resources in your area. They'll be happy to help – after all, it's in their interests for you to become a regular cyclist!

1 – Kitting out

For short trips on a warm sunny day, you need very little kit to enjoy cycling – maybe a lock and some lights if you're due back after dark. You can get away with wearing normal clothes: sling a bag over your shoulder and you're off. But don't let the threat of bad weather put you off as, with the right protective clothing, you can be warm and dry whatever the sky throws at you. Don't be put off by the expense either. You definitely don't need to rush out and buy everything in this chapter all at once – just pick up what you need when you need it.

Choosing a bike: hybrids

There's a good chance your bike choice might already have been made as you might have inherited something that works or you might have bought one previously. But at some point in your future cycling career you may well find yourself having to choose a machine that suits you. It may be new or second-hand, but either way you'll find yourself having to make some decisions.

The range of models on display can be overwhelmingly confusing. So we'll start by having a look at some of the general types on offer and going through the reasons for choosing one over the others.

The four basic choices are a hybrid, a folder, a road bike or a mountain bike. Your decision will depend on a range of factors. For example, you may want to do more than just commuting on your bike. If you fancy a bit of off-road riding, then it's worth getting a mountain bike and fitting slick tyres on it for road use. If you want to get fit, a road bike with its narrow smooth tyres means you can sprint around the countryside at weekends, burning off calories in the process. Folding bikes are perfect for longer commutes as you can ride to the train station or the bus stop and hop aboard with your steed. But, if your bike's main use is going to be riding backwards and forwards to work, it's a good idea to choose something that's been designed for the job. Hybrids originally got their name because the first generation of

this type of bike was a hybrid between a chunky, strong mountain bike and a fast, lean road bike. Since then, however, they exist in their own right, designed to be comfortable and quick around town and to take the punishment out of riding around in the city.

One great advantage of a hybrid is the riding position. Straight bars and a high front end put you in a great position to check out what's going on around you. Brake-levers and shifters are both accessible without taking your hands off the bars. The wheels are slightly larger than mountain bike wheels. This helps you ride over lumps and holes in the road without the wheel dropping in and out of every dip. The frame will have braze-ons for mudguards, rear racks and possibly front racks as well, making it easy to bolt accessories securely straight to the frame. Hybrids have a wider range of gears than road bikes. They are spaced out evenly with enough gears in the high end of the range so that you can speed down hills or sprint for the lights without your legs having to spin ridiculously fast.

Specialized Crossroads

Choosing a bike: folding bikes

Folding bikes have experienced something of a renaissance recently. Previously, they were considered a bit of a joke: unwieldy to collapse and ungainly to ride.

This change in perception is mainly a result of pioneering design work by Brompton Bicycles, which proved it was possible to construct an altogether more satisfying bicycle for a sensible amount of money. With any folding bike, there will always be a compromise between its folding capability, the quality of the ride and its price. You might need to fold and unfurl your bicycle every single time you ride it, but only ever use it for short hops. Or it might spend almost all its time shaped like a bicycle and only get packed away during flights to exotic locations. Whatever you want, somebody out there has made a design with you in mind.

If you're plagued by bicycle theft, a folder could be the ideal solution as packed away it can go with you wherever you are. You can leave it tucked under your desk or take it in at night and park it under your bed. And it's great for days when you decide you're too knackered to cycle home as you can easily take it back with you on a bus or a train. If you find the potential for punctures and other mechanical problems puts you off commuting, again,

a folder might well be the answer. It means you can finish your journey and then sort the problem out at your leisure.

Smaller wheels are one of the distinguishing features of folding bikes. There are plenty of tyre choices around now, with as many puncture-resistant bands and reflective strips as you could hope for. Tyre pressure is even more critical with smaller wheels than with the standard 700C (hybrid) or 26-in (mountain bike) sizes – let them go soft and you'll feel like you're running in wellies. A decent track pump is a great accompaniment to a folding bike.

Using a folding bike to swap between cycling and public transport increases your range and flexibility considerably. Once folded, the bike seems to count as innocent luggage, rather than the perception of bikes as a potential fire hazard or terrorist threat that the standard configuration seems to inspire in authorities. For further disguise, a bag that covers the whole folded machine is handy. It also means you can more easily slip the thing into luggage racks, taxi boots and between seats.

Brompton folder

Choosing a bike: road bikes

Racing bikes come in all shapes and sizes, but they share some common features. The frames are light with a long, low shape that encourages you to ride in an aerodynamic, stretched-out position. The wheels are narrow with skinny tyres designed to be pumped up to high pressures. Drop handlebars accentuate your tucked-in position and the brake-levers and gear shifters are combined into one unit so that you don't have to take your hands off the bars to make quick gear changes.

Racing bikes aren't usually the most practical choice for city commuting. The frames and wheels are relatively delicate and the brakes are designed for lightweight – rather than emergency – stops. The range of gear ratios is narrow, so if you find yourself climbing a steep hill you have no choice but to get up off the pedals and pull yourself upwards. But if you like going quickly, they're really good fun.

The lightweight frame and tight angles mean that they will accelerate in an instant and they make easy work of hills for the same reasons. The aerodynamic position minimises your wind resistance, saving your energy. And, if you've still got any left after commuting to work all week, a racing bike is an ideal steed to escape from the city on. Once you've left the traffic behind,

you can spin along country roads and enjoy some fresh air.

Racing bikes often don't have the capacity to attach mudguards, which makes journeys in the rain a bit more of a palaver as you can't just pop out in your normal clothes and expect your mudguards to protect you from showers. Even if you have the braze-ons for a rack – so that you can bolt the rack fittings directly to the frame – the narrow tyres and skinny wheels will be less stable under load and less durable in the long term if you carry heavy loads around.

But there's no denying that they're quick and nippy and, if your normal route is hilly, you'll notice the lighter weight. And, while nothing is immune to bike thieves, the bendy bars seem less attractive than the universal currency of the mountain bike.

Specialized Dolce

Choosing a bike: mountain bikes

When mountain bikes first began appearing on city streets, it was common to hear non-cyclists say things like, 'What's the point? There aren't any mountains around here.' Traditional cyclists said things like, 'What's the point? They're so heavy.' Of course, both of these points were true unless you actually did live near some mountains or spent unfeasible amounts of money. But – heavy and clunky as they were – they proved to be exactly what urban commuters were looking for.

Robust and tank-like with brakes that actually worked and gears you could use without taking your hands off the grips, mountain bikes made it easy for people to ride bicycles without having to be cyclists.

Of course, many of the factors that make a bike great for mountain biking weren't ideal for urban use. Big, chunky mud tyres on tarmac feel like trying to run in treacle. Frames don't need to be strong enough for you to ride down flights of steps and a gear range suitable for climbing mountains will leave your legs spinning wildly in top gear when you try to sprint to beat the lights. But the best aspects were borrowed for a new generation that became hybrids or city bikes.

This doesn't mean there's no room for mountain bikes round town. If you ever find yourself wanting to take your bike off road, it's great to be able to swap your road slicks for a pair of knobbly tyres and slip off into the countryside. Equally, if you carry a lot of weight around on your bike, the slightly smaller 26-in wheels are stronger than 700C hybrid ones and will take a wider, more protective tyre.

And, if you're just hard on bikes, a mountain bike is that much tougher. There are a huge range of slick tyres on the market and this is the only real change you'll need to turn a trail machine into a tarmac tank.

Specialized Rockhopper

What to wear: jackets

Your raincoat is your first line of defence against the elements. Unless you live somewhere with year-round sunshine, you'll need something that stops you getting cold, wet and miserable. Cycling around town makes an extra demand on your cycling clothing as you're usually going somewhere, rather than cycling around in circles just for the fun of it.

This means you have to consider what the jacket looks like off the bike too – a skintight tube of fluorescent yellow might be very efficient, but it's not an attractive item to wear to the pub at the end of the day. Jackets perform three functions. They keep you dry when it's raining and warm when it's windy or cold. Also, since purpose-made cycling jackets are so often used as an outer layer in the wet, they often have reflective stripes or tabs. These are especially valuable in the rain, since that's when car drivers seem to concentrate least on who they're sharing the road with.

While any jacket will provide you with protection, something bike-specific will do the job better, simply because it's made for the job. These are some of the features you'll want to look out for:

Cut

Cycling clothes are designed to fit you properly when you're sitting on the bike, so they often look odd when you're standing up. A cycling jacket will have a longer back to ensure your kidneys don't get cold and wet. It will also help protect your bottom from the spray that comes off the road if you don't have mudguards. The arms are slightly longer than normal since you're generally reaching forward to the bars. If the sleeves were of normal length, your wrists would be exposed and get cold and wet quickly. The front of the jacket should be cut short so your legs can move freely. If the jacket reaches down as far as the front of your thighs, you'll find your legs lift up the jacket with every pedal stroke, sucking cold air in.

Sealing

The neck, wrists and around the waist need to be draughtproof. Best of all are toggles that you can pull tighter and release with one hand so you can keep your ventilation and warmth balance just right.

Pockets

There's a conflict here. When you're wandering around off the bike, you definitely want pockets at the front of your jacket. You can put your keys in them or your hands to keep them warm. However, front pockets are a bit of a pain when you're riding along. Anything in them weighs the front of the jacket down, misshaping it so that it creates a big draughty space inside the jacket instead of fitting warmly and snugly with no gaps. You may also find that precious things drop out of your pocket as you ride along. A good solution is to put the pockets on the back. It goes against your instincts at first, but means that anything you put in your pocket will stay there.

Features

Pockets, storm flaps, extra zips and hoods are all good, but any features you add to the jacket make it more bulky. This is fine if you know it's definitely going to rain, because you will sling your jacket on anyway. Trouble starts on 'just-in-case' days. A jacket with fewer features that packs smaller is more likely to be used. A larger, bulkier one is more likely to get left at home in a dose of optimism where it will be no good to anyone.

Safety is more important than vanity: bright clothing is essential on dark days since it will keep you visible on your bike; reflective piping and tabs are more than useful at night since they help you stand out in headlights

Colour

If you're going to be riding in town, then anything that helps drivers to see you is an advantage. Bright yellow is obviously the best in terms of visibility, although some people struggle with the idea of riding around looking frighteningly like a banana. Jackets need to be versatile enough to cope with being worn off the bike as well as on it and sometimes that means compromise in the visibility department.

Fabric

There is a bewildering array of different fabrics available. Generally, all claim to be the best at everything. There are a few key things you need to look out for. The level of waterproofing is often the deciding factor. There are two distinct types: waterproof and water-resistant. Water-resistant will protect you from showers. Waterproof is more expensive and will keep you dry for longer. In fact, better fabrics, such as Gore-Tex, will keep you dry all day. Water-resistant jackets will keep you dry on shorter journeys – up to about 40 minutes in a shower or 20 in heavy rain. After that, they'll start to leak, usually through the seams first. But if your average commute is 20 minutes or so, a water-resistant jacket will do the job just fine, saving you a large chunk of money.

It's essential that the fabric of the jacket is breathable. However casual you are about cycling, there will be times when you're working hard enough to get hot and sweaty. Breathable fabrics are made so that the moisture you generate can easily pass out of the jacket, stopping you from ending up swimming in a puddle of your own making.

Windproofing

This is more important than it sounds. You're constantly moving through the air, so effectively when you're cycling it's always windy. On hot days this is great as it keeps you cool. On cold, damp days, you'll get cold very quickly and the faster you move, the colder you'll get, especially on long downhills when you're not working hard enough to keep you warm. Luckily, windproof fabric can be made very thin and light. A shell that you can throw on during chilly days won't take up much room in your bag and will even fit in your pocket.

Hoods

Generally, they're rare on cycling jackets since many people wear a helmet. A better option is usually a hat as it turns with your head. The experience of glancing back at traffic before a perilous manoeuvre and getting a clear view of the inside of a hood puts people off them quite quickly.

What to wear: lower half

Weather protection depends on the length of your journey and the climate. In mild weather you can cycle around in whatever you normally wear – high heels can be a little unstable and jeans are quite sweaty, but pretty much anything will work. Trouser legs need to be either rolled up or strapped out of the way of chain oil with a trouser clip. But if it's hot, cold or wet, you'll need to think through your lower-half options.

Proper cycling shorts look ridiculous on the rail in the shop and feel ridiculous the first time you try them on as the padding makes it feel like you're wearing a nappy. But they're not designed to be hung on a rail or stood about in. They only make sense when you realise that you can happily sit in the saddle all day, then go on to sit on something more conventional like a chair without wincing. More expensive shorts are specifically designed for men and women's different anatomies, although even the most basic will make your saddle more comfortable. Your saddle should be comfortable. Don't listen to anyone who tells you that you should 'break a new saddle in' or that 'you'll get used to it'. If it's not comfortable, get some proper cycling shorts or a new saddle, or both.

Clockwise from left: shaped seamless chamois will keep you comfortable on the saddle; baggy shorts are more flattering; grippers round the bottoms of the legs stop fabric from riding up

Choosing shorts can be quite confusing. The expensive ones look almost identical to the ones that cost a quarter of the price, so it's difficult to understand what you're getting for the extra money. One of the major differences is the fabric – pricier shorts are made of more breathable material, like Coolmax, which keep you cool and dry. They will also be made up of more, smaller panels, so that the shape of the short will follow your contours as you cycle. Padding is more sophisticated in expensive shorts and can be more supportive and comfortable without being too thick.

If you're commuting on hot days you'll probably want to change when you arrive. It's a good thing to share the warm glow of your commute with your colleagues, but you don't want to become a health hazard. And unless you work in a particularly casual environment, cycling shorts don't make you look professional. Enlightened employers provide showers, lockers and changing facilities, but even a lavatory can be pressed into temporary service.

Good, comfortable shorts are made of Lycra, Coolmax or similar stretchy materials. This works well, but for most of the population it isn't particularly flattering as it emphasises every curve in ways most of us would rather not. However, there is absolutely no law against wearing whatever you want over your cycling shorts such as baggy shorts, a skirt or whatever you fancy.

Nobody need ever know that you're sporting a skintight layer underneath. You can even get bike shorts that have a baggy outer layer concealing a proper pair of cycling shorts underneath. There's a final thing about cycling shorts that nobody ever tells you: they're designed to be worn next to the skin, with nothing underneath.

Cold weather

In some ways, very cold weather is easier to deal with than in-between days. You can just put on everything you own and then cycle as fast as you possible can to keep warm.

Tights should go over shorts, not the other way around for the Superman look. Tights always have a seam in the middle, which you don't really want to be sitting directly on as the shorts are there to protect you from that.

Once it gets colder, choose tights with a fleecy lining. This traps the heat generated by the work your legs are doing and keeps everything snug. Make sure you choose a pair that are long enough to cover your ankles even when your legs are bent. As with your wrists, this is where your blood is carried close to the surface of your skin, so once it gets chilled you tend to get really cold. The same goes for the waistband at the back and, when you're sitting on your bike, this should come up high enough to overlap your jacket as exposed skin will chill quickly.

Knees are complex joints and need to be taken care of as much as possible. Cycling is rarely bad for knees on its own, but it can aggravate other injuries if not treated with care. Keeping your knees

Overtrousers should be wide enough to fit easily over your shoes: but make sure they are breathable or your legs will get horrible and sweaty inside them

warm on chilly days makes a big difference. If you hurl them out into the cold and expect to be able to stamp up hills without any warm-up, they'll protest. If you've had a history of knee injuries, wear leggings until it's really warm or get three-quarter length shorts as these come right down over your knees.

Wet weather

Rain causes a bit of a dilemma about what to wear on your legs. Your legs are the part of your body that's working the hardest, which will mostly keep them warm even if they're wet. So getting your legs wet shouldn't be as much of a problem in the rain as not having a proper jacket. This is fine if your trousers fit fairly close and you don't have to spend the rest of the day standing around in them. But wet, loose trousers that flap about never warm up, no matter how hard you work. Waterproof trousers, therefore, are useful for keeping your normal trousers dry, even if your legs don't need it. But, unless you have very breathable waterproofs, they get horrible and sweaty inside and you'll end up wishing you hadn't bothered to try and keep dry. Waterproof trousers over shorts seems like an odd combination, but they work much better than you expect as long as you have somewhere to change out of your shorts at the other end.

Choose a pair of waterproof trousers with reflective tabs. If it's cold the chances are it will be wet and dark as well. They should be baggy enough so that there's room for your knees to bend and so that you can pull them on over your shoes by the side of the road – if you have to take your shoes off you will probably step in a puddle, which spoils the point of putting on waterproof trousers to stay dry. Long zips that come most of the way up your calves or a wide pleat at the bottom that can be cinched in tight with Velcro tabs both work well, especially if you can get them open and closed without taking your gloves off.

What to wear: shoes

Many people who cycle as their main form of transport prefer to wear as many of their normal clothes as possible. This makes it easier to arrive at places without looking like you've just won a stage of the Tour de France and to leave places without spending half an hour fiddling around with gadgets and gear.

However, it's often the shoes that give people away as more serious cyclists than they'd care to admit to being. The realisation that cycling kills normal shoes is often a major push towards specialist shoes. Any pedal that's got enough grip to keep you securely connected to your bike will tear away at the soles of your shoes. It also makes cycling shoes appear much cheaper when you realise how much longer they last than trainers.

The other reason for choosing shoes that have been specifically designed for cycling is that they have very much stiffer

Good shoes needn't be ugly

soles than ordinary shoes, making you more efficient. All of the precious energy that you use to push your feet around goes into turning the pedals, rather than being wasted scrunching up the soles of your feet.

Cycling shoes also support your feet much better across the whole width of the sole, so that you don't get sore patches under the balls of your feet where the pedals sit. You don't need to ride around looking like you've got crisp packets on your feet, however. There are plenty of options that look very much like trainers so you can get away with wearing them without looking overdressed. There's also a real advantage to having stiff soles in very hot

Specialized trail boots

and very cold weather. If the whole sole of your foot is supported, you can relax it. In cold weather this means that blood can flow freely all the way to your toes, keeping them a bit warmer. In hot weather air can flow around your skin, keeping your feet a bit cooler.

Clipless pedals

Clipless pedals lock securely into cleats on the soles of your shoes, yet release instantly when you twist your feet. The cleat is a metal key, fitting precisely into the release mechanism of the pedal. The cleat will only fit onto the bottoms of shoes that have been specifically designed to take them and you cannot fit them onto ordinary shoes. Luckily, there is something that approximates to a universal standard for attaching cleats to cycling shoes so you're not stuck with using pedals, shoes and cleats from the same manufacturer. The most usual set-up is that used by Shimano, which consists of two bolt holes deeply recessed into the sole. A range of different manufacturers make pedals and cleats that fit into this shoe pattern.

This universal standard applies only to shoe/cleat combinations, however. It doesn't apply to pedal/cleat combinations. A set of clipless pedals will come with its own cleats and is only designed to work properly with those cleats. This means that, once you've fitted your cleats to your shoes, you can't automatically jump onto somebody else's bike and use their clipless pedals unless they're the same make and, in some cases, the same model.

Be sure to try on a range of shoes before you choose, especially if you have, or are thinking of using, clipless pedals. You need a pair that fits snugly around your feet. It's important that your feet can't twist around in the shoes, otherwise, when you come to try and release your shoe from the pedal by twisting the shoe, you'll find that your foot will slide around inside the shoe without releasing.

The SPD-type clipless pedals are by far the most common. Their biggest advantage is that the cleat is recessed into the sole so that you can walk easily. There is another type of pedal, typically used on racing bikes. These have a larger cleat that protrudes out from the surface of the sole. However, they're not a great idea for using round town as the cleat makes the shoes very slippery to walk on, especially if it's wet.

Cleats must be bolted to the soles of the shoe

What to wear: overshoes and gloves

Cold weather makes extra demands on your feet as they're stuck way out on the end of your body, a position which tends to leave them exposed when the temperature plummets. As you pedal, they're spinning around as well as moving along so the wind chill factor is exaggerated.

The most obvious solution is overshoes. These are booties made of neoprene, Gore-Tex or nylon that you pull on over your shoes. They have a cut-out window in the sole for the shoe to grip the pedal or, if you're using clipless, for the cleat to poke out. Velcro secures them tightly around your shoes and they usually have some retro reflective strips on the back.

These keep the wind and water off your feet and have the added advantage of keeping your shoes dry, essential if you have to spend the rest of the day walking around in them. They do look a bit daft, but that seems like quite a small price to pay for comfy toes. Take them off as soon as you get off the bike. If you walk around in them, the soles wear quickly and once they're torn they don't stay on your feet properly. They're especially useful if you don't have a front mudguard. Water from the road gets picked up by your front tyre and carried a little way around the wheel by its rotation. Soon enough, however, it sprays off the back of the tyre and gets dumped all over your feet.

If you really can't imagine yourself being seen in overshoes, you can get waterproof socks. There are a few different brands, but the best are made by SealSkinz. You wear them instead of ordinary socks. They're a little bit stiffer than normal socks and so feel a bit strange, but keep out both the wind and the water. They're thicker than normal socks too, so make sure there's enough room in your shoes. If it's too much of a squeeze, you'll restrict the circulation of warm blood down to your feet, which will then get cold anyway. Wear your largest shoes.

Cycling shoes come with variable amounts of ventilation. Some are almost all mesh, which is great for hot weather, but useless in winter. If you're mainly dealing with the cold, look for a pair that has few or no mesh areas.

These overshoes have plenty of reflective piping, front and back

Gloves

Keeping hands warm is a number one priority from the beginning of autumn to the end of spring. There are a few things to look out for in winter gloves. The material obviously needs to insulate your hands. But windproofing is equally important as your hands are really exposed, sitting up out front on your bars in the full force of the wind. If they're wet as well, the wind will strip the heat from your skin. Even if your gloves aren't waterproof, choose something windproof. Fully waterproof gloves tend to be expensive as the complicated shape of your hands tends to mean lots of seams, all potential routes for water to get in.

The thickness of the material is also an issue and you'll always find yourself in situations where you have to operate keys or fumble for your phone. It's no good having a lovely warm pair of gloves and then having to rip them off every time you want to do something. You'll also appreciate padding on the palms to absorb vibration from the road. Cycle-specific gloves have padded palms, to protect hands from vibration. This is especially worthwhile if you work at a computer for hours on end as jumping onto the bike at the end of the day can leave you with sore wrists, elbows and shoulders.

Summer gloves with short fingers fit quite snugly. Try on a few pairs since different manufacturers put the padding in different places and they seem to suit different people. What's comfortable depends on how your hands approach your bars.

Full-finger gloves keep you warm. Mitts protect your palms even on really hot days

What to wear: thermals, layers

This page is primarily about cold weather. Warmer weather is usually easier to deal with, but there's something satisfying about bundling yourself up against the elements and cycling around all snug in your cocoon. Sometimes, if the weather's really bad, you cycle past a bus queue and you can see that someone in it has seen you and feels sorry for you. But if you've got the right gear, the chances are you're warmer than they are. You'll probably get where you're going first as well.

The basic problem with very cold weather is that you need to be able to change the amount of insulation you're wearing quickly and constantly. When you first step out of the front door on a cold day, you need enough on to keep you from freezing until you've jumped on your bike and got moving. Halfway up the first hill you come to, especially if it's a little bit steep, you'll be all hot and bothered. The first downhill after that is always the moment when you find out if you've managed to dress yourself appropriately. You head downhill and suddenly it gets easier so you don't have to pedal. You're not working yourself warm, but you're moving faster so the wind starts cutting into you and all that sweat that you worked up getting up the hill suddenly starts freezing onto your skin. That's when you get really cold.

The key to beating this scenario is layers. Layers are good for two reasons. The first is that it's vital to be able to remove and replace thin layers, so that you can regulate your temperature precisely, and not get too hot going uphill. The second good reason for layers in cold weather is that each layer serves a different purpose.

Base layer

The layer directly next to your skin is there to make you comfortable. Its most important task is to wick moisture away from your skin, keeping it dry and comfortable. For anything other than really relaxed cycling, cotton T-shirts just aren't up to the job. They absorb and hold sweat, which means that the layer next to your skin is always damp. If any draught can get to it, the damp cotton will feel instantly chilly. Modern fabrics, like Coolmax, wick moisture away from your skin, keeping you warmer and dryer.

Wicking base layers keep you dry

Coolmax summer jerseys make great winter vests. There's no need for a completely new wardrobe for the winter – you just have to make more use of the stuff you've already got.

Another great fabric for this is merino wool, which is making a comeback after years of being thought of as an old-fashioned fabric. Wool has another great advantage – it's evolved over millions of years protecting sheep to become an unappealing environment for the kind of bacteria that make you smell after exercise, and so won't retain odour in the same way as synthetic fabrics. It's great for arriving at the office without foisting the full joy of your breakneck commute upon all your work colleagues. This doesn't, however, mean that it never needs to be washed. Catalogues for merino cycling clothing frequently carry tales of epic adventures by intrepid explorers, who boast about how many months they survived in the jungle/Antarctic/mid-ocean with no change of shirt. Merino wool will smell less after this kind of punishment than Lycra, but it's not the kind of boast that your work colleagues are likely to appreciate. Modern wool garments don't need outrageous amounts of washing care – they survive fine on normal 40° washes in the washing machine.

Mid layer

Your mid layer is purely for warmth. If it's below freezing, a fleece is a great idea as you'll need to choose something that's not too bulky. For in-between days, a long-sleeved jersey – in Coolmax or similar – over your vest is fine. It doesn't have to be cycling-specific as any breathable fabric will do. Just make sure that the cut is generous enough so that you can stretch out over your bicycle without exposing flesh at your wrists and across the bottom of your back.

A full zip is always a better idea than a short zip or no zips at all as you can open it easily while riding along for instant ventilation. Again, cotton fabrics are no good; they will just get wet and then cold. They're much better saved for putting on when you're home, warm and dry. Several thinner layers will always be better than one thick one so that you can regulate your temperature easily. The annoying thing about cycling in cold weather is that you actually spend a fair amount of time trying to keep cool when you find yourself suddenly working hard to overtake a bus or sprint up a hill. Full zips make instant ventilation much easier. As long as they fit, your mid layers don't have to be cycling-specific. If you've already got gear from another sport or exercise, it'll probably do a fine job – as long as the fabric is breathable.

Outer layer

Your final layer of clothing is all about the weather. It's there to keep the wind and the rain off your body. Jackets with full zips are best as again, like mid layers, they allow instant blasts of ventilation. Your jacket is also an essential place for keeping keys, wallet and so forth, so choose one with pockets. These are often positioned at the back to stop the weight of items inside dragging the jacket out of shape. Hoods are rare as it's generally assumed that you'll be wearing either a helmet or a hat anyway. Hoods can be really tricky too as, however well designed they are, they still tend to cut down on your all-round vision.

When you're choosing a jacket, it's best if you can try it on while you're actually sitting on the bike. If you can't, try stretching out in your riding position. Make sure the arms are long enough to cover your wrists and that the material isn't stretched tightly across your shoulders. The back should come down low enough so that your kidneys aren't exposed. The front of the jacket shouldn't sag forward too much. If there's too much space, the wind will get in underneath, exposing you to a constant draught.

It's not always so cold that you'll need a full jacket. Autumn and spring bring days when you can easily get away with a sleeveless gilet, which keeps your torso warm while leaving your arms free. These usually have windproof panels at the front and thinner fabric or mesh – and perhaps some reflective tabs and a pocket – at the back.

Layer compatibility

Your layers will only work if they fit together well. A warm fleece that pokes out below the bottom of your jacket at the back will act like a wick, soaking up moisture from the cold outside air and drawing it slowly up your back into the warm gap between

A base layer keeps your skin dry, while a mid layer insulates you. Outer layers protect you from the elements. You need to make a judicious selection of layers if you want to stay warm and dry without getting sweaty

your body and your jacket. The same goes for sleeves that poke out of the ends of your jacket. Bulky layers won't fit properly underneath others, restricting your movement and making you feel colder than you are.

Breathable jackets will only work if all the layers underneath the jacket are also breathable. The jacket fabric is designed to rapidly transport moisture from its inside surface to the world outside, but it can only do its job on moisture that reaches the inside surface, which is another thing to think about.

Safety gear: helmets

There are always arguments for and against using safety gear. There's a point of view that says that cycling is so good for you anyway that you can survive the occasional prang. However, if you do end up coming off your bike occasionally, that argument begins to look very unconvincing, so stay safe in the saddle.

Consider your options, but don't get so wrapped up in thinking about cycling as dangerous that you start to treat your journey to work as an extreme sport. Essentially, it's just a way of getting about. Helmets are the most obvious piece of cycling-specific safety gear. There are many convincing arguments for wearing one and they will protect your head in certain types of collisions. Helmets are a legal requirement in a lot of countries. Kids, in particular, should always wear one, even in countries where they are not legally required to, because they have softer skulls and can often make inexperienced decisions. It is also important to remember, however, that helmets won't stop you having accidents.

One of the reasons people used to cite for not ever wearing a helmet was that they were heavy, sweaty and uncomfortable. This just isn't true any more. Modern lids are light enough to wear without you noticing them and have good big vents, which let in plenty of air. There's no need to use comfort as a reason not to wear one. It's essential to go to a shop and try on a few different types before you buy one as they are all different shapes. It's not until you start trying helmets on that you realise some people's heads are very round, while others' are much more oval. Just knowing whether your head is small, medium or large will not be enough to secure you the right helmet. Within each size, there will always be some adjustment to make, but if the basic shape doesn't match your head, try another make.

Big vents in the helmet make it a lot more comfortable, but you lose most of your heat through your head and a helmet without vents will stop this from happening.

If you've got a particularly large or particularly small head, your helmet choice will be rather more restricted and generally involve more expensive makes. The cheaper versions tend to restrict themselves to medium sizes. Giro make a huge range of helmets and their size range for adult helmets goes from 51 to 63cm (20 to 25 in), which should be enough to cover most people's heads.

Before you use a new helmet for the first time, take a bit of time to fit it properly. There's a single strap under your chin, which splits into four parts – two on each side, one leading forwards, the other backwards. There needs to be even tension in each strap with the helmet sitting level on your head. Check this in a mirror as a common mistake is to position the helmet too far back on the head. This makes it fairly useless as a safety device since, if you hit something hard, it will just get pushed off backwards, leaving the strap still wrapped around your neck. Similarly, to work properly, the strap under your chin needs to be reasonably tight so that, if you open your mouth, you feel the helmet pressing down onto the top of your head. When you first try this, you'll probably find it too uncomfortable to wear. But when you get on your bike, you'll find that you generally ride around looking forwards and upwards, which loosens off the strap to a point where it should feel comfortable. The straps are a little bit fiddly but you only have to set them up the first time. After that, the helmet will only need an occasional tighten as the straps work loose. It's essential to get it right, however, as a badly set up helmet won't stay on your head and protect you in a collision.

If you don't like riding around with a smelly head, you may want to know that the pads inside the helmet are generally secured with Velcro. This means you can pull them out and stick them in the washing machine. You can also buy replacement pad sets and use them to customise the fit of your helmet.

Helmets are ideal for increasing your visibility. Go for a bright one

Safety gear: be safe, be seen

Visibility gear is one of the things that really mark you out as a cyclist. Reflective strips on your body or your bike use the light given off by car headlamps and bounce it back into the driver's eyes. Any time lights are pointed in your direction, you give everybody a chance of noticing you're there.

Reflective bands and strips don't need batteries and don't usually get stolen. Reflective strips worn on your body pick out your silhouette so that you stand out clearly as a person. Even if this only makes it a little bit harder for car drivers to cut you up too close, it helps. If you're sticking reflective strips or stickers onto your bike, remember to give them a quick wipe occasionally as they don't reflect light when they're dirty. Reflective trouser clips are especially effective from behind because they bob up and down as you pedal, making them and you much more visible.

Nothing marks you out as a cyclist more than a Sam Browne belt. There's no mistaking your mode of transport with one of these about your person. They're more expensive than you'd expect, due to the high cost of the reflective material. The combination of Sam Browne belt and a rucksack doesn't work at all since you're covering up the important bit at the back. If you're going to wear a rucksack, make sure that it's got its own reflective strips or tabs. Even better, get yourself a rucksack cover with visibility strips on it. They slip over your bag like a shower cap, and also keep the rain off.

In traffic, your helmet is one of the best places for a little extra sparkle. Your head is above the level of much of the traffic, so if it's bright enough, people will be able to see you weaving about in a line of stationary cars. Light-coloured helmets are easier to pick out than dark colours and those designed for use round town will have silver reflective stickers or logos. You can supplement these with a reflective band that sits around the widest part of the helmet like those made by Respro. For extra visibility, many LED lights are small enough to ziptie onto the back of your helmet, without the weight dragging it out of balance.

The above are the obvious bits of protective gear and probably the ones you need most, but there's a couple of other bits of kit that are more useful, less often. As well as keeping your hands warm and dry, a pair of gloves will protect your palms if you have a spill. It's amazing how much a single layer of fabric will help.

Sun cream is an accepted part of being outdoors now, but you burn in odd places on a bicycle. The tops of your thighs and the backs of your calves get more exposure than you'd expect, as do the backs of your hands, which is another good reason for wearing fingerless gloves. If you're not wearing a helmet, be careful with the top of your head, the back of your neck and your ears.

Contact lens wearers – and many other cyclists – find that a bit of eye protection stops grit getting stuck onto their eyeballs, especially on windy days. Sunglasses are fine for the summer, but are a bit gloomy for the winter. Try a pair of light-enhancing lenses instead. They're like sunglasses, but make everything just a little bit brighter on gloomy days, dark evenings and early mornings.

Above left: pause for reflection with the Sam Browne belt; below: glasses for light relief

Make yourself visible: small, neat extra lights can be hung from your rucksack or bag straps

29

Top safety tips

Cycling itself is a relatively safe activity – it is normally only the other road-users who make it dangerous. There are things you can do to stay safe in the saddle. However well you maintain your bike and use the road, it's very important that you look ahead and make allowances for other people's potential bad driving. Cycling shouldn't be treated as a scary, dangerous activity, but at the same time a few simple tips will reduce your chances of a collision, or a near-miss.

◎ Don't be bullied by considerations of fashion – if it makes you feel safer to wear a helmet or dress up like a Christmas tree, then do it.

◎ Make sure you're as comfortable as possible. If you're busy thinking about how cold, wet and miserable you are, you're not thinking enough about what you're doing or about what the traffic is doing.

◎ Lights and reflectors can seem like a bit of an imposition on the simplicity of cycling, but without them, you are effectively invisible. Be as visible as you can and not just at night – a flashing light will mean you can be seen from further away in all kinds of bad weather.

◎ Car drivers don't have the same relationship with the road surface that you do, and so will be taken completely by surprise if you swerve to avoid a wet drain cover or a piece of fast-food roadkill. Maintain a predictable line, rather than swerving about.

◎ Take your space. If you're creeping along in the gutter, you don't have any manoeuvrability. If there isn't room for a car to pass you safely, don't give them so much room that they're tempted to squeeze past. Instead, move out and take the centre of the lane. Once there's enough room for both of you, move back over so they can pass you.

◎ Beware drivers opening the doors of parked cars without warning. In fact, be vigilant around any vehicles with people sitting in them since people frequently don't look behind them before acting. This is also true of moving vehicles if you're near train stations or cash points where passengers have a habit of flinging themselves from cars in slow-moving traffic queues.

◎ The single most dangerous type of traffic is lorries. Never mind how many mirrors they have, treat them as if they can't see you. Never try sliding down the inside of them. If they turn across you, you'll have no exit. They're bigger than you are so leave them well alone.

◎ Make sure your bike is roadworthy – especially the brakes. Traffic and pedestrians often do unpredictable things. If your brakes are working, you can avoid them and give them a hard time. If they're not, you'll hit them.

◎ Headphones and headsets are a really bad idea. You can't hear what's going on around you. Headsets onto your phone are an even worse idea because you can't concentrate on what's going on around you. If you really can't switch off the iPod for as long as it takes you to do your trip, take the bus and let somebody else drive.

◎ Safe cycling means being alert. If you're not in a fit state to concentrate properly on what the traffic is up to, you shouldn't be cycling.

◎ Filtering through traffic. If you're going up the outside, remember motorists don't expect you to be there and are prone to cutting unexpectedly through gaps in the oncoming traffic. They don't expect you to be moving up the inside lane either, so watch for them turning into side streets.

Golden rule: don't take risks on your bicycle

Fitness and health

We're constantly being encouraged by doctors and governments to take more exercise, but it's hard to know how to fit this into our hectic lives. It's all too easy to join a gym enthusiastically and be full of optimism about classes or going to the pool for a fortnight or so. But if you turn round in a couple of months and realise you've wasted your membership, you're in good company.

Estimates suggest that around £200 million was spent on unused gym memberships in 2004. Cycling is a much more reliable way of getting the exercise you need. Instead of using the bus or the car, make it a habit to hop on your bike. You'll probably get there more quickly, saving time rather than spending it. And, along with walking and swimming, cycling is an ideal form of exercise – energetic enough to make your heart and lungs do some work, but still low-impact, which minimises the chance of you injuring yourself.

Fitness

Cycling is a great form of exercise to start off with. It's low-impact and if you don't feel sporty you can go pretty much as slowly as you like. If you're trying to get or keep fit, you should aim to go fast enough to get out of breath occasionally, but mostly you should still be able to carry on a conversation. It'll seem like hard work at first, but gradually your strength and stamina will improve. This doesn't happen immediately, but – if you persevere – within a couple of months you'll find yourself bemused to remember how your initial trips left you out of breath. "Regular cyclists enjoy a fitness level equal to that of a person 10 years younger," says the National Forum for Coronary Heart Disease Foundation.

Reduce the risk of heart attacks

There has been plenty of research into the health benefits of cycling. One of the most significant findings is that regular cycling can cut the risk of a serious heart attack by over 20 per cent. And the amount you have to cycle to feel the benefit isn't outrageous. A regular commute is enough to move you up into a lower risk band. This is what the British Heart Foundation has to say about it: "Cycling at least 20 miles a week reduces the risk of heart disease to less than half that for non-cyclists who take no other exercise."

Control your weight

Cycling won't make you instantly thinner, but it's an easy way to get the kind of regular exercise that diet programmes always seem to recommend. Government guidelines suggesting you should get 30 minutes' exercise five times a week aren't that strenuous to achieve. If you commute to work, a 15-minute bike ride each way each day means you've reached your target. Fifteen minutes should be enough time to get you about three or four miles. If that's within range of work or the train station, then perfect. If you're new to cycling, start slowly. Do it maybe once a week or cycle to work and leave your bike there and then reverse the journey the next day. Cycling at a fair clip will burn calories fairly effectively – around 450 to 550 an hour. At lower speeds, the satisfying efficiency of a bicycle means you're not working hard enough for your weight to plummet, but it's got to be more energetic than sitting in your car.

Stress

It might not seem like it on busy days when you have to discuss the finer points of the Highway Code with sleepy bus drivers, but regular exercise helps alleviate anxiety and stress. And some days are positively exhilarating: the first few days of spring or beating your train journey time for the first time or just getting out of the office and blowing the cobwebs away can be enough.

I often find that it helps me work problems through, too. If there's something that's been bothering me, just riding along helps me sort things out in my head. There's something about the need to keep the pedals turning around that helps keep your thoughts turning over as well. And sometimes you arrive at your destination knowing exactly what you need to do next.

Pollution

Some days the air quality is so bad you can see it out of a car window. But if this puts you off getting on your bike, think again – car drivers suffer much worse from bad air since they're sitting still in their vehicles. As a cyclist, you're moving through the traffic, rather than being stuck in a jam directly behind someone else's exhaust pipe. And, at lights, you're most likely to be found at the front of the traffic queue, where the pollution levels are lower. Then again, some people have it worse than car drivers – kids in buggies on the pavement are at just the right height to breathe in the worst of the fumes and are most likely to suffer from the effects. At least if you're on a bike, you're not adding to the problem.

31

2 – Getting comfortable

This chapter explains how your bicycle can be adjusted so it's comfortable. Riding your bike should be fun, and make you feel great. If sitting on it makes you miserable, you'll soon find excuses to avoid using it. Everybody is a different shape, so it can take some experimentation to find the right combination of saddle height and handlebar shape to adapt your machine to suit your needs. You may need to swap saddles, pedals or handlebars for differently shaped versions.

Choosing a saddle

One thing that stops people who cycle a little from cycling a lot is an uncomfortable saddle. If it's not comfortable, it's not likely to suddenly get any more comfortable. You're just going to find it unpleasant to ride around and it will put you off.

The solution is to swap your saddle for one that matches your own shape. If you're buying a new bike, the saddle it comes supplied with was chosen to make the bike look appealing on the shop floor. This might mean that the manufacturer has fitted some lean, mean strip of hard plastic to make the bike look racy and weigh as little as possible. If they're aiming for the leisure market, the bike might well come with a big squashy cushion that gives when you press your thumbs into it. That's all very well if you're going to practise handstands on your bike, but bottoms are a very different shape to thumbs – something that feels forgiving to your thumb will be far too soft and unsupportive to ride far on. Just as if you were going to buy a mattress, don't trust any judgement other than how a saddle feels when you're sitting on the bike. It doesn't actually matter at all what it looks like – nobody can see much of it while you're riding along. And, if you find a saddle that suits you, there's no reason not to take it with you if you decide to get a new bike.

Men's and women's saddles

Men and women have different-shaped pelvises, so your saddle is one part of your bike that it's absolutely essential to get right. New bikes generally come fitted as standard with a men's saddle. On request, any bike shop with any sense will swap this for a women's one if you ask them to when you buy the bike. Women's saddles are slightly wider and slightly shorter. The extra width is necessary because women have wider 'sit bones'.

You need enough padding on a saddle to cushion you from road shocks without it being so soft that you sink into it and wallow around. This is a very personal choice and depends on your mileage, your position on the bike and your shape. Softer saddles are better for short trips. If you're sitting very upright, you'll also need a softer saddle and

may also want to consider a suspension seat post, since your bottom will be taking most of your weight. The better types have gel cushions under each sit bone, supporting you exactly where you need it most.

In a longer, more stretched-out position, your weight is shared out more equally between bars, saddle and pedal, so your saddle can be firmer without being uncomfortable. A thin layer of gel will reduce vibration from the road and a narrow cutaway shape will allow you to pedal efficiently without the sides of the saddle chafing on your thighs. Extra comfort can come from having hollow or titanium saddle rails. These flex just enough to

Brooks leather saddle

give you just a little bit of suspension. A leather upper is more expensive than standard synthetic covers, but will breathe better, which you'll appreciate on hot days or when you're working hard.

Although almost everybody uses a foam- or gel-covered saddle now, some people swear by old-fashioned leather ones. They're rock-hard to begin with, but once you've ridden them for a few hundred miles, the leather breaks into your shape and they fit you perfectly. They need a little more care than normal saddles, but will last for years if not decades.

Men's saddle

Women's saddle

Saddle position

You can make a saddle at least twice as nice to sit on by spending a little time getting the position exactly right. You get to play with three different adjustments – its height, its angle and the length between the bars and the front of the seat. Try to change one at a time, rather than fiddling with everything at once, so that you can pinpoint which adjustments make your bicycle more comfortable.

Saddle height

You would imagine that getting the seat height adjusted correctly would be everyone's first port of call, but the streets are full of people wobbling about because they're perched atop their bicycle as if they were on stilts or because they've got their knees wrapped around their ears. There's no excuse for this and it just makes your entire journey much less comfortable than it should be.

To check your seat height, find a place where you can sit still on your bike in your normal cycling position, leaning against a wall. Look down at your feet. When you're cycling normally, you'll find that the most efficient position for your feet to be in is with the ball of your foot directly over the pedal axle. But just for the purposes of measurement, sit with the heel, rather than the ball, of your foot over the axle. If your seat is at the ideal height, your leg will be almost straight – not locked out, just extended.

Seat height is adjusted at the bottom of the seat post using either an Allen key (4mm, 5mm or 6mm) or a quick-release lever, which you loosen until you can move the post freely.

Fore-and-aft positioning

This is quite a subtle adjustment and it can take a fair amount of fiddling about to find the right place. The fore-and-aft position of the saddle determines how much length there is between the saddle and the bars, and so how upright your sitting position will be when you're holding the bars.

Bringing the saddle forwards will make you more upright and is in many ways equivalent to raising the handlebars. A forward position is often favoured by triathletes – it makes use of similar muscles as running, and so makes the change from one to the other less of a shock. Women also often favour a saddle in a more forward position, placing the pelvis more directly over the pedals. A further aft position will stretch you out more, which you may find more comfortable on long journeys. Change the position of the saddle by loosening the clamp bolt until you can free the saddle rails enough to slide it along in the clamp. Tighten the clamp bolt firmly when you've finished. You'll find that quite small adjustments to the position will make your bike feel quite different, so change it a little at a time.

SADDLE ANGLE

Step 1: In almost all cases, the most comfortable angle for your saddle will be with the top of the saddle either horizontal, or very close to horizontal.

Step 2: If your saddle tips backwards, you'll be pulling yourself forwards with your arms every pedal stroke to counteract the tendency to slide off the back. This can lead to sore shoulders.

Step 3: There can be times when tipping the front of the saddle downwards relieves unpleasant pressure, but an exaggerated angle indicates that either your saddle is the wrong shape for you or your bicycle is too long or just too big. If the saddle tips too far forwards, you'll have to be pushing yourself up and back with your feet constantly, making journeys much more tiring than they need otherwise be.

Choosing pedals

Pedals usually get the shortest shrift when you're thinking about comfort on your bicycle, but remember, along with your hands and your bottom, your feet are in contact with the bicycle all the time. Choosing pedals needs a little care since they have to perform two opposing functions.

Most of the time pedals have to grip your feet firmly so that you stay securely attached to the bicycle. If you stand up off the pedals to sprint up a hill and the soles of your feet slip, you're really going to hurt yourself. If you're stumbling to find a secure position when you set off from the lights, you're going to struggle to accelerate into the stream of traffic. But equally, as soon as you stop, you need to be able to get your feet down and onto the ground as bicycles only hold you upright as long as you're moving along.

Traditionally, this dilemma was solved in two ways. If you considered getting off, safety was paramount which meant you stuck with a pair of flat plastic or rubber pedals that gripped your feet well enough, but assumed you were never going to try to do anything unexpected or sprint about, so the perils of your feet slipping off were low. If you wanted a little more power or were touring and so didn't expect to be getting on and off your bike all day, you strapped yourself into toe clips and straps. These did a great job of keeping your feet attached as long as you cranked the straps tight, but that meant that you needed a moment to anticipate stopping so that you could reach down and loosen the straps as you slowed down.

Neither of these two options is ideal for commuting since occasionally you need to be able to get up off the pedals and sprint, knowing you'll stay up off the pedals. But you can't always anticipate stopping, which means a couple of new solutions had to be pinched from different areas of cycling.

BMX-style pedals are designed for an extreme version of the same purposes as commuting – you need your pedals to stick securely to your shoes even if you're six feet off the ground and upside down. But you need to be able to get your feet free in an instant as soon as it becomes apparent that the whole six-feet-off-the-ground-upside-down thing isn't

panning out as well as you'd hoped. The pedals, therefore, have big wide platforms so your feet grip only as long as they're anywhere near the pedals. Studs or pins stick upwards, stopping your feet from sliding sideways. In theory, this is perfect for commuting, but in practice, a toned-down, BMX-lite version is a better option as the spiky grip surfaces are just too harsh. If you happen to catch your shins on the pedals, they'll really hurt – BMXers don't seem to care about this as they often wear shin pads – but they're also so sharp they'll rip up the soles of your shoes in no time at all – BMXers don't seem to care much about this either; you wouldn't want to be seen in last year's shoes anyway. But the influence of BMX means plenty of wide, flat pedals with enough pins to keep you attached are available now.

Pedal design has also been stolen from mountain biking. Clipless pedals emerged first in road racing, but there you generally don't have to get off your bike until after a road race has finished so there was never any reason to design the pedals in order to walk in the shoes. Mountain biking created a different need as people wanted to stay securely attached to their pedals, but they also wanted to be able to get off the bike and walk or run or lift it over things they couldn't ride past. This prompted the development of clipless pedals where the cleat is recessed into the sole of the shoe so that it's safe to walk on. The cleat on the sole locks into a sprung mechanism on the pedal, but is shaped so that the action of twisting your feet sideways will unlock the cleat from the pedal instantly. The unlocking movement is an easy, natural twist of your foot, but has to be learned. Once you've got the knack, you don't have to think about it, but during the learning curve there is certainly potential for situations where you don't get your feet out in time.

Left: BMX-style pedals; right: a normal pedal surface on one side and a clip on the other make these perfect for city riding

Pedals: learning to ride clipless

Learning to ride with clipless pedals takes you right back to learning to ride your bike in the first place. Before you can do it, it's impossible to imagine yourself succeeding in this, but after you've worked it out, it seems so simple that you can't remember what it was like not to be able to.

Ensure that the bolts are greased and tightened securely

First, fit the new pedals. The left and right pedals are different, and marked 'l' and 'r'. The left-hand pedal has a reverse thread so undoes clockwise and is refitted anticlockwise. The right-hand pedal has a normal thread. Tighten both pedals securely into the cranks. Pedal spanners are thinner than normal ones in order to fit into the gap between crank and pedal, and longer to give you enough leverage to tighten the cranks firmly.

Since you need to have the right size shoes for your feet, you usually have to commit yourself to the clipless pedal idea before you've really had a chance to try them. You'll need a pair of shoes in your size and a pair of clipless pedals. The clipless pedals come with the cleats, which need to be attached to the bottom of the shoes – almost always with a 4mm Allen key.

When new, shoes often (but not always) have a cover hiding the attachment holes on the sole of the shoe. If you're lucky, the cover comes off with a couple of Allen keys. More typically you have to cut a chunk of the sole out of your new shoes – which always seems a bit bizarre. It's also a little tricky – take good care as you do this since you'll need a sharp knife to cut through the rubber and it's all too easy to cut yourself. You'll see the patch to be cut off as soon as you turn the shoe over. Cut neatly around the edge with a sharp knife, then pull off and discard the cover.

Next, it's time for cleat positioning. It's essential that you take a bit of time and care to get the cleat position right. If you ride around with your feet strapped into awkwardly positioned cleats, you can damage your knees. This seems to be particularly problematic for people who've played sports like football which involve lots of knee twisting. If you find yourself getting pains in your knees after fitting cleats, take yourself back to your bike shop and get some advice about cleat fitting. Fit the cleats when you've got enough time to test and readjust them – not just before you set off on a big ride.

The cleat should fit just under or just behind the ball of your foot. It can be tricky to locate where this is on the sole of the shoe, so put your shoes on and have a feel around where your feet fit inside the shoe. Use a bit of tape to mark on the top of the shoes where the middle of the ball of your foot fits and then line the centre of the cleat up with the tape. You'll be able to slide the fitting plate backwards and forwards along the sole of the shoe to find the right place.

It's essential that the cleats point in the right direction. Sit yourself on the edge of a table so that the lower halves of your legs hang vertically and your feet dangle above the floor. Look carefully at the angle your feet hang at as they won't necessarily both point the same way. A good starting point is to set the direction of the cleats so that your feet replicate the angle that they naturally hang at.

Once you've chosen the angle, pop the greased bolts through the cleats including any washers that came with the pack and tighten firmly. Since you'll have to test the cleat position, it's tempting to leave the bolts loose while you do this, but don't because, if the cleats aren't properly tightened into the sole of the shoe, they'll tear out as you try to release your feet.

Then the hard part – you have to teach your feet to get into and out of the cleat. Take a look at the cleat and pedal before you start so that you know what you're trying to do. Lean your bike up against a wall, then try one foot at a time. At first, it takes ages to find the right place for your foot – you have to feel about to engage the front of the cleat and then push down hard to click the back in. Once you're locked in, twist your heel outwards to release. Practise this with both feet separately before you even think about going anywhere. You have to get to a point where you can release your feet without looking or thinking. Once you're confident, take yourself to the park and practise clipping out and then coming to a stop. Don't venture out into traffic until you can come to an emergency stop and get your feet out every time. You'll probably want to readjust the cleat position. Take an Allen key with you on your first few rides and remember to tighten the cleat securely every time. This may seem long-winded, but once you've taught your feet how to do it, they never forget.

Handlebars

Getting the shape and height of your bars right is essential to your comfort. If you're sitting in a position that doesn't suit your body, this will soon make itself known through a sore neck, shoulders, wrists or back.

It can often take a bit of time and a few alterations to the saddle, stem and bars to work out what's wrong. It might be enough simply to change the angle, or height, of the bars. If that doesn't do the job, it may be worth looking at changing bars for a different-shaped pair, although it's difficult to imagine what another pair will feel like until you've had a chance to try them. Part of the problem with positioning is actually aesthetics. People who make and sell bicycles tend to have a fairly clear idea about what a bike should look like: they use words like 'sleek' and 'streamlined'. So they fit flat, straight bars that make the bike look like the kind of thing you want to buy, but isn't necessarily best for your riding style. Bar shape is just as important as position, although the two are intimately connected. If you're looking for an upright position with your back relatively straight, the most comfortable shape for the bars is usually with the grips swept backwards at 30–45º. This means you can grip the bars comfortably without sticking your elbows out. It may seem like a straight bar would be ideal, but the shape of your hands means they grip best at an angle. To see what I mean, find a straight bar, roughly the same diameter as a handlebar and longer than the width of your hand. Hold out your arm in front of you and grip the bar with one hand. You'll see that it doesn't rest comfortably at 90º to your arm as its natural resting position is at an angle to the rest of your body. That's the kind of angle you want the bars to be swept back to so that they drop neatly into your palm.

Straight bars

If you're looking for a position that's perhaps a bit more aerodynamic and sporty, you tend to lean further forward over the bars with your arms a bit bent to absorb the shock. This shifts the angle so your palms sit inwards a little and a straighter bar is a more comfortable option. Even then a slight sweep to the bars – between 3º and 6º – will make a big difference. And the angle that this

points in can be critical. There was a fashion for a time of angling the sweep so that the bars pointed downwards. It may or may not have looked cool, but it was gruesomely uncomfortable. With relatively straight bars, look carefully at the angle of the sweep. The bars should point up and back, so that the angle of the grips sits neatly into the angle of your palms.

City bars

For pottering around town aerodynamics is one of the least of your concerns and comes some way behind being able to see where you're going and giving other people the best chance to see you. For this a curved, swept-back bar is ideal, bringing the grips upwards and backwards so that you sit more upright. This makes it much easier to turn your head and look behind you. It also makes you tall, so drivers can see your head clearly above traffic when you're busy weaving between lanes.

City bars provide a comfortable, upright position

Drop bars

Being stretched-out and low-down has its advantages too. It makes you less of a target for the wind, saving your energy. In terms of comfort, it also spreads your weight out much more evenly since, instead of being concentrated on your bottom, it's divided between handlebars, saddle and pedals.

Getting the position right takes some fiddling, since the position of the brake-levers is crucial. Many people fit the bars, but leave the bar tape off for a few rides until they've had a good chance to adjust the angle and level of the levers perfectly.

Straight bars give you precise control for nipping through traffic and make you that bit more aerodynamic

Drop bars make you aerodynamic with a range of hand positions. They also make you less of a target for the wind

Altering the handlebar position

Sometimes all you need to do to get a comfortable position is to fiddle with the angle of the bars. You'll have to climb on the bike to test a new position, but remember to retighten the stem bolt each time before you put your weight on it as it's all too easy to forget what you're doing and bear down on the grips, only to have loose bars twist out from under you.

You'll have to loosen off the stem to move the bars. There are different styles. The simplest have a single bolt, which is the easiest to deal with as it simply needs to be retightened to secure the bars. There's another more complex style. Stems with two or four bolts – front loaders – are designed so the front plate can be removed completely, allowing you to remove the stem from the bars without taking the controls and grips off the handlebar. This makes stem changes much easier, but the stem bolts need to be refitted with care so the tightness of the bolts is as even as possible.

If you're moving the bars in the stem and have a front-loading stem, it's worth taking the opportunity to take the face off and clean the interface between stem and bars. If this gets dirty, the bars will creak under pressure, which is annoying. This procedure works just as well for drop bars as for straight or curved bars.

Brake-lever and shifter positions

Once you've got the handlebar angle right, you'll have to shift the positions of the controls so that they fit comfortably in your palms. The brake-levers are the most important, since in an emergency you need to be able to reach them without thinking. You can only really find the right place by sitting on the bike and experimenting with angles. I like the brake-levers set fairly low, so that I don't have to lift my fingers too far to get up and over them, but it's a matter of personal preference. You'll have to loosen the bolts that secure the levers to the bars, which will almost always need a 5mm Allen key. Loosen them so the levers can move freely, since it's important not to create weak spots by scratching the surface of the bar. As a rough guide, start with the levers sitting at an angle of between 30° and 45° to the ground. It's fine to leave some room between the brake-levers and the grips if you've got large hands – it gives you some breathing space. Once you've done adjusting, tighten the bolts that secure the levers to the bars. Check that the levers can't twist around.

Once the brake-lever position is sorted, tuck the shifters up close to them. Triggershifters should be angled so they sit close up under the brake-levers. Twistshifters may be designed so that the barrel-adjuster sits over the brake-lever rather than under – check by ensuring that the indicator numbers are clearly visible.

SHIFTING BARS WITH 2- AND 4-BOLT STEMS

Step 1: Remove the bolts that hold the bars to the stem and pull the front plate of the stem away. Use degreaser to clean the inner surfaces of the stem and the part of the bar that's clamped into the stem. Dry them off. Clean the bolts and dab a little grease on the threads and under the bolt heads. As well as preventing corrosion, this makes them turn in the threads more smoothly, making it easier to gauge how tight they are.

Step 2: Reassemble the stem, adjusting the angle of the bars until the grips sit comfortably in your palms. It's important to do the bolts up evenly. With two-bolt stems, tighten both bolts until there is an even gap between the main body of the stem and the front plate. Then tighten each bolt half a turn at a time until both bolts are firm. Tighten four-bolt types in a cross pattern as shown above.

Step 3: With four-bolt types, check as you tighten that the gap is even at the top and the bottom and on either side. This matters because it means that the bolts will go in straight and will be stronger. If the bolts enter the main part of the stem at an angle, they'll be stressed and thus more likely to snap. Sit on the bike to test your new bar position. You'll have to shift the position of controls, bells, light brackets etc.

Handlebars: adjusting stem height

Lift your bars up a little to get a better view of the traffic, or drop them down to tuck yourself out of the wind and make yourself more energy-efficient.

There are two types of headset, each of which requires a different procedure to change the bar height. The older-style threaded headset has a narrow stem emerging from two nuts at the top of the headset. These are the easiest to adjust – see the three steps below. The newer, non-threaded Aheadset type has the stem directly bolted to the top of the steerer tube. You can't simply adjust the height of these by moving the stem up and down, but adjustable versions are available that allow you to alter the angle. The instructions below show you how to do this. If your Ahead stem is not of the adjustable type, the only way to change your handlebar height is to replace the stem with one of a different shape – see page 39.

ADJUSTABLE AHEADSET STEMS

Step 1: Adjustable stems have hinges, held in place by an Allen key bolt. When locked down, splines prevent the hinge from moving. The one pictured has the bolt on the side, but yours may be under the stem. If you're not sure, check your bike manual. Loosen it until the stem moves easily; you may have to wriggle the bolt to release the splines. Change the stem angle, then retighten the bolt firmly.

Step 2: Shifting the stem angle will rotate the bars so that they point at an awkward angle. Undo the stem bolt(s) and rotate the bars so that the grips fit nicely in your palms. Retighten the stem bolts. If there are two or four bolts, tighten them evenly so that there's as much gap above the bars as below.

Step 3: Now you'll need to swing the controls round on the bars too. Loosen shifter and brake-lever bolts, climb onto the bike and roll the controls around so that they're within easy reach. The brake-levers should be low enough so that you don't have to strain your hands to lift your fingers up and over them every time you want to brake. Tighten the bolts on the brake-levers and shifters.

THREADED HEADSET STEMS

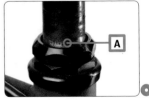

Step 1: Undo the expander bolt at the top of the stem. This almost always needs a 6mm Allen key, but you might need to prise off a rubber bung first. Undo it four complete turns.

Step 2: As you turn the bolt, the head rises up out of the stem. Tap the Allen key with a rubber mallet or block of wood (not a hammer as this will damage the bolt head), so that the Allen key drops down flush with the stem again. This releases the wedge that holds the stem in place.

Step 3: Once the stem is loose, adjust its position. It mustn't be raised so high that you can see the safety marks, usually a row of vertical lines around the stem (A). Point the stem forwards, so it's directly in line with the front wheel, and tighten the 6mm Allen key bolt firmly. Check it's tight by standing in front of the bike and gripping the wheel between your knees. If you can twist the bars, retighten the stem bolt.

Grips

Grips come in all shapes, sizes and colours, but you don't tend to think about them until they've completely worn out and are falling off your bike. When the time comes to change them, you need to consider more than just your colour scheme.

Thin ones are ideal for smaller hands and also a good idea if you tend to ride with gloves on. Thicker, more squidgy versions absorb more vibration and are more comfortable on longer rides. Price is an issue. It's one of those occasions where the cheap ones look identical to the expensive ones, and so it's difficult to work out what makes the expensive ones cost twice as much. The answer tends to be rubber quality – expensive ones have a denser layer next to the bars to absorb road shock and then a thinner, softer layer on the outside that moulds into your palm, spreading the load out over your whole hand rather than concentrating it in small zones.

Getting grips off can be a bit of a nightmare. It's tempting to cut them off, but not a good idea. The material bars are made of is very thin, which makes them lighter and also means that they flex slightly as you ride, giving you a bit of suspension. But it also makes the material very vulnerable to scratches on the surface – these grow easily into cracks, which should be avoided.

It's better to get old grips off by sliding something relatively soft – chopsticks are the ideal shape and size – between the grip and the bar. You'll have to squeeze past the brake-lever clamp. Lift the end of the rubber up just enough to spray underneath. Degreaser works well, as does warm water. Wriggle the chopstick about to break the seal between grip and bar and slide it gently

further into the gap. Spray some more water in. You should then be able to twist the grip off the end of the bar.

Fitting grips isn't difficult, but you need to make sure that, once fitted, they stay on. The grips are the same size as the bars, and so won't slide on without lubrication. You need something that wets the surface long enough to slide them on and then dries and sticks. Options include products like Renthal grip glue from motorbike shops, hot water – drop the grips in for a few minutes and then slide them on, but don't burn your hands – as well as less obvious things like hairspray. Don't use spray oil or solvent as they will make the grips slip on easily, but they'll never really secure themselves safely.

Barends

These are less popular than they used to be, perhaps because they look slightly odd fitted to riser bars, rather than flat ones. They allow you to vary your riding position, swapping between the grips and the barends as you get tired. Short, stubby ones allow you to ride with your wrists turned outwards; longer curved ones give you a stretched position. Tighten them securely and check the stem fitting bolts. You can get enough leverage from the barends to twist them on the bars or the bar in the stem.

FITTING GRIPS

Step 1: You'll have to make room on the end of the bar first. Undo the bolts that clamp the shifters and brake-levers onto the bars and then slide a chopstick under the grip. Spray or drip water into the gap between the chopstick and the grip, and roll it round to loosen the grip. Slide it further onto the bar, leaving enough room for the barend, and tighten the brake-lever and shifter bolts.

Step 2: Undo and remove completely the barend fixing bolt. Slide a screwdriver into the gap and use it to open out the clamp slightly. This will prevent the barend from scratching and so weakening the bar. Slide the barend onto the bar. If there isn't already a barend plug, fit one – they're there to prevent you making holes in yourself if you fall off onto your bike.

Step 3: Sit on your bike, and roll the barends around to a comfortable angle. A good place to start is usually around 30–45° to the ground. If you find yourself wanting to point them steeply upwards, you might be better off looking at a higher stem. Tighten the barend fixing bolts firmly and then test by standing in front of the bike and pushing both barends down firmly. If either the barends or stem rotate, tighten them.

3 – Out and about

A bicycle opens up a whole world of possibilities, whether it's simply getting to work or setting off on an epic adventure. For some trips your bike is all you need. But as you venture further afield, you'll end up accumulating the kind of accessories that make your life easier. Lights and locks are usually the most vital, but a rack and some panniers are also a great investment. Getting your family cycling with you means you can plan days out, while negotiating with your employer for some basic facilities might help you cycle to work.

Security: which lock?

People who live in big cities often quote security as their single biggest cycling headache. If you like your bike, there's always a worry that someone else will like it enough to make off with it. However careful you are, a moment's inattention or an alert thief with a van full of heavy-duty tools can be all it takes.

People stealing bits and pieces off your bike is often just as irritating as losing the whole thing. For starters, there's nothing superfluous on bicycles, so generally if someone walks off with some of it, you're walking home, pushing or possibly carrying the remains. Getting spares can often be really annoying as, even if the part doesn't cost much, your shop may not have it in stock and you'll have to wait for replacements. It's also not unknown for people to steal parts off your bicycle that make it dangerous to ride. It's all too easy to leap aboard your trusty steed only to find that somebody has whipped your quick-release skewers. It's also upsetting because their chances of being able to use a part that they've stolen off somebody else's bicycle for themselves are fairly slim. To take just one example, seat posts are available in about 30 different common sizes and a handful of weird ones.

All this sounds very depressing, but there is a lot you can do to increase your chances of hanging onto a complete machine. There are two main types of solution – technological and behavioural. To maximise your chances, you must use both of them. Page 45 looks at the kinds of lock you need to have, while page 46 deals with making sure your locking strategy covers all the bases.

Your final line of defence against the dark forces of bicycle thievery is insurance. It won't bring your bike back, but if you're properly covered it softens the blow. Make sure you keep all receipts, take a photo of the bike and keep it with the receipt. Double check with your insurance company when you first buy the bike that it's properly covered in the circumstances you intend to use it and make sure you've understood all the small print. There are all sorts of odd exclusions including policies that won't cover your bike if it's locked up out on the streets after 10pm. Presumably they're expecting upstanding citizens to be tucked up in bed as soon as it's dark, but it seems to miss the point that a bicycle is the best way of getting home once public transport slows down or stops. Make a note of the frame number, too. It doesn't seem to make much difference in terms of the police recovering your bike and returning it to you, but if you don't have it, you may find that your insurance company uses it as an excuse to delay or refuse your claim. If you live somewhere interesting, you may find that quotes for insurance are absolutely outrageous. If you feel like they're taking advantage, you might want to consider a DIY alternative: pay the premium into a savings account instead of to the insurance company. Keep going until the savings account has enough money in it to replace your bike and then just leave it alone until you need it.

Lock it up

However peaceful and sleepy your neighbourhood, you do always need a lock of some kind. An unlocked bicycle is just too tempting and you'll kick yourself if you lose it. The amount you need to spend on a lock depends entirely on where you are – better locks are more expensive and heavier to carry around. U-locks – also called D-locks, depending on which way round they're facing – can be really depressing to buy. The cheaper ones look very much the same as the more expensive ones and it's a chunk of money you spend on your bike that makes it feel worse, rather than better. The quality of lock you need will also depend on how you use your bike. If you leave it outside all day, you'll need something stronger than if you can take it in with you at the end of your journey. If you have to leave it outside your home as well, you'll need something stronger again. As a general rule, you should look to spend around 10 to 20 per cent of the cost of your bike on a lock – so if your bike cost £200, spend £20–40 on a lock.

The people who work at your local bike shop will know most about the level of security you need to have in your local area. Ask them which locks they recommend and use themselves – they get to choose from a vast range of options and don't want to lose their bikes any more than you do.

Lock your bike to some sturdy street furniture

Different kinds of lock

Because security is so important, your main lock should be a substantial, heavy-duty lock. You've got a basic choice between the more common U-locks and chunky motorcycle-style chains. In any price bracket, both styles offer a similar level of security and have advantages and disadvantages.

Chain-style locks are easier to pass around odd-shaped bits of street furniture. U-locks are easier to fit onto your frame and will usually come complete with a bracket that you can use to attach them. Some people prefer U-locks because it seems a bit mad to carry a heavy lock yourself when you have a bicycle that will do the job without complaining. Cyclists worry about carrying big chains around their waist because of the danger of landing on them if they fall off their bike. But it's all down to preference.

Your best bet with a U-lock is to go for one of the big brands – Kryptonite, Abus, Trelock, or Squire. Each manufacturer has its own testing regime, but there isn't a universally accepted test that can be used to compare locks of different brands. If you're insured, check that your insurer doesn't stipulate particular locks before you buy something – a lock may be perfectly good and strong, but if it wasn't on their approved list, they may refuse to make a payout. If they do insist on particular locks, keep the receipt when you buy one to prove that you had one of the acceptable kind. All decent locks are heavy by comparision with your light bike, which is a fairly depressing fact of cycling life.

Your main lock – whatever shape it is – should be used to lock your frame and one of your wheels. This leaves your other wheel vulnerable to theft, so a second lock is a good idea. Quick-release wheels are the easiest to steal, while old-fashioned wheels with nuts mean that the thief needs a spanner. But spanners aren't

A U-lock is easy to fit round your frame and stops opportunist thieves

difficult to get hold of, so in some ways quick-release wheels are an advantage because they stop you from being complacent about locking your wheels up properly. A simple cable is usually sufficient for your second lock. The easiest to use are the extension cables with a loop at either end. Your main lock locks the frame and a wheel with the extension cable looped around the other wheel, slipping the extension cable loops onto your U-lock before closing it. If the extension cable is slightly longer, you can use it to secure your saddle as well. Thread the extension cable through your saddle rails and then pop one end of the extension cable through the loop at the other end. Pull all the way through. When you come to lock up, pass the free end through your back wheel and then stretch it forwards. Thread your U-lock through the frame, the front wheel and some substantial street furniture. Then slip the free end of the extension cable onto the U-lock and close it. When you're unlocking, disentangle the extension from the back wheel, but leave it wrapped around the saddle rails – use a toestrap or a Velcro strip to keep it from hanging into the back wheel as you ride along, or wrap it around your seat post. An alternative to using an extender lock is to use a coil lock as your secondary security. If the thought of having two separate keys is too confusing, the coil lock could be a combination lock.

There are, obviously, myriad little gadgets you can buy to make your bike more secure. The most common of these are security skewers for your wheels. These can only be released with an Allen key. The more sophisticated systems use custom shapes and sizes of Allen key, so you can only release your wheels if you have the special key that comes with your skewer set. These are a great idea, but do make sure they're tightened securely as far too many people cycle around with loosely attached security skewers.

Many new bikes come with a quick-release lever that you use to adjust the seat height. These are especially common on mountain bikes when you often find yourself in situations where it would help to be able to change the seat height quickly. For instance, you might want to lower your seat before riding down a steep slope or jumping off a ledge. Riding around town, there are very few occasions when you need to change your seat height. If you're buying a new bike and it has a quick-release seat post, get it swapped for one that requires an Allen key. It won't completely stop your seat and seat post being stolen, but it does make it a little more difficult.

Combination locks are quick and easy to use and don't require a key

Locking your bike securely: where and how

You can buy all the locking and security devices in the world, but it's not worth as much as taking a little bit of care about where and when you lock up your bike. A lock won't do any good unless you use it every time. Otherwise, you're providing the light-fingered with a swift means of escape and depriving yourself of the means to chase them down. Even if you can run fast enough to keep up with somebody sprinting off on your bike, it's unclear what you would do if you actually caught them.

Safety in numbers: park your bike in busy places

of your bicycle. If you're commuting to work every day and you always work in the same place, it's worth investing in a second lock. Two locks are too heavy to carry around all the time as they'll make your bike feel sluggish and unexciting, but you can leave the heavier one locked up at work and just use it when you get there. Even better is if you can negotiate getting your bike into your work – perhaps there's a few of you that all cycle to work and you could get together and ask for somewhere safe to leave your bike during the day.

If you're on the street, crowded places are better than back streets, where somebody can fiddle about with your bike undisturbed.

The recent explosion in CCTV everywhere doesn't seem to help much in the fight against bicycle theft, but it might help psychologically to park somewhere that's obviously in full view of a camera.

If you're locking your bike to railings in the street, it pays to spend a while considering the best spot. On a busy road, the outside of railings is often a good bet. Anyone attempting to fiddle with your lock or your bike will have to contend with the risk of being run over. Even better are central reservations. They're very exposed, in full view of both passing pedestrians and car drivers. Avoid narrow pavements, where your locked-up bike will impede pedestrians pushing buggies or carrying lots of shopping. You'll annoy people, which is bad, and your bike may get damaged as people push past.

Finally, if you're forced to lock up somewhere that looks dodgy, lock your bike near someone else's that looks flashier in the hope that thieves will ignore yours and go for the eye candy.

You've got to lock to something solid as well. A bicycle that's locked to itself is impossible to ride and fairly difficult to carry, but it's the work of a second to sling into the back of a van, where it disappears instantly. Signposts need a little care as it's easy enough to lift a locked bike up and over the top of shorter ones. Choose something tall with a big sign on the top.

Thefts that happen when your bike is locked to itself or not locked at all are usually the work of opportunists, who can't resist an easy lift. If you're leaving your bike for longer, you need to think about the more professional approach to depriving you

Bike etiquette

Here is a subject guaranteed to raise hackles. Bicycles occupy a tricky middle ground between the vulnerability of pedestrians and the arrogance of motorists. We can all too easily get squashed, but we're also capable of scaring the unwary.

As cyclists we have many different perceptions of ourselves, but almost all non-cyclist thinking about cyclists boils down to just two issues: pedestrians get angry about near misses with cyclists on the pavement and motorists get angry about cyclists jumping red lights. This naturally bewilders most cyclists, who don't usually cycle on the pavements – for a start, they're full of pedestrians who just get in the way – or jump red lights. This obsession with the pavement/red light thing is because the rest of the time we're completely invisible.

So the only time pedestrians and drivers are aware of us, it seems like we're being antisocial. From there it is just a small step to assuming that all cyclists are inconsiderate, pavement-hogging, red light jumping delinquents.

The problem is that bicycles approach quickly and quietly and so have a tendency to surprise innocent passers-by. From the cyclist's point of view, even before you start to think of the ethics of running over an innocent road-user, the selfish argument keeps you on the safe side of too close – running over a pedestrian would hurt too much, let alone what it would do to them, and it is, of course, illegal. Be particularly wary of kids and small dogs as you can never tell what they're going to do next.

The red light issue is slightly thornier. That's because it's perfectly common in busy towns and cities for cyclists to behave as though red lights don't apply to us.

If it's cold and raining and there's no one in sight, it's tempting to just slip across. But it's not really very helpful and it does wind motorists up out of all proportion, especially if the roads are congested. It must clog your arteries to be sitting in stationary traffic in a tin box that's cost you half-a-year's salary and be overtaken by some fit, happy-looking person on a contraption that they can easily pick up and carry onto the pavement if the road jams up too badly.

The times when it's most tempting to pop a red – it's late, you're late, or whatever – are also the times when you should most resist the urge to do so since they're not generally times when your judgement is at its peak and, even if you're well lit, a bicycle is fairly invisible from the side.

It's just not acceptable to jump lights because you're late – that's when accidents happen. Nor is it acceptable to jump them because you can't be bothered to stop or because you don't care. All in all, it's a bad habit to fall into.

Running a red light in any situation is illegal and is just as much against the law as if a car driver chooses to run a red light. For some reason, cyclists have always had an unnecessarily antagonistic relationship with pedestrians, who are the next size down on the food chain. People on foot may generally be slow, rude, oblivious and step out into the road while talking on their mobile phones, but they're just as squashable as us.

But this habitual conflict is good news for the motorist. While we're bickering among ourselves about who has the higher moral ground, we're not looking at the most important issue: many motorists behave in ways that are selfish and dangerous.

If we want to change this, we have to do our best not to alienate ourselves from our natural allies. If we frighten pedestrians, they'll spend the rest of the day complaining about how they 'nearly got run over by another cyclist' regardless of the absence of an actual opportunity for collision.

My suggestion is for you to arm yourself with a bell. It won't get through the soundproofing of anything but the oldest and tinniest car, but it will alert those on foot to your approach, in the nicest possible way of course.

The good part is that it's unlikely to convey anything more aggressive than 'excuse me, please', and gives them a chance to give you enough room. And maybe the next time they're looking for a scapegoat for the bad day they're having, then they won't add you to their list.

All new bikes must have bells – it's the law in the UK

Luggage: pannier options

The existence of panniers makes bicycles about twice as useful as they would otherwise be. Suddenly, they're not just great for carrying you around – they take care of all your goods and chattels as well. Backpacks and shoulder bags are all very well, but they're not ideal on a bicycle. They leave you with sore backs and shoulders and big sweaty patches wherever they sit on your body.

Panniers, however, swallow all your stuff and sit securely on your bike. Good ones will hardly alter the handling and, unlike plastic bags slung from your bars, they won't get caught in the spokes as you pedal.

There is, of course, a vast price range. Your choice will depend on how far you travel and how much you carry. Simple, cheap, nylon panniers are fine for short trips and are cheap enough to replace if they give up the ghost after a particularly enthusiastic shopping trip. The weather will have an effect on your decision too as, if you ride in the rain and carry papers, documents or a laptop, you'll need a waterproof pannier – wrapping things in plastic bags should work but it never does. A secure fitting also gets more important if the contents of your bag are valuable. More sophisticated bags have a locking clip, rather then a simple hook that clips under, as well as over, the tubes of the rack.

If you have to lug the bags around at either end of your journey, it's worth searching for something with a shoulder strap. Panniers work best on the bike in pairs, but once you've left your bike, you've got one in each hand, which doesn't leave room for you to carry anything else or to use your front door keys to open the door. Look also for reflective strips on the backs and sides of the bags as these are remarkably effective in car headlights. If you're intending going camping, the more traditional type of bags with a smattering of differently sized and shaped pockets make it easy to organise your possessions. Bright, cheerful colours help you stand out against the traffic and a light-coloured fabric inside the bag makes it very much easier to see what you've got in there.

One of the shortcomings of panniers is their well-established dislike of neat, flat A4 paper. They have an amazing capacity for making a sheet of it look like a piece of teenage homework finished on the school bus. If this kind of thing doesn't enhance your status at work, consider swapping one of your panniers for a briefcase/office-style bag. These are stiffened to keep the contents looking as they should and double up as a respectable executive-type bag. A combination of a normal pannier on one side – for your clothes, lunch or whatever – and a briefcase on the other balances the load on your bike and keeps smart things away from potentially wet and messy things. Padded inserts mean they'll carry a laptop, too.

A) Secure pannier hooks have an extra tab that locks under the tubing of your rack.

B) Reflective stripes or patches stand out well as they present a broad face to traffic coming up behind you.

C) Handles are essential as full bags are unwieldy otherwise.

D) Hooks at the base of the pannier allow you to compress your load with the shoulder strap, keeping the contents from flopping about and throwing you off balance.

E) Rugged, water-resistant fabric. These panniers have waterproof fabric with welded seams.

F) Watertight closure. Waterproof fabric won't do you any good if the rain can leak in through the openings. In this case, a roll-type fitting means that you can throw the bag in the sea without getting the contents soggy.

G) Wide, square shapes give plenty of capacity.

H) D-loops for a shoulder strap – essential when you have two panniers.

Racks

Racks are an essential first step before you can fit panniers and are also dead handy for strapping random bits of stuff to. For cheap theft-proofing use zipties to strap a second-hand shopping basket or fruit box to the top. It's perfect for slinging shopping into and makes your bike look instantly less appealing to the light-fingered.

There are myriad different rack styles, but luckily most work in the same sort of way. A leg on either side bolts onto the back of your frame, just above the rear wheel axle, and a pair of 'stays' – metal arms – reach forward from the front of your rack and bolt onto the top of the seatstays.

Almost all modern bicycles have special lugs or eyelets to attach racks and mudguards to. They take two forms: a hole may be drilled in the frame and then threaded so that you can screw a bolt into it or a small extra piece of metal may be attached to the frame with a threaded hole already in it. These lugs make rack fitting easier and more secure. In some circumstances, your bike may not have the correct lugs for fitting a rack to. It may be quite old, or it may be a road bike that's designed for racing, when the manufacturer will not be expecting you to fit a rack. All is not lost as you can get special rack brackets from your local bike shop that wrap around the frame and replace the lugs. These are fine if you're going to be carrying shopping or panniers but are not secure enough if you're intending to fit a child seat to the rack. You'll have to think again and either buy a child seat where the bracket bolts directly to the frame or carry your child around on a different bicycle.

Rack (and mudguard) bolts have a tendency to work loose over time. Check them regularly and especially before you set out on a long trip. If you find they have a habit of working loose, apply a small drop of threadlock to the threads before you fit them. Don't overdo it – the screws are very small so a tiny drop will do the trick. If you don't have any threadlock, nail varnish makes a fine substitute. Also, always fit a washer directly under each bolt head since, without one, the bolts will work loose much more quickly. Since racks are mostly made of soft aluminium, tightening the bolts down too hard without a washer will damage the rack around the bolt hole.

Racks will come supplied with a selection of hardware for fitting to your bike. Since nuts and bolts have such a well-known tendency to rattle loose, they're supplied with shake-proof nuts. These look like ordinary nuts, but have a thin plastic ring tucked in above the threads. The inside of the ring is slightly smaller than the bolt diameter, so that, as you tighten the bolt, the nylon ring grips it. It's confusing when you try to fit the nuts since, when you thread the bolt through the shake-proof nut, it moves easily at first and then gets stiff, which makes you think it's the wrong size. Don't worry, it's meant to be like that, but you'll have to hold the nut with a spanner while threading it onto the bolt.

If you're going to be carrying panniers, choose the type of rack that has a dog-leg. This means that the rear leg of the rack is bent backwards and stops the bottom corner of the pannier from getting caught in the back wheel as you ride along. You'll also need to set the rack up so that the top is flat and so that it's set far enough back to ensure the backs of your heels don't hit the front of the pannier as you pedal.

Occasionally, you'll find that the threads that the rack bolts screw into have become clogged with paint and you won't be able to get the bolts in. You'll need to clean the threads out with a small tool called a tap. It's like a bolt, but with sharp threads. You may want to take this to your bike shop to get done. Don't be tempted to just force the bolt into the threads as the chances are that it will snap off in the clogged thread and be a nightmare to remove without damaging your frame.

The 'dog-leg' of the rack stays stop your panniers from getting caught in your back wheel

Shoulder bags and backpacks

For short journeys, where you're stopping and starting constantly and have to rustle about in your bag for keys, the A–Z, packages or whatever, a shoulder bag is perfect. You can swing the bag around your body and get into it really easily. This makes a shoulder bag perfect for messengers.

Messenger
bags are convenient
for short trips

For the rest of us there is a big limitation as carrying a heavy bag slung over one shoulder tires your back out. Messenger bags are handy as the subdivided pockets and various flaps, clips and tabs make it easy to keep things organised, but you're still putting unnecessary stress on your body. If you insist on a shoulder bag, make sure it has a comfortable, padded strap and don't overfill it.

The ideal solution is always panniers – why buy a bike then go to the trouble of carrying stuff yourself? But for lighter loads a rucksack is a lot more convenient, since it gets off the bike when you do and needs no extra hands to carry. A well-designed rucksack will spread the weight evenly between your shoulders and the better ones have raised padded areas down either side. These keep the weight off your spine and allow air to circulate between the bag and your back, to prevent that sticky, sweaty feeling.

If you're going to use a rucksack on your bike a lot, choose something that's been specifically designed for cycling. Camelbak, Karrimor and Deuter (shown here) all make a range of cycling rucksacks. These usually have a waist strap, which are more important for cycling than for walking. When you're stretched out over the bike, a waist strap will reduce the tendency for your bag to roll across your back as you ride. It also spreads the weight more evenly between your shoulders and your waist.

Other useful features round town are loops of webbing that

you can clip an extra back light onto. These always appear to be too low down when you try the bag on, but lower is better when you're on the bike, leaning forwards, since they point the light right backwards. Waterproof covers, especially if they're in bright colours or have reflective strips, are great for bad weather as even if the rucksack fabric itself is waterproof, rain can leak into the bag through seams and zips. Good rucksacks often have a special little pocket for the rain cover separate from the rest of the bag, so that, when you arrive at your destination, you can tuck the wet rain cover away without soaking the rest of your belongings.

Most cycling backpacks are designed so that they can be used off-road. The idea of designing rucksacks specifically for cycling is another result of the influence of mountain biking. Rucksacks were pressed into service for carrying flexible plastic bags of water with a tube coming out the bottom that you can attach to the rucksack strap near your mouth. The bags quickly and inevitably came to be called bladders and the idea turned out to be very popular. On longer rides, they allow you to sip water frequently without having to stop riding and therefore encourage you to drink more water, instead of getting dehydrated.

This is a great idea for whole days in the saddle, but perhaps excessive for a simple commute where, if you suddenly realise you're thirsty, you can pop into a shop and buy something to drink. Rucksacks often come with a bladder and, if they don't, there will be a compartment at the back which you can use to slip a bladder into. Round town, the bladder compartment should be the perfect size and shape to pop a newspaper into.

Rucksacks spread
the weight across
your back

Trailers

Panniers, rucksacks and the like are all very well for the normal day-to-day loads that you're going to have to carry about with you. But some days you'll find yourself needing to move about something that's particularly large, heavy or even just an awkward shape – basically, unsuitable for either pannier or rucksack.

It's a bad idea to use your back for transporting heavy loads – that's what you have a bicycle for. Some loads are not particularly heavy – they're just a bit larger than pannier-sized. Fruit and vegetables are an obvious example as they don't weight much, but the stuff at the bottom will suffer if you stack it into a pair of panniers and then bounce down the road on your bike.

Trailers are a great option for these loads. When it comes to heavy stuff, they spread the weight out over more wheels. Lugging too much stuff about in your panniers will prematurely age your back wheel and tyre. Trailers have smaller wheels, which can take more weight without buckling. A larger, stiff base area allows you to stack your produce in a thinner layer so you don't squash soft or fragile items. The lower centre of gravity also means that the load doesn't sway about alarmingly if you stand up off the saddle to climb a hill.

People often worry that they will jackknife a trailer going round corners. Provided the trailer isn't overloaded and the load is secure, this is actually quite difficult to do. The real problem is forgetting that the trailer is there since, once you've got used to having it tagging along behind you, you won't notice it unless it's very heavy. This is fine until you try to slip between some bollards, whereupon you'll get brought to a halt quite abruptly. If the pavements are busy with pedestrians, watch out for people waiting to cross by the side of the road. They'll let you and your bike go by and then step out into your trailer. Fit a bell to your bars and use it often when it's busy as it seems to shake pedestrians out of whatever dream they're having and encourage them to actually look at you.

Trailers at night need a bit of thought as they're much lower than drivers expect, so fit as many lights to them as you can. Many come with

a flag on a thin pole – at night, fix a light to the flagpole because the flag itself won't be visible.

Single-wheel trailers are the simplest and the best-known are made by BOB. These come with a special replacement quick-release skewer for your rear wheel. The trailer has an arm on either side at the front, which hooks over the slots on the special skewer and locks into place. It's very quick to attach or remove. The single wheel makes it very manoeuvrable and the narrow width means you can slip through the gaps in traffic. It's no wider than an average set of handlebars, so the trailer follows you through any gap. A single-wheel trailer is the only option if you want to go off road as two wheels are always too wide.

Two-wheeler trailers are more stable when riding along and also when parked as they're easier to load and unload. But they do take up more space, which can be an issue if your home isn't vast. Folding versions take care of this and the best will pack flat in seconds. Burley makes a great cargo trailer that unhooks from your bike and folds flat in a couple of minutes. Trailers have a downside in that decent ones will set you back a lot more money than a pair of panniers and, unless you're delivering heavy stuff on a regular basis, you won't need them that often. But if you can find a group of people to share one between, they're great fun.

A trailer will carry much more than panniers. The load is close to the ground which makes it very stable

Baskets, bar bags and toolbags

Panniers, briefcases and rucksacks are all very well and solve most simple transport problems, but sometimes something a little more specialized is called for in the luggage department.

Baskets are right up alongside an expensive U-lock on the list of effective theft-proofing devices. They seem to work as camouflage, blinding others to the value of your steed. The wicker versions are particularly good at this, but the wire mesh versions aren't bad either.

They're also great for short-hop shopping trips, when they'll swallow all sorts of odd-shaped packages without you needing to worry about clipping and unclipping your luggage every other step. Bigger baskets – deeper than about 35cm – need to be supported from underneath to stop them drooping onto the front wheel. A front rack does the job perfectly, but you can also get specific basket supports that clamp on either side of your front wheel. Smaller baskets, where there isn't as much potential for overloading, can clip onto the bars. The Busch & Muller one in the picture has a quick-release fitting, so will snap on and off the bike very easily.

Baskets make shopping trips easy and keep everything where you can see it!

Tool packs

An emergency tool pack and a tube make you self-sufficient in an emergency, but the rest of the time they're just heavy and clutter up your bag. The tools also tend to be grubby, so need to be kept separate from the other contents of your bag, like paperwork and sandwiches.

If you're lucky enough to be able to leave your bike somewhere secure, rather than having to lock it up all the time, the best option is a seat pack that sits under your saddle since it keeps everything in one place and means it's always all there, rather than you having to remember to pack it every time you leave the house. A tool pack keeps the extra weight off your back and on your bike and, if you have the misfortune to come off your bike, tucking all the hard sharp tools away under your saddle makes you less likely to land on them. They're just the right size for tools and a tube and will keep everything together neatly even if you end up having to take it off your bike and stuff the whole thing in your bag occasionally.

Barbags

Barbags are traditionally the preserve of those highly organised and intrepid bands of long-distance cycle tourists, but need to be rehabilitated for town use. Smaller than a pannier, they're the perfect receptacle for all those urban essentials, like phones and front door keys.

The bag sits right in front of you where you can see it and they always have a clear map case on the top, which works just as well for your A–Z as it does for Outer Mongolian route maps.

Modern versions have simple one-handed quick-release brackets, rather than stiff leather straps and a shoulder strap leaves you hands-free off the bike.

Despite their association with drop handlebar road bikes, the bracket will clamp perfectly neatly onto more common flat or curved bars. They're also a handy box shape, so the stiff sides stop your cakes from getting squashed.

Seat packs are perfect for carrying tools as well as a spare tube

Front racks

A rack at the back is plenty for normal amounts of luggage. You can fit a good big pair of panniers to it and unless you need to lug an unusual amount of stuff around with you, they will carry more on your bike than you can manage on foot. But some circumstances require a slightly different approach.

You either need a front rack because a back rack on its own isn't enough or because you haven't got room for a back rack. If you regularly drop your child off at school on your way to work, your child seat fills the space that your panniers would otherwise fit into. You can't easily sling a rucksack or shoulder bag on your back, because it'll sit in the tiny gap between you and them at their head level. A front rack may be your only option for stowage and will help to counterbalance the weight of your child at the back of the bike.

If you're touring by bicycle – rather than simply getting to work and back – you may find that your rear panniers won't hold enough gear as tents, sleeping bags, warm clothes and food take up a fair amount of space if you're off for more than a couple of days. Front panniers spread the weight evenly over the whole bike, which makes it feel more stable and corner more easily.

In either case, best results are achieved if the centre of gravity of the panniers is as close as possible to the front-wheel axle. This is much more important for the front wheel than for the back wheel, because the front wheel of the bike has to be able to move easily from side to side. The big movements – for example when you steer around something – are the most noticeable, but you're also rocking the front of the bike constantly from side to side as you pedal. If the weight of the panniers hangs much higher than the wheel axle, the wheel will tend to flop from side to side. Once it starts moving in one direction, it will tend to carry on over and needs to be wrestled upright, rather than self-correcting back towards the centreline.

This means that good front racks have a slightly different design to rear ones. Instead of having a platform on the top, there's a much simpler frame that holds the pannier away from the wheel on either side. The hooks on the pannier fit over the top of the frame and are prevented from sliding off the front or back by small lugs. This type of rack is called a 'low rider'.

Since they're lower to the ground, front panniers need to be quite a lot smaller than rear ones. This is a good thing, since it prevents you from overloading them, which will make steering hard work however well you've balanced the loads. But smaller panniers can be great when you're camping – separating out some of the essentials you need to be able to access quickly without rummaging through all your various pieces of luggage.

Front panniers come in two different types. The most solid type is called 'custom'. These bolt directly to each fork leg, but can only be used if the fork legs have the right rack fitting – a threaded hole about halfway up the leg and an eyelet before and behind the bottom of the fork leg beside the dropout. There's a square loop frame on either side with a separate stiffening hoop that connects the fronts of the two frames over the top of your tyre.

If you don't have these threaded fittings, all is not lost – as long as you have an eyelet near each dropout, you can use a slightly clunkier version of the same thing, which uses a threaded U-bolt around each fork leg to attach the frames to the fork legs.

Once you've fitted the racks, adjust the positions of the pannier hooks, so that the bag fits as evenly as possible on the rack and the hooks can't slide from side to side. Tuck up any loose trailing straps since the last thing you want is for these to get caught in the front wheel.

You can take everything but the kitchen sink with you

Front lights

Lights tend to be thought of as an added extra, but I can't see the point of having a bicycle if you're only going to use it in daylight. Front lights have two purposes which are equally important when the sun has gone down. They allow you to see along an unlit road and they also allow other road-users to pick you out in the dark.

On busy urban streets, the latter is much more of an issue. Generally, streetlights allow you to pick out enough detail around you to see where you're going, but those same streets also contain so many distracted drivers that a bright light is essential to attract any scraps of their attention. Flashing lights have a chequered legal history, but can help pick you out in busy traffic as drivers have seen enough of them by now to begin to know what they mean. It's difficult to be sure whether a flashing light is better than a steady light, but if in doubt, go for both – you can't have too many lights and one of each gives you a backup in case the other fails.

Your local bike shop will be full of front light options. Basic battery lights are best for occasional use, being relatively cheap. They usually come supplied with their own quick-release bracket, which is essential since there are as many different types of brackets as there are makes of lighting. If you've got more than one bike, pick up a spare bracket at the same time. Sadly, you can't necessarily assume they'll still be available as spares later.

If you're using the bike more than occasionally at night, it makes sense to think about rechargeable batteries. Using endless disposable ones is expensive. The best come with their own charger, so you just have to plug the lights in, rather than worry about taking the batteries out. This may not seem much of a problem, but generally lights have to go on charge just as you get home, while you still remember. In the winter it can just end up being one mission too many when you come in out of the cold, so you forget and then go out again with half-charged lights and get caught out.

For really serious commuting and long rides on unlit roads, look to the night lights that have been inspired by mountain bikers riding off road. Although much more expensive than standard bike lights – three or four times the price – these have a separate battery pack that straps on your frame or under your stem with a cord that leads to a small neat light unit on the bars. The separate parts mean that they're much more time-consuming to take on and off your bike and heavier to carry around, but you get enough light out of them to make oncoming drivers sit up and take notice as well as enough battery life to get you home. Once you're out of range of streetlights, the extra brightness means you can pick out potholes and loose road surfaces before you're upon them. The faster you travel, the brighter your light needs to be to keep up.

Rechargeable batteries are made in different ways – some need to be run down completely before they can be recharged, others should be switched off as soon as they dim. A new light will come with battery care instructions which will extend battery life considerably. If your usual commute is in busy traffic, think about a helmet light. Your head is usually high up enough above cars to allow a light to be seen. This is particularly useful when you need to ensure you're visible to drivers pulling out of side turnings. If you're negotiating gloomy sidestreets, a helmet light means you can illuminate dark corners before you get there. LED versions are powerful enough to show you where you're going, without eating up batteries or giving you a headache from the weight.

Be seen at night

Lights and computers

Your rear-facing red light has a much simpler task than the front light – it's just there so nobody runs you over. As with the front light, the best answer as to whether you should have flashing or steady lights is that you really should go for both as you really can't have too many rear lights.

The other advantage of having two separate lights is that you can't see them when you're riding along, so an extra set is insurance against one of them running out of batteries, bouncing off or switching off.

Carrying panniers with rear lights is often a bit of a tricky combination as one tends to obscure the other. Get somebody to stand behind you and tell you whether you can be seen from behind or not – if the tops of the panniers obscure the light, it will have to be moved upwards or backwards. Sometimes this can take a little ingenuity, so ask your bike shop for help as they'll probably have a little drawer of odd brackets that could be adapted to extend your normal light fitting. Panniers sometimes come with light pockets that face backwards and have a clear plastic panel your light shines through. They're a great idea for eliminating bracket hassles.

Lights on your rucksack or shoulder bag can be a mixed blessing. They have the advantage of always being there and don't have to be taken off your bike every time you leave it. But the positioning is tricky – far too many people cycle merrily around with a bright red light pointing directly up at the sky, which is useless unless you need to make emergency signals to aircraft. If you go down this route, get somebody to stand behind you and check which way you're pointing. Bags and rucksacks often have a webbing loop that lights can be clipped onto, which often but not always point in the desired direction.

Check and replace batteries on rear lights regularly as a subtle red glow under your saddle is not enough to wake up dozy drivers approaching from the rear. Dirty lenses don't help either – give them a wipe sometimes.

Your bike shop will probably have a daunting array of different back lights, all looking very similar but carrying different price tags. A more expensive light will contain more LEDs, and so be more visible from further away, which is worth paying a little bit extra for. You'll also get a more robust construction and bettter weatherproofing.

A good bright light gives motorists plenty of time to see you

Computers

Computers are exactly the kind of thing many people ride bikes to get away from, but if it's important to know how fast you're going or how far you've gone, they're a handy little gadget. They're most useful if you're claiming mileage as work expenses and are also handy for navigating on longer trips. If you're reading the map and know that your next turnoff is in five miles, it helps to know when to start looking.

They calculate how far you've travelled by counting the number of times a little magnet fitted to your spokes passes a sensor fitted to your forks and multiplying that by the distance around your wheel. This means the computer needs to know how big your wheel is, so you usually have to spend a bit of time with a new computer setting it up and calibrating it. Once you've done that the first time, you shouldn't have to fiddle again.

Some computers have amazing features such as altitude measuring, heart rate monitoring and the like. Don't get so carried away when you're riding along that you forget to look where you're going. Normally, the fitting is relatively painless, although the initial calibrating can be confusing. Keep and follow the instructions – each model needs to be calibrated in a particular way. Wireless models use a radio signal from the sensor to the computer. They're more expensive, but easier to fit, neater and you don't have to worry about wires getting caught up and torn.

55

Dynamos

Dynamos are a seriously underrated piece of kit. Far too many people have a memory of really ancient versions, fitted to dodgy Seventies shopping bikes that barely cast the faintest of flickers on the road while adding enough resistance to your tyre to slow you down to a crawl.

It doesn't have to be like this! Decent, modern dynamos use very little of your power – some versions quote 0.5 per cent of your output – and are efficient enough to light up the road ahead of you as well as or better than a good set of battery lights. They have other advantages too: dynamos are always fixed to your bike, so you never get stuck without lights because you've stayed out later than you expected to. You never realise that you've left your dynamo behind on a pub table. If you're concerned about your effect on the environment, anything that reduces the number of batteries you use has to be a good thing, so rechargeable ones are better than disposables but no batteries is better still. Finally, the little hum they give off is kind of reassuring when you're rolling along quiet streets on your own late at night.

There are two basic types. Sidewall dynamos are bolted onto your bike, either onto the frame at the back or onto the forks at the front. They can be fitted to almost any bike, although folding bikes and suspension bikes often require a little inventiveness. Their advantage is they're simple and can be swapped from bike to bike. You do need to keep an eye on the sidewall of the tyre as the head of the dynamo will wear away at it slowly. Swap tyres over front to back or just reverse them every few months.

A second, slightly more complex, option is available. Several manufacturers, including Schmidt and Shimano, make hub dynamos. These replace your front hub with a generator so that electricity is produced continuously as you ride along. This may seem like a waste, creating drag during the day when you don't need light, but in fact they draw so little power that you'd be pushed to notice the dynamo is there. The drawback is that the hub is integral to your front wheel – you can't just bolt the unit onto your bike. The best time to convert to a hub dynamo is when you need a new front wheel as it makes the extra cost of the dynamo unit a bit less painful.

Either way, once you've got a generator attached to your bike, you've got to think about the actual lamp units and then connect it all together. If you're going to be riding a lot at night, it's worth considering the type of light where the lamp unit collects a little extra store of energy and keeps on shining for a couple of minutes after you've stopped moving. This is useful when you're waiting at traffic lights or turn across the traffic in the middle of the road.

It's well worth having a spare bulb for your dynamo lights. The front and back are usually different voltages and there are also a couple of different fittings, so keep one of each in hand and replace blown bulbs straight away. If you don't, all the power that was meant for both lights goes through the remaining bulb and will blow that as well.

Earthing

This is a bit of a diversion in a book about mechanics, but if we're talking about dynamos, we have to spend a moment on wiring. The whole dynamo wiring thing is made out to be a bit of a complex matter, requiring at least a degree in physics. It's actually remarkably simple. The electricity is generated in the generator. It must flow out to the bulb, then back to the generator. The part where it flows back is essential – if there isn't a complete circuit, the electricity will not flow. The section of the circuit from the generator to the bulb is called the 'live'. The section back from the bulb to the generator is called the 'earth'. The live section is always a wire. In many cases, instead of having a separate 'earth' wire, people use the frame of the bicycle instead because, if it's made of metal, it will conduct electricity. The back of the bulb is connected to the frame or the metal stay of the mudguards and so is the generator. This works perfectly well in theory, but doesn't tend to be as reliable as a wire. A separate earth wire means a little bit more wiring on your frame, but as long as you're tidy about it, it takes up no extra room. If you're running both a front and a back light, they will each need a separate circuit from the generator to the bulb and back. For details on how to fit a dynamo to your bike, see page 232.

Front light, generator and rear light – self-sufficiency in the darkness

Mudguards

Countries with a long history of cycling as a means of transport and a healthy amount of rain, don't seem to be affected by the aesthetics of mudguards. There are, however, many places in the world where the humble, hardworking mudguard is regarded with something approaching scorn.

However, if you have to look smart when you arrive at your destination and there's a chance of rain, fit full mudguards. Once they're fitted, you don't have to think about them again, they don't need adjusting and they will last for years without wearing out. If you think they look ugly, there's a chance that the person thinking about stealing your bike thinks so too, so that's a bonus.

Don't be tempted to leave off the front mudguard. In wet weather, your front tyre picks up water as it rotates. Once you pick up speed, this is scooped up by the tyre tread and sprayed off backwards, where it's neatly aimed at your shoes. A front mudguard will keep your toes drier and make your shoes last a little longer.

Mudguard bolts do have a habit of rattling loose and leaving their stays – the thin rods that connect the mudguard to the frame – flapping in the wind where they're in danger of becoming entangled in your spokes. Deal with loose stays straight away. Make sure there's a washer under the head of all stay bolts and drip a drop of threadlock onto the threads before you fit them. If you don't have threadlock in your toolbox, nail polish makes a very effective substitute, irrespective of shade.

If you really can't bear the thought of proper mudguards, but

If you're using your mountain bike for commuting and you need to be able to strip it down for off-road use at a moment's notice, clip-ons suddenly become the sensible choice. Mountain bikes may also be missing the threaded eyelets you need to bolt mudguard stays onto, which reduces your options to clip ons. In which case choose something that follows the profile of the wheel as closely as possible.

Quick-release fittings

Narrow versions are available that are specially made for road bikes where there may not be enough room between frame and fork for anything to fit through. Here, the mudguard is attached to the stays via two plastic blocks, one on either side. These can be secured with small rubber straps for maximum speed of removal. For a slightly more permanent temporary fit, they can be ziptied onto the stay, which reduces irritating rattling.

Front mudguards need to be taken particular care with. It's all too easy to treat them casually as, after all, there's no getting away from the fact that they're a cheap piece of plastic. But they live out their lives perilously close to your front wheel. If they're allowed to flap about, they'll get caught in the gap between your tyre and your fork, bringing you to an unscheduled halt and probably bringing you off your bike in the process. However little your front mudguard cost and however ugly it makes your bike look, it must be secure. Take hold of it and wobble it about – if you can get the tail end of it to touch your tyre, there's a possibility it will get caught. If it can be secured, do so before you ride. If it can't, take it off altogether.

Mudguards should fit close to the wheel

still want to ride your bike in wet seasons, plastic clip-on ones will do the job better than nothing as a last resort. They're not as long or as close-fitting as proper ones, but can be popped on and off according to the weather forecast. Of course, if you take them off, chances are you'll lose them before it next rains.

Storing your bicycle inside

If you're not in the habit of using your bike regularly, you have to find ways to make it as easy as possible to just pop out on it. When you find the journey turning into a mission, the chances are you'll find some other means of transport. Give yourself as much chance as possible by making your bike as ready as it can be.

Living on the ground floor with a big hallway makes life easy as you can park inside the door and just wheel out whenever the urge takes you. But if you live up several flights of stairs or don't have a hallway big enough for your bike, it can take a bit of planning and investment.

Lifts are generally easy to deal with as all but the oldest are designed for wheelchair access and you can get a bicycle into any space you can get a wheelchair into. You'll have to roll the bike up onto its back wheel, so that it's balanced vertically – this sounds unwieldy, but once it's there, use your back brake to control it.

If you live in an older block, look around and see if there are any unused rooms that could be converted to bike storage on the ground floor. This often requires some negotiation. Most success seems to come from approaching other cyclists in your block and making a joint case to your landlord – perhaps you can get a new lock fitted to an old boiler room, with security keys given out in exchange for a deposit.

Storage in shared narrow halls can be a bit of an issue as bicycles fill places very quickly. As well as problems with fire exits, your pedals and handlebars always end up sticking out sideways, ready to bite the unwary non-cyclists who share your entranceway. It's best if you can get the bike up off the ground, where it won't snag anyone's ankles or fall over. A simple hook in the wall might be the solution but this will depend on the exact shape of your hall. Here are some starting points.

If there's an out-of-the-way corner, hang your bicycle vertically in it. A simple hook coming out of the wall at shoulder height is about right as it should point sideways, so that you lift your front wheel up and slide it in under the end of the hook. Your bike will hang there happily, pointing straight upwards as if you were cycling directly up the wall. You can get these from bike shops or hardware stores and you're looking for a hook that's big enough to fit easily around your front tyre.

Wall racks that lift your bike right up and out of the way keep hallways clear. Success depends mainly on what your wall is made of and whether it has the strength to support your bike. Storage racks and hooks usually come supplied with fixing bolts or screws, but this is no guarantee that they'll be suitable, or big enough, for your wall material. If your walls aren't particularly sturdy, swap the screws supplied for longer ones or for the appropriate type of fixture for the fabric of your building.

For narrow hallways even lifting your bike upwards doesn't necessarily help since, if it hangs parallel to the wall, the width of your bars will mean that it may well stick out inconveniently across the hall. A device that hangs the bike off the pedal, like a Mountain Ledge, can be just the right thing – keeping the pedal close in to the wall means that the bike hangs against the wall at an angle. With the wheels tucked in close against the wall, the bars stick outwards, but as long as you get the whole bike high enough the wide bits will be above head height.

Whichever type of indoor storage you use, think about security. Shared hallways seem to provide an abundant harvest for opportunist bicycle thieves. Lock your bike to something solid so that it doesn't get 'liberated'.

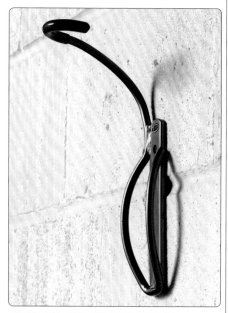

Hanging your bike on a bike hook can solve storage problems

Storing your bicycle outside

Unless you live somewhere that's blissfully free of bicycle theft, outside storage has to be a last resort. As well as the risk of your bicycle disappearing, it also leaves your machine exposed to the weather. If you have to leave your bike locked to a railing or lamp-post outside your house, consider investing in a second lock.

It can be as heavy and chunky as you like as you don't need to worry about carrying it around with you – just leave it locked up outside your house ready for when you come home. That way – when your bike is outside overnight – it can be locked with that lock as well as your normal lock. The rest of the time, just use your normal lock. The same applies if you have to leave your bike outside when you're working – invest in a second lock that you leave attached to whatever you regularly leave your bike secured to.

Lockers are the ultimate outside solution. These are commercially available, you don't have to get them individually made and the local cycling campaign or transport authority will know where to get them from. They're great because you can leave everything in them ready to go and you don't even have to strip the lights off your bike. You can leave a basic tool kit and a pump in there in case of emergencies. They protect your bike and kit from the weather as well. They're not cheap to buy, but as with everything are better in bulk. Again, if you live in a block, get together with other cyclists or potential cyclists to lobby for secure parking. If you're negotiating with landlords or employers, ask them how much they spend annually on car park maintenance. You'll probably be shocked by how much this costs. By comparison, a little cluster of lockers, and the land you need to stand them on, will suddenly start looking cheap.

If you have to leave your bike exposed to the weather, it will need extra attention. The first priority is to make sure that the chain is well lubricated – once it starts to go rusty, it will always be more reluctant to run smoothly or change gear easily. This doesn't mean that the chain needs to be drowning in a thick slick of oily gloop – just apply the normal amount, but make sure that you wipe clean and reapply at least once a month, whether you're using the bike or not. This is especially true if the bike gets wet. Salty air will accelerate any corrosion so be especially attentive if you live near the sea.

Tyres need to be kept pumped up and preferably in the shade as bright sunlight will make tyres and brake blocks deteriorate more quickly. But the best way to take care of your bike is to make sure it gets a regular spin as bikes hate being left still for long periods. It's irritating, but if you service your bike and then ignore it for more than a few months it will always need another service when you haul it out of retirement.

Cables suffer when left exposed to the elements – follow the instructions on page 157 to expose the parts of the cable that are normally concealed under outer casing so that you can clean and lubricate them. Moisture and dirt tend to accumulate in the little space between the cable and the outer casing. If you're riding the bike regularly, the cables all shift constantly in the casing and prevent this coagulating into a sticky paste. Left alone, the cables soon become gummed up. Gear cables suffer particularly badly since accurate shifting depends on the cable being able to slip smoothly through the outer casing. Sticky cables mean sluggish shifting and increased transmission wear where the chain sits awkwardly on sprockets or chainrings.

Saddles and grips or bar tape should be protected. Cover saddles with a cloth – an old T-shirt works just fine – and then a plastic bag as a plastic bag on its own will just attract condensation.

If you can, protect the whole bike by covering it in tarpaulin. You can get specially shaped ones that fit neatly over your bike and tie underneath – bicycle pyjamas. As well as protecting your bike from rain and sunshine, a cover will give it a little extra camouflage and make it more difficult for people to casually steal bits off it.

If your bike's outside regularly, it'll need to be locked to something substantial. If there isn't already a good solid anchor point, set a ring bolt in concrete, or get a chunky rawl bolt (14mm [½ in] or so from a hardware store) and lodge it securely, so that you can thread a U-lock through it.

Bikes left outside need frequent servicing

Your first commute

Maybe you're a seasoned bicycle traveller and are quite confident about launching forth and getting to work under your own steam. If that's the case, you can skip this page quite happily since it's for people who haven't commuted before and are maybe a little bit daunted by the idea.

If you haven't got one already, you'll need to get your hands on a bicycle. Perhaps you should borrow one in the first instance. It's tempting to wonder whether you're really going to cycle regularly or whether it's just a passing phase that you don't really want to invest too much money in.

If it's the latter, many people take themselves off to the nearest second-hand market and purchase a rattling death-trap. Please don't go down this route.

If you're really confident and experienced, you can probably negotiate the traffic on any old machine. However, if you're new to it all, it really makes a big difference if you have a bicycle that works properly. Brakes and gears need to be reliable and tyres need to hold air long enough to get you all the way to work and grip wet roads. Your steed doesn't have to be new, expensive or glamorous, but it has to function reasonably well. Take a cycling friend with you if you're going to buy something. Better still, see if they have a second bike that they might be prepared to loan you for a couple of months while you find out if you're going to enjoy it or not. If you're hauling a disused machine out of the garage, get it fully serviced by your local bike shop before you start.

Once you've got a bike, take some time to do a little bit of planning. Getting to work by bike may be as quick as or quicker than your normal transport.

But you don't want to be scouring the map for a route on your first trip – or worse, getting lost and arriving late. It's a great idea to do a trial run, the weekend before. If some enthusiastic cyclist out there spent ages persuading you to take up cycling, get them to come on the trial run with you.

You can get familiar with your route and have a good idea how long it will take you. Unlike car and bus journeys, bike journeys take pretty much the same amount of time, every time. If you've got a local cycle club or a local campaign group, contact them as they may have a 'bike buddy' scheme where experienced riders agree to accompany novices until they're confident.

If you've got somewhere you can change at work, leave a spare set of clothes there the week before. You might decide you don't need them and that you're quite happy cycling in your normal clothes, but it's worth having them there just in case. If you have to wear smart shoes, leave a pair there so that you can cycle in something more comfortable, like trainers.

And, before you set off, have a proper breakfast to keep you going until you arrive. This checklist is just to give you ideas as some points may not apply to you.

◎ Lock or find somewhere secure to leave your bike. Most bikes are stolen from new cyclists who haven't yet learned to be cynical and vigilant. Lock it whenever it's out of your sight.
◎ Helmet. If you're new to cycling, ignore the helmet politics and get yourself a proper lid that fits you properly and wear it consistently. Once you've been cycling for a couple of years, you'll know where you stand on the should-we-or-shouldn't-we thing.
◎ If it's likely to rain, a light jacket. Unless it's very cold you're more likely to get wet from perspiration coating the inside of a jacket than rain soaking through, so don't wrap yourself in something too heavy.
◎ A bag to carry essentials. Panniers are ideal, but a rucksack will do fine at the beginning.
◎ If you're not confident about the route, a map.
◎ If you know how to use them, a spare tube and a pump. Otherwise, a lock and the cab fare.

That's about it! Leave plenty of time for your first trip, especially if that means you can reward yourself with breakfast or coffee when you get there.

Once you've done your first trip, don't overdo it. If you've not cycled a lot before, remember that you don't have to do it every day at the beginning. You could start doing it one or two days a week and see how you get on.

You might find it tiring the first few weeks so build up to it gradually, only increasing the number of days when you can do so without arriving knackered.

It's supposed to be something you enjoy. If you find yourself hating it, cut back and ride in on fewer days. If you can leave your bike somewhere secure overnight, you don't have to ride both ways – ride in one morning, then get the bus home. The next day, reverse it so you take the bus in and ride home. And if you wake up and the weather is really horrible, it's fine to skip days. If you find yourself loving it, there's plenty of time later for buying the kind of gear that makes even the nastiest weather a pleasure to ride through.

Getting your employer on board

In terms of mileage, a regular cycle commuter will slowly but surely clock up a mileage far in excess of that covered by an average Sunday cyclist, who might drive to an event every couple of weeks, get their bike out of the car, do a 10-mile race or a 40-mile ride and then drive home. But many regular commuters seem to think that, just because they don't cycle around dressed like crisp packets or have long tedious conversations about what gear ratio they use, they're not 'real cyclists'. We need to change this idea.

If you work in the same place every day, your employer is usually the person who can make the difference between it being really easy to cycle to work and it being awkward and unsatisfactory. You've got a big advantage if there are a few of you, so get to know the other cyclists in your building, work out between you what you need and ask for it as a group. Many areas have a local cycle campaigning group. It's worth making contact as they may have had experience with other employers in your area that they could share.

Security is one of the things that an employer can usually provide fairly easily. If they provide car parking, it's usually a fairly small step to get secure bike parking provided too, mainly because providing and maintaining car parking is actually a remarkably expensive thing for your employer to do. Bike parking takes up far less valuable, expensive space and you can get 10 bikes in the same space as a car. If there is secure car parking, see if there's a corner of it that could be given over to bicycles – there's usually a designated motorcycle space. If there isn't a guard, try to get the bike area located somewhere where it's overlooked by a busy window, rather than tucked away in some obscure corner where nobody will notice anything going on. Even better is a room inside the building – if there are enough of you to justify this, try to identify an underused storage room or basement that could be converted to bike parking and get racks installed so that you don't have to lean all the bikes up in a big pile.

Showers, lockers and a changing area are a major plus in an office. Lockers allow you to leave a pile of clean clothes at work at the beginning of the week and cycle in something more comfortable. If you have to look smart at work, cycling in your work clothes won't do them any good anyway.

You may have to use some careful arguments to persuade your employer to spend money on secure cycle parking, installing changing rooms and so on. See how many other people you can get on board – non-cyclists that you work with might appreciate being able to go for a run or to the gym at lunchtime and having somewhere to change. A local or national cycle campaigning group may be able to help here as some areas with a lot of congestion have schemes to persuade big employers to discourage car commuting and they may have details of tax breaks for employers who can show they're doing their bit. These are generally known as 'Green Travel Schemes' and are becoming more common in busy cities across Europe and the US.

There can be other positive spin-offs for your employer, too. One option to consider would be a 'pool bike' that anyone in your workplace can use to make short local trips. It could supplement a pool car, or save time on trips that would otherwise be walked. It will inevitably get used more in the summer than in the winter, but may gradually convert occasional users into regular cyclists.

You should be able to set up a maintenance contract with a local bike shop to keep the machine in good working order and replace worn or broken parts. The pool bike will need some basic kit so that it's always ready to go, but this needn't be extensive. A helmet, some lights, and a lock with several keys is a great start.

Arguments that work well for employers are statistics that show that cyclists are generally healthier than non-cyclists and so lose fewer work days to sickness. Whether this is because of an increased level of fitness, not being a sitting target on public transport for whatever bug is currently going around or just being cheerful self-motivated folk is unclear. Getting to work on time seems to present less of a problem, too. A 2004 survey by the Chartered Management Institute found that the most reliable way of getting to work is by bicycle. The CMI survey examined the levels of disruption experienced by managers travelling to work by car, bus, motorbike, train, the underground and bicycle to find that those travelling by cycle experienced the least amount of delay. As a cyclist you're blissfully unaffected by public transport strikes. The occasional puncture delay seems insignificant by comparison.

Cycling with young children

Trips with kids and bikes are great as they get some exercise, wear themselves out and get to see the world going by under their own steam. Bestowing a habit of exercise can only be a good thing, especially if they associate it with something they've enjoyed with you. There are many ways to find the right balance between getting them to provide a bit of pedal power and keeping them safe in traffic.

Most kids love riding around in child seats, but you have to wait to put them in a child seat until their neck muscles are strong enough to hold their heads and a helmet upright This is definitely not before a year old and many osteopaths recommend waiting until 18 months. The helmet debate is much simpler with young children than it is with adults – kids' skulls are too soft and their brains too busy growing not to wear one. Luckily, unlike the rest of their bodies, their heads grow very slowly so the same helmet will last for years. The same applies to kids' helmets as adults – if the lid gets a knock, it needs to be replaced. This counts for the helmet falling off tables or bumping down flights of stairs too.

Baby seats come in both front and back versions. The front versions mean that you can keep a close eye on the child and they can chat away and see where they're going. Front seats have another advantage as well – they're very effective as a windbreak, keeping your torso just that little bit warmer. Great for you, but make sure you wrap the little one up especially warm – they're not doing any work, so haven't got the muscle glow that you have.

Rear seats are easier once they get a little bit bigger and it starts to get tricky to see over the tops of their heads. It takes practice to load them up effectively – once the child is in the seat, you can't let go of the bike until you're on it. Your bike doesn't have enough stability to leave bike and child leaning against a wall and if they move suddenly the whole thing tumbles down.

Kids often fall asleep on bike seats as the movement is reassuring. This seems to work just as well in busy traffic as it does on quiet streets and country lanes, so make sure they're strapped in securely before you start – your balance gets a little tricky if they slump sideways in the seat and, if their heads loll over the side of the seat, they pass a little too close to the wing mirrors of parked cars for comfort.

There is also an issue with how much they weigh. Many seats are rated up to around 40kg (80 lbs), but don't use this as an absolute guide. If you're big and tall, it's fine, but a loaded child seat begins to get too unwieldy for safe cycling as soon as the child weighs half as much as you do.

Fitting child seats onto smaller bikes can also present problems, and you may find that if your frame is smaller than about 38cm (15 in) you may not be able to fit a child seat on the back securely.

There are several brands of bike seat that work particularly well. Co-pilot makes a couple of different types, one of which comes off the bike and doubles as a baby chair. Two European makes – Hamax and Bobike – are solid with sturdy brackets to fit the seat to the frame and adjustable harnesses. Always follow child seat fitting instructions very carefully and get your bike serviced. You're adding a lot of extra weight to your machine, so make sure brakes, wheels, tyres and gears are in tip-top condition. Make sure your rear light is clearly visible with the seat in place, and that it's got enough battery power to give a good bright glow. Attaching the light near the top of the seat means it will give maximum visibility, and also help emphasise to drivers that you have a childseat on your bike. Puncture-resistant tyres are a great idea – especially for the back, where the extra weight increases the likelihood of flats. Fixing a puncture by the side of the road is also less appealing than ever when you have to keep an eye on junior at the same time.

The period after your children have grown out of a child seat is the most difficult to deal with. By the time they've got to that age, they're generally big enough to be taught how to ride a bike, but still too young to deal with busy traffic on their own and not strong enough to cycle very far under their own steam. The most useful solution I've come across for this age are trailer bikes. These clamp onto the back of your ordinary bike, turning it into a temporary tandem. The trailer bike just has one wheel at the back and follows the main bike's path. They have their own set of pedals and, on fancier models, their own gears. It makes a huge difference to your combined speed when they pedal – although sometimes this takes some persuasion because it's just as easy to sit on the back and be towed along! But pedalling keeps them warm and makes hills a lot easier for you. If you're dropping them off at school, the trailer bike part unhitches in seconds, so you can leave it locked up ready for you when you come back. It's no effort to leave it hitched on the back and tow it empty, but it does bounce around a bit and people in the street amuse themselves by shouting to you that you've lost your stoker. They retain their resale value and so can be passed on to the next cohort once they get to the independent stage.

Teaching kids to ride

It's such a cliché that once you've learned to ride a bicycle you never forget how, but it seems to hold true. Most people also have a clear memory of the first time they managed to balance on their own and the instant feeling of freedom.

If you're teaching kids to ride, earlier rather than later is easier, not particularly for their sake, but more for yours. There's no real way round spending a session running around and holding them upright until you decide they're ready go solo and, the smaller and lighter they are, the less exhausting the whole process is. Younger kids have often not yet learned to be scared of things and so are far more relaxed about the whole process, which helps them balance better. They seem to bounce better, too, and so are less disheartened by the occasional spill.

Learning to ride a bicycle is a particularly complicated process for kids because it requires them to master four separate skills – pedalling, steering, balancing and braking – simultaneously. This is a bit of a tall order because you can't really learn any of them until you've already mastered the other three. Stabilisers are a quick fix, avoiding the question of balance, but at some point you're going to have to tackle it and sooner is better than later since, the more they grow, the harder work it is to run beside them keeping them up. Besides, stabilisers are usually badly made and fall off at the smallest excuse.

Instead of fitting stabilisers, one idea is to take pedalling skill out of the equation and use the bike as a scooter at first. Remove both pedals. You'll need a 15mm pedal spanner. Remember that the left-hand pedal – as you're sitting on the bike – has a reverse thread and so undoes clockwise.

While you've got the spanners out, have a check of the brakes as well. Kids have smaller hands and much less strength than you. Check that the brakes are easy enough for them to use by pulling each lever with just one finger. If the brake lever has a reach adjust screw, wind it in so that the lever blades rest close to the bars. You'll probably find that you have to readjust the brakes after this – see the brakes chapter.

Pump up the tyres to the maximum printed on the tyre walls, so that the bike rolls easily. If the bike has gears, shift into an easy gear and leave it there.

Now you're ready for the maiden voyage. Take the pedals you've removed, the pedal spanner and a spanner for adjusting the seat height. Choose an open space, as big as possible so that you don't have to worry about bumping into other people. Drop the seat down far enough so your child can get both feet flat on the floor. They should be able to sit on the bike and scoot themselves about quite safely. At this stage, you need to teach them about steering and braking. Even without the pedals,

they'll begin to be able to feel the effects of steering to the left and right. As they turn corners, the bike will lean into the corner. Encourage them to try left- and right-hand bends.

Before they've worked out quite how fast they can go, teach them how to brake effectively. It's important that they learn to start using the brake levers straight away, rather than just dragging their feet along the ground.

And if you're not in a hurry, you can leave the bike set up like this for as long as it takes for them to get confident. As they get more confident, they will begin to experiment with going a little faster and cruising downhill and during long boring straight bits. There's no hurry with the next bit – wait until they're completely confident with steering and braking before you refit the pedals. It might be the same day, but another day is just fine too.

Check your pedals and work out which is left and right. It will be stamped on the axle. Screw in the right-hand pedal clockwise (as if you were sitting on the bike). The left-hand pedal screws in backwards, so anticlockwise. Raise the saddle slightly to give them room to turn the pedals, but make sure they can still reach the ground easily on both sides.

Now you have to do the running along beside the bike bit. Choosing a very slight downhill slope certainly helps and don't be impatient to let go too soon as a crash will put them off. The key to balance often seems to be getting them to look forwards, rather than down at their feet. Enlisting a helper to stand a few metres away and act as your target helps, giving them someone to look up at and if necessary be caught by.

Most kids get the hang of this in an afternoon, but don't despair if it doesn't happen straight away – it might be worth having the pedals off again and going back to scooting along until they feel more confident about their balance.

With practice, they will learn to use the brakes, how to pedal and steer effectively. Keep the saddle low at first to give them a chance to practise these basic skills, so that, if it all begins to go wrong, they can put both feet solidly on the ground. Raise the saddle gradually as confidence grows. Although it's harder to put feet down with a higher saddle, it's easier to put more power into the pedals. First bikes don't have to be new, or have gears, or be particularly lightweight. The most important things are that the brakes should work well and the bike shouldn't be too big. It's much easier and less frightening to learn to ride if the chld knows that s/he can put her/his feet down at any moment.

Holidays: tents and bicyles

Enough of all that sensible stuff about using your bicycle to get to boring old work. They're the perfect vehicle for having fun on, too. The great advantage is that, on a bike, you move quickly enough to be able to get to new places, but slowly enough to experience the area you've come on holiday to.

It's remarkable how few essentials there are when you're camping and how your perception of 'essential' changes when you're carrying everything up every hill under your own steam.

There are no real limits to the places people choose to go cycle touring, but any combination of temperate weather and quiet roads is likely to be a winner. Hills and mountains make for interesting scenery but are hard work, so when planning, take elevation into account as well as distance – steep terrain might halve your mileage. Plan some day trips before you set out to give yourself an idea of how far you can comfortably go in a day. Then it's just a case of poring over maps of faraway places and setting off! Some useful things to take with you:

- A decent map and some kind of plan.
- A compass is always handy – it doesn't have to be an expensive version, but being able to tell where North is helps.
- Tent. If you've got company, share the tent between you, otherwise they're bulky. If you have to pack it up wet, strap the outer cover to the top of your panniers, so that you don't soak everything else as well.
- Sleeping bag and sleeping mat – the Thermarest style that inflate themselves are expensive but well worth the investment. After pedalling all day, you'll appreciate a decent night's sleep. They pack up small, too.
- Camping stove. If you're flying, think through your fuel options – you can't put pressurised canisters on the plane, so, if your stove uses them, make sure you can pick up a bottle at the other end. Check for fuel availability at your destination as this varies from country to country.

- Instant food that can be cooked in a single pan if possible. Soup, rice, potatoes, fruit and plenty of emergency tasty bars to eat during the day. Food gets a magic flavour of its own if you've carried it all day, so there's no need for anything fancy – just choose things that are easy to warm up.
- Water. Clean drinking water isn't always easy to come by and water purifying tablets and kits are essential in remote locations.
- A small first-aid kit. Hopefully you won't need it, but it helps to be self-sufficient. Pack some insect repellent.
- An emergency tool kit. The one listed on page 75 will get you far, but if you're going to be travelling far from any towns big enough to have a bike shop, add spares from page 74.
- Clothing depends entirely on where you're going, but wherever it is, layers work best. Thin layers will pack smaller and be more flexible than bulky layers. If you're expecting rain, fabrics that dry quickly are vital. If your campsite has a launderette, use the dryers. Especially good on cold days is putting your clothes into the tumble drier for a few minutes before you put them on.
- If you ride with clipless pedals, your feet will appreciate something to change into at the end of the day.
- Sun cream. Even on cloudy days, it's easy to underestimate the strength of the sun because you're constantly being cooled by the air flowing past you. Backs of necks, tops of heads, knees, calves and the backs of your hands all need plenty of protection.
- A coil lock. It's easy to be carefree because you're on holiday, but your bike is still a tempting target if you leave it and wander off somewhere.

There's nothing like the freedom to travel at your own pace and go wherever you want...

Charity bike rides

For many people, charity bike rides are their first exposure to long-distance cycling. If you've got one coming up and you're feeling daunted because you've never ridden that far before, this page is for you.

You might have got talked into it over a couple of beers, it might be something a bunch of your mates are doing, or maybe you just see it as a way to kick-start a healthier, fitter lifestyle. The key to an enjoyable day out – and still being able to sit down without wincing the next day – lies in preparation, for both you and your bicycle. If you're borrowing a friend's bike, or dusting off something from the garage, take it to a bike shop for a service, so that you can be sure the brakes are working properly and that it's in a safe condition. If your chosen ride is local, get it in well in advance – lots of their other customers may have the same idea at the same time and they'll be inundated in the run-up to a popular event. As well as getting your bike serviced and the tyres pumped up, take a little time to get your riding position adjusted, too. Check out Chapter 2 for tips on getting the seat and handlebar height right, and think carefully about how comfortable the saddle is. If it doesn't suit your bottom, you'll know about it the day after the ride. Invest in a perch that doesn't make you hurt before the big day as you'll be spending a fair amount of time sitting on it.

Once your bike is sorted out, it's time to concentrate on the engine – you! Your enjoyment of the actual ride will depend on how fit you are, so get out as often as you can in the weeks and months before the ride. A frenzied burst in the last couple of weeks won't do you any favours at all. A better approach is to wind up your mileage gradually over the 10 or 12 weeks before the ride. Try to get out at least three times a week, but if you've given yourself enough of a run-up, you don't have to go mad – start with 20-minute rides and keep the pace up enough to make you feel like you're working, but not so you can't hold a conversation. In fact, if you're finding it hard to get motivated, make a regular date to pedal around the park with a friend. It makes it seem less like hard work and more like something you'll look forward to. If you live near your work, you could think about using your commute to get you in shape. Try riding to work a couple of days with a longer trip at the weekends. As you get nearer the day, increase the length of one of your trips every week, until in the last couple of weeks before the ride one of your rides is around half as long as the proposed route. Then you'll be ready.

On the day itself, take it steady for the first few miles. It's tempting to charge off and exhaust yourself. If it's not a race, take time to enjoy and stop for a rest whenever you feel like it.

Take plenty of water with you since, although you may find that the organisers hand it out, you don't want to be waiting for the next official stop when you're thirsty. Plain water is almost always your best bet as, unless you're used to them, sports and energy drinks can make you feel queasy rather than sprightly. Snacks, that are easy to eat and tasty even if they get squashed, are essential. Nuts, fruit, muesli bars and so on will keep your energy levels up throughout the day. Eat little and often so you don't have a chance to get hungry.

Similarly, the organisers may provide mechanical back-up, but it's well worth your while taking a basic tool kit, a spare tube and a pump. The kit list on page 75 should cover most emergencies.

Arrows will have been put up to show you the way on bigger rides with marshals at busy intersections, but they'll usually provide a map too. Keep this as you'll then know how far you've got to go. Don't forget to stop occasionally on the way and have picnics and take pictures too – your sponsors will always pay up more readily when they see the evidence of your adventures!

When you get to the finish, stretch tired muscles while they're still warm and drink plenty of water. If your legs feel very tired, they'll thank you if you walk around for a little after you stop riding. Don't forget to take a picture of you under the finish line! And – if you did enough training to enjoy it – you might well find yourself thinking that you've found yourself a whole new way of getting about that means you arrive quicker and feel healthier, all at the same time!

Although the vast majority of bike rides are day trips you can take yourself further afield as well – many of the larger charities will take you off for a couple of weeks to somewhere hot, sunny and exotic, as long as you pledge to raise a minimum donation. All the same rules about preparation apply to longer trips as well as day trips, just writ large – get your bike thoroughly serviced and set up before you start training and set enough time aside so that you're fit enough to cover the daily mileage without suffering. Try to get your body used to the idea of exercising every day before you go as in many ways the frequency is more important than the intensity or length of your training sessions.

Your charity's tour operator will have plenty of information about where you'll be going and what you should expect, but if in doubt, ask for a kit list – they always contain good ideas. Ask if they'll put you in touch with people who've previously done the trip, who may be able to pass on invaluable tips.

Bicycling holidays

Your bicycle is a great way to explore new places. Camping is fun, but for an easier holiday, pack your bike up and take it with you and use it to make day trips out from wherever you're staying. This means you only ever have to carry a few hours' worth of supplies with you, rather than everything you need for your whole trip.

Page 67 gives you tips on how to pack bicycles onto a plane, but they can be thrown onto many other forms of transport too. Trains may require negotiation, since every country and rail operator has its own list of regulations about when and where they may be carried, but as long as you follow the rules, bicycle carriage is often free or cheap. The same goes for ferries and it's even possible to get bicycles onto coaches – although it's more likely to have to involve you in charming the driver as your bike will have to go in the narrow trunks under the coach.

The most important thing to remember is that just because you're on a cycling holiday, you don't have to ride every day. You're supposed to be enjoying yourself, so make time in your schedule to spend a day on the beach, sightseeing or just chilling out. If you come home more exhausted from your holiday than you set off, you've done too much!

Where to go depends on what kind of experience you're after. Many mountainous areas in Europe and America have set themselves up as off-road holiday venues. In some cases, like certain areas of the Alps, they're ski resorts in the winter and mountain bike destinations in the summer. This means that all the infrastructure is there for you – chalets, bars and connections to airports and big train stations. Ski lifts are great for bikers, too – you can spend days and weeks just riding downhill and then using your time on the lift to catch your breath in time for the next gravity-assisted blast downwards. Many of the more extreme areas are best appreciated with full-suspension bikes, full-face helmets and body armour – but don't worry if you're not fully equipped since all of this can usually be hired from local companies, which saves you the bother of lugging it with you as well as the expense of buying it. Popular destinations in Europe include Verbier and Chamonix in the Alps and the Picos De Europa in northern Spain. As befits the birthplace of the mountain bike, the USA has more classic destinations than it's possible to list, but Moab in Utah and the nearby upstart biking hub in Fruita offer a lifetime's worth of getting lost and dirty on two wheels.

Unless you're a fairly experienced mountain biker and very organised, you'll probably appreciate using an established company to sort out your holiday. You can choose what level of nurture you need – some will simply book you suitable accommodation, point you at the trails and be available when and if you need them. There's a lot to be said for getting a guide, however. If you're only in an area for a week or so, it's impossible to find all the best trails for yourself. A guide will know how to link good routes up and will also have experience of the weather conditions – which can change very quickly in the mountains and catch you out if you don't know what to look for.

Clearly, holidays are not simply the preserve of the knobbly tyre. A road bike lets you eat up the miles between towns, enabling you to enjoy the scenery between refuelling in coffee shops. Popular destinations are usually hilly rather than flat. For those who enjoy looking at the scenery, mountains tend to be more interesting to look at and for those who are concerned solely with improving their performance on the bike there's no substitute for gradient. Areas like Northern Italy, with thriving local road clubs, are ideal destinations as there are always plenty of well-equipped bike shops and bike-friendly cafes. Plus, drivers are used to coming across groups of cyclists on the roads. Again, going to a tour operator is the easiest way to arrange a holiday if you've not done it before as they'll have a network of places to stay that are bike-friendly with secure places to leave your bike.

Both of those options are quite energetic, but if you're after something gentler, a bike is the perfect way to enjoy flatter destinations as well. Holland, Germany and Scandinavia all have well-developed networks of cycle routes, many of which are completely separate from other traffic, making them ideal places to take kids for a low-stress active holiday. Efficient signposting makes navigation less of a worry and you can intersperse days on the bike with other activities, or just have rest days!

Bikes can take you far from the madding crowd

Bikes on planes

Getting away on holiday with your bike is great, but getting your bike there safely with you can be a bit of a headache. There are a few steps to take before you start packing, though. Airlines vary over how willingly they each accept bicycles as luggage. You have most bargaining power when you're just about to buy a ticket – once you've handed over your cash, you'll have to take your chances with their guidelines and the check-in staff.

Ensure they know that you're taking a bike when you buy your plane ticket. If you buy the ticket in person, get them to write down that your bike comes too and take the piece of paper with you when you check in. If you buy the ticket on the phone, write down exactly who you spoke to. If it's on the internet, email them and find out what the situation is: if they say yes, print out the email and take it. Many airlines will take a bike free of charge as long as you stay within your weight limit, but check when you buy the ticket. Once you arrive at the airport, you're too committed to argue effectively against unforeseen charges for sports equipment.

A few days before you fly, get on the phone to the airline and find out how they prefer to have the bike packed. They might not have an opinion. On the other hand, they might have a very strong opinion about whether it has to be boxed or not. This may seem like a lot of effort and mostly you'll just be waved through the gate, but occasionally some back-up can make all the difference.

Packaging to protect your bike in transit is essential. This comes in two forms: expensive and free. Easiest to lug about are bike bags. Made of thick Cordura, usually with padding, these come with thick shoulder straps. A more glamorous and protective version is a hard case. These are made of fibreglass and have wheels. They have plenty of space for all your other cycling paraphernalia (helmets, shoes or whatever) and are the most protective option. The problem with both hard and soft bags is what to do with them on holiday. If you're staying in one place, fine: they're not much bother. But if you're moving around, they're a bit of a pain.

A lower-tech option is to re-use the cardboard boxes that new bikes arrive at bike shops in. You can generally pick these up for free or very cheap as they're bulky rubbish that shops are glad to get rid of. And your bike will fit into one with a little careful packing, sometimes with enough room left over for shoes and helmets. Once you get to the other end, you can sometimes find a left luggage to store them in. Alternatively, abandon the box on arrival and scout out another on your way back – most towns big enough to have an airport will also have a bike shop.

When the box arrives at the far end, it doesn't usually come out of the same baggage carousel as the rest of the bags. Search the airport for something like an 'oversize luggage' depot. Check

the box straight away and, if it's damaged, get a claim form as it's very much harder to convince airlines that they've damaged your property once you've left the airport.

Packing your bike into the box takes a little care as the boxes are only just big enough.

- ◎ Remove the pedals. The right-hand pedal has a normal thread and unscrews anticlockwise. The thread on the left-hand pedal is a reverse thread and unscrews clockwise.
- ◎ Remove the front wheel and, if it has a quick-release skewer, remove it completely from the axle.
- ◎ Next the bars will have to come off. It's easier if you have a front-loading stem where there are two or four bolts on the front of the stem, which you can remove to separate the bars from the stem. Replace the front face of the stem and the bolts so you know where to find them.
- ◎ Let a little bit of air out of the tyres. Airlines always ask you to do this as there seems to be an urban myth that tyres will explode in the hold. Leave enough air in the tyre to protect the rim – the tyre should be soft, not floppy.
- ◎ Turn the forks to face backwards. If you have disc brakes, pad the calliper by taping bubble wrap or cardboard around it. Do the same with other delicate parts like shifters.
- ◎ Turn the left-hand pedal to point forwards and up and then slide the front wheel over the crank from the front, so that the wheel sits beside the main frame of the bicycle with the crank sitting between the spokes.
- ◎ Tie or tape the wheel to the left side of the frame, and the handlebars to the right side, making sure not to kink or bend any of the cables.
- ◎ Remove the seat and seat post.
- ◎ If you have a fork brace (a short strip of plastic that wedges into the fork dropouts to protect them), fit it now.
- ◎ Drop the bike into the box – it should just fit. Tape together or bag up the bits you've removed like the saddle, pedals and quick-release skewer. Include in the box everything you need to reassemble the bike such as pedal spanner, Allen keys and the pump necessary to re-inflate the soft tyres.

4 – Basic tools and equipment

One great thing about modern bicycles is that a large proportion of the fitting, adjusting and replacing of components can be done with a fairly small selections of tools. You don't need to spend a fortune to go a long way towards being self-sufficient. This chapter takes you through some of the more common tools, explaining what they're for and when you need them. At the end, there are a couple of pages that should help you avoid needing to fix your bike. Checking it over regularly will help avoid annoying and expensive breakdowns.

The language of bicycle parts

People who talk about bikes sometimes sound like they're speaking a foreign language. Some words they use are unfathomable and bizarre, while others sound familiar but often mean something completely unexpected. The language of bikes isn't just a way of keeping in the clique, however. It's vital to be able to identify specific parts, so you can work out what's wrong, explain the problem to somebody else or buy the right replacement when some part of your bike breaks or wears out.

A) Disc brake callipers (aka disc brake units): These are bolted to special disc mounts on your frame or fork. Operating the lever forces thin, hard pads onto your rotor (the metal disc attached to your hub). Powerful and lightweight, these can be daunting to service because they're new technology. However, they respond well to treatment with a few basic tools. Mechanical versions use normal V-brake levers and cables; hydraulic disc brakes use an oil-filled hose to force brake pads onto the rotor.

B) Cables and hoses: Connecting brake levers to callipers or V-brake units, these need to be kept in good condition to transmit an accurate signal. Speed control, as well as raw braking power, is vital. Steel cables run through lengths of outer casing from brake levers to V-brakes. Hoses are the stiff plastic tubes that transfer hydraulic brake fluid from hydraulic brake levers to callipers.

C) Chainset: This consists of three chainrings bolted together. Like the cassette sprockets, choosing a different-sized chainring gives you a different gear ratio. Larger chainrings give you a higher gear, which is harder to push, but propels you further on each pedal stroke. Smaller chainrings give you a lower gear, allowing you to climb steep hills. Chainrings will wear out over time as the valleys between the teeth stretch until the chain slips under pressure.

D) Cassette and freehub: Your cassette consists of a set of different-sized sprockets bolted together. Currently nine-speed cassettes are most common and combine with the three chainrings on your chainset to give you 27 gears. Smaller cassette sprockets give you a higher (harder) gear for maximum speed, while larger sprockets give you a lower (easier) gear for climbing. The cassette is fitted to a freehub on your rear wheel. Your freehub body is attached to your wheel, and is a ratcheting mechanism that allows the rear wheel to continue spinning freely when you stop pedalling.

E) Chain: The chain connects your chainset to your cassette so that the back wheel goes around when you pedal. It needs to be strong so it doesn't snap when you stand on your pedals and stamp up a hill, but it must also be flexible so that it can shift from side to side across the cassette and chainset. Chain width needs to match your cassette. For example, nine-speed cassettes have narrower, more closely spaced sprockets than older eight-speeds so you need a narrower chain.

F) Headset: The main bearing at the front of your bike, the headset connects your forks to your frame. This part is often ignored because it's mostly hidden in the frame. This bearing must be adjusted so it turns smoothly without rattling — any play or binding will affect your bike's handling. There are two types of headset: the newer 'Aheadset' type shown here has almost completely superseded the older threaded headset. Regular servicing keeps bearings running smoothly and helps your headset last longer.

G) Bottom bracket: Bottom brackets are another component that is out of sight and frequently forgotten about. The bottom bracket axle connects your two cranks together through the frame. If worn and loose, the bottom bracket can lead to front gear shifting problems and cause your chain to wear out. Worn bottom brackets can be spotted by checking for side-to-side play in your cranks. Usually supplied as a sealed unit, this part must be replaced when worn or stiff. This repair needs a couple of specific, but inexpensive, tools.

H) Wheels: Your wheels take most of the punishment as you ride around. If they're straight and round, they'll last much longer. Adjusting the spokes so that they're as strong as possible takes some patience, but once you've learned how to do it, you'll save yourself money and time. Tyres keep your grip on the road and protect your inner tubes from punctures.

I) Hubs: Well-adjusted hub bearings let wheels spin freely and save you energy. When properly adjusted, your bearings will be tight enough to prevent any side-to-side play without being so tight they slow you down. Occasional servicing to clean out any grit and dirt that has worked its way in will keep your wheels turning smoothly. Fresh, clean grease helps keep moisture out of your hubs. Jet washing your bike at the garage is tempting, but will drive water in past your hub seals, flushing out the grease. This is a bad idea.

 J) Suspension: Suspension makes your ride smoother. Many new city bikes come with front suspension forks and full suspension bikes (with front suspension forks and a rear shock unit) get lighter and cheaper every year. A cheaper alternative is a suspension seat post. There isn't much of a weight penalty

and they don't need much maintenance. The suspension keeps your centre of gravity moving forward rather than up and down, reducing the jarring of uneven road surfaces. Front forks and rear shocks need setting up for your weight and riding style.

 K) Pedals: Clipless pedals are more efficient for longer journeys: a key-shaped cleat on the bottom of your shoe locks into a sprung mechanism on your pedals. The idea of clipless pedals is daunting for the first-timer, but you'll appreciate the extra power once you are used to them. Because your shoe is firmly attached, all your energy is used throughout the pedal stroke. Clean, oiled cleats will release your shoe instantly when you twist your foot. For shorter journeys many people prefer flat pedals, which don't require you to wear special shoes. Flat pedals need enough grip to stop you sliding off them in wet weather.

Specialized Rockhopper

71

Tools

Your toolkit will inevitably start as a few basic tools. Gradually, as you get more confident in fixing your bike, you'll find yourself needing more specialized bits of kit. Your toolkit then grows until you reach the happy point where you can tackle complicated jobs without investing in any more equipment.

Some tools, like screwdrivers, are useful for all sorts of jobs. Others are highly specific and do only one task, or even just one task on a particular make and model of component. These can be annoyingly expensive, especially if you don't find yourself needing to do the job they're made for very often. On the plus side, these also tend to be the kinds of jobs that it costs most to get done, so the cost probably evens out in the end.

The first batch of tools – the essentials listed opposite – are the most commonly used ones and should allow you to carry out simple tasks like fixing punctures, fitting brake blocks and adjusting your bike to fit you comfortably. It's worth owning all these tools, so that you can do running repairs without having to make emergency sprints to the tool shop or the bike shop in the middle of a job. The list on page 76 consists of more specialist kit that you'll want to acquire gradually as you get more confident as a mechanic.

Page 75 contains a list of tools that you might want to take with you for roadside repairs. As your toolkit grows, you'll want to keep these completely separate from your workshop tools. Roadside repair tools need to be light and preferably foldable, so

that they take up the minimum of space in your bag and don't stab holes in your spare clothes or your sandwiches. Workshop tools are best if they're as big and chunky as possible – so you get more leverage and they last as long as possible. If you keep your neat, lightweight tools separate, it saves you from leaving them behind in your toolkit by mistake – it's inevitable that you won't realise your loss until you're stuck by the side of the road and find yourself walking home for the want of a tyre-lever.

Manuals and instruction books

All new bikes and parts come with manuals or instructions – it's not just manufacturers being nice, the law says they must. For some reason it's traditional to throw them away without reading them. Don't do this. Keep them all together so that you can find them when you need them. They're part of your toolkit. It's particularly important with any suspension components as fitting and set-up instructions vary between make, model and year. Write on them too, noting down any suspension measurements or pressure settings, so that you can reuse ones that work for you and improve on those that don't.

Toolbox

Keep all your tools together in one place. Plastic toolboxes are cheap, help keep things tidy and you can sit on them if the ground's wet, but a cardboard shoebox will work perfectly well. Keep the contents dry and sort everything out every so often so you know what's there. Finally, don't lend your tools to anyone. If you like someone enough to lend them a spanner, fix their bike instead. If you don't like them enough to fix their bike, don't trust them with your precious spanners either.

The first rule of owning a bicycle: instruction manuals should always be kept. It is a sin to throw them away!

Toolbox essentials

Always get the best quality you can afford. Good tools last for years and are an investment. Cheap ones let you down and can damage the part you're trying to fix.

A) **Allen keys.** The best starter packs are fold-up sets of metric Allen keys that include 2, 2.5, 3, 4, 5, 6mm sizes. You can use the body of the tool as a handle and bear down on it hard without hurting your hand. For the workshop, choose a set with a wider range of Allen key sizes rather than the type which come with screwdrivers as well – those are more useful for parcelling up and taking out with you. If you have to fix your bike a lot, invest in good-quality separate Allen keys with long handles and a ball end as they're a lot easier to use for fiddly jobs.

B) **8mm Allen key.** Most current cranks bolts use this size. You'll need one with a long handle for leverage – about 200mm (8 in) is right. There are a couple of variations for crank bolts – 10mm Allen keys make an appearance and older bikes still use a 14mm socket. You'll need to go to the bike shop for one of these as the standard socket that comes in ordinary toolkits is too fat to fit in the recess in the cranks.

C) **Screwdrivers** – a couple of flat heads, with blades about 3 and 6mm, and a number two Phillips crosshead.

D) **Metric spanners** in 8, 9, 10, 15 and 17mm. These are the most useful sizes, although you can't go wrong with a metric spanner set with all sizes from 7 to 17mm. The best are combination spanners with a ring at one end to grip securely around the nut and an open end at the other to get into awkward spaces easily. Imperial equivalents won't do as they're not close enough in size to make adjustments without damaging the nuts you're trying to turn.

E) **A big adjustable spanner.** One that opens out to at least 35mm is a good size. Always tighten the jaws firmly onto the flats of the nut or tool before applying pressure to avoid damage to both the component and the spanner jaws.

F) **Good-quality, bike-specific wire cutters.** Not just pliers, which will damage inner cable and outer casing if you try to cut it. You'll be able to get cutters from your bike shop. This tool always seems expensive and it's tempting to think that you can get away without it, but you can't.

G) **Chain tool.** This is another tool where quality really makes a difference. It's easy to damage an expensive chain with a cheap chain tool. For ease of use, durability and reliability go for Park chain tools.

H) **A sharp knife with a retractable blade.** Essential for getting into packaging (this can be the most challenging part of a simple mission to change your brake blocks), reusing zipties, etc.

I) **Puncture kit.** Essential, even if you carry around a spare tube. If you bring a punctured spare home, you can patch it in comfort in front of the TV and carry that around as your new spare. A patch kit in your toolbox means you're not tempted to steal the one out of your emergency kit.

J) **Tyre-levers.** You'll often be able to get tyres on and off without these, but they're worth having for the occasional stubborn tube or moments when your thumbs don't feel up to it.

Useful extras: ◎ **Track pump.** For getting a tube up to pressure – so you have fewer punctures – nothing beats a track pump.

◎ **Notebook and pen** – they're useful for making quick sketches of things as they come apart, and noting suspension pressures and tyre pressure etc.

◎ **A rubber or plastic mallet.** These come from hardware shops. The correct emergency alternative is a block of wood.

◎ **Chain wear measuring tool.** One of these will pay for itself in no time at all, showing you when your chain has developed enough wear to start damaging other components.

◎ **A pair of pliers.**

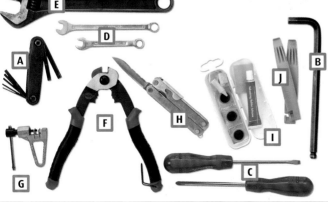

Tools: your spares box

As well as tools, it's handy to have a box of essential spares, so that you don't have to make a trip to the bike shop in the middle of a job to pick up some small piece of rubber. The exact contents will depend on your bike, but here are some suggestions for starters.

A) A couple of tubes that are the right size for your bike and have the correct valves as well. There's no reason why they shouldn't be old tubes that you've patched.

B) Brake blocks or brake pads for disc brakes. Cantilever, calliper and V-brakes all use different types of block. Disc brakes are even worse – you'll need the correct type for the exact make, model and year of your disc brake. Keep them wrapped in plastic until you need them to avoid accidental contamination with oil.

C) Two brake cables and a length of brake outer casing. It makes sense to buy a few metres of it and then cut off what you need as you need it.

D) Two gear cables and a length of gear outer casing.

E) Ferrules (the end caps for outer casing). Brake and gear need different sizes – 5mm for brake, 4mm for gear.

F) The correct chain-joining pin (8, 9 or 10 speed) for Shimano chains.

G) Zipties. What did we do before these existed? They join anything to anything else and no toolbox should be without them.

H) Electrical tape. Preferably black.

End caps (not pictured). These go on the end of brake and gear cable once it's fitted, adjusted and excess cut off the end. They prevent the end of the cable fraying.

Emergency roadside repair tools

Your roadside toolkit is what you carry around in the hope you'll never have to use it. Keep it separate from your normal toolkit and replace anything you use.

However diligent you are about maintaining your bike, there will inevitably be occasions when it lets you down by the side of the road. This is often listed as a reason why people don't commute to work by bike, but with a little bit of preparation you can sort out most of the kinds of problems that occur without too much fuss. Bicycles do have a great advantage over cars in this respect since, if it does all go horribly wrong, you can just stick the whole thing in the back of a cab, finish your journey and then sort out the problem at your leisure.

There are other solutions too – walking home takes a while, but is usually possible and free. If you're carrying a decent lock and are within striking distance of civilisation, lock it up where it is and find some public transport. Do make sure you know how to find your way back to it, however.

There's always a balance between the amount of time you spend carrying emergency tools around and the amount of time you actually spend using them. During the 'carrying about' period, you tend to curse them because you feel like you're carrying around a ton of unnecessary weight. During the 'using' period, you curse yourself for leaving behind essential kit, the weight temporarily forgotten. You'll have to decide for yourself where the balance lies.

Roadside tool pack

A) Spare tube in the right size with the correct valve (thin Presta or fat Schraeder).

B) Pump with the right fitting for your valve. Double-action pumps inflate your tyre as you pull them as well as pushing them, refilling the tyre more quickly. They're more expensive, but you'll thank yourself as soon as you have a puncture.

C) Patch kit. Take one of these even if you already have a tube. They don't weigh much or take up much room. Once you've broken the seal on the glue it dries up within about six months, however tightly you screw the lid on, so replace it regularly. You can buy glue separately.

D) Tyre-levers. Plastic ones are much better than metal ones, which will damage your rim.

E) Fold-up Allen key/screwdriver set. These keep everything neat and fold the sharp tools out of the way so they don't stab you if you fall on your bag. The handle makes the tools easier to hold and to apply pressure without hurting your hands. They're handy to have floating around in your bag, too, as you never know when you might have to make emergency repairs to things like flat-packed furniture.

F) Chain tool and, if you have a Shimano chain, the correct replacement chain pin. It's a good idea to practise using the tool before you need it for real: spend a bit of time with an old scrap of chain and the instructions on page 160.

G) Zipties. I don't know exactly what you're going to find these useful for, but I can guarantee there will be a moment when you appreciate having carried them around.

H) Duct tape. Stick it round your pump until you need it. (Not pictured)

A comprehensive toolkit

As you start to tackle major jobs, you'll need more specialized tools. Most of these will have to come from a bike shop, rather than a tool shop. The following are just examples, but often the exact type of each set of tools will depend on your bike. If you can, take it with you to the shop to make sure you're getting the right tool. Specialist tools can get expensive and you don't need them very often. But if you know a group of other people who enjoy fixing their bicycles you might consider forming a tool pool.

Brakes

Disc brakes – brake bleeding kit, brake fluid. If you have disc brakes, you'll need brake fluid to bleed or refill the system. You can improvise a bleed kit using plastic tubes or buy a complete one as most brake manufacturers make their own bleed kit. Check the type of brake fluid you need – mineral oil and DOT fluid are not compatible with each other.

Cable brakes. A decent pair of wire cutters is essential for chopping inner cable and outer casing cleanly and neatly.

Left: brake fluid;
above: cable cutters;
right: disc brake bleed kit.
Below: bottom bracket tools;
below right: headset spanners

Bottom bracket tools

The most common fitting by far is the Shimano splined pattern. You'll also need a large adjustable spanner to drive the tool. Remember when using it that the right-hand side of the frame has a reverse thread. This means that the right-hand cup is removed by turning it clockwise. The left-hand cup has a normal thread and is removed by turning it anticlockwise. Older versions of this tool have a smaller hole in the middle, just big enough for the axle to poke through as you use the tool. Although the splines on the cups of newer, splined tools are the same size, the axle won't fit through the hole in the tool so you'll need to buy the newer version.

Headset spanners

You'll only need these for older, threaded headsets, which come in three sizes: 32mm (which used to be standard, but is now much less common), 36mm (still called oversize but actually standard now) and, very occasionally, 40mm. These days, typical headsets or threadless headsets are adjusted with standard Allen keys, so you won't need a headset spanner for them.

Transmission

Chain-cleaning brushes. Keep these separate from those that you use for rims or disc rotors, so that you never accidentally transfer oil to a braking surface.

Cassette-remover and chain whip. The cassette-remover fits into the splines on the lockring in the middle of the cassette. You'll then need an adjustable spanner to turn the tool. The chain whip fits around a sprocket and is used to prevent the cassette turning as you undo its lockring. You won't need the chainwhip for refitting the cassette as the ratchet in the middle of the cassette stops it turning.

Freewheel tool. Before cassettes were invented the sprocket and ratchet arrangement was combined into a single unit that simply threaded onto your rear hub. You'll need a freewheel tool to unscrew it, but be aware that there are quite a number of different patterns of remover, some with splines, some with two or four pegs that fit into notches in the freewheel. The Shimano pattern shown here is the most common.

Crank extractor. Essential for removing cranks and chainsets and accessing your bottom bracket. Two sizes are shown here – the one with the smaller head is for older, square-tapered axles. The larger size is for larger-diameter, splined axles. You will also need a large adjustable spanner to drive the tool.

Wheels

Cone spanners. These are very thin, so that they can fit into the narrow spanner flats on the cones. Common sizes are 13, 15

Clockwise from top left: chain-cleaner, splined and square-taper crank-extractors, chain-cleaning brush, freewheel tool and cassette-remover; immediately above: chain whip. Below left: spoke key and cone spanners; below right: pedal spanner

and 17mm, but there are no hard and fast rules – measure the distance across the spanner flats or take your bike to the shop with you before buying the sizes you need.

Spoke wrench (also called a spoke key). This tiny tool allows you to adjust the tension in each spoke, balancing them so that the wheel runs round and true.

Pedals

Almost all makes of pedal use a 15mm spanner. Pedal spanners are narrower than normal spanners, so that they slot into the gap between pedal and crank. They're extra long so that you can get enough leverage to fit the pedals snugly – otherwise, they'll work loose, ripping out the crank threads as they go. Expensive! Just occasionally you'll come across a pedal that doesn't have spanner flats outboard of the crank. For these you'll need to get an Allen key in the very end of the pedal axle where it emerges from the back of the crank. Again, you'll need an Allen key with a long handle to get enough leverage.

Lubricant and grease

Keeping your bike running cleanly and smoothly will make all your components last longer and work better. Different potions for different uses can make it seem like you're shelling out a lot of money on bike cosmetics, but you don't need very much of anything. A small bottle of good-quality chain lubricant, used sparingly, will last all year and double the life of your drivetrain.

Chain lubricant: this is an essential. Everybody has a favourite type: ask the mechanics in your local bike shop what they use. Different lubes work in different climates. If you ride in a very wet and muddy place, you'll need a different lube from someone that rides in hot, dry climates. A dry climate requires a dry lubricant to keep the drivetrain running smoothly while attracting minimal muck. In muddy, wet conditions you need a wet lube. These are stickier so they stay on in extreme conditions, but attract more dirt so you must be conscientious in your cleaning routine.

The important thing about chain lubes is that they should be applied to clean chains. Putting oil on a dirty chain is the first step towards creating a sticky paste that eats expensive drivetrain components for breakfast. If you haven't got time to clean your chain first, you haven't got time to oil it. Whatever you use for oiling the chain will also do as a more general-purpose lubricant for cables, brake pivots and derailleur pivots – anywhere two bits of metal need to move smoothly over each other.

I always use drip oil rather than spray oil. Spray is messy and wasteful and it's too easy to get it on rims and disc rotors by mistake, which makes your brakes slippery rather than sticky.

Cleaning: bikes get dirty but are quite sensitive creatures. Common cleaning products, like washing-up liquid are rather salty and will accelerate the usual tendency to rust. Specialist products actually work much better – car shampoo is fine, but try also bike-specific liquid cleaner. Three good makes are Finish Line Bike Wash, Muc-Off and Fenwick's. All of these contain additives that protect the components you're cleaning.

Degreaser: for really stubbornly dirty components use degreaser. Again, Finish Line stuff is best. It comes both as a spray and in a bottle. The bottle means you get to apply it carefully and accurately with a brush rather than just spraying it wildly about. Take care when you're working on any part of your bike not to let the degreaser seep into nearby bearings where it will break down any grease it comes across. Degreaser may need rinsing off when you're done. Check the instructions on the pack.

Grease: confusion surrounds the difference between grease and oil. Essentially they're both lubricants, but grease is solid and oil is liquid. Grease is stickier and can't be used on exposed parts of the bike; dirt sticks to the grease, forms a grinding paste and wears out the bike rather than making ⊘

it run more smoothly. Grease is used inside sealed components like hubs. You don't get in there often so the stuff is required to last longer and remain cleaner. In an emergency almost any grease will do, but as you don't actually need much of it, get the good stuff from your local bike shop. As your confidence grows, invest in a grease gun. This will keep your hands and grease stock clean. For a clean and simple system, use the ones that screw onto the top of a tube of grease. To get the last bit out, however, you usually abandon the gun and cut open the tube.

Polish: this might seem like a bit of an extravagance, but a layer of polish on the frame and forks will provide a smooth surface that protects your paintwork and stops a new layer of dirt from sticking quite so easily. Plus, it makes your paintwork easier to clean next time. You can get a bike-specific polish from your bike shop, but car paintwork polish does exactly the same job.

Specific lotions

As with your toolkit, start with a stock of essential consumables and build up as you tackle specialist jobs. You won't need any of these in the course of routine repairs and, depending on your bike, you may never need them.

Disc brake fluid: use only the fluid specified for your brake system. There are two types – mineral oil and DOT fluid. The two types are not interchangeable in any way. The type you need will be marked on your brake. The brakes you're most likely to come across are Shimano. These use mineral oil, which is available from bike shops in small, convenient bottles – there isn't actually much space in your hydraulic brake system, so you never end up using much of the stuff. DOT fluid, an autoparts trade standard, deteriorates once the bottle has been opened so buy in small amounts and open as you need it.

Suspension oil: this is formulated to have damping as well as lubricating properties. Its 'weight' is critical and depends on the make and model of your fork or rear shock. Damping occurs by oil being forced through small holes. Lighter, thinner oil (e.g. 5wt) passes through more quickly. Heavier, thicker oil (e.g. 15wt) takes longer. Your fork or shock only works properly with the correct weight of oil: if you're taking forks or shocks to pieces, check the manual (which is, of course, neatly filed in your workshop). You may mix

two weights of oil to make an intermediate weight, but don't mix brands.

Antiseize (also called Ti-prep or, if you buy from a hardware shop rather than a bike shop, Copperslip): this prevents reactive metals from sticking together and is especially important for titanium components, which react and seize whatever they touch. Avoid skin contact with antiseize as this stuff is not good for you.

Vaseline: this is often the best substance for applying to seat posts in carbon frames. Check with the frame manufacturer's recommendations.

Loctite glue: the generic name is threadlock, although the Loctite brand is pretty good. It's used where bolts cannot rattle loose and between parts that may corrode together if moisture gets in, like rear hubs. Different colours indicate different strengths. Threadlock '#222' is red and is usually applicable up to M6 (6mm diameter) threads. The most common – threadlock '#242' – is blue and used for bolts M6 and above. Threadlock '#290' is green and used for holding pivot bushes.

Suspension oil,
brake fluid, antiseize
and plastic
lubricant

Your workshop

A proper work stand is probably your most expensive investment. Almost all the procedures listed in the main part of this book are easier if the bike is held steady with both wheels off the ground. For some repairs, such as adjusting your gears, you need the back wheel up off the ground so you can turn the pedals and watch the effects of changing gear. A work stand – or its equivalent – is essential.

Working standing up is easier than working crouched on the ground. Take care where you clamp the bike into the stand. The best place is the seat post. Try to avoid clamping onto the tubes — these are thin and you can dent or even bend them too easily. Wipe the jaws of the stand before you clamp the bike into it so you don't scuff the paintwork. If you're tight for storage space, look for a work stand that folds up when you're not using it.

The next level down from a full work stand is a prop stand, which keeps the back wheel off the ground and holds the bike upright. This is exactly what you need for working on your drivetrain, rear wheel repairs, brakes, bottom brackets and indeed most common repair and maintenance tasks. These are relatively cheap compared to a work stand and a good compromise if you're not ready to commit to a work stand.

If you have nothing, then improvise. Avoid turning the bike upside down — bikes don't like it and behave differently from when they're the right way up. Instead, find a friend who will hold the bike upright and off the ground at appropriate moments.

You need enough light to see by, especially for close-up jobs such as truing wheels. Most repairs are messy so if you're working indoors spread an old sheet on the floor for protection. Ventilation is important as well. Any time you use solvents or spray you need enough air circulating to dilute chemical fumes to harmless levels. Anything powerful enough to sweeten your bike will probably damage your body.

The same goes for bodily contact with substances. Consider wearing rubber gloves like those used by mechanics. This saves loads of time cleaning your hands and reduces the quantity of chemicals absorbed through your skin. Lots of jobs involve removing something dirty and then either cleaning it or replacing it, before fitting it. You must have clean hands for the last part of the job as there's no point fitting a clean component with dirty hands.

A biscuit box

One of the most irritating parts of bike repair is being thwarted in a simple task because you need a simple but very specific part. Bike shop workshops always have racks of plastic drawers full of tiny little parts, many of which are essential for just one job. This is a luxury you're unlikely to have. Your biscuit box is essential but, like a good compost heap, it must grow over time and cannot be bought wholesale! Start one now. A biscuit box is any container into which you drop odd nuts and bolts left over from other repairs. Then, when you shear off an essential bolt after the shops have closed or a vital part escapes as you're trying to refit it and finds asylum under the fridge, your box of bits can save your bacon. The box should be bike-specific — surplus woodscrews and outdated distributor caps don't count. Useful things include M5 (5mm diameter) bolts in lengths from 10mm to 45mm, crank bolts, Aheadset caps with rude slogans, odd washers, valve caps, ball bearings and scraps of chain. If you're buying things like ball bearings or bolts for a repair, get an extra packet and pop it in your biscuit box for later.

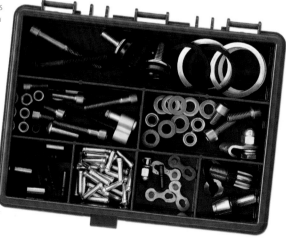

Torque

In order to measure how firmly we are tightening bolts we use torque. There are two methods of doing this: the instinctive, common-sense version and the scientific. Both have advantages. Traditionally, the manufacturer of a part indicated to the mechanic how firmly things should be tightened by fitting an appropriate bolt.

Delicate parts, which just need holding in place, come equipped with small bolts. The spanners that fit these bolts are short, so that you don't have enough leverage to overtighten the bolt. Parts that need to be clamped down firmly come with a big bolt that you can attach a nice hefty spanner to and lean on. This used to work well enough, but as riders we're demanding lighter equipment all the time so manufacturers are designing components with less room for error. For example, replacing steel bolts with aluminium ones will save weight, but aluminium bolts are far less forgiving of overtightening: once stressed, they can snap without warning.

Overtightening bolts can also strip the thread that you're bolting into. This is a common problem with aluminium parts. For example, overtightening the bolts that hold the stem to the handlebars can damage the thread inside the stem so that the bolt rotates uselessly rather than securing the bars.

The reverse problem, undertightening bolts, has a more obvious consequence: whatever you're trying to secure will rattle or work loose. Crank bolts often suffer from this — the left-hand one in particular needs to be tighter than people imagine. The first warning is usually a regular creaking noise as you pedal. If you ignore it, the crank bolt works loose, allowing the crank to shift about on the bottom bracket axle. This damages the mating surface between bottom bracket and crank, so that even if you retighten the crank bolt it works loose constantly.

As a consequence it's becoming more vital to know exactly how much force you're putting on any specific bolt. This is especially true for suspension forks where the bolts that hold the moving parts together are constantly being stressed by the cycling – moving up and down – of the fork. Many components now come with a tightening torque specified for every bolt.

Since torque specifications are a relatively recent obsession, most come quoted in Newton-metres (Nm). The Imperial equivalent unit is the inch-pound (in-lb). To convert inch-pounds into Newton-metres, multiply by 0.113.

However, it's one thing to find out how tight a bolt is supposed to be and quite another to be able to tighten it to exactly that amount. There is a workshop tool that allows you to do this — a torque wrench. It looks like a ratcheting socket handle and works in a similar way. Standard socket heads fit onto the wrench, which can then be set to the specified torque by turning a knob at the base of the handle. The wrench is then used to tighten the bolt as normal. When you reach the correct level the handle of the wrench gives slightly and you hear a distinct click, telling you to stop.

These tools are simple and reliable to use and are becoming more and more common in bicycle workshops. A well-equipped workshop will have two torque wrenches. A small one with a range from about 4 to 20 Nm (35 to 177 in-lb) covers delicate applications such as cable clamps and disc brake rotor-fixing bolts. A larger one with a range from 20 to 50 Nm (177 to 443 in-lb) covers those that need more force, like crank bolts. The two sizes are necessary because the tools always work best in the middle of their range. However, they are expensive to buy, relatively delicate and could be considered overkill for a home workshop.

If you don't own a torque wrench of your own but get a chance to borrow one, use it to tighten a selection of the bolts on your bike to the specified torque setting to get a feel for how tight they should be. Many mechanics use torque wrenches to set bolts to the correct level regularly to remind themselves what the correct torque feels like.

When working by feel, be aware of the size of the bolts you're tightening and use this as an indication of the amount of force you should be using. Small bolts take small spanners (or thin screwdrivers) and so should be tightened firmly but not excessively. If you're overenthusiastic with a delicate bolt, you'll strip the thread, snap the head off or round off the key faces. Large bolts, or those that have to be tightened with chunky tools, like bottom bracket cups, should be wedged home with vigour.

The best place to find torque specifications is on the instructions that came with the component, which will have the right torque for your specific make and model. New bikes come with a pack of booklets and leaflets, covering all the parts fitted to your bike. You may have to ask for it when you buy the bike. If you haven't got the instructions any more, use the Park Tools website to reference general torque specifications. It is www.parktool.com and the page address is www.parktool.com/repair_help/torque.

All specified torques assume that the bolt you are using has been greased so that it turns easily in the threads and that both parts of the thread are clean and in good condition. A dirty, damaged bolt will be harder to tighten than a clean one and so will give a false torque reading.

Twelve routine safety checks before you ride

Checking your bike every time you ride it can seem like a lot of effort and it can also seem a little bit boring. However, it needn't take more than a few moments and occasionally you'll appreciate the time it takes because you'll pick up problems waiting to happen, which are far easier to fix before you set off than halfway through your journey. Looking carefully at your bike on a regular basis makes it more familiar, so it's easier to spot when something is wrong.

Specialized Enduro

It's worth having a routine for checking your bike. Doing it in the same order every time means you're less likely to miss something. It's worth going through a mental checklist at the same time to ensure you have everything else you need for a ride. Your needs will depend on how far you're going, but might include things like a puncture kit, a lock (and its keys!), lights if you're going to be home after dark, a helmet if you wear one and so on.

1) Quick-release skewer: check both wheels are securely attached. Quick-release levers must be firmly folded to line up with the fork blade or rear stay, otherwise they can snag on anything they're leant against and open accidentally. Most levers have 'open' and 'closed' printed on opposite sides. Fold the lever so the 'closed' side is visible.

2) Tyres: check tyres for bald patches, tears and sharp objects. Things like glass and thorns that cause punctures often take time to work through the tyre casing. Inspect your tyres frequently and pick out foreign objects. It's tedious but quicker than fixing the punctures they cause!

3) Spokes: check for broken spokes. Gently brush your fingers over the spokes on both sides of both wheels. Even one broken spoke considerably weakens a wheel. A permanent repair is also much easier if the wheel hasn't been ridden on.

4) Front wheel: lift the front end off the ground and spin the front wheel. Check it runs freely and doesn't wobble between forks.

5) Rim brakes (not illustrated): check the brake blocks don't touch the tyre or rim as the wheel turns. Rubbing blocks wear quickly and slow you down. Check the position of the brake blocks. Each block should be parallel to the rim, low enough to avoid hitting the tyre but not so low that any part of the brake block hangs below the rim.

6) Disc brakes: check disc pads. You should have at least 0.5mm (1/50 in) of pad thickness on either side of both brakes.

7) Brake-levers: carry out a simple brake check every time you ride. Stand beside the bike, push it gently forward and then pull on the front brake. The front wheel should lock on and the back one lift off the ground. If this doesn't happen, don't ride!

8) Brake-levers: use a similar test for the back brake. Push the bike forward and then pull on the back brake. The back wheel should lock and slide along the ground. Again, if this doesn't happen, do not ride.

9) Chain: check the drivetrain. The chain should be clean and should run smoothly through the gears without falling off either

side of the sprocket or the chainset. Turn pedals backwards and watch the chain run through the derailleur. Stiff links flick the derailleur forward as they pass over the lower jockey wheel. It's worth sorting them out before you ride your bike since they can cause your gears to slip under pressure.

10) Cables and hoses: check all cables (brake and gear) for kinks in the outer casing or frays in the cable. Frayed cables should be replaced immediately. Clean and oil rusty or dirty cables. Check hydraulic hoses for damage; inspect the joints between hose and calliper and hose and brake lever for oil leaks.

11) Stem: check that the stem and bars are tight. Stand over the front wheel, gripping it between your knees. Try turning the bars. They shouldn't move independently. Try twisting the bars in the stem too. If you have barends, lean down on them. Tighten any loose steering components.

12) Pedals: for flat pedals, check that the pedals are clear of debris – you don't want to slip off a muddy pedal. For clipless pedals, make sure you can clip into and out of both sides of both pedals easily.

It's essential to use the correct procedure when fitting quick-release skewers – if you've not done it before, get your bike shop to show you how it all works

Regular cleaning routine

Cleaning your bike is the best time to spot worn or broken parts that could otherwise let you down just when you're trying to get somewhere important. Beware of jet washes though. The power hoses on garage forecourts can leave your bike looking very shiny without much effort but, no matter how careful you are, they force water in through the bearing seals, flushing grease out. This shortens the lifespan of bottom brackets, headsets and other components radically. I prefer to use a bucket of water and a rag – it takes a little longer, but there's less chance of accidentally causing damage. In general, it's best to start with the dirtiest bits and work up to the cleaner ones. That way, you minimize the amount of recleaning you may have to do.

Full-suspension Marin

Take the wheels off your bike. If you can, hang up the frame so that you can get to everything easily. Otherwise, turn the frame upside down and stand it on bars and saddle.

A) Begin with the chain. There's no need to remove it from the bike. For the best results with the least fuss, tip a little degreaser into a small jar. Use a toothbrush or washing-up brush dipped in degreaser to scrub the chain clean. You'll know it's clean enough when you can read the numbers stamped onto each link in your chain. Rinse off the degreaser nice and carefully.

B) If your sprockets and chainset are oily, clean with degreaser. Oil is sticky and picks up road dirt as you ride along, which will begin to wear out the drivetrain over a reasonable period of time. As above, use a little degreaser and work it delicately into the sprockets and chainset with a brush. It's very important to rinse things very carefully afterwards to remove all traces of degreaser.

Once everything is clean and dry, relubricate the chain. I prefer drip oils to spray types because that way you can direct the oil much more precisely. Drip a little onto each link. Leave the oil to soak in for approximately five minutes, then carefully remove any excess with a clean rag. Luckily, you don't need to worry about relubing other drivetrain components as they need no more than is deposited by the chain onto the sprockets.

C) Next, clean the wheels. Rim brakes work much better on clean rims. They pick up dirt from the road and from the brake blocks, which stops the blocks from gripping the rim effectively. Washing-up liquid will shift the dirt, but specialist bike cleaning products work better and will protect the material of your rims. Wipe or spray on, leave to soak, and scrub off – nylon washing-up pads are ideal for this job. While you're there, check for bulges or cracks in the braking surface. These indicate that the rim is worn out and needs replacing urgently. Disc rotors should be cleaned with specialist bike wash like Muc-Off. If they have become oily, clean the rotors with isopropyl alcohol (from chemists), which doesn't leave a residue.

D) Brakes next. For rim brakes, release the V-brakes by pulling back the black rubber boot and pulling the curved metal noodle out of the hanger on the brake unit. Clean the block surfaces. Use a small screwdriver to pick out shards of metal. If the block surface has become shiny, use a strip of clean sandpaper to roughen it. When looking at the brake blocks, check they aren't excessively or unevenly worn. For disc brakes, wipe the calliper clean. Check hydraulic hoses for oil leaks. Look into the rotor slot on the calliper, and check that the brake pad is at least 0.5mm (1/50 in) thick.

E) Pedals are often forgotten, even though they get more than their fair share of abuse. For clipless pedals, use a small screwdriver to clear any detritus from around the release mechanism. Make sure you do both sides of both pedals. Grit and dirt gets forced into the springs every time you clip in with your shoes, building up until you can no longer clip in and out properly. Lubricate the moving parts sparingly with a light oil, like GT85 or WD40.

F) Wipe clean all reflectors and lights.

G) Clean the frame and forks. You need a sponge and a bucket of warm water to rinse everything off afterwards. All components work better and last longer if they're not covered in grime. To finish off, they need a quick polish. Wax-based polish helps stop dirt sticking to the frame, keeping it cleaner for next time. Saddles also benefit from a polish – you might as well while you've got the polish out. Refit the wheels, reconnect the brakes. This is a good time to pump up the tyres, just to finish the job off neatly.

A simple chain-cleaning routine

It's tempting to ignore your chain until it's a claggy oily mess, then attack it with harsh chemicals like degreaser to get it working again. But if you can make time to give it a quick wipe down once a week, you can keep it sufficiently clean so that it never needs a major overhaul. Once a week seems like a lot, but it really should only take a few minutes, and will make your chain last a lot longer. The other advantage is that a clean chain won't deposit oily patches on your trouser legs as you ride.

Lean your bike up against a wall, with the chain in the largest chainring, and the largest sprocket. Take a scrap of cloth, and spray some light lubricant into it – SuperSpray lube, GT85, something like that. Wrap the cloth around the bottom stretch of chain, where it runs between the bottom of the rear derailleur and the bottom of the chainring.

Hold it there, and pedal backwards for a couple of minutes. Move the cloth around, and repeat a couple of times. Once you've got the worst of the dirt off, drop a little good-quality chain oil (e.g. Finish Line Dry Lube) onto the top of the chain as you pedal. It only needs the smallest amount, don't go wild. This next bit is the most important – leave the oil to soak in for five minutes, then wipe excess oil off your chain, in the same way, with a clean bit of cloth. This cleaning up process is essential, as it prevents excess oil from collecting more dirt.

5 – Punctures

This chapter leads you through the process of getting your wheels off, removing the tyre and tube, fitting a new tube and replacing the wheel securely and safely on your bicycle. It concentrates on the rear wheel, which is more prone to puncture. It's also slightly more complicated to work on because it has to be disentangled from the transmission. But don't be daunted. Learning how to fix your own punctures makes you more self-sufficient and means you don't have to worry that a puncture might leave you stranded when you're in a hurry.

Punctures

Punctures are one of the factors that people cite most frequently as a good reason not to cycle to work. This is a shame since, if your tyres are good quality, relatively unworn and pumped up hard, you're unlikely to get many punctures.

Many people returning to their bikes after a long break have a perception of punctures as a constant feature of cycling, but, in the intervening years, tyre quality has improved dramatically. Puncture-resistant tyres are effective, last for thousands of miles and don't cost the earth. If you're still worried, follow the steps on page 94 to minimise your chances of getting a flat.

Quick-release skewers

Many bikes designed for commuting come with quick-release skewers. These have advantages as well as disadvantages. If you have a flat, it means you can get the wheel off to fix it without having to carry a spanner around with you the whole time. On the other hand it also means that a wheel left unlocked can be stolen by an opportunistic passer-by without them having to have a spanner on them either. As long as you always lock your wheel, this needn't be a problem, but it requires you to be a little more vigilant about security.

Quick-release skewers can be replaced by versions that require an Allen key or more sophisticated ones that can only be opened with an individually shaped tool supplied with the skewers. These are a great idea round town. If you're leaving your bike at the shop for repairs, remember to leave them with the release

tool, otherwise they won't be able to get your wheels off.

But for ease of getting your wheel off, nothing beats a quick-release skewer. Used correctly, they'll secure your wheels without the need for tools. It's essential to learn how to use them in the right way. The most common problem is when people try to close them simply by twisting the lever until it feels tight. This won't work as you cannot tighten the lever enough to be safe.

The quick-release skewer has a lever with a cam mechanism on one end and a threaded nut – the acorn – on the other. Correct fitting of the skewer is done in two parts. The initial tightening is by holding the lever still and tightening the acorn until it's just finger tight. Then the skewer is secured by folding the lever, flipping it so the handle of the lever passes over the centre of the end of the axle. This will tighten the end of the skewer properly onto the outsides of the forks, gripping your wheel. If you're not confident about it, take your bike to your bike shop and ask them to check what you've done. Quick-release skewers work well, but it's essential that they're used correctly.

Fancy lightweight quick-release levers are available, but some people prefer Shimano ones as they're well made, the cam mechanism is perfect and they hold your wheel on more securely than some of the more glamorous and expensive alternatives.

FITTING QUICK-RELEASE LEVERS SECURELY

Step 1: Flip open the quick-release lever by pulling it away from the frame. This should loosen it enough so you can hold the lever still and undo the acorn nut on the other end a few turns. This should give you enough room to remove the wheel from the dropouts. Front wheels may have lips at the bottom of the dropout. If so, undo the acorn nut enough to clear the lips.

Step 2: The acorn nut, the face of the cam mechanism and both locknuts should have deep, sharp serrations that will grip the soft faces of the dropout. There will be a small steel spring – called a volute spring after the similarly shaped seashells – on each side. Both of these should sit outside the frame and point inwards towards the hub. Push the wheel firmly into the dropout, so that the axle is as far in as it will go.

Step 3: Hold the quick-release lever so that it sticks out at 90° to the wheel. Tighten the acorn nut finger tight. Close the lever folding it over (not twisting it). The lever has to be loose enough to close by hand, but tight enough so it leaves an imprint on your palm when you close it. If it closes too easily, flip the lever open, tighten the nut a quarter-turn, and repeat. If it won't close, flip it open, loosen the nut a quarter-turn, and repeat.

Punctures: removing the rear wheel

The job of fixing a puncture is split into three parts – getting the wheel off, replacing or repairing the tube and finally replacing the wheel.

The most difficult part of fixing rear punctures is getting the rear wheel out past the chain, because it's looped around the cassette. To make the job as easy as you possibly can, change gear so that the chain is in the smallest chainring and the smallest sprocket. If your tyre is too flat to ride the bike, stand next to the bike, lift the back wheel up, change gear, then reach down and turn the pedals so that the chain can shift into the correct place.

Turn your bicycle upside down. This is the only time you need to do this, so make the most of it. If you're on tarmac or concrete, try to find something soft to balance your seat on – a piece of paper, a screwed-up plastic bag, your hat, whatever. This will save you from scratching the cover.

REMOVING THE REAR WHEEL

 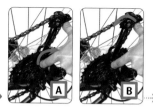 

Step 1: If you have a back wheel with nuts, undo the wheel nuts on both sides. If there are any washers between the nut and the frame, pull them outwards so that they're not stuck to the frame. If you have quick-release levers, release them by flipping the lever outwards and then hold the nut still and twist the lever undone by a few turns. If you're not sure how quick-release levers work, see page 88.

Step 2: Stand behind the bike. Take hold of the rear derailleur as shown above and pull the body of the derailleur (A) backwards while pushing the tab behind the tension jockey wheel (B) – the one that would be closest to the ground if the bike was the right way up – forwards.

Step 3: Lift the wheel upwards out of the dropouts. You should find that pulling the derailleur backwards has created enough slack in the chain that you can ease the back wheel upwards without it catching too much – you may have to wiggle it a bit. Once you've cleared the dropout, twist the top of the wheel slightly to the right. You should then be able to lift it up and out past the top of the chain, freeing it completely.

Getting the front wheel off

This is a whole lot easier than the rear wheel! As above, turn the bike upside down. Unless you've got disc brakes, release the brakes so that there's room for the tyre to pass between the brake blocks. If you've got disc brakes, you can ignore them for now. Undo the wheel nuts or the quick-release skewer. In either case you'll find that you have to keep undoing the fixings a couple of turns after you've loosened them off – the bottoms of the dropouts have little lips, called lawyer tabs. They're there to keep the wheel from falling off if the fixings become loose while you're riding along. In the case of quick-release skewers, it means that you'll have to hold onto the nut on one end of the quick release and twist the lever on the other end a few times, until there's enough of a gap. Then pull the wheel upwards and outwards, freeing the axle from the dropout.

Front wheels should be no bother

Punctures: removing a tyre

Removing the tyre and tube is the same for both front and rear wheels. Some combinations of tyre and wheel are, however, harder to separate.

Generally, wider tyres are easier to get off than narrow ones, mountain bike wheels are easier than hybrids or racers and full-size wheels are easier than the smaller sizes used on shopping and folding bikes.

The easiest way to get back on the road is to fit a new tube, saving the old one to patch at your leisure and become your

spare tube in its turn. If you're worried about getting punctures on your commute, carry a spare tube of the right size around with you so that you're always ready for emergencies. Read the correct size off the sidewall of your tyre – the standard mountain bike size is 26 inches, while hybrids are 700C. The diameter measurement matters much more than the width, so most ⊘

REMOVING A TYRE

Step 1: Removing a tyre is easiest if you've got rid of as much of the air left in the tube as possible. Even if you've punctured, it's worth getting the rest out. With Schraeder valves, remove the valve cap and push down the pin in the middle of the valve – a fingernail, small screwdriver or a pen lid should do the trick. For Presta valves, remove the valve cap, then unscrew the top thumbnut a couple of turns and press it downwards.

Step 2: While pressing the valve pin down, roll the tyre around and massage it with your hands, until you can't hear any air coming out at all. Work your way right round one side of the tyre, pushing the side of the tyre away from the rim wall so that it sits in the dip in the middle of the rim, directly over the spoke holes, as in the picture. This creates extra slack in the tyre bead, which will help you get the tyre off easily.

Step 3: Hold the wheel facing you with the side of the tyre where you've loosened the bead nearest to you. Start near the valve, and lift the tyre bead upwards. If you choose a small enough area, you should be able to lift the tyre bead up and towards you over the side wall of the rim. Once you've cleared the rim, drop it down so that it gets hooked over the outside of the rim.

Step 4: Work gently around the tyre. Starting from the section you've lifted out already, lift a little bit at a time, until the whole of one side of the tyre falls away from the rim. Reach inside the tyre and pull out the tube. Wiggle the valve loose from the rim so that the tyre comes away completely. You should then be able to lift the other side of the tyre easily off the wheel.

Step 5: If you find that you can't lift the tyre off by hand you'll be forced to use tyre-levers. Start with a single lever. Choose a spot away from the valve and in line with a spoke. Push the tyre bead away from the rim and tuck the tyre-lever right into the gap under the tyre bead. Fold it gently outwards until you can hook the other end of the tyre-lever under a spoke, which will keep it in place.

Step 6: Just next door to the lever you've already got, and in line with the next spoke but one, tuck your next tyre-lever right under the tyre bead and fold it back so you can tuck the end behind the spoke. Repeat the same distance along with your third lever. Then take out the middle of these three levers, because it's now redundant, and repeat one step along from lever number two. Repeat until the tyre falls off the rim.

diameter tubes cover a range of widths. For example, a 700C tube might cover widths from 28–38mm (1⅛ in–1¼ in). There are also a couple of different types of valve to contend with. The common types are Presta (the thin racing valve) and Schraeder (car type). Mostly, in terms of riding your bike, it doesn't matter which one you use, but it makes sense for both the valves on your wheels to be the same, because many pumps either do one kind or the other, but not both.

Once you come to fit the tube, especially if it's an old tube you're fitting back in after repairing a puncture, it can seem like it's far too big to fit inside the tyre. Don't panic, this is normal. Just make sure to tuck the excess in as evenly as possible as you fit it, rather than leaving a big bulge at the end and stuffing it all into one section of the tyre.

The instructions here show you how to lift your tyre off without tyre-levers. This is a pretty useful trick to learn for two reasons. The first is that it saves you from having to remember to carry tyre-levers around with you all of the time, which is handy if you're as forgetful as I am.

The second is that, unless you're careful, you can nip the tube with the tyre-lever as you struggle to get the tyre on or off. This isn't too significant if you're taking out a tube that you're going to discard, but if you're fitting a new tube back in, it's really quite annoying to puncture it before you've even had a chance to ride it. So give it a go by hand before you resort to levers. But even with the strongest of thumbs, some tyres are tighter than others, so don't despair if they resist your efforts.

REFITTING THE TYRE

Step 1: Once you've got the tyre off, it's time to check carefully around the inside of the tyre for whatever it was that caused the puncture in the first place. This is the most important step of all, easily ignored but worth taking time over. Look around the outside surface of the tyre too, and pick out anything you find. Check that the rim tape covers all spoke heads/spoke holes.

Step 2: Now you're ready to refit the tyre. Start by folding one side of the tyre gently onto the rim by hand, so one tyre bead sits in the rim well all the way around – you should be able to get it all on there without using tyre-levers. Put a little bit of air into the new tube (or old tube, patched) – everybody puts too much in at this stage, which makes it harder to refit the other side of the tyre.

Step 3: Locate the valve hole, then fold back the loose side of the tyre so that you can see the hole. Push the valve through the valve hole, then tuck the rest of the tube back under the tyre. It may seem a little bit big, especially if it's not a fresh one. Space it out as evenly as you can, without any big lumps.

Step 4: Starting at the valve hole, fold the loose bead of the tyre back onto the rim. It will go easily at first, then get tighter. You may want to let out more air at this stage, which will help. Keep tucking the tube well under the tyre, so that you don't catch any tube under the bead. You'll get to a point where you only have a few centimetres of tyre left outside the rim. Taking a little at a time, use both thumbs to gently lift the tyre up and over the rim.

Step 5: As it gets more difficult, let more air out of the tyre. Massage the far side of the tyre so that the tyre bead comes away from the inside surface of the rim and drops into the rim well, giving you a little extra slack to work with. If you have to resort to tyre-levers, just use them to lift a tiny bit of the tyre at a time, to reduce the amount that you have to stretch the bead to a minimum. You should only have to use one tyre-lever.

Step 6: Once you've got the whole tyre back in place, push the valve right upwards into the tyre, to make sure that none of the tube is trapped under the tyre bead. Once you're sure there's no trapped tube, pull the valve back down out of the rim. Pump the tyre back up to the pressure on the sidewall. If there was a valve stem nut, refit it now and hand-tighten. Refit the valve cap. See page 92 to refit rear and front wheels.

Refitting the rear wheel

You've fixed your puncture and now you need to get your back wheel on again. This can seem daunting! Don't panic as it's much easier than you'd expect it to be.

The most important thing is to have practised the procedure before you find yourself needing it in an emergency otherwise it might be all too easy to get confused.

The first time you manage it, it's a huge relief and you'll get a real feeling of achievement. By the time you've repeated the task four or five times, you'll be wondering what you ever worried about. While the bike is still upside down, check that the rear derailleur is set so that it is as far out from the centre of the bike as is possible.

You'll have to reach down to the shifters and fiddle about until it's in the right position. Then stand behind the bike with the wheel in your right hand, cassette facing to the left.

REFITTING THE BACK WHEEL

Step 1: The next step is to open it out to make space for the cassette in the loop of the chain. Take the derailleur with your left hand and put your forefinger on the knuckle of the derailleur at its furthest forward point. Put your left thumb on the tab behind the tension jockey wheel (with the bike upside down, it's the one furthest from the ground). Keep your thumb still and pull your finger backwards, opening out the derailleur.

Step 2: This makes a generous loop in the chain. Guide the back wheel down into the frame and between the brakes. Aim the smallest sprocket of the cassette so that it sits on top of the lower loop of the chain. Once the chain has meshed with the sprocket, guide the axle into the dropouts – it's the dropout nearest the cassette that will require most of your attention. Push the wheel firmly so that it's seated in the bottoms of the dropouts.

Step 3: Check the position of the wheel. There should be an equal amount of space between the tyre and the frame. Check by the seatstays and by the chainstays. Shift the axle slightly in the dropouts if necessary. Tighten the wheel nuts or quick-release skewers firmly. If you need reminding how quick-release skewers work, see page 88. Finally, re-attach the brakes. Spin the back wheel, checking that the brakes don't rub.

Refitting a front wheel

This is much simpler than fitting a rear wheel, but your first attempt may still be daunting. With the bike still upside down, lower the wheel into the forks. If you have disc brakes, guide the disc gently into the gap in the calliper. Sit the axle into the dropouts and give the wheel a wiggle to ensure that the axle is resting as far in as it will go. If you've got an axle with nuts, make sure there's a washer on the outer face of each dropout and then firmly tighten the axle nuts down. If you've got a quick-release axle, tighten it firmly (page 89 if you're unsure how to do this correctly). Then look at the gap between the tyre and the fork on either side, which should be even. If there's more gap on one side than the other, loosen the axle nuts or quick release, wiggle the wheel to centre it and retighten it firmly. Finally, refit the brakes! It's easy to forget this part. Spin the wheel to check that the brake blocks don't bind on the rim or snag on the tyre.

Emergency kit

An emergency kit needs to be small and light enough so you don't resent carrying it around all the time, but also contain everything you might need in an emergency. Obviously, you can't take every possible contingency into account, but a few basic tools should prove sufficient most of the time. After all, there's no point in carrying the kitchen sink around with you everywhere you go.

If something goes wrong that you don't have the tools to fix, either push it to the nearest bike shop or lock it up and take the bus to wherever you're going and come back for it when you have time to deal with it.

The most common emergency you'll come across is a puncture. It's easiest to practise dealing with this before you get caught out by the side of the road and need to do it for the first time in the cold and the dark. Do a trial run at home and make sure everything you had to use goes in your emergency tool bag.

The easiest way to deal with punctures by the side of the road is to fit a new tube, rather than trying to locate and patch the hole. Don't discard the punctured tube, though – take it home, find the hole, patch it and carry it around as your new spare tube. Mini-pumps are the only sensible solution for carrying around. They make harder work of putting air into the tyre than a larger-sized version, but hopefully you'll spend much more time carrying it than using it, so size it for that. Check your valve type. Many pumps now come in versions that will pump either type of valve, but if not, make sure yours is set up appropriately.

Most minipumps come with a couple of brackets that allow you to fit the pump to the frame. These are useless unless you never have to lock your bicycle up and leave it, because somebody will find it irresistible and walk off with it. Luckily they're small enough to fit in the bottom of your bag. I quite like the type with an integral pressure gauge; they're not particularly accurate but they give you something to look at and aim for while you're doing the boring getting-air-in-the-tyre bit.

If you've got wheels with nuts, you'll need to carry a spanner around with you in order to get the wheels off. Front and back wheels often have different-sized nuts – the back is almost always 15mm, whereas fronts may be 13, 14 or 15mm. Multi-spanners (with a range of different sizes stamped onto a flat piece of metal) seem like an appealing option, but they're more irritating than helpful: their shape makes them awkward to use and you can never get enough leverage on them to tighten nuts up properly. A small adjustable spanner is a much better option – pick up a good-quality one from a tool shop or hardware store.

A bunch of Allen keys is an essential – you can raise or lower seats, retighten pinch bolts that have worked loose, or refit

accessories. Best are the fold-up sets, with a range of sizes that tuck out of the way when you're not using them. A basic set with a 4, 5 and 6mm Allen key plus a flat and crosshead screwdriver should be sufficient for most problems. Just like Swiss Army knives, you get versions with more and more different gadgets on, but there does come a point where they just become too heavy to carry around and too awkward to use.

A chain tool is handy to have if you're confident about using it – beg a scrap of old chain to practise on off your bike shop if you can. Page 158–159 takes you through the process of splitting and rejoining a chain. If you're using a Shimano chain, you need to carry around a special replacement pin to have any hope of rejoining it. These come in different sizes depending on the number of sprockets on your cassette. See page 160 for more detail.

The last item on the list may seem extreme, but rubber gloves weigh nothing and take up no space in your emergency tool kit. They just save you getting covered in grease if you have to fix something by the road. It starts on your hands, then you get stuff out of your bag and cover it in grease, then you put your hands on your bars and cover the grips in grease, which comes off on you the next few times you ride your bike. You'll curse yourself.

Keep all your emergency kit together in a separate bag, so you're not tempted to raid it for an Allen key when fixing your bike at home. A bag that keeps everything dry will stop your tools corroding, and a tough material like Cordura will mean the tools don't wear little escape holes as you ride along. You'll find yourself adding to your emergency bag as you go along; mine always contains a couple of zipties because they come in so handy for non-bicycle emergencies as well.

Emergency tool checklist

◎ Spare tube (in the right size and the right valve type)
◎ Pump
◎ Puncture kit
◎ The right-size spanners if you have wheels with nuts
◎ Allen keys – at least 4, 5, 6mm
◎ Chain tool (with relevant Shimano replacement pin if necessary)
◎ Rubber gloves or wet wipes

How to avoid punctures

It's easier to prevent punctures than to fix them. Follow the simple steps here and you'll reduce your punctures significantly. Some measures have beneficial side-effects too – keeping plenty of air in your tyres means they roll more smoothly and don't wear out as fast, so as well as having fewer flats, you'll save money and energy.

◎ Keep your tyres pumped up hard. Soft tyres are far more susceptible to punctures than firm ones. A hard tyre will roll over without the glass having a chance to stick whereas a soft tyre won't. The maximum pressure that your tyre will take is stamped on the tyre wall. Use a bicycle pump with a pressure gauge – the ones in garages aren't that accurate because they're designed to be used with car tyres, which have a much larger volume.

◎ Inspect the surface of both tyres regularly. Pieces of glass, flint and so on may take a couple of weeks to work their way through the thickness of rubber on your tyres. If you regularly pick out anything that looks suspicious, you won't give it a chance to take hold.

◎ Replace worn-out tyres. Once you've lost most of the thread, the surface of the tyre will have begun to get scarred and damaged, giving much more chance for something to work its way through.

◎ Use puncture-resistant tyres. These have become so much more effective in the past few years, dramatically reducing the number of punctures people get. An extra layer of tough material under the tread will prevent all but the sharpest scraps of glass, stone or whatever working their way through. They're not foolproof. You may still occasionally get punctures, so don't think you're let off the hook from carrying around your puncture kit – but it reduces the frequency dramatically.

◎ If you find yourself getting more than your fair share of flats, invest in tubes that are pre-filled with sealant. If these get a puncture the sealant flows into the hole and then dries instantly, sealing the hole. The pre-filled versions are far less messy than the type where you have to get the stuff into the tubes yourself. There are a few different makes, but Slime make a good range. They're great

for smaller holes, but a big tear in the tyre will defeat the sealant, which will then spill out of the tube and spread itself all over the place. If this happens, try to clean it off your bike before it dries.

◎ Check the sidewalls of the tyre as well as the tread. You're looking for cuts or splits, where the tube may bulge out under pressure.

◎ If you carry a lot of weight, such as heavy panniers or children, use the largest-diameter tyres that will fit on your wheel and in your frame.

◎ Avoid riding right in the gutter. This is where larger pieces of broken glass tend to collect. Once you're out into the road, you're in the zone where car tyres constantly crush up any road detritus so that it's too small to do any damage. But at the same time be aware of the dangers of swerving about to avoid patches of broken glass. Car drivers don't ever really look at the road surface so they won't be expecting you to be pulling out into their path.

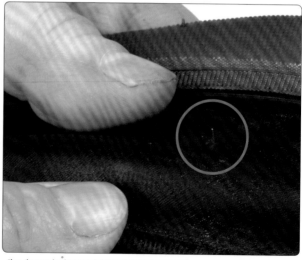

Glass, thorns and tacks can work their way slowly through your tyre

Punctures: fixing a flat

Fixing a puncture is not actually that difficult – it's just a bit of a nightmare to do the first time by the side of the road. You do also get more punctures in the rain; this is not just your paranoia: rubber is easier to cut when it's wet so tyres are more susceptible to damage with rain. If you can, fix emergency punctures by fitting a new tube. Take your punctured tube home, repair it in comfort and then carry the repaired one with you as your new spare.

Fixing the puncture

Before you can fix your puncture, you'll have to find it. It's worth having a quick check of the outside of the tyre before you remove it – you may be able to spot the culprit still sticking out of the tread. Keep track of the suspect area as you remove the tyre from the wheel. It gives you a good idea where to start searching. If you're unsure how to get the tube out of the wheel, follow page 90 as far as step 4 to get the old tube out. To replace the tube, follow the same set of instructions, using your repaired tube instead of the new one.

Once you've got the punctured tube completely out of the tyre and off the wheel, pump it up. It will get fatter and bigger. In fact the tube will get so big that it looks like it would never have fitted in the tyre. You'll need a fair amount of air in the tube to locate the puncture easily – the tube should be 6–8cm (2⅜–3⅛ in) across.

You may hear air hissing out of the hole, which makes it easy to find. If not, feel gently around the surface of the tube. If there's still no sign of it, pass the tube gradually in front of your face as the skin here is more sensitive and you may feel the rush of air more easily. If you still can't find the hole, you'll have to resort to the traditional bucket of water. Immerse a short section of tube at a time in the water, squeezing it and watching for bubbles. If it's a slow puncture, you may only get one or two little ones. Don't miss out the valve – if bubbles pop out of it, replace the whole tube.

If none of these work, put more air into the tube and try again. Even if you find a hole, check all the way around the tube in case there's more than one hole. Once you've marked up the tube, let the rest of the air out of the valve.

A patch kit doesn't take up very much space at all and keeps you on the road

Once you've located the hole, mark it straight away by drawing a ring around it – biro works well. Dry the tube off if necessary. If your patch kit came with a scrap of sandpaper, use it to roughen the area around the hole to help the glue stick, but don't go mad. Take your glue and spread it gently around the hole. It works best if you start on the hole and then work gradually out in a spiral. Be generous with it as you don't want to leave any bare patches. Make sure the area covered by glue is a fair bit bigger than the size of your patch. Then leave the glue to dry completely. It needs at least five minutes and up to 10 minutes in cold weather. The patch will not stick if the glue appears to be wet.

The patches themselves come trapped between two sheets – usually clear plastic over the patch with foil underneath. It's important not to touch the underside of the patch as you handle it since the oil from your fingers won't help it stick. Peel the foil off the underside of the patch, but leave the plastic on there to give you something to hold on to.

Lay the patch carefully on your glue patch. Don't move it once it's made contact. Leaving the plastic on the patch, smooth the edges down carefully. Pinch the patch firmly onto the tube and hold it there to give it a chance to start drying. The plastic is usually perforated so that you can break it and peel it off, but I don't usually bother. However careful you are, sometimes you end up peeling off the patch as well. There isn't much of a weight penalty for leaving it on. If your puncture kit came with a little block of chalk, grate some onto any excess glue to stop it sticking to the inside of the tyre. It's not essential, so if you don't have chalk, don't worry. Don't stress the patch by pumping the tube up to check it – it will only stick properly once the pressure of being inflated squashes it against the inside of the tyre.

In cold weather, give the glue a little bit of extra help in sticking by holding it between your palms to keep it warm, or if it's so cold that your hands need to be in your pockets, trap the patched area of the tube between your arm and your body. Make sure the patch is flat on the tyre, and keep it there for a couple of minutes until the glue has stuck well enough for you to be able to manipulate the tube without peeling the patch straight back off.

6 – Brakes

The brakes on your bike probably need more attention than all the other components put together. It's an inevitable part of city cycling that you'll need to do lots of stopping and starting, and that some of this will need to be done in a very short distance at very short notice. Learning how your brakes work, and how to adjust them, means you can ensure they're always giving you as much control as possible. Constant use will wear your brake blocks out at regular intervals, giving you plenty of opportunity to practise replacing them.

Brakes: how they work

If there's any one part of your bike that needs to be working properly all the time, it's your brakes. Luckily, they're also the easiest piece of maintenance you'll have to tackle – everything is fairly exposed and it's obvious when you've not quite got the adjustment right.

Before you even get round to thinking about the differences between various types of brake, it's important to think about the similarities. Callipers, V-brakes and disc brakes all work by pushing a lump of material onto a rotating wheel, either onto the rim or onto a disc in the centre of the rim. If you use your bike regularly, the single biggest enemy of effective braking is contamination of the braking surfaces. Any dirt or grime that comes between the braking surfaces will make your braking less effective and will wear out surfaces, which will eventually prove expensive. The most important maintenance for your brake system is regular inspection of the rim or rotor and regular inspection of the pads.

Rim brakes tend to get much dirtier than disc brakes. Your rims are nearer the ground – where they get wet and dirty – and also much nearer your tyres, which dump dirt onto braking surfaces. By comparison, a disc rotor is safely out of the way and far enough from your tyres to stay much cleaner.

Which brake lever operates which brake?

This may seem obvious, but each brake lever operates just one brake. As a general rule this depends on which side of the road you legally ride, so brakes are set up according to which country you're in. There's a good reason for this – it's generally assumed that the trickiest manoeuvre you'll commonly do in traffic is turning across the oncoming lane. If you're signalling, you'll have one arm out in the air, leaving you only one hand to cover your brakes and steer with while you wait for a gap in traffic. In these cirumstances, it's better to use your back brake than your front, which is more difficult to control with one hand. In the UK, turning right means pulling across the traffic, which leaves only your left hand on the bars and, therefore, your left brake-lever operates your back brake. In the US and all other countries that drive on the right, it's usual for the brakes to be reversed, so that the right-hand brake-lever operates your back brake.

But it's still worth checking this before you start working on a bike and before you ride an unfamiliar bike, since a fair few will be set up unexpectedly. It's also important to be aware of which one is which, because hauling in on the front brake can throw you over the bars. Working out which is which is simple: check the brake-lever and follow the path of the cable that emerges from it – or, in the case of hydraulic brakes, the brake hose – and see where you end up.

Dirty rim brake blocks can wear all the way through the rim, until the point where the rim is no longer strong enough to support the pressure that the tyre exerts on the inner-rim wall. Once they're this worn, the rim will have to be replaced, and the cheapest way to do this is to buy a new wheel.

A cleaning routine for your braking surfaces

Rim brakes need most attention. If you live in the city, you'll soon see the black grime building up on your rims. This is made up of the rubbish that gets pumped out of the back of car exhausts. It will wear your rims out, and make your brake blocks slide around on the rim rather than gripping them and bringing you safely to a halt. The problem is, it needs to be removed regularly. How often will depend on the weather more than anything else – for example, rain mixes the exhaust fumes into a sludgy paste and welds it to your rims. Getting it off consists mostly of using a good deal of elbow grease. It's easier to remove if done regularly, before it's had a chance to accumulate.

The best things for cleaning rims are green nylon wire washing-up pads. They're abrasive enough to remove dirt, but not harsh enough to damage the aluminium of your rims. Otherwise, rag or kitchen towel is fine. You'll need some chemical assistance. Washing-up liquid in warm water is better than nothing, but a specialist bike cleaner such as Muc-Off or Finish Line Bike Wash will do the job better. If that still doesn't do the trick, use degreaser. Scrub rims until they're completely free of road dirt. Wipe dry with a clean cloth.

Brakes: comparing rim and disc

This chapter is split into sections depending on which type of brake you have. There's a basic division between two types of brakes: rim brakes, which are designed to employ the rim of the wheel as a braking surface, and disc brakes, which use a separate disc in the middle of the wheel as a braking surface. Rim brakes have been around in various forms for many years, whereas disc brakes are a more recent introduction to bicycles. First we'll look briefly at rim brakes since they're the more traditional type.

RIM BRAKES (V-, cantilever and calliper brakes)

Rim brakes fall into three basic types. Road bikes – with very light frames and drop handlebars – will typically use calliper brakes. These are simple and light, but not particularly powerful and are designed more for going fast than for slowing you down. But they're the simplest of all the types to maintain and the easiest to deal with when it comes to replacing brake blocks and brake cables. They need extra care if you don't have mudguards, since all the pivots sit directly above the middle of the tyre, right in the firing line for anything thrown up off the road.

V-brake

V-brakes are still the most common system on mountain bikes and hybrids, although they are slowly being superseded by disc brakes on mountain bikes. V-brakes were originally introduced as a replacement for cantilever brakes and one of their selling points was that it was supposed to be easier to fit brake blocks onto them than onto cantilevers. However, although it's not difficult, it's still quite fiddly the first time you do it.

Cantilever brakes are commonly found on touring bikes and cycle cross bikes and also on older mountain bikes and hybrids. The brake blocks last well, but the units take a little time to set up correctly – the brake cable branches into two just above the brake unit and the angle that the branches make with each other is crucial to effective operation of the brake. There isn't a wide range of models currently available if you want to replace the brake units – just very cheap ones or very expensive ones. Luckily, the cheap ones work perfectly well.

Calliper brakes are found on racing bikes. They're not particularly powerful, but they're light and neat. If you're not using mudguards, they

Cantilever brake

can get clogged up with road dirt that gets flicked off the tyre, making your braking sluggish.

DISC BRAKES (mechanical and hydraulic)

Disc brakes use scaled-down technology adapted from motorbike brakes. They were originally used for mountain bikes, but are creeping into use on hybrids. Their big selling point

Calliper brakes

on mountain bikes is that they are much more powerful than V-brakes. But your average commuter will actually do far more mileage than a recreational mountain biker, who might easily only go out once or twice a month. So commuters are in more of a position to appreciate the other advantage of disc brakes, which is that braking doesn't wear out your rim. From this point of view a separate rotor makes much sense.

Mechanical disc brakes work by using a cable to force the brake pads inside the calliper onto the rotor. In many ways mechanical discs are perfect for riding round town. Many parts are the same as V-brake parts and they fit

Mechanical disc brake

onto the same disc mounts on your frame and forks as hydraulic brakes.

Hydraulic brakes are more powerful still and are mainly found on mountain bikes. Instead of using a cable to operate the pistons, the calliper and brake-lever are connected by a thin hose filled with incompressible oil. Pulling the brake-lever squeezes the pads together, trapping your rotor.

Hydraulic disc brake

V-brakes: naming the parts

People often ask what the 'V' stands for in 'V-brakes'. It stands for 'vertical' – the position of the brake units. They're also known as 'linear pull'. They're light and powerful and, with a bit of practice, can be set up quickly. The accurate positioning of the brake blocks is critical and cables need to be kept in good condition, too. For almost all the jobs you'll need to do, like adjusting and replacing brake blocks or cables, you'll need little more than a couple of Allen keys and a pair of wire cutters.

A) Successful brake adjustment depends on the precise angle at which the brake blocks strike the rim. Most of this angle adjustment is carried out by shifting the brake block around on the brake unit. The brake block consists of a rubbery pad and a threaded metal stud. A selection of curved washers slide onto the stud and are held in place with an Allen key nut. Before the Allen key nut is completely tight, the curvature of the washers allows you to fiddle with the angle of the block. Once you've got it right, you can tighten the Allen key nut up completely, thus securing the brake block exactly where you want it. This simple description can be a little misleading and, the first time you try it, it may take a few attempts to get the position right.

 B) The brake units rotate around a stud that sticks out of the frame called a brake pivot. Each unit can only rotate in a circle around the brake pivot. Pulling the brake lever draws brake cable through the outer casing and pulls the tops of the two brake units together. Since the wheel rim runs between the brake units, pulling the brake units together forces the brake blocks attached to the units onto the rim, stopping your bike.

 C) Once you've finished braking, you release the brake-levers. What needs to happen next is for the brake blocks to spring back from the rim, releasing it so you can pedal away without the blocks dragging. But cables are very flexible – they have to be in order to wind their way from the lever to the brake unit – so they can only pull the units together: you can't use the cable to push the units apart again. Therefore, each brake unit has a spring that's always working to push the blocks away from the rim. When you pull the brake-lever, you can feel the resistance of the spring as soon as you start to pull. When you release the cable, the spring in each unit is free to push the blocks back off the rim, ready for next time. You can usually see the spring running up the side of the brake unit (as shown in the picture opposite). Don't worry if you can't locate it since brakes occasionally have a coil spring tucked up out of sight in the bottom of the brake unit.

 D) The spring has to be fairly thin and spindly, and so it needs all the help it can get to be able to push the blocks smartly away from the rims. As well as pushing the brake blocks away, it has to pull the cable you drew through when you braked back to where it started and pull the brake-lever back to its starting position ready for next time as well. Any friction in the cable means the spring

has to work harder. Kinks and bends in the cable or outer casing won't help. The cable will also feel rough if dirt and grit have got drawn into the outer casing, clogging up the hole that the inner cable is supposed to run through. Since most dirt will have been thrown up from the tyres, each brake has a black rubber boot (also called a gaiter) that covers the section of cable that runs closest to the tyres, between the brake units.

 E) As it approaches the brake unit, the last part of the brake cable fits into a curved metal tube called a noodle. This ensures that the cable leads smoothly into the brake unit. The very end of the noodle is tapered and fits neatly into the pivoted nest on the brake unit. It fits into a special key-shaped hole, which prevents the noodle from popping out of the nest if there is any tension in the cable – so your brakes cannot spontaneously release.

 F) Each brake unit has its own return spring. When you pull the brake-lever, you're hoping that the springs will be evenly balanced, so that the brake blocks on either side touch the rim at the same time. However, this is often not the case as one spring may be slightly stronger than the other and will hold its own brake block off the rim. This allows the weaker-sprung brake unit to move first, only starting to operate when the other is already jammed against the rim. This puts uneven pressure on the rim and twists it to one side every time you brake. The strength of the spring on either brake unit can be adjusted separately to correct this, allowing you to match them up so they operate simultaneously. Follow the procedure on page 107 to balance the units.

The noodle fits into a key-shaped hole, so your brakes can never spontaneously release

V-brakes: quick-release mechanism

V-brakes have a quick-release mechanism, so you can get the wheel on and off without deflating the tyre. Don't forget to reattach the brakes after refitting the wheel!

Releasing and refitting the brakes doesn't change their adjustment at all. This makes getting the wheel back in simple, since you won't have to readjust the brakes afterwards. There's an important point to remember here, however: it's essential when you're refitting the wheel to check that you've fitted it fully and centrally into the dropouts. If you've fitted the back wheel

in at an angle by mistake, the brake units won't strike the rims at the correct angle and the blocks may even rub on the tyre or pass under the rim and get stuck between the spokes. Even though this is a procedure to quick-release your brakes, it's best not to try to do the refitting bit too quickly. You should take a little time afterwards to ensure correct brake operation.

RELEASING BRAKE

Step 1: There's a small black rubber boot across the centre of the cable, between the two brake units. Pull it towards the cable pinch bolt, exposing the end of the noodle. The brake units must be squeezed together to create some slack in the cable. Once you've squashed them together, reach across and hold them as close to the rim as you can with one hand.

Step 2: Next, while holding the brake units together, pull the noodle away from the cable pinch bolt and up out of its pivoted nest. The end of the noodle will release from its key-shaped hole and you can ease the cable up through the slot in the nest. Sometimes it needs a little wiggle to free it. Once the noodle is free from its nest, the brake units will spring back so they're completely clear of the wheel.

Step 3: To reattach the cable, pull the brake units together, and guide the noodle into the nest. You may have to squeeze the units together tightly, close enough so you can slip the section of cable that emerges from the noodle into the narrow slot in the top of the nest. Make sure that the very end of the noodle sticks out beyond the nest, as shown. Spin the wheel and check that the tyre doesn't rub on the brake blocks.

How to release the noodle easily when brakes are set very tight

This is quite a common problem. It's especially difficult if your hands are cold or not as big as they're expected to be. It can also be caused by the brake modulators that get fitted onto front brake cables to stop you pulling the brake so hard that you lock the front wheel and fly over the handlebars. These consist of a spring tucked into a small metal barrel on the cable, which limits how hard you can pull the lever. It's crude, but it works. Sadly, it can also mean that you can't pull the brake units close enough together to release them. The solution is to set up the brakes as normal, but to make sure that, when you've finished adjusting the cable tension, there is at least 4mm (⅙ in) of

exposed thread showing at the brake-lever barrel-adjuster. Then, when you come to release the brakes, release the locknut from the barrel-adjuster and roll the barrel-adjuster into the brake-lever, slackening the brake cable. Squeeze the brake units together and release them, as above. When you come to refit the brakes, use the procedure above to refit the cable. Then roll the barrel-adjuster back out of the brake-lever, tightening the cable back up. When the adjustment is correct, wedge the locknut back against the brake-lever to stop the barrel-adjuster rattling loose. This sounds more complicated than it is and is a lot easier than struggling to squeeze the brake units together.

V-brakes: the most effective set-up

You're looking for a specific adjustment for your brake blocks. They need to be set up so that, when you pull the brake-levers, the brake blocks hit the rim when the levers have travelled about halfway to the bars. The brake blocks themselves need to be set up so that they hit the rims flat, square and with the front of the brake block touching just before the back does. The front has to touch before the back to stop the brake from squeaking.

It's important how the brake feels when you squeeze the lever. The lever should pull easily – without resistance – and you should be able to feel through the lever when the brake block strikes through the rim.

If the cables are dirty so that the cable struggles to slide through the outer casing, you won't be able to feel what's going on at the brake through your fingers and it's important that the cables can transmit a signal clearly. If your brakes are tough to pull on, you have to start thinking about changing your cables. See page 108.

Equally, when you've finished braking and have released your brake-levers, the brake blocks should spring back from the rims smartly, so that you can set off again without any resistance from the blocks dragging on the rims. A sluggish return indicates that it's time to service your brake units as well as to check the condition of your cables. See page 112.

Finally, there's the actual slowing down bit. When you pull the brake-levers, your bike should come to a halt quickly, but in a controlled way. If your bike continues to slide forwards, even when you haul on the anchors, you need to look at the condition of your brake blocks. Even if they look like they still have quite a lot of thickness left on them, they may have become dirty or contaminated or have worn unevenly. See page 110.

Key things to look out for

One of the most common brake block problems that occur with V-brakes is uneven wear. V-brakes are powerful and can push the blocks onto your rims with a fair amount of force. This means that the material of the brake block will wear out quite quickly. During braking, the unit itself moves closer and closer to the rim as the brake block becomes thinner. The brake unit moves in an arc around its pivot, so the height at which the brake block hits the rim will gradually change. This means that, even if the position of your brake blocks was originally set up perfectly, they will need regular checking to ensure that they're still striking the rim flat and centrally.

If they're allowed to wear down without being adjusted, the brake blocks may erode to such an extent that the lower part of the block no longer strikes the rim. This is a problem for two reasons. Firstly, the area of your brake blocks is fairly small to begin with – two blocks front and back, each about the size of your thumbprint, is not a lot of area to rely on to stop you. The second reason is a longer-term issue. Only the part of the block that strikes the rim will wear out. The part that hangs uselessly underneath won't wear. Over a period of time, this will create a lip at the bottom of the brake block that will pass under the rim as you brake and catch on the underside of the rim when you release the brake-lever, preventing the brake unit from returning smoothly.

You'll be able to see quite clearly whether your brake blocks are wearing unevenly. Squeeze on the brakes and look at how they hit the rim. The entire face of the block should hit the rim. If there's any of it visibly hanging under the rim, you need to take action.

If you've caught it in time and a lip hasn't yet formed, you're in luck and can simply readjust the position of the brake blocks so that they're hitting the rim fully. Follow the instructions for adjusting brake block position on page 105. If a lip has formed, you have two options.

The easier is to replace the brake blocks with fresh ones (see page 110). If the lip is small and there's enough life left in the rest of the brake block, follow the instructions on page 110. Once you've removed the blocks, carefully cut the lip off the brake block with a sharp knife.

To do this, stand the block up on a hard surface and cut downwards as the blocks are too small to hold safely in your hand while you cut. Make the surface as flat as you can, then follow the rest of the instructions on page 110 for refitting the brake blocks.

Finally, if you're struggling to get your brakes adjusted correctly, check that your wheel isn't out of true. Spin the wheel slowly, and watch the gap between the brake pad on one side and the rim. The size of the gap should remain the same as the wheel turns. If the rim wanders from side to side as it spins, see page 192 for instructions on getting the wheel straight before you start altering brake block positions.

V-brakes: adjusting cable position

Fitting new cables and brake blocks to your bike are both procedures that you'll have to set aside a fair amount of time to do since they're fiddly to get right and you'll probably need to make a trip to the bike shop for spares. In either case, once you've fitted new parts you'll want to adjust your brakes so they feel right and you get the most stopping power with minimum effort.

You'll also need to adjust your brake cables as your brake pads wear, taking up slack in the cable to move the remaining pads closer to the rims. Most of your final adjustment will be done by moving the barrel-adjusters. If you're not sure how these work, read through the step sequence below. Once you're confident about your brake adjustment, you'll be able to make fine adjustments without too much fuss, taking up slack in the cable to make brakes feel exactly how you want.

You're searching for an ideal position with your brake adjustment. The brake blocks need to be close enough to the rim so that when you pull the brake-lever you can lock the wheel when the brake-levers are about halfway to the handlebars. On the other hand, you need your brake blocks to be far enough away so that they don't rub on the rim as you ride along, since this will both slow you down and wear out the brake blocks unnecessarily, which you don't want.

Being able to achieve this adjustment depends partly on your rims being reasonably round. If they wobble from side to side as they spin, it will be hard to get the brake blocks into

a position where they will brake effectively without rubbing. Before you start, it's worth checking how round your wheels actually are. Pick up one end of the bike at a time and spin the wheel gently and slowly. While it spins, look carefully at one side of the wheel. Concentrate on the gap between the brake block and the metal rim. If the wheel is perfectly round, this gap will not change in size as the wheel spins. A little bit of movement is acceptable and – in anything other than a brand-new wheel – almost inevitable. But if the gap changes in size by more than a couple of millimetres during a revolution of the wheel, it will be a struggle to adjust the brake blocks. If so, it's best to true the wheel before you attempt to adjust the blocks. If you're feeling confident, instructions for doing this are on page 192. But truing wheels is something you get much better at with practice, so decide how deeply you want to commit yourself: it is perfectly reasonable to get your wheels trued by your bike shop and then adjust your brakes yourself. Keeping your wheels true doesn't only make it possible to adjust your brakes effectively – true wheels are much stronger than wobbly ones and last much longer.

ADJUSTING CABLE POSITION

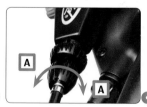

Step 1: Spin the wheel, watching the gap between the brake blocks and the rim. If the brake blocks touch the rim, the cable is too tight. Use the barrel-adjuster (B) on the brake-lever to loosen it slightly. Turn the lockring (A), so it moves away from the lever body, then turn the barrel-adjuster clockwise so it moves towards the lever body, loosening the cable until the wheel can spin freely. Wind the lockring back, wedging it against the lever body.

Step 2: You may find that there isn't enough adjustment on the barrel-adjuster. If you wind it all the way in and the blocks still touch the rims, you will need to let out a bit of cable at the brake unit. Hold the cable as shown then undo the cable clamp bolt with a 5mm Allen key. Let out a little bit of cable – maybe 5mm (⅕ in) – and retighten the brake cable firmly. Now go back to step 1 and make fine adjustments with the barrel-adjuster.

Step 3: If the lever pulls too far back before the brake blocks bite, wind the lockring away from the lever body and then turn the barrel-adjuster anticlockwise to wind it out of the lever body and tighten the cable (A). When you're done, wedge the lockring back against the lever body. If the barrel-adjuster threatens to fall out of the lever body go to step 2, but pull more cable through rather than letting it out.

V-brakes: brake block position

The key with your brake blocks is to ensure that they strike the rim with as much of their surface and force as possible. The first time you try to adjust them, it seems to take ages to get it right. Don't worry – you will get better with practice.

The key is to undo the Allen key bolt that secures the brake block just enough so that you can move the brake block around – sliding the whole block up and down in the slot in the brake units and rotating the blocks. Once the Allen key is slightly loose, the curved washers allow you to swivel the block quite easily, changing the angle at which it approaches the rim. Once you've finished you tighten the Allen key bolt firmly, which secures the brake block wherever you've set it. Check once you've finished by taking hold of the block and twisting it firmly. If you can move it, you need to tighten the Allen key fixing bolt some more.

Here's a rogue's gallery of common errors!

Too high
The brake block should strike the rim centrally so that there is as much rim showing above the block as below. The block in this picture is set too high and will rub on the tyre, quickly puncturing it.

Too low
This brake block is set too low. The bottom part of the brake block falls below the rim. It won't wear out like the rest of the block. Eventually this will form a lip, which will stop the brakes from functioning correctly.

Angle of approach not 90°
The brake block should strike the rim so the threaded metal stud fixing the brake block to the brake unit lies at 90° to the surface of the rim. Here, the block approaches the rim from above, rather than square on.

Blocks at different heights
The brake blocks have been set at different heights: when you look at the brake head on, the brake blocks' positions should look even. Uneven blocks will twist the rim as you brake.

Wheel out of alignment
Here, the wheel alignment wasn't checked before the brake block position was adjusted. The wheel sits off to one side in the forks. You should check wheel alignment before adjusting your brakes.

Twisted block
When looked at from the side, the brake block should follow the curve of the rim. This block is twisted, with the back too high and the front too low. The blocks will wear unevenly.

Toe-in
Finally, the gap between the brake block and the rim needs to be about 1-2mm ($\frac{1}{25}$-$\frac{1}{12}$ in) bigger at the back than at the front.
This is called 'toeing-in' and stops the brakes squealing as you pull them on.
It also helps to reduce vibrations when you are braking – it's always better to get a direct response when you need to stop in a hurry. Both front and rear brake blocks need to be toed in.

Barrel-adjusters and lockrings

They may well seem like very small parts of your bike to allocate a whole page to. But they're essential tools for getting brakes and gear cable tension perfect.

There are often occasions when you need the cable tension on your bike to be precisely adjusted. A perfect example comes when you're indexing your rear derailleur – setting the tension in your gear cable, so that each time you shift gear the chain moves precisely from one sprocket to the next. Equally, it's nice to be able to adjust the tension in your brake cable so that the brake blocks bite on the rim – or disc rotor – when your hands are about halfway to the bars.

You could make these precise adjustments by unclamping the gear or brake cable from under its cable-pinch bolt, pulling through or letting out a very small amount of cable and then retightening the cable clamp bolt firmly. You still find old bikes, cheap bikes and kids' bikes that don't have a barrel-adjuster option.

But there are a couple of reasons why this is not very satisfactory. One is that it is really quite difficult to be precise, judge exactly how much cable you need and then hold that adjustment while you retighten the cable. Another is that, if you have to have several goes at the adjustment, you end up undoing and retightening the clamp bolt several times – squashing and damaging it a little bit each time. It's a prime location for the cable to fray anyway so it's best to avoid weakening it. It also means you can never make a quick adjustment – you'll always have to find some tools to do the job.

Barrel-adjusters exist to allow you to make quick, precise and easy adjustments to cable tensions.

The barrel-adjuster (B) on your brake-lever is the easiest to understand. Take a look at it: it's the part that the brake cable goes through as it enters the brake-lever. A barrel-adjuster consists of a deep cup with a threaded portion at the end. The outer casing fits neatly into the cup, with the cable passing all the way through. The extra ring on the threaded portion (A) is the lockring – ignore that for now.

The outside of the barrel-adjuster is knurled – it has grooves that make it easy to grip and turn with your hand. Because the barrel-adjuster is threaded, as you turn it the whole barrel moves in and out of the brake-lever. As you move the barrel-adjuster out of the brake-lever, you're making a little bit of extra distance between the end of the outer casing and the brake-lever – a little bit of extra distance that the inner cable has to travel. The inner cable hasn't got any longer, so it has to get a little bit tighter because it's stretched over a slightly longer distance. Turning the barrel so that it moves out of the lever makes the cable tighter, and vice versa.

Once you've set the ideal position for your barrel-adjuster, you want it to stay there, not to rattle loose as soon as you go over a pothole – which is why you have a lockring. While you're adjusting the barrel you turn this out of the way – wind it up the barrel-adjuster so that it's not touching the brake-lever. Once you've finished, wind it back down and wedge it against the brake-lever to prevent further movement.

Gear cables work in exactly the same way – turning them so that the barrel moves out of the gear-shifter or derailleur makes the cable tighter; winding them into the shifter or derailleur makes the cable looser. If there's a barrel-adjuster on both the shifter and the derailleur, it doesn't matter which one you use.

Barrel-adjusters for gears also have a means of stopping the barrel rattling loose, although it's not immediately obvious how it works. The most common version has the whole barrel-adjuster covered in a plastic sleeve, which has a little spring inside constantly pushing the sleeve onto the body of the derailleur. Notches on the sleeve fit into dips in the body of the derailleur so that the barrel can't turn easily unless the sleeve is lifted slightly away from the derailleur. The barrel-adjuster at the shifter works in exactly the same way.

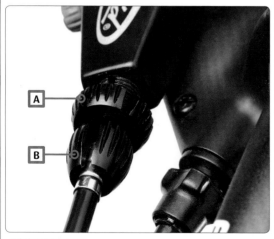

Brake-lever barrel-adjuster

V-brakes: balance screws

Each V-brake unit has a balance screw. You'll find it at the bottom of the unit, usually a crosshead bolt but occasionally a small Allen key.

The balance screw adjusts spring tension

The end of each bolt rests on the end of the brake-return spring so that the spring is forced against the bolt when you squeeze the brake unit towards the rim. Turning the balance screw alters the preload on the spring, pushing its starting point further around the unit for a stronger spring action and releasing it for a weaker spring action. The confusing part is remembering which way to turn the screws for the effect you need.

Turning the balance screw clockwise (A) pushes it further into the unit, increasing the preload on the spring, making it springier and pulling the attached brake block away from the rim.

Turning the balance screw anticlockwise (B) unscrews it from the unit, decreasing the preload, softening the spring and allowing the brake block to move nearer to the rim.

Since the two units are connected together by the cable across the top, adjusting one balance screw will affect both units: if one unit is pulled away from the rim, the other will be drawn towards it to compensate.

To adjust the balance screws, look first at each brake unit from face on. If the balance screws are badly adjusted, the units will point off to one side, rather than being parallel and vertical. There will be an uneven distance between brake blocks and rim, perhaps with one closer than the other or even with one brake block dragging on the rim. To correct the problem locate the balance screws. Start with the unit that's closer to the rim and wind the balance screw in clockwise a couple of turns. You'll need to squeeze and release the brake-lever every time you make a balance-screw adjustment to resettle the position of the spring. Look again at the angle of the two units. You should find that the adjustment has both pulled the closer brake block away from the rim and pulled the other block closer.

One confusing thing about the balance screws is that turning the screw has a different effect at different points – sometimes a couple of turns seems to make no difference at all, sometimes a quarter-turn makes a radical change. You'll have to experiment, adjusting the balance screws a quarter-turn at a time to find the central position.

Lever modulation

Modulation is just a fancy word for 'how far the cable travels when you pull the lever', which depends on the distance between the point that the cable attaches to the lever blade, and the pivot that the blade rotates around. Increasing this distance means more power, but also more lever travel. Some models of brake-lever allow you to adjust the modulation. In the picture, the red thumb nut on the lever adjusts the position of the cable nest. Turning the thumbscrew clockwise moves the nest further from the pivot of the brake-lever, so more cable is pulled through the lever when you move the lever blade. Turning the thumbscrew anticlockwise moves the nest nearer to the pivot, so less cable is pulled through when you move the lever blade. Adjust the lever modulation so that it gives you a comfortable amount of lever swing. This will depend on the size of your hands.

V-brakes: fitting a cable

Before you start, you should remember the benefits of a decent pair of cable cutters. This is one place where you can't afford to be stingy.

A decent pair of cable cutters will probably cost you at least £20 and it's tempting to think that you could get away with using an old pair of pliers, or tinsnips or whatever. But a great deal of the quality of your final product will depend on how cleanly you can cut both the outer casing and the inner cable. Wire cutters must be good enough to cut through a cable in a single bite. Chewing through the cable a strand at a time will leave you with a messy frayed end that won't pass cleanly through the outer casing. It matters just as much when it comes to the outer casing. You need to be able to make a clean cut without leaving a tang of metal that hangs across the end of the outer casing. When you look down into the cut end of the casing, you should see a neat 🔽

FITTING A CABLE

Step 1: Snip the end off the cable with cable cutters. A clean cut is important: if the end is frayed it will damage the inside outer casing as you draw the cable through. The cable is trapped between the top of the brake unit and the washer that sits under the cable pinch bolt. The washer is usually shaped, so that it doesn't turn with the clamp bolt, preventing damage to the cable. Release the cable pinch bolt and pull the cable free.

Step 2: Release the noodle from its pivoted nest by pulling it away and up, working the cable up and out of the slot in the nest. Pull the black rubber boot off the end of the cable and then the metal noodle which should all come away in one piece. If it leaves behind a section of lining, pull that off too and feed it back into the noodle. Pull the old cable out from each section of outer casing, a bit at a time. Leave the outer casing in place.

Step 3: Once you've got back to the lever, pull the outer casing away from the lever, exposing the barrel-adjuster. It's made up of two parts – the barrel-adjuster itself and a lockring that keeps everything in place. Each has a slot in it as does the lever body. Turn the lockring so it moves away from the lever body, then turn the barrel-adjuster and lockring so all the slots line up. If you're not sure how barrel-adjusters work, go to the box on page 106.

Step 4: Pull the brake-lever towards the handlebar. Pull the cable gently out of the lined-up slots. Keeping the brake-lever pulled back, wiggle the cable nipple out of the key-shaped hole in the brake-lever. You'll need to line the cable up with the little slot in the nest. Clean out the nest if necessary. Release the brake-lever.

Step 5: Now that you've removed the old cable, check each section of the outer casing carefully. You're looking for kinks, parts where the plastic casing has worn away or sections that are so short that they only just reach. Remove damaged sections one at a time and replace with new sections, making sure you replace any ferrules.

Step 6: Take the new cable and drip a small drop of oil on the junction of the cable and the nipple. Pull the brake-lever back so that it touches the handlebar and hold it there. Wiggle the nipple back into its nest in the lever, then draw the cable back through the aligned slots in the brake-lever, barrel-adjuster and lockring. Turn the barrel-adjuster slightly, so that the cable can't slip out again and release the brake-lever.

circle with none of the metal of the casing overlapping the centre of the circle. The casing is lined all the way through the middle with a Teflon tube. This usually gets squashed as you cut the cable and appears to seal the end of the casing. Use a sharp knife to open out the end of the casing at either end.

Ferrules are another essential, and it's worth having a handful living in your toolbox. There are two sizes: 5mm ones fit brake casing, while 4mm are usually for gear casing. Ferrules are important because they stop the ends of the brake casing from splaying out under pressure and ensure that the ends of each section of casing fit snugly in the cable stop, barrel-adjuster or noodle that it ends in. Each end of each section of cable will need a ferrule with the exception of the very last section, where the

outer casing fits into the noodle. This will only need a ferrule if one fits neatly in there. If you can't get a ferrule in there because the end of the noodle is too narrow, it doesn't need one.

A handful of cable ends is another useful thing to have in your toolbox. You slip them over the end of the cable when you've finished and squash them on with pliers. They stop the cable fraying or unravelling, which is messy. It can be painful too – strands of frayed cable are sharp and have a habit of stabbing your fingers if you ever get accidentally close to them. Cable ends are one-use only. You have to cut them off and discard them next time you want to work on the cable. It's worth oiling the new cable as you fit it, to stop it corroding inside the outer casing. Don't go mad though – you only need a little bit.

Step 7: Feed the end of the cable back through each section of outer casing in turn (there will only be one section if you're working on the front brake). Wiggle each ferrule into its cable stop to make sure it's nice and secure. As you feed the cable through the casing make sure it moves smoothly. If it's a struggle to get it through or it feels gritty, pull it out again, check the outer casing and then replace any suspect sections.

Step 8: Once you've got the cable through the outer casing, feed it carefully through the noodle. Sometimes the curved noodle resists the brake cable. If so, pull the cable out and bend it about 3cm (1⅓ in) from the end, then try feeding it through again, twisting it as it goes. Slide the noodle up the cable so it fits snugly onto the outer casing and refit the black rubber boot loosely onto the cable, but don't cover up the end of the noodle yet.

Step 9: Feed the end of the brake cable under the cable pinch bolt so it sits between the washer and the brake unit. To check it's the right place, there will be a groove cut into the washer or the brake unit. Pull through most of the slack. Refit the noodle back into the nest in the brake unit. Make sure that the end of the noodle protrudes through the nest. Push the black rubber boot back over the exposed end of the noodle.

Step 10: Pull the slack end of the cable through until the brake blocks almost touch the rim. Tighten the cable clamp bolt. Pull hard on the brake-lever to settle the cable in. You may find there's now a lot of slack in the cable – the brake-lever may pull back to the bars. If so, undo the cable pinch bolt, pull through cable until the blocks almost touch the rim, and retighten. Leave 10cm (4 in) of spare cable, cut off the rest and fit a cable end.

Step 11: You need to make a fine adjustment to the cable. Lift up the wheel and spin it gently. If the brake blocks are touching the wheel on one side but not the other, turn the balance screw gently, a quarter-turn at a time on the side that the block touches. You'll need to squeeze and release the brake-lever periodically as you adjust to settle the balance screw into place. For more details on balance-screw adjustment, see page 107.

Step 12: Adjust the cable tension (see page 104 for more detail). Spin the wheel gently, then pull the brake-lever. If both brake blocks rub on the rim, the cable is too loose. If the brake-lever moves too far before the blocks bite, the cable is too tight. Roll the lockring away from the lever. Turn the barrel clockwise to move the blocks away from the rim, anticlockwise to move them nearer. Wedge the lockring back onto the lever.

Fitting brake blocks

Learning how to fit new brake blocks to your bike is probably the single most useful place to start wielding your spanners as a budding bike mechanic.

For all the advantages of V-brakes – they're simple and relatively cheap – they do have an Achilles heel and that is that you'll find yourself wearing out brake blocks fairly frequently. You can minimise this by keeping your rims clean (see page 85), but replacing the blocks is still a job that needs doing a couple of times a year. Learning how to do it yourself is an investment that will repay itself quite quickly, saving you the labour costs as well as the hassle of getting your bike to the bike shop when you're busy.

There are several possible indications that your brake blocks are worn out. The most obvious is when your brakes don't stop you properly any more or suddenly start making a scary squealing noise whenever you pull the levers. Don't ignore these signs! They mean that you have worn all the way through the rubber part of the brake block and are forcing the metal stud embedded in the brake block against the rim every time you pull on the brake-lever. This won't stop you safely when you need to and will wear out your rim in no time at all – an expensive thing to neglect.

You shouldn't be waiting for these signs that your brake blocks have worn out completely. Instead, you should change them before they've worn right down. Don't be stingy about brake blocks. They're much cheaper than the damage you'll do running into things that you wouldn't have run into if your brakes had been working properly.

Manufacturers of decent brake blocks will always print or mould some kind of brake wear indicator onto brake blocks, usually a line or an arrow. If your brake block originally had slots in it, the brake blocks are worn out when you have reached the bottoms of the slots. In any other case, replace the blocks when they've worn down to half their original depth.

Unlike disc brakes, where each make, model and year of brake calliper is only compatible with its own unique brake pad, replacement V-brake pads are almost universal. This means you can fit brake blocks from any manufacturer to brake units made by any other.

This helps keep brake blocks cheap. There's a little price to pay for this universal compatibility, however – the manufacturers don't know the exact size and shape of your rims or the dimensions of your brake unit. Each brake unit, therefore, has to come with a selection of different sizing washers so that you can manipulate the position of the brake blocks precisely.

This is fiddly and seems to be something that puts people off fitting new brake blocks for themselves. It's important to follow the instructions for assembling the washers carefully. The washer set consists of some flat washers, some curved washers and some dome washers. For a secure fit, ensure that a dome always fits into a curve, and that a flat washer always faces the block, the Allen key nut and either side of the brake unit.

NEW BRAKE BLOCKS

Step 1: Use an Allen key – almost always 5mm – to remove the nut that holds on the old brake block. Lift off any washers under the nut, then wiggle the brake block out from behind the brake unit, along with the rest of the washers from between the brake units and the brake block. Remove the other brake block in the same way.

Step 2: Before fitting the new brake units, it's important to ensure that the brake units are correctly aligned. Looking at them face on (as in this picture), they should be parallel and vertical.

Step 3: If the brake units aren't parallel, undo the cable pinch bolt and let cable out or in until they are. Tighten the cable pinch bolt firmly. If the brake units are slightly curvy, you will have to estimate the correct position.

Step 4: If the brake units are parallel but both point off to one side or other, you will have to use the balance screws to correct the angle. Choose the brake unit closer to the rim and gently screw in the balance screw a quarter-turn at a time, squeezing and releasing the brake-lever to settle the balance screw into place. If you're unsure, read page 107.

Step 5: Next, sort through the collection of washers that came with your new brake blocks. You will need a cup washer and a dome washer between the brake unit and the brake block. There are two sizes to choose from – a fat cup washer and a thin cup washer. Choose the size that means the brake block just fits between the brake unit and the rim.

Step 6: The cup washer goes onto the brake block first with the cup showing. The dome washer goes on next with the curve of the dome facing into the cup. Try fitting the brake block between the brake unit and the rim. If it looks like the other-sized curved washer would be a better fit, take the brake block back off and swap them over.

Step 7: Push the threaded stub of the brake block through the brake-lever. Slide a domed washer over the threaded stub with the curved side facing you and the flat side against the surface of the brake block. Then slide on your remaining cup washer with the curved surface of the cup facing the domed washer. Next, fit on any remaining washers and thread on the Allen key nut loosely.

Step 8: The curved washers mean that, as long as the Allen key nut is a little bit loose, you can slide the brake block around to adjust the angle at which it strikes the rim. You can also change the height of the brake block by sliding the whole brake block up and down in the slot on the brake unit. When in the right position, the brake block should strike the centre of the rim and be parallel to it.

Step 9: The front of the brake block should be slightly closer than the back, so when the front touches the rim there is a gap of 1-2mm ($\frac{1}{25}$-$\frac{1}{12}$ in) between the back of the brake block and the rim. Once you've found the right position, tighten the Allen key nut firmly. Hold the brake block and twist firmly. If you can move the brake block, retighten the Allen key nut. You'll need to see page 104 for fine adjustments to the cable.

Cartridge-type brake blocks

Cartridge-type brake blocks are designed in two parts. The rubber braking surface is a separate block that fits inside the metal shoe, which is the part that clamps onto the brake unit. The block slides inside the shoe from the back and is held in place with a retaining pin. To change the blocks, pull the retaining pin out upwards with a pair of pliers and simply push the rubber block backwards. Your new replacement blocks may be marked up to show that they're left- and

right-specific. They'll also have a slot at the back where the retaining pin secures them, so push the other end in first. You'll need to squint through the retaining pin hole and wiggle the position of the block around until you can see light through the other side. Push the retaining pin in firmly and check to see that the end has protruded slightly out of the bottom of the metal shoe. Ensure that the opening in the shoe where you slide the rubber block faces backwards.

V-brakes: servicing

Brake units are relatively inexpensive and usually come complete with a fresh set of brake blocks, so if you get halfway through servicing your set and realize that they've become very worn, it's worthwhile simply to replace the units.

Compatibility is not really an issue as V-brakes will fit onto any bike with brake pivots on the frame or fork.

The first sign that your brakes need some attention is that the

return spring will start to struggle to snap the blocks smartly away from the rim when you release the brake-levers. If you want to make a really thorough job of it, then replace – or at

SERVICING V-BRAKES

Step 1: Your first step is to quick-release the brake units – see page 102 if you're not sure how to do this. Take a moment to check the condition of the brake cable. Follow it back to the lever, looking for kinked cable or casing, holes in the casing or frayed cable. Damaged cable or casing will need to be replaced (see page 108).

Step 2: Cut off the cable end and undo the cable pinch bolt enough so that you can slide the cable out from underneath the cable pinch bolt. There's usually a specially shaped washer between the cable pinch bolt and the cable. The one in the picture has two little claws that sit either side of a tang on the brake unit. These are there to stop the washer twisting as you loosen or tighten the cable, which would damage it.

Step 3: Now that the cable is detached from the unit you can remove the brake units. The brake fixing bolt is the lowest one on each brake unit and may be a little stiff to move at first. The bolt heads often become full of dirt. If this is the case, clean them out carefully with a small screwdriver before you start so that the Allen key fits snugly. Remove the bolts completely.

Step 4: Next, pull the brake unit off the brake pivot. The unit may take some persuasion, especially if it's been on there a while. If it's reluctant to come off, pull the unit firmly away from the frame with one hand, while rotating the unit backwards and forwards – as if you were applying then releasing the brakes – with the other hand.

Step 5: Now you can get at the brake unit and give it a proper clean. Use a small brush and some bike wash, or degreaser if it still won't come clean. Clean inside the pivot hole that runs through the brake unit. Unhook the top of the spring from behind the tab on the brake-lever. Work the spring back and forth to see how the two parts of the brake-lever move against each other. Drip oil into this gap, wiping off excess.

Step 6: Clean the brake pivot. If it's rusty, take a small strip of wet-and-dry paper and rub it smooth. Clean dirt out of the three small holes in the frame beside the brake pivot. Drip a small amount of oil onto the brake pivot, and spread it around.

least clean and lubricate – your brake cables at the same time. The pictures here show a front brake, but the rear brakes are serviced in exactly the same way.

The rear brakes just need a longer piece of cable to reach all the way from the handlebars to the back of the bike and are, therefore, even more sensitive to gritty cables and worn or gummed-up brake units.

Servicing the unit won't affect the position of the brake blocks, so they won't need readjusting after you've finished, but you will probably need to readjust the balance screws.

This is usually the case if one of the brake units had previously been getting stiffer and the balance screw was adjusted to compensate for this. Once you've cleaned them both out, they'll

move more easily and will need to be rebalanced. If you decide to replace your brake blocks, choosing new ones can be a bit confusing, since the cheap ones look pretty similar to the more expensive versions, and it's hard to work out where your extra money is going.

The main difference is that, since the more expensive ones are made more accurately, they are a lot easier to adjust precisely, and will keep their adjustment for longer once you have put them in place.

Another advantage is that you'll also find that the springs, bolts and washers will last longer without corroding. So it's worth spending a little bit of extra cash, rather than choosing the bargain basement model.

Step 7: Next, look carefully at the back of the brake unit. You'll see a short stud about 1mm across (½₅ in) and 5mm long (⅕ in) sticking directly out of the back. Slide the brake unit back onto the brake pivot and, as it gets close to the frame, ensure that this little stud fits neatly into the middle of the three holes next to the brake pivot. Rotate the brake unit around its pivot, checking that it moves smoothly.

Step 8: The brake fixing bolts must not be allowed to rattle loose, especially the front ones. If they do, the brakes will shoot off the front of the pivots instead of stopping you – dangerous. Pop a little drop of threadlock onto the threads of each brake. You can see the spring flapping loose in the picture. Take care to get the fixing bolts securely in place before you refit the spring.

Step 9: Lift the spring back up to the brake unit and slip the top of the spring behind the tab that keeps it in place. Put a small drop of oil onto the tab, so that it lubricates the interface between spring and tab.

Step 10: Push the brake unit so that the brake block is forced against the rim and then release it. The unit should move smoothly and spring back smartly. If it's rough or gritty, remove it again, re-clean, re-lubricate and reassemble. Repeat the whole procedure from step 3 with the other brake unit.

Step 11: Remove the cable pinch bolt completely and clean the threads, the bolt head and washer and the top of the brake unit. Refit the bolt with a drop of oil on the threads and locate the shaped washer so that it won't rotate around the bolt. Slide the brake cable back under the washer. You'll be able to locate the right place. There will be a groove cut into the washer, the brake unit or both, indicating where it goes.

Step 12: Pull the brake cable through under the pinch bolt until the brake blocks are almost touching the rim, then tighten the pinch bolt firmly. Squash on a new cable end and tuck the stray end of cable behind the spring tab. Test the brake adjustment by squeezing the brake-lever firmly – the brake should lock on when the lever is about halfway to the handlebars. For detailed cable adjustment, see page 108.

Curing squeaky brakes

Squealing brake blocks are annoying. The racket makes you wary of using your brakes, and it's not even good for alerting pedestrians about to step out in front of you – you've already braked by then. The squeal tends to come and go, so you think you've fixed it, only to have it return. All types of brakes suffer from it, but luckily the same few causes are responsible for most noises. Rim brakes – V-, cantilever and calliper – can all be cured the same way. Disc brakes need a slightly different approach.

Rim brakes

◎ The most common culprit is dirty braking surfaces. If you ride in town, your rims pick up a sticky layer of black grime. Once stuck to the aluminium of your rims, it prevents brake blocks from gripping. They slide over the surface instead, making that awful noise. Dirty rims will quickly wear out your brake blocks, too. The best implement is a nylon washing-up sponge – it's abrasive enough to do the job without scratching your rims. Stubborn stains must be removed with bike wash, or even degreaser.

◎ Dirt on your rims quickly gets transferred to the surface of your brake blocks. If your brakes aren't stopping you sharply, check the surfaces of the blocks and pick out anything that shouldn't be there with a sharp knife. Smaller particles, too small to be seen individually, will make the brake block surface hard and shiny rather than grippy – lightly sand the surface with fresh sandpaper.

◎ Even without obvious contamination, brake blocks do just get harder over time, especially if your bike is left out in all weathers. Brake blocks should be changed every couple of years, whether they've worn away or not.

◎ If your brake surfaces are clean, and you still get noisy brakes, look at your brake block alignment. All rim brakes – V-, cantilever and calliper – should be set up in the same way. The front of the brake block needs to touch the rim just before the back. This is called 'toeing in', and is essential for silent braking. The difference should be around 1–2mm (½₅–½₂ in). The adjustment method varies according to brake type – see the appropriate section on brake block alignment – page 110 for V-brakes, 123 for cantilevers, 116 for callipers. If you haven't done this adjustment before, don't be put off by how fiddly it seems – leave yourself plenty of time the first time and it will get quicker and easier every time you do the job.

◎ If none of the above suggestions works, check the brake unit(s). Wobble each one back and forth. There will often be a little bit of movement – perhaps 3mm (⅛ in) – but any more than that is probably the source of the squealing. Check the brake units are tightened securely to the frame. It often helps to remove the brake unit, clean the interface between brake unit and frame, oil it and replace the unit.

Squeaky brakes are annoying but easy to cure

Disc brakes

◎ Disc brakes suffer less from surface dirt than rim brakes – the rotor is further up off the road surface. But that doesn't mean they should be ignored. Disc rotors and brake pads will slide over each other without slowing you down if either get oily. Clean disc rotors with bike wash or isopropyl alcohol. Replace brake pads that have become contaminated.

◎ Many people believe that squeaky disc brakes should be cured with a dab of grease on the back of the pad. I tend to avoid this solution – the heat of braking will melt the grease, and it will eventually work its way onto the braking surface.

◎ Check the alignment of the callipers very carefully. Spin the wheel and make sure that the rotor doesn't touch either side of the calliper slot – as well as making an evil noise, contact will wear the rotor out. Adjust the callipers so that there is an even gap between rotor and brake pad on either side, and the pads are parallel to the rotor.

◎ If cleaning the surfaces and aligning the caliper doesn't work, the most likely problem is that the disc brake mounts on the frame or fork aren't precisely flat or parallel. Milling them flat will cure the problem, but it's a job for your bike shop – the correct tool is rather expensive.

Checking rims for wear

The single best argument for using disc brakes rather than rim brakes around town is the speed at which dirty rims will wear out. Riding in town involves a whole lot of stopping and starting, so your braking surfaces work hard. Having a rim sidewall blow suddenly is very alarming. People can think they've been shot when there's a loud bang and suddenly they're lying on the ground, just like in the movies. Because of the pressure inside the tyre, the sidewalls don't give way gracefully.

Over time the sidewall gets thinner and thinner. One part of the sidewall gets too thin to hold in the tyre. Then you brake suddenly and the moment of reckoning occurs! Once one section of the rim starts to give way, it cannot support the next section, so within a fraction of a second most of your sidewall is ripped off. This punctures your tube, the resulting mess usually jams on your brake and you fall off the bike.

Rims can also give way when you're pumping your tyre up. The extra tyre pressure on the inside of the rim sidewall is all it takes for the rim to finally collapse. This is just as alarming and may also shower you with rim shrapnel.

Some newer rims come with indicator marks that show when the rim is worn out. The rim will have a small hole drilled from the inside, but not all the way through. The position of the hole is marked by a sticker on the rim with an arrow pointing to where the hole will appear. As you wear away the sidewall, the bottom of the hole appears from the outside; look carefully and you can see your tyre through it. Time to get a new rim. Another type of rim indicator consists of a groove milled all the way around the braking surface of the rim. When the rim is worn away to the base of the groove, it is worn out and should be replaced. To help you see it, the bottom of the groove will be a different colour to the sidewall of the rim. For example, a silver rim will have a black groove in it, and a black rim will have a silver groove.

If you don't have a wear-indicator, check the condition of the sidewall by running your fingers over it. It should be flat and smooth, without deep scours and ridges. Check both sides because one sidewall may be far more worn than the other. Curvy, bulging or scarred rims are due for replacement. If they look suspect, ask your bike shop for an opinion – you'll know straight away once you've seen enough of them. If you find any cracks in the sidewall when you inspect, stop riding immediately.

It's also worth checking the join where the two ends of the rim meet. It's usually directly opposite the valve hole. Good-quality rims will have a milled sidewall. The wall is made slightly too thick and welded together in a loop. The surface is then ground off flat. Cheaper rims are simply pinned together, relying on the spoke tension in the built wheel to push the joined ends properly together.

Sometimes the ends don't meet exactly, making a bump in the rim that knocks against the brake blocks. Small imperfections can be filed flat, but if the join protrudes by more than 0.5mm (1/50 in) take the wheel back to your bike shop for inspection because overenthusiastic filing will just weaken the joint. Also check for cracks around the spoke holes and the valve hole. These are less dangerous but still mean the rim should be replaced.

Rims can be replaced in two ways. Usually the cheapest way is to buy a whole new wheel and transfer your old tyre, tube and rim tape onto it. For a rear wheel, you (or your bike shop) will also have to transfer the cassette (sprockets) from the old wheel to the new one as rear wheels don't come complete with gears. However, if it's just the rim that's worn out and the hub is of good quality and in good condition, you may wish to consider rebuilding the wheel with a new rim and fresh spokes on your old hub. Building wheels takes some practice so, unless you're very keen, get your bike shop to do it for you. If you're feeling brave and fancy tackling it, get a book about wheel building and give it a go. Rebuilding is a more expensive option because you'll have to pay for labour, but you can choose a better-quality rim and a properly handbuilt wheel will last longer than an off-the-shelf machine build.

Deep scours, ridges and curved braking surfaces indicate worn rims – if you find any cracks in the sidewall, stop riding immediately

Calliper brakes: adjustment

For best performance, calliper brakes must be adjusted so that your wheel will run cleanly between the blocks without touching either block.

However, the blocks must be close enough so that when you pull the lever the blocks bring the wheel to a stop when the brake lever is somewhere near the middle of its travel.

You shouldn't be able to pull the brake-lever back far enough to touch the handlebars. This means you haven't got enough power to bring the bike safely to a stop. Some prefer a little bit of movement of the levers before the brake blocks bite as it means they can get a proper grip on the lever.

This adjustment will only work if the wheels are aligned centrally in the frame. Check that the gap between the tyre and the frame or fork is the same on either side of the wheel and realign the wheel if necessary.

CALLIPER BRAKE ADJUSTMENT

Step 1: Before you adjust anything, make sure the brake cable isn't seized or sticky. Undo the cable pinch bolt so that it's not gripping the cable at all. Pull down gently on the cable and squeeze the brake-lever at the same time. You should feel the cable pulling upwards. When you release the brake-lever, a gentle tug should pull the cable smoothly back through again. If the cable feels rough or gritty, then change it. (See page 118.)

Step 2: Check where the cable lies as it clamps under the pinch bolt. There will always be a groove marking the correct place and there will always be a washer – often a specially shaped one – between the cable and the pinch bolt. Squeeze the brake blocks onto the rim with one hand while pulling through any slack cable with the other. Let go the cable, but keep hold of the block and tighten the pinch bolt firmly.

Step 3: Squeeze the brake-lever firmly several times to settle slack out of the cable. You may now find that you can pull the brake-lever all the way to the bars. If so, you need to pull through slack cable at the calliper again. Hold the cable just where it emerges from under the cable clamp bolt, undo the cable clamp bolt a couple of turns, pull through any slack cable and retighten the cable clamp bolt firmly.

Step 4: Check the gap between the brake blocks and rim. Spin the wheel gently. The blocks shouldn't touch the rim. Squeeze the brake-lever – you should be able to get about halfway to the bars. Make minor adjustments with the barrel-adjuster. Turning the barrel-adjuster out of the calliper will bring the blocks closer to the rim, turning it into the calliper moves the blocks further away. Experiment to find the best position.

Step 5: You may find that the brake block on one side touches the rim, while the other block doesn't. Newer callipers have a balance screw that allows you to readjust the angle of the whole calliper. Try to remember which way the balance screw turns; just experiment as different mechanisms have opposite effects. Turn the screw gently – quarter of a turn at a time – until the rim runs centrally between the blocks.

Step 6: You may find the blocks are way off to one side, further than the balance screw can correct, or you may have a calliper without a balance screw. If so, you'll have to adjust the position of the whole calliper. Hold it as shown and undo the calliper fixing bolt until the calliper swings freely. Correct its position and retighten the calliper bolt firmly. If you've got a balance screw, use it now to make final adjustments.

Calliper brakes: fitting blocks

Calliper brake blocks don't wear out as quickly as V-brake blocks, but they'll still need occasional attention.

The calliper mechanism means you can't apply as much force to the block to stop you as you can with a V-brake, so it's worth investing in good-quality brake blocks and replacing them when they're worn. Good makes include Aztec, Shimano and Kool-Stop. Of the three types of rim brake, calliper blocks are the easiest to change. Give your rims a good clean at the same time, and check them for wear

(see page 115). There are only two types of fitting for brake pads – most common are 4 or 5mm Allen keys, but some need a 10mm Allen key. You may decide when you've got the old brake block off that it will survive a little longer – if so, clean it up carefully. Use a sharp knife to pick out any bits of metal or glass, then flatten the surface with sandpaper. Refit in the same way as a new block.

FITTING BRAKE BLOCKS

Step 1: Start by removing the old brake block. Undo the bolt at the back and slide the block downwards and outwards. Inspect the surface of the block. You may decide that it will survive a little longer, in which case follow the instructions above to clean it up and then refit as below.

Step 2: If you've got the kind of brake blocks that have replaceable pads, undo the screw on the back of the pad. The old pad should then slide backwards out of the brake shoe. Clean up the shoes then slide the new pad in and replace the screw. It is very important to replace the brake blocks the right way round: the opening on the block *must* face towards the *back* of the bike.

Step 3: Check for marks indicating the direction the new blocks must face. The block may be marked 'left' and 'right' or be curved, in which case the shape of the curve must match the shape of the rim. The block may come supplied with shaped washers. If so, fit the cup-shaped washer so that the flat side rests against the brake flock. Fit the domed washer so that the curve of the dome faces into the cup of the washer you just fitted.

Step 4: Wriggle the brake block into place. It should be parallel with the rim, but not so high that it will touch the tyre nor so low that any part of it would hang down below the rim. The curvature of the fitting washers will allow you to make minor corrections to the angle. Once you've got it in place, hold the block still with one hand while you tighten it with the Allen key, or spanner.

Step 5: Next, check the toe-in. Pull the brakes and watch the gap between the rim and the brake block. The front of the block should touch the rim just before the back – the difference should be about 1mm (½5 in). If it's not correct, loosen the fixing bolt slightly, adjust the angle of approach and tighten the fixing bolt firmly. Check that the brake block is at the right height as you pull and release the brake-lever.

Step 6: The new brake blocks will probably be a different thickness to the old ones, so you will need to adjust the clearance between the brake block and the rim. It should only be a minor adjustment, so use the barrel-adjuster on the calliper. Loosen the lockring slightly to get it out of the way, then adjust the clearance using the main part of the barrel-adjuster (see page 116 for details). Retighten the lockring.

Calliper brakes: fitting cables

Road bike brake blocks won't be as sharp as V-brakes or disc brakes even when new, so make sure your cables are in good condition for the best possible braking.

The back brake in particular has a long cable, and both cables are routed under the bar tape, so they're forced around tight turns. Once the cables start to deteriorate, you'll find that the levers become steadily harder to pull, and the brake blocks don't spring easily back from the rims once you release the levers. Replacing the cable makes a massive difference.

If the outer casing is kinked or damaged, it should be replaced at the same time as the cable. Use the old sections to measure out new sections, taking care to cut the ends clean and square. New bits of casing need a ferrule at each end of each section. The exception is the last one, where the casing enters the calliper. There may not be room for a ferrule, in which case it doesn't need one.

FITTING BRAKE CABLES

Step 1: Make sure you have the right kind of brake cable before you start – road bikes use a different type from the ubiquitous mountain bike with a pear-shaped nipple on the end rather than a barrel-shaped nipple. Once armed with the correct type, cut the cable end off your old brake cable. You'll need a decent pair of cable cutters – a pair of pliers isn't good enough as you'll just end up fraying the cable.

Step 2: Feed the brake cable back up through the outer casing. You can leave this in place, but check each piece as you pass it through since sections that are kinked or crushed, or have patches of the protective plastic coating missing, will need to be replaced. If the cable feels gritty as you remove it, it's also worth replacing the casing.

Step 3: When you get up to the handlebars, you'll have to pull the lever back to expose its innards. Push the cable through the casing from the other end. You should see it emerging gently from the lever. Keep pushing though until a handful has emerged, then pull the whole lot out. Watch as you extract the last bit of cable so that you can clearly see the nest where the new cable has to go into.

Step 4: Now the tricky bit: getting the new cable back into the lever. Success depends on having a neat, non-frayed end on your new cable. Keep the brake-lever pulled back against the bars and feed the cable back into the nest in the brake-lever. Once it's through the nest, feel for the hole in the back of the brake-lever. You should be able to see the brake casing under the bar tape, which will give you an idea what you're aiming for. Feed through.

Step 5: Once the cable emerges from the outer casing, pull it through until only the last 10cm (4 in) of cable sticks out of the lever. Keeping the brake-lever against the bars, drip a drop of oil onto this last bit and pull through completely. For the front brake, the cable goes directly into the front brake. Ensure as you route the back brake that there is enough slack in the outer casing for the handlebars to turn freely. Oil the cable as it passes through the outer casing.

Step 6: On the brake calliper, pass the cable through the barrel-adjuster. Set this so it's about halfway through its travel (see box on page 106). Check the cable pinch bolt – there will be a clear groove where the cable rests. Sit the cable in place and squeeze the brake blocks against the rim. Pull through the cable to take up slack. Release the cable, keeping the blocks against the rim, and tighten the cable pinch bolt. See page 116 for final adjustment.

New outer casing and bar tape

You may find when you're replacing the brake inner cable that it feels gritty as you feed it through the first section of outer casing – this runs from the brake-lever under the bar tape to the frame, in the case of the back brake, or directly to the front brake unit. If this is the case, you will need to peel back the bar tape and replace the outer casing as well as the inner cable. It's an irritating job, but will make your brakes feel much crisper and more responsive.

There are other circumstances in which you might want to replace the first section of outer casing. You may want to raise the bars and find that the casing isn't long enough to do so without forcing it around tight bends. You may also have found damaged or kinked spots in the casing.

Either way you'll need to get some fresh bar tape before you start. It is possible to reuse the old stuff, but it's sticky-backed so doesn't often come off without tearing and tends to refuse to lie flat when you wind it back on again. Treat yourself to new tape – it makes your bike look much smarter too.

Best results come from changing the whole lot at once. Peel off the old stuff gently. You're trying to lift off as much of the sticky glue as you can as you go along. Remove the bar-end plugs. Clean up the bars as best you can, but take care not to scratch the bars as small scratches can form the roots of cracks in the material.

Now you're free to work on the brake cable and casing. You'll have to tug the old brake casing out from inside the back of the brake levers. Look carefully to see if the cable finishes in a ferrule – if it does you'll need to remember to refit the new casing with a ferrule.

Measure up the new casing and then cut it carefully to length, making sure that the cut end is a clean cut and that there isn't a tag of metal cutting across the hole through the middle of the casing. Replace any other sections if necessary and feed the inner cable through the middle. Pull through any slack in the cable, clamp it under the cable pinch bolt and pull the lever firmly to settle the new outer casing into place. You may find after this that you have a fair bit of slack. Loosen the calliper cable pinch bolt again, pull through more slack and tighten the bolt firmly.

It may be a little bit of a struggle to get the new outer casing to sit properly into the brake lever. It can help to loosen the bolt that clamps the brake lever onto the handlebars in order to give the casing a little bit of space. The bolt may be in one of two places. Pull the lever towards the bars and look into it from in front. You may see the head of an Allen key bolt at the back – often a 5mm. You should be able to wiggle an Allen key in there.

If the fixing bolt isn't inside the lever, it will probably be on the side of the lever, under the rubber lever cover. Again, it will usually be a 5mm Allen key and will be on the outer side of the lever (the right-hand side of the right lever and the left-hand side of the left lever). Loosen the fixing bolt, wiggle the brake casing home and then retighten the fixing bolt firmly.

Tape the brake casing onto the front of the bars with three strips of electrical tape to hold it neatly in place. Three strips of tape on either side should do the job.

Once you've got everything taped together it's time to refit bar tape. Start by filling in behind the brake levers. This is always too wide a gap for the bar tape to cross without leaving gaps. Your new pack of bar tape may have come with a couple of extra short strips. If not, cut two strips about 7cm (2¾ in) long off the end of the bar tape. Fold back the rubber brake lever hoods so they're out of the way and wrap a horizontal strip around the bar from one side to the other. Leave the brake hoods out of the way. Start at the bottom end of the handlebar. Start with a strip of tape facing down on the inside of the bar with about half the width of the tape overlapping the end of the bar. Wrap so that each new layer overlaps a third of the last layer. When you get to the brake lever, wrap up to the short strip you already put there and then head diagonally upwards in one layer. Don't be tempted to weave the tape back down again as you'll just make the bar feel really bulky behind the brake lever. Once you get above the brake lever, carry right on up towards the middle of the bar – you'll need to finish about 5cm (2 in) from the stem. Cut off the tape so that it finishes underneath the bar and then tape neatly in place with black electrical tape. Bar tape sometimes comes with little plastic grip ties, but they're more fiddly than they're worth and a layer of tape does the job better.

If you've been careful with wrapping the tape around the bottom section of the bars, you may find there's enough to increase the overlap on the top section. This makes the bars more comfortable when you're sitting in a more upright position. Fold the end of the tape into the ends of the bars, and refit the barend plugs. As well as keeping the ends of the bars neat, the plugs protect you from cutting yourself on the end of the bar in case of a spill.

Servicing calliper brakes

Without mudguards, calliper brakes are right in the line of fire for anything your tyre picks up off the road. Dirt ends up on the pivots that hold your callipers together and stops them moving freely. This is one of those satisfying jobs that looks much harder than it is and makes your bike feel much better as soon as you've done it.

Like your gears, your brakes are operated by a combination of a cable and a spring. Cables are great for transmitting a signal through all the curves from your handlebars to your brakes and they're light and strong, but they can only pull, not push. Once you've used the cable to pull your brake blocks onto the rim, you release the brake-lever and rely on a spring in the calliper to push the blocks back off the rim so that you can ride and the blocks are back in their original position. However, your hands

Front calliper brake – Brompton folding bicycle

are generally much stronger than the little coil of wire that does the springing-back job. The effect of this is that, once your calliper pivots start to get all clogged up and sticky, you will still be able to pull your brakes on, but they'll be more reluctant to spring back away again. Leave it longer still and it will start to be hard work pulling the brake levers on. Luckily, it's not difficult to clear away the muck and apply a little oil, but the sooner you do it, the more effective it will be. Dirt that's left long enough will start to corrode the pivots, the washers and the calliper. Once the surfaces that rub against each other become rough and damaged, there's a limit to how much improvement you can make.

It's possible to give the callipers a quick wipe over without removing them from the bike, but it's not difficult to take them off completely and it means that you can really get in properly behind the calliper. An old toothbrush is the perfect size. You can try using plain water if your brakes aren't too bad, but if you've been riding in wet conditions or around town, you'll probably need something a little stronger. Bike washes like Muc-Off or Finish Line Bike Wash should do the trick. For really stubborn, caked-on dirt – a sign that you really need to invest in mudguards! – try some degreaser. Pour some in a jar then dip the toothbrush in and scrub. Spray-on degreaser is much too messy and wasteful for this kind of job, where you need precise application. Don't forget to rinse off carefully afterwards.

As with the degreaser, when you come to lubricate the pivots, drip oil is much better than spray. Take particular care not to get any oil at all on your brake blocks as it will spread all over your rims in no time and you'll lose most of your stopping power. The gaps that need lubricating are easiest to see with the calliper off the bike. Squeeze the blocks together as if you were squashing them onto the rim and watch how the brake mechanism moves. Anywhere where two sections of calliper move against each other needs the gap between lubricating. After you've dripped oil into the gap, squeeze and release the brake unit a few times to work oil into the space and then wipe off excess.

You may find, once you've got the calliper off and you've started cleaning it, that it's too corroded to be worth servicing. If this is the case, replace it. You'll need to get the right size – measure the distance between the middle of the hole that the calliper bolts into and the middle of one of the braking surfaces on the rim. This distance is called the 'drop'.

Servicing calliper brake units

Follow these instructions if your calliper brakes clog with road dirt, if the brake-levers stick or if the brake doesn't return smartly when you release the brake-lever.

Always do one brake at a time – that way, you've always got a complete one to refer back to if you get stuck in the middle of reassembly. Take particular care to clean road grime away from around the return spring. There isn't much of a gap between the spring and the calliper arms, so it doesn't take much of a build-up of detritus to make everything feel sluggish.

For the full spring clean effect on tired brakes, combine this service with a new pair of blocks and a new brake cable. Once you've got all your tools out, it doesn't take much longer to do the whole lot at once, and you'll feel the difference in increased braking control straight away. Fresh brake blocks are easier on your rims, minimising wear so that they last longer.

SERVICING CALLIPER BRAKE UNITS

Step 1: Start by cutting off the cable end on the brake cable, undoing the cable pinch bolt and pulling the brake cable and casing out of the barrel-adjuster. If you're thinking of fitting a new cable or cable and casing, do this now by following instructions on pages 118, 119.

Step 2: Undo the bolt that attaches the calliper to the frame/fork. It's either a 5mm Allen key or a 10mm nut. If you're doing both brakes at once, don't get the front and back mixed up – the pivot bolt that sticks out of the back of the front calliper and through the fork is slightly longer. Clean and inspect the fixing bolt – the 5mm Allen key type is called a sleeve nut – for cracks. Clean and inspect the bolt hole.

Step 3: Turn the calliper over and have a look at the back surface. You don't usually get to see this side of it and it tends to collect grit. Clean it thoroughly with degreaser or bike wash and a scrubbing brush. You can see the return spring clearly from here. Get right in close and clean up all around it so it can move freely. Squeeze the brake blocks together a few times to work out stray bits and pieces of dirt or grit.

Step 4: Turn the calliper so you can see the top and give this a good scrub, too. Again, squeeze and release the calliper and clean all the bits that squeezing it reveals. Once the whole calliper is clean, rinse off all the degreaser. Drip a little drop of oil down into the gaps between each part of the mechanism and squeeze the calliper to work the oil in. Wipe off excess – it will only collect dirt. The calliper should feel much smoother.

Step 5: Pop a drop of oil on the calliper fixing bolt and slide the bolt back through the frame/fork. Make sure you replace any washers that sat between the calliper and the frame. These are there to stop the back of the calliper getting jammed on the frame/fork. Refit the fixing bolt.

Step 6: Hold the calliper as shown so the wheel runs centrally between the blocks and tighten the fixing bolt firmly. Wiggle the calliper to check the fixing bolt is secure – otherwise it will work itself loose. Feed the brake cable back through the barrel-adjuster then under the pinch bolt washer. Hold the blocks against the rim, pull through any excess cable and tighten the pinch bolt firmly. For final cable adjustments, see page 118.

Cantilever brakes

Cantilever brakes are still found on many town bikes and older mountain bikes. They're not just an anachronism, however. They're also favoured on new touring bikes because the brake blocks last far longer than those on V-brakes and they retain their adjustment without the need for constant fiddling.

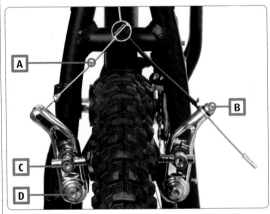

Cantilever brake with link wire

Take care to use the correct brake-levers for cantilever brakes because they are not compatible with V-brake-levers. V-brake-levers are designed with a greater distance between the lever pivot and the nest that the cable nipple sits in. This means that more cable is pulled through the lever with V-brakes than with a cantilever brake-lever. You can see the difference if you compare a V-brake-lever with a cantilever brake-lever. For a cantilever brake to work properly, the distance between brake-lever pivot and cable nest needs to be around 30mm (1¼ in).

Although cantilever brake blocks usually last much longer than V-brake blocks, they will wear through eventually, so check them every month.

Check for wear by looking on top of the block for a wear-indication line. Usually stamped in black writing on the black surface of the block, they can be hard to spot and you may be able to feel the line with a fingernail more easily than see with the naked eye. There may not be an indication line: in this case replace blocks before they've worn down to the base of the grooves moulded into the blocks. Leave it too late and you risk wearing through to the metal bolt that the block is moulded around. The bolt will scrape the surface off your rims. Even if they're not visibly worn down, they'll need changing every couple of years as the rubber hardens

and ceases to work well after a while. This seems to be especially true if your bike lives outside or in outbuildings that get cold in the winter.

The way in which the brake block is clamped onto the brake unit takes a little bit of looking at to understand. There are a handful of assorted bolts, Allen key nuts and curvy washers that all have to be assembled in the correct order. They allow you to control the position of the brake blocks very precisely. You'll get maximum braking power if you can set up the brake blocks so that they hit the rim flat and square, with the fronts of the block touching just before the backs.

In order for you to be able to set them up correctly the brake block is held in place by an eye bolt (C). The stub of the brake block passes through a hole in the eye bolt, which in turn passes through a curved washer and then through a slot in the brake unit. On the other side of the brake unit is another curved washer, then a nut. When you tighten the nut it pulls the eye bolt through the brake unit, squashing the stub of the brake block against the first curved washer and holding it securely.

This design means that, when you loosen the nut on the end of the eye bolt, you can move the position of the brake block in different and useful ways. You can move the eye bolt up and down in the slot on the brake unit, so that the brake block hits the rim higher or lower. You can push the stub through the eye bolt, moving the brake block towards or away from the rim. You can roll the stub in the eye bolt so that the block approaches the rim at an angle. You can also twist the eye bolt on the curved washers so that the front or the back of the brake block touches the rim first. Use this flexibility to get the block precisely positioned.

The vital adjustment for the brake cable on cantilever brakes is setting the position where the main cable splits into two, just above the brake units. The split can be made with a straddle hanger bolted onto the cable, with a straddle wire that passes from one brake unit to the other via the straddle hanger or with a separate link wire (A) through which the main cable passes and then clamps to the brake unit. Either way it's important that the two branches of straddle cable – or the two arms of the link wire – are set at 90° to each other.

Cantilever brakes: brake blocks

A regular check on the condition of your brake blocks means you'll spot worn ones before they have a chance to do any damage. It's worth being vigilant.

Brake blocks will often have a wear-line indicator on them. It will be fairly small so you'll have to wipe the block clean and get in close to see it. If the brake block has slots cut into it, your brake block is worn out when you've reached the bottom of the slots.

You don't need to wait until the brake block is visibly worn away to replace it – if your brakes seem to be becoming ineffective, a new pair of blocks can instantly make them more responsive.

It may seem like there's a bit of a detour in the middle of this process. Start by removing the old brake blocks and then fitting the new ones loosely in place. Check the brake cable is correctly set up. Only then return to the process of aligning the brake blocks with the rim.

FITTING BRAKE BLOCKS

Step 1: Use an Allen key to hold the end of the pinch bolt and a 10mm spanner to undo the nut hidden behind the brake unit as shown. A couple of turns should be enough. It only needs to be loose enough to allow you to ease the old brake block stud out of the hole in the eye bolt and slide a new brake block into place. Push the new brake block all the way in and tighten the nut just enough to hold it in place.

Step 2: Next, adjust the straddle position using the cable pinch bolt. For straddle wire types, adjust the height of the straddle hanger and the length of the straddle wire, so that the two halves of the straddle wire are at 90° to each other. Link wires types are much simpler: undo the cable clamp bolt (B, page 122), pull in or let out until the two arms are at 90° and re-clamp. Most link wires are stamped or printed with a helpful guide line.

Step 3: Next, the balance screw (A, above). Cantilevers only have one. Pull brake-lever and watch the units. If one sits closer to the rim, adjustment is needed. If the unit with balance screw is closer, turn screw clockwise to strengthen spring and move it out. If it is further away, turn balance screw anticlockwise. At first there's no effect and then the spring gets sensitive to quarter-turns, so move slowly.

Step 4: Now that the brake unit is set up correctly, return to the brake blocks. Loosen the nut on the back of the unit slightly so that you can manipulate the brake blocks. Push in each one until it's almost touching the rim. Each block should hit the rim at 90°, midway between the top and bottom of the rim. Use the curvature of the washers and the length of the slot that the pinch bolt sits in to manipulate the angle of the blocks.

Step 5: The front of the block should be about 1mm (¹⁄₂₅ in) closer than the back. This is called 'toeing in' and helps to prevent the brakes from squealing. People often mess about with bits of cardboard stuck behind the back of the brake block. This just makes work for you — look at the brake block and the rim and set the angle of the brake block so that it's slightly closer to the rim at the front than at the back.

Step 6: Hold the block in place with your hand and tighten the 10mm nut gently. Once it is fairly secure, hold the eye bolt still with a 5mm Allen key and tighten the 10mm nut firmly. Try to waggle the brake block from side to side to check that it's secure. If you can move it, retighten. Now that you've got the brake blocks on, you may find that the cable needs further adjustment – see pages 124–125.

Cantilever brakes: changing cables

Replacing brake cables is very satisfying as new ones make your bike feel a lot better for not very much money. You may find yourself distracted along the journey by the need to adjust the positions of your brake blocks. Both cable and blocks need to be positioned correctly for optimum performance, so be prepared to detour.

There are two different styles of cable fitting – link wires and straddle wire. The straddle wire type was the original style. These have a triangular metal hanger that is clamped to the brake cable. A separate straddle cable passes over a hook on the straddle hanger with each end connected to a brake unit. These are less common now than the newer 'link wire' type. This is because the link wires are safer. If your brake cable breaks with the straddle wire type, the springs on the brake unit will pull the straddle wire down onto your tyre, locking the wheel and throwing you off. The link wire type will simply unravel without getting caught in your wheel.

But the principle of adjusting the straddle wire type is just the same, only more fiddly – the straddle hanger must be positioned at a precise height on the brake cable so that the two sides of the straddle wire can form their 90° angle. It's essential to ensure when you've finished that the pinch bolt on the straddle hanger is very secure – with all the fiddling, it's far too easy to leave it loose by mistake.

These instructions take you through the process for the far more common link wire type, but if you have the straddle type, there's no reason not to replace the straddle with a link wire.

Take you bike to the shop with you when you buy a new cable so that they can sell you the right size.

Link wire

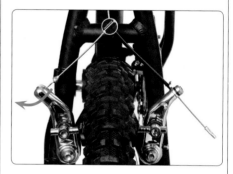

The brake units on either side connect separately, one to each branch of the brake cable. On the quick-release side, quick-release the end of the link wire from the brake unit by pulling it downwards and outwards as shown

CHANGING CANTILEVER BRAKE CABLES

Step 1: Quick-release the link wire from the brake unit as above. On the other side, cut off the cable end and undo the cable clamp bolt, so that you can slide the cable out from underneath it.You should be able to pull the v-shaped link wire off the brake cable completely. Unless it's kinked or frayed, keep it and reuse it – they don't wear much.

Step 2: Slide the old cable out through each section of outer casing in turn, leaving the cable attached to the frame. Inspect each piece as you go along. If there are frayed or damaged sections, take them off with care and cut a replacement section of casing, refitting new ferrules wherever the old casing had ferrules.

Step 3: When you get all the way to the brake-lever, turn the lockring on the barrel-adjuster so that it winds away from the brake-lever body and you can turn the barrel-adjuster easily. Line up the slots on the barrel-adjuster and lockring with the slots on the body of the brake-lever. Pull the old cable gently out of the lined-up slots.

Step 4: Keeping the brake-lever pulled back against the bars, you should now be able to wiggle the old brake cable nipple out of its nest in the brake-lever. The nipple sits in a key-shaped hole and you'll have to align the cable with the key slot. Clean the nest if it's dirty and slot the nipple of the new cable back in its place.

Step 5: Gently fold the new cable back through the slots in the brake-lever, barrel-adjuster and lockring and then turn the lockring slightly so that the cable can't fall out. Turn the barrel-adjuster so that it sits about halfway into the brake-lever. Feed the cable back through the outer casing with a drop of oil on any sections that end up inside the outer casing.

Step 6: When you get back to the brake unit, feed the cable through the link wire joint. You'll see that the hole in the link wire that the cable passes through is in two parts – one end of the hole is much easier to push the cable through because it lines up with the exit hole. Push the cable through this end and then move the brake cable over so that it rests in the other section of the hole.

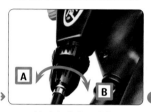

Step 7: Pass the free end of the cable back under the cable clamp bolt, leaving it fairly slack. Then refit the other branch of the link wire onto the opposite brake unit. Go back to the cable clamp bolt and pull the cable through until the two branches of the link wire are at 90°. Tighten the cable clamp bolt firmly.

Step 8: You will probably find you now have to readjust the position of the brake blocks to hit the rim level, square and toed-in. Use a 5mm Allen key to hold the front of the eye bolt, and a 10mm spanner to loosen the nut on the back of the eye bolt enough so that you can shift the blocks. When the position of the blocks is perfect, hold the eye bolt still with the Allen key and tighten the fixing nut firmly – see page 123 for more detail.

Step 9: If the brake blocks touch the rim, wind the barrel-adjuster into the brake-lever clockwise (B) to loosen cable. If the brake-lever moves too far before the blocks bite on the rim, roll the barrel-adjuster anticlockwise (A) to tighten the cable. Once the adjustment is correct, wedge the lockring against the brake-lever body. Test the brake before riding – pulling the brake lever should lock the wheel when the lever is halfway to the bars.

Adjusting straddle or link wire angle

The angle at which the cable connects the two brake units is critical since it determines how powerfully the brake blocks are forced onto the rim when the brake cable is pulled. Readjusting your cable angle will help you stop more quickly, but once you've done it, you may have to readjust your brake block positions.

Step 1: The link wire is too low. Loosen the nut on the back of each brake unit and pull the brake blocks back from the rim. Undo the cable clamp bolt, pull through cable, tighten bolt, readjust blocks.

Step 2: The link wire is too high. Undo the cable clamp bolt, release the cable until the angle between the link wires is 90°, retighten the bolt, then readjust your brake blocks so they sit closer to the rim.

Step 3: Just right! The pictures show a link wire type, but the principle is the same for straddle wire types. Play with the position of the straddle hanger until the two sides are at 90°.

How disc brakes work

The key difference between disc brakes and rim brakes is, obviously, the braking surface. A separate rotor, bolted to the hub, is used. The brake pads are housed inside a calliper, attached to the end of the fork or to the back of the frame. The diameter of the rotor is much smaller than that of the rim, so the brake has far less leverage and, because of this, must be much more powerful to get the same stopping power. But you can get lots of power out of the callipers.

They're bolted on near the end of the stays, near the part of the frame that the axle is bolted through, so they can't flex much, even under full braking. The rotors are made of very hard material so the brake pads can be made of a hard material as well, which also allows them to be very thin. This means that they don't feel at all squidgy when you use them and the brake pad is so thin that it won't compress.

There are two different types of disc brake – mechanical and hydraulic.

Hydraulic brakes use motorbike and car technology, forcing the brake pads onto the rims with oil. Squeezing the brake-lever forces hydraulic oil down the thin tubes to the brake callipers. It's incompressible so the pistons respond instantly to the pressure. They sit inside the callipers, facing each other, so when the oil backs up behind them, they're pushed out of the piston and move towards each other. Each piston has a brake pad stuck to the top, so when they move together the rotor gets caught between the pads, stopping your wheel.

Mechanical disc brakes used to be thought of as a poor relation, more expensive and heavier than V-brakes but not as powerful as hydraulics, but mechanical brakes have got a lot better in the last couple of years and now represent better value. They're less daunting than hydraulics since cables are a familiar technology. The brake-levers and cables are exactly the same as those used for V-brakes and so are compatible. The callipers also work by squashing the rotor between two sets of brake pads, but usually only one of the pads moves. The piston is fixed into the calliper body on a spiral groove, so that as the brake cable pulls, the piston around it also moves sideways towards the rotor – they're neat little mechanisms inside.

Both types are susceptible to contamination of the pads with oil or grease. Take care to avoid both the pads and the rotors with anything oily – another good reason for using drip oil on your chain rather than spray oil, which will quickly find its way onto your rear brake rotor unless you're very careful.

Disc brake pads usually last much longer than V-brake pads. The material in the disc rotor is much harder than the material in the rim, allowing the disc brake pad to be much harder as

well. Were you to use the material in the disc brake pad as a rim brake, then the rim would wear away in next to no time. The harder material also means that the pad can touch the rotor as the wheel spins without slowing down significantly and you don't have to worry about a slight rubbing noise when you spin a wheel with a disc brake. Pads may wear unevenly, and should be replaced when either of the pads has less than 0.5mm (1⁄50 in) of thickness left from any direction. You may need to take them out to check how they're surviving. If in doubt, follow the procedure for removing them – see page 128 – and refit them if they have life left. Clean your rotors whenever you fit new pads.

Make sure you get the right pad for the brake as the fittings and shapes vary between makes and models even from the same make. Take the old ones along to your bike shop for comparison if you're not sure. Even if you know the make, the shape will vary from model to model and from year to year. After fitting, new pads need to be burnt in as they don't work properly until you've braked a few times. Once you've got the new pads in, find somewhere you can ride the bike safely with limited braking power. Ride along slowly, haul on the brakes and bring the bike to a halt. Repeat at increasing speeds until you're satisfied. This may take 10 or 20 repetitions.

Disc brake pads are hard and thin

Mechanical disc brake cables

People like mechanical disc brakes because they're so simple to take care of. They use the same levers and cables as V-brakes, so spares are easy to get your hands on.

Most mechanical disc brakes work in the same way – the cable only moves one of the pads, the one furthest away from the wheel, the primary pad. Pulling the cable forces this pad onto the rotor, distorting the rotor slightly and bending it towards the other, stationary, pad. As you pull the cable slightly harder, the rotor becomes trapped between the two pads, stopping the

wheel. This sounds like quite a clumsy arrangement, but the discs are actually flexible enough for it to work very well.

The position of the stationary pad needs to be adjusted quite carefully. It needs to sit as close to the rotor as possible to minimise the amount which the rotor has to flex. But it needs to have enough clearance not to rub constantly.

ADJUSTING DISC BRAKE CABLE

Step 1: You'll know you need a new cable if it's got kinks and becomes unresponsive. Front and rear cables work in the same way, but your back cable is longer and so needs changing more often because it will suffer more from friction. To change the cable, first cut off the cable end and undo the cable pinch bolt. Thread the cable back through the casing, working back towards the brake-lever.

Step 2: Inspect the outer casing as you come to each piece. Damaged sections or those that feel gritty must be replaced. Cut the ends of new sections of casing cleanly without leaving a tang of metal across the hole. Use a sharp knife to open out the lining that runs through the middle. Fit any new sections of casing back on the bike.

Step 3: At the lever, turn the lockring on the barrel-adjuster and then the barrel-adjuster itself, so that the slots on the lockring, barrel-adjusters and lever all line up. Squeeze the brake-lever in towards the handlebar and pull the cable gently out through the slots. Wiggle the cable nipple out of its nest on the brake-lever and fit the nipple of the new cable back into the nest, then lay the cable back through the lever, lockring and barrel slots.

Step 4: Feed the new cable all the way back through the outer casing. When you get back to the calliper, feed the cable through the calliper barrel-adjuster (if there is one) and then under the cable clamp bolt. There will be a clear groove under the pinch bolt that shows you where the cable should go. Tighten the clamp bolt, pull the cable through and then pull the brake-lever firmly a couple of times to settle the cable into place.

Step 5: Loosen the cable clamp bolt again. While drawing through the cable, use the other hand to push up the actuation lever so that the primary brake pad is almost touching the rotor. When you're close, tighten the cable clamp bolt firmly. Use the barrel-adjuster on the lever to make fine adjustments to the clearance between the primary pad and the rotor – see page 106 if you're not confident with barrel-adjusters.

Step 6: Finally, set the position of the stationary pad. You'll have to feed an Allen key through the wheel to reach the back of the calliper – it's usually a 5mm. Turn the Allen key clockwise to move the pad closer and anticlockwise for more clearance. You'll have to adjust a little bit and then take the Allen key out to spin the wheel and check the pad doesn't rub on the rotor. Cut off spare cable and fit a cable end.

Fitting mechanical disc brake pads

Disc brake pads usually last much longer than rim brake pads. They can be made of harder material to match the steel rotor that they have to clamp onto.

You'll have to take care to get the right replacement brake pads – the fittings and shapes vary between makes and models. Take your old ones along with you to your bike shop if you're not sure. After fitting, new pads need to be 'burned in'. Once you've got new pads fitted, take your bike somewhere where you can ride safely. Ride along slowly, haul on the brakes, and bring the bike to a halt. Repeat at increasing speeds until you're satisfied. This may take 10 or 20 repetitions.

When you're checking to see if your pads are worn, take care to inspect both pads, since they often wear unevenly. They should both be replaced when either pad has less than 0.5mm (¹⁄₅₀ in) of thickness left in any direction.

FITTING BRAKE PADS

Step 1: Drop the wheel out of the frame and look at the calliper. The pads will normally be held in place with a retaining pin that passes through the calliper and holes in both pads. There is usually something that stops the pin dropping out – either a spring clip over the end or, as in this picture, the split pin must be bent straight so that it can be drawn through the hole.

Step 2: Pull out the retaining pin and keep it safe, because you need to fit everything back at the end. In some cases, there may be two retaining pins. Look carefully at how the old pads fitted in the calliper before you start to remove them.

Step 3: Gently pull the pads out, either by grabbing the little ears that poke out of the slot or by pulling on the corners of the pads. If you're not sure of the correct replacement pads, take the old ones to your bike shop to match them up.

Step 4: The pads may have a retaining spring – make a note of its position and orientation and refit it with the new pads. Take care when fitting the new pads that the arms of the spring sit beside the pads, not over the braking surface. It's easiest to squash the spring between the pads and then fit both into the slot together, rather than trying to get the pads into the slot one at a time.

Step 5: Slide the new pads back into the calliper, pushing them in until the holes in the pad line up with the retaining pin holes in the calliper. Refit the retaining pin or pins, bending over their ends or refitting spring clips so that the retaining pins don't rattle out. Then pull the pads firmly to make sure they are held securely in place.

Step 6: Refit the wheel, wiggling the rotor back into the gap between pads. You may need to readjust the cable because new pads will be thicker than the old ones. Spin the wheel. It should spin freely, without binding. But it's fine if you can hear the pad rubbing slightly on the rim as this won't slow you down. If the rotor drags or the brake-lever pulls back to the bar without braking, go to the adjustment section on page 127.

Fitting hydraulic disc brake pads

Brake pads must be changed if they're worn down to less than a third of their original thickness, so replace them if you only have 0.5–1mm (¹⁄₅₀–¹⁄₂₅ in) of pad left.

You will also need to replace them if they've become contaminated with oil. This could be the result of spilling brake fluid on them or of careless chain lubrication for the rear brake.

The way pads fit is similar enough with most models for it to be possible to give a general overview, but each model is also slightly different. It's worth having a good look at your calliper

before you start taking out the old pads. If you haven't got a photographic memory, draw a sketch to remind yourself how to put it all back together again.

All pads for all makes and all models are different, which is irritating. You have to get exactly the right kind, so keep a spare set in case you need them when the shop's closed or has run out of your type.

FITTING PADS

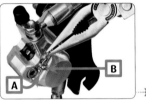

ADJUSTING CALLIPERS

Step 1: The pads will be held in place with some kind of retaining pin. With Shimano brakes this is usually a split pin, which you have to bend straight with pliers before you can pull it out. The Hope brakes pictured have a spring clip (A) on the end of the retaining pin (B), which you must pull off with pliers before you can unscrew the retaining pin.

Step 2: With the retaining pin removed you'll be able to pull the brake pads out of the slots. They may come out downwards through the calliper as in this example or upwards through the top of the calliper slot. Some have a spring that sits between the pads and holds them apart. Keep the spring and note its position as you need to reuse it. If the left and right pads are different, make a note so you know how to refit them.

Step 1: The new pads will be thicker than the old ones so you have to manually press the pistons back into the calliper. It is important not to damage them. If the surface of the piston is flat, a plastic tyre-lever is ideal. Have a good look inside before you start and choose your implement carefully. Push the centre of both pistons firmly so that they sit evenly in the calliper.

Step 2: Clean carefully inside the callipers. If dirt works its way in between the piston and calliper, the pistons will leak, allowing oil out and air in. The ideal implement for this task is a cotton swab. A twist of very clean rag also does the job. Don't use harsh solvents or brake fluid, which will destroy the delicate piston seals. Water is perfect. If you must, use some mild detergent.

Step 3: If there was a spring between the old pads then set it between the new ones, checking the orientation if left and right pads are different. Hold the pads and spring together, making sure the arms of the spring are beside – rather than on – the surface of the brake pad. Slip the pads into the slot in the calliper. Push them home until the holes in the brake pad line up with retaining pin holes.

Step 4: Refit the retaining pins and then refit the spring or P-clips or bend back the ends of split pins so that they can't fall out. Tug the pads outwards to check they are securely fitted. Refit the wheel. Pump the lever a few times to settle it into place. The pads will take a few goes to bed in, so take the bike for a test ride and brake at gradually faster speeds until you feel the pads bite properly.

Bleeding hydraulic brakes

Bleeding isn't a regular task and, as long as the system remains sealed, you can mostly ignore it. However, it does need to be done if there's been any break in the seal that might allow air in: for example, if you cut the hose to shorten it or you crash and pull out a hose. If you use your bike hard – riding fast and stopping abruptly or carrying heavy loads in your panniers – the fluid will eventually become worn out from heating up too many times.

Hydraulic brakes are designed to work with one of two different types of fluid – DOT fluid (a standard car spare) or mineral oil. The correct type of fluid must be used for each system – they are not interchangeable and cannot be mixed up. The correct replacement fluid will be printed on the brake-lever. The procedure is the same regardless of the fluid, although DOT lasts longer – a year if you work it hard, four years with normal use. Mineral oil doesn't last so long, but it discolours when worn out, making it obvious when a change is needed. Pop the lid off the reservoir every six months or so, look at the fluid and change it when it is cloudy.

Don't be drawn into thinking bleeding has to be done routinely – you won't get an improvement in performance by bleeding unless something is actually wrong. If you have to bleed your brakes frequently, then there is something wrong. Look for leaks at all the joints and inspect the hoses carefully. The smallest split in a hose will let out oil and suck in air, making the brakes feel spongey.

Regardless of the specifics, the point of bleeding is the same: you are opening the system to release air bubbles, replacing the air with oil and then sealing the system again without letting in air. Here are the general guidelines, followed by specific examples.

Arm yourself appropriately. Most importantly, you need at least one, sometimes two, short plastic hoses to pump oil into the system at one end and to route surplus oil away from the bleed nipple at the other. With open-topped reservoirs, the surplus will spill over and you will need plenty of rags to mop up. Brake fluid is corrosive and will damage your paintwork if you let it spill onto frame or forks.

The easiest connectors come with Shimano and Hope types, which have a simple bleed nipple over which you can slip the end of the plastic tube. Other types of brake require a specific connector. You may have been supplied with the right connector when you bought the brakes or with the bike if the brakes were already fitted.

However, life sometimes isn't that simple so prepare for the bleeding operation by ordering the part from your bike shop. Plastic hose is easier to obtain because hardware stores stock it. Take the connection or your bike with you to ensure you get the right size. The larger common size of bleed nipple – like that found on the Hope brakes – is the same size as standard car

brake bleeding nipples, so you will be able to use bleed hose from car shops.

Plastic syringes are very useful for pumping oil into the system. You can improvise by taping the plastic tubes onto plastic bottles you can squash, but it's easy to slip and introduce air into the system, causing the bleed operation to fail.

Once the syringe is filled with oil, hold it upright and tap the syringe to persuade air bubbles to drift upwards, just like in the movies. You may feel slightly foolish doing this, but it works. Once all the air has collected at the top of the syringe, squirt it out onto a clean rag so that the syringe contains only oil.

Surplus oil will be expelled from one of the tubes, so tape a bag or bottle to the end to catch it. Don't use thin plastic bags with DOT fluid as it's mildly alarming how quickly the brake fluid melts the bag. The tape is necessary to prevent it falling off as the weight of the oil increases, which can spread the stuff everywhere and spoil your bleed.

All systems have a port at the lever end and a port at the calliper end. Some systems, like Hayes, prefer to be filled through the calliper with the surplus coming out at the lever end.

Others, like Hope and Shimano, work best filled at the lever end with the surplus coming out through the bleed nipple at the calliper. Check your bike shop or your instruction book for the appropriate method for your particular brakes.

Air bubbles make disc brakes spongey

Bleeding Shimano Deore brakes

The brakes used in this example are Shimano Deore hydraulic brakes. Although the principles behind all hydraulic brakes are the same, different makes respond to different bleeding methods, so be sure to refer to the manufacturer's specific instructions.

The oil comes in single-use packs, which contain enough fluid for one fill. Conveniently, this means that the container doesn't sit around absorbing water.

You'll be pouring fresh mineral oil into the reservoir, which can be messy. Wrap a cloth or kitchen towel around the lever before you start as a pre-emptive mopping exercise. The bleed nipple is narrower than the standard car size so you'll need narrower plastic tube. You can find it in hardware shops, or buy a kit. Clear plastic is best as you can see the oil and air bubbles emerging from the bleed nipple.

BLEEDING SHIMANO DEORE BRAKES

Step 1: Start by removing the wheel and the pads of the brake you want to bleed to prevent them becoming contaminated by spillage. If you are bleeding the rear brake, remove the front wheel as well in case fluid spills out of the reservoir at the lever.

Step 2: Loosen the brake-lever fixing bolts and twist the lever so that the top cover of the reservoir is level. You may have to swing the bars about a bit to find the right place. Remove the top cover of the reservoir and the rubber diaphragm. Put these aside on a sheet of paper so that they stay clean.

Step 3: Shimano recommends you remove the calliper from the bike and let it hang from the lever. However, bleeding seems to work well enough as long as you keep the bike propped up so that the lever is higher than the calliper. Fit an 8mm ring spanner around the bleed nipple and then push a piece of plastic hose over the nipple. Tape the other end into the mouth of a bottle, and tape the bottle to your frame or fork.

Step 4: Push the pistons gently back into the callipers, ideally using a tyre-lever. Wedge them in place with a block of clean cardboard. Fold it over until it's a nice tight fit to get in there. Open the bleed nipple a quarter-turn. Pump the brake-lever gently, while keeping the reservoir topped up.

Step 5: Flick the hose to encourage air to bubble up and escape through the open top of the reservoir. Shaking it sometimes helps too. Close the bleed nipple and gently pump the lever to help the bubbles rise. Keep adding oil and pump the lever gently until the lever goes stiff and only moves a quarter of its travel.

Step 6: Pull the lever back, close the bleed nipple, release brake-lever, fill reservoir to the top and replace diaphragm and reservoir top. Fluid will overflow as you replace cap, so be ready to catch it. Tighten the reservoir screws. Remove tube from bleed nipple and replace cover. Remove the brake-spacing pad and refit pads and wheel. Pull and release the brake several times to test.

131

7 – Transmission

This chapter deals with your transmission – all the parts of your bike that transfer your pedalling power to your back wheel. It explains how to adjust your gears so they change smoothly and quickly, and how to replace parts that are worn out or damaged. The parts that make up your transmission are relatively simple, but are exposed to the elements. They have to be lubricated to work efficiently. If you don't clean your transmission, oil and dirt will form an abrasive grinding paste, which will quickly eat into your transmission components.

Transmission: naming the parts

You need to know what all the parts of your transmisssion are called before you can start fixing them; it makes going into bike shops and asking for replacement components a whole lot easier. The appearance of each mechanism may vary from bike to bike, but don't worry too much about the detail for different components: all do the same jobs regardless of what they look like. All the parts here are dealt with in more detail later in this chapter.

A) Shifters

It's all very well having a million gears to choose from, but you need to be able to decide which one to be in, without taking your hands off the bars. Shifters put the controls where you need them – directly under your hands. The shifter unit might be integrated with the brake-levers, making a slightly lighter combination than two separates. However, there are a couple of advantages to having separate brake-levers and gear shifters as you can adjust them independently and also replace them independently if they wear out or break.

B) Cables and casing

This is often neglected, but is much easier to replace than you'd imagine. A new set of cables and casing is the cheapest and most effective way to make your shifting much crisper. It makes you feel much faster, but also helps to make your transmission last as long as possible. Fresh cables means that your chain will run neatly over your sprockets and chainrings, rather than rubbing constantly and wearing itself out. The inner cable is the metal wire that runs all the way from the shifter to the derailleur. The outer casing is the plastic-covered tubing (usually black) that the cable runs through in short sections. The casing protects the cable and guides it around bends and curves.

C) Chainset

Your chainset is the block of gear wheels on the right-hand side of your bike, along with the pedal arm that it connects to. The individual gear wheels are called chainrings and your bike will have one, two or three of them. Road bikes normally have two: hybrids and mountain bikes three. Hub gear bikes will have a single chainring at the front. Like the rest of your transmission, chainrings will wear over time and aren't cheap to replace, but can be made to last much longer if kept clean.

D) Cassette

This is the cluster of sprockets in the middle of your back wheel. Derailleur geared bikes may have five, six, seven, eight, nine or 10 sprockets packed into the space between the frame and the back wheel. If the sprockets are all similar sizes, getting slightly larger as they get nearer the back wheel, your gear ratios will be very close together so that each is only slightly harder or easier than the next. Hybrids and mountain bikes tend to be fitted with cassettes that cover a wider range with larger steps between each gear.

E) Rear derailleur

This cunning piece of kit shifts the chain gently across your sprockets when prompted by the right-hand shifter on your handlebars, via your gear cables. These cable movements are quite small and precise, so the quality of your shifting is dependent on the condition of your cables and the fine adjustment of the cable tension.

The rear derailleur also performs a handy second function – the lower of the two jockey wheels keeps the chain tensioned, so that you can use a chain long enough to go around the big sprockets, without it dragging on the ground when you shift into small sprockets.

F) Front derailleur

Front derailleurs are much simpler than rear derailleurs since they just perform a single function: as you operate the left-hand gear shifter, the derailleur pushes the chain from side to side across your chainset.

Its simplicity as a mechanism means that it rarely needs attention and is usually quite straightforward to service, or replace. The trickiest part is usually ordering the correct replacement – there are a handful of different sizes, depending on your frame size and cable routing.

Rear derailleur overview

Your rear derailleur is in many ways the most complicated mechanism on your bicycle, and so can be quite intimidating. But the job it does is relatively simple. Being able to adjust it can seem fiddly the first few times you do it, but with practice, it becomes easier to dial in your shifting so it's exactly how you like it.

The derailleur responds to signals from your handlebars, transmitted by the gear cable. This has to travel a long way and the signals – changes in cable tension – are very small and very precise, so accurate adjustment is essential. Clean, non-frayed, lubricated cable also helps. Worn pivots on old derailleurs make them difficult to control, since they'll slip into any available position, rather than sitting exactly where you want them.

The most visible parts of the derailleur are the two jockey wheels – small black (or occasionally red) toothed wheels, hanging below the derailleur body with chain wrapped around them. They look the same but perform completely different functions. The top jockey wheel – the guide jockey – is mainly there to move the chain sideways across the sprocket.

The lower jockey wheel (also called the tension jockey) looks similar but has a completely different function – it pulls the chain backwards all the time, taking up slack. This allow you to use different-sized sprockets without the chain either dragging on the ground when you're using small sprockets or being too short to reach large sprockets.

The derailleur has to be able to move sideways across the sprockets. Four main pivots in the derailleur allow this by connecting the central section of the derailleur to the knuckles at either end. They're simple vertical pins. The front two are easiest to get to whereas the back two tend to be more difficult to access, but they all need regular lubrication.

There is also a spring inside the derailleur between the four pivots. The spring acts to folds the derailleur up, so that it draws the chain towards the smallest sprocket when you release cable tension. If the spring becomes full of dirt, it will not be able to pull the derailleur back so that the chain runs over the smaller sprockets.

The shifter works by increasing and releasing tension in the cable. The rear derailleur cable is the longest on your bike and so needs more attention than the others. Any dirt in the cable will slow your shifting down and make accurate adjustments difficult.

The most common place for a shifting problem to occur is in the final stretch of cable between the rear derailleur and the frame. Here, the cable runs through a short section of outer casing. It's near the ground, has to make a sharp bend and sticks out just enough to get caught in things. It's worth replacing this section of outer casing whenever you replace the inner cable. Check as you do so that it's long enough – it should make a smooth curve from frame to derailleur and approach the barrel-adjuster on the back of the derailleur in a straight line. The most obvious sign that the old one was too short is a bend just as it enters the barrel-adjuster. Don't forget ferrules – one on each end of the casing.

All the instructions for adjusting cable tension tell you that you have to concentrate on getting the shifting right between the two smallest sprockets. This works because all the sprockets are evenly spaced and so are the clicks on the shifter. If you get the smallest two right, the others should automatically be aligned correctly.

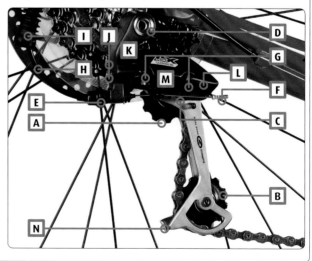

Derailleur close-up

Rear derailleurs deserve particular mention. If treated right, they'll give you precise, perfect shifting, but if they're neglected or incorrectly adjusted, they'll get their own back on you. You need them to drop the chain precisely from sprocket to sprocket when you change gear and the rest of the time you need them hanging vertically under the centre of your chosen sprocket, offering as little resistance as possible to your pedalling force.

Although it looks rather complicated, the derailleur has been developing in its current form for over 50 years. Campagnolo brought out a model called the 'Gran Sport' as long ago as 1951, which is instantly recognisable as a direct ancestor of the modern version on the page opposite.

A) Guide jockey wheel: this controls the position of the chain, moving it sideways across the sprockets as you click the shifters.

B) Tension jockey wheel: although it looks like the guide jockey wheel, the tension (lower) jockey wheel has another job – it's sprung so it's always pushing backwards, taking up the slack on the chain.

C) Rear gear cable: when you work the shifters, this pulls the cable clamp bolt towards the barrel-adjuster, spreading out the derailleur and so moving the guide jockey towards the larger sprockets.

D) Derailleur fixing bolt: this attaches the derailleur to the frame.

E) Barrel-adjuster: this allows you to adjust the cable tension precisely, indexing the gears so that each click of the shifter positions the cable accurately under a sprocket.

F) Cable end: protects the cable from fraying or unravelling.

G) Front pivots: the derailleur rotates around these. There are two more at the back of the derailleur, parallel to these two.

H) Outer casing: leads the gear cable smoothly around the loop from the cable to the barrel-adjuster. It is flexible so that the derailleur can move freely.

I) Rubber boot: helps prevent the ingress of dirt into the cable. This one has been positioned out of the way up the outer casing, so that you can see the barrel-adjuster.

J) End-stop screws: these can be adjusted so that the derailleur can move the chain all the way across the cassette, but no further, so there's no danger of it falling into the gap between the cassette and the frame or the cassette and the wheel.

K) Rear knuckle: this part is bolted to the frame and doesn't move when you change gear.

L) Front knuckle: the swing arm is connected to this part, which moves from side to side as you pull and release the cable.

M) Spring: you can't see this, but it's tucked into the body of the derailleur.

N) Tabs: these prevent the chain from skipping out of the swing arm.

Reverse derailleurs – also known as low-normal and rapidrise

All the instructions shown here refer to 'normal pull' rear derailleurs, where increasing the tension in the cable moves the derailleur from a smaller to a larger sprocket. These constitute the vast majority of derailleurs. However, there are a few about that work in the opposite direction – so that increasing the tension on the cable pulls the chain towards a smaller sprocket. There are a variety of reasons bandied about why this should be better, none of which are particularly conclusive.

In many ways, a rapid-rise derailleur is just the same as a normal one and all the parts are compatible. The cables are the same, they fit onto the bike in the same way, you can even use the same shifters – the numbers will work backwards, so that a high gear will be numbered 1, and a low gear will be numbered 7 or 8 or whatever, but it makes no difference whatsoever to the function. But the instructions on page 138 for adjusting cable tension don't apply, because increasing the tension has the opposite effect. You just have to remember that all adjustments have to start from the low gear rather than the high gear. When adjusting the cable tension, start with the chain running around the largest sprocket, because this is its default position – where it goes if there's no tension in the cable. Check the cable tension is correct by shifting into the second biggest. If it won't shift or moves reluctantly, the cable is too loose and must be tightened by turning the barrel-adjuster anticlockwise.

Rear derailleur: adjusting the cable tension

Adjusting the cable tension on your rear derailleur is one of the most important things that you can learn to do on your bike. You won't need any specialist tools, and it doesn't take very long to get it right. But it takes a little practice to learn what effects your adjustments are going to have.

Your rear derailleur should respond instantly to the right-hand shifter, pushing your chain smoothly across the sprockets as soon as you click for a new gear. This means you have to set the cable tension precisely so that the positions of the sprockets exactly match the positions of the clicks on your shifter.

The distance between each sprocket is small, so it only takes a very small cable pull to move from one to the next and a little bit of extra tension or not quite enough tension will make a big difference. It's not just important when you're changing gear, however, as the correct adjustment means that when you're pedalling the chain runs straight and vertically from the sprocket to the guide jockey, reducing wear and preventing those annoying clattering noises.

You have to start by checking that the end-stop screws are correctly adjusted. This may seem like an odd place to begin but it saves a lot of confusion later on. If they're not quite right, pages 144–145 take you through the adjustments in detail.

You may find that, even if you follow the instructions, you can't

get the gears to index reliably. If this is the case and you've tried the adjustment several times, the chances are there's another problem which will have to be sorted out before you can come back and readjust the cable tension. Likely candidates are the condition of the gear cable (frayed or dirty cables are difficult to adjust) and the derailleur hanger alignment – see page 146.

One part of the adjustment process that you'll become increasingly familiar with is adjusting the cable tension using the barrel-adjuster. Turning it one way increases the cable tension, whereas turning it the other makes the cable slacker.

Almost all barrel-adjusters have a small plastic sleeve that covers the part of the barrel that you turn. This has a dual purpose as it gives you something that is easy to grip, but also has a hidden anti-shake device. There is a tiny spring that pushes the plastic sleeve onto the derailleur body, and both sleeve and derailleur body have interlocking notches so that the barrel cannot shake itself out of adjustment. When turning the barrel-adjuster get into the habit of pulling the plastic

ADJUSTING CABLE TENSION IN THE REAR DERAILLEUR

Step 1: Start by checking that the end-stop screws are correctly adjusted. Turn the pedals, and shift into the smallest sprocket. Then without turning the pedals, push the section of the derailleur that the guide jockey is attached to away from you. This creates a little bit of slack in the gear cable. Choose a section of casing as it enters a cable stop and pull it away from the cable stop, as shown, then out of the slot in the cable stop.

Step 2: Now, the cable should be so slack that it won't affect the position of the derailleur. Turn the pedals and watch the chain. It should drop neatly into the smallest sprocket. Looked at from behind, the guide jockey wheel should be directly under the smallest sprocket. If the chain doesn't drop down to the smallest sprocket or goes too far, you must adjust the high end-stop screw before you go any further – see page 144.

Step 3: Next, check the adjustment on the low end-stop screw. While continuing to pedal with your right hand, hold the back of the derailleur and use your left thumb to push the guide jockey wheel towards the wheel, as shown on p145 step1. The chain should climb steadily up the cassette and reach the largest sprocket, where it will run smoothly. If it doesn't do this, adjust your low end-stop screws – see page 145.

sleeve slightly away from the derailleur body, so that you don't wear out the notches. You'll feel the notches clicking every quarter-turn – when you've finished making your adjustments, rock the barrel-adjuster gently to locate its notches.

The instructions tell you to do the adjustments in the smallest two sprockets. The sprockets are evenly spaced and so are the clicks on the shifter. If you get the adjustment right for these two, the indexing should work across the rest of the cassette.

This is a job where a work stand or a friend who is willing to lift the back wheel off the ground at opportune moments is essential. You need to be able to turn the back wheel and change gear, so that you can see the effects of your adjustments. Turning the bike upside down is a last resort as it makes the derailleur hang differently which affects the adjustment.

If you can't get the cable tension right

This adjustment does take a little practice to get right, but if you're struggling to find the correct cable tension, it's worth having a check in case there are other problems preventing the chain from shifting smoothly. A dirty or kinked gear cable is a common culprit; unless the cable is clean and smooth it will stick in the outer casing when you release the cable tension, leaving the chain floating in no man's land between one sprocket and the next. See page 140 for gear cable replacement instructions.

Another common reason for derailleurs refusing to be adjusted is excessive wear on your cassette or chain. This will prevent the chain from sitting easily in any gear, causing it to slip about however precise your adjustment is. See page 166 for tips on checking your chain wear.

Step 4: Once you've made sure the end-stop screws are correctly adjusted, refit the cable. You'll need to push the derailleur towards the wheel again to create slack in the cable. If you struggle to get the section of outer casing that you removed back into its cable stop, check all the other sections of casing are correctly lodged in their cable stops or barrel-adjusters as they sometimes get dislodged.

Step 5: Next explore your shifter and work out which way you have to move it in order to make the cable looser. Take hold of an exposed section of outer casing and pull it gently away from the frame. Hold it still and operate your right-hand shifter. You'll feel that with each click the cable either gets tighter or looser. Move step by step through the range of the shifter and then back to the position where the cable is slackest.

Step 6: Turn the pedals gently. The chain should run smoothly in the smallest sprocket. If it won't sit on the smallest sprocket, the cable is too tight. Turn the barrel-adjuster gently into the derailleur as shown – looked at from behind, the barrel should move clockwise. Keep turning until the chain runs smoothly on the smallest sprocket and the guide jockey hangs directly below the sprocket.

Step 7: Turn the pedals and click the shifter one click tighter. The chain should shift smoothly onto the next-largest sprocket. If it won't get up onto the next sprocket or only just makes it, the cable tension is too slack. Turn the barrel-adjuster anticlockwise a half-turn at a time. Click the shifter so that the chain returns to the smallest sprocket and try again, turning the barrel-adjuster until the chain shifts smoothly.

Step 8: You may find that the cable is far too slack so you run out of barrel-adjuster – it may be wound all the way out of the derailleur and still not be making a difference. If this is the case turn the barrel-adjuster back into the derailleur body so that it's about halfway through its range. Undo the cable pinch bolt and pull through some cable, maybe 5mm (¼ in). Tighten the clamp bolt firmly and go back to step 7.

Step 9: Once you've got the chain moving smoothly from the smallest to the next sprocket and back, shift into the second from smallest and look at the chain and sprocket from behind. Using the barrel-adjuster, set the position of the derailleur so that the chain sits exactly vertically under the second sprocket. Then, click through the gears one at a time to check they're all working correctly.

Rear derailleur: the fine art of cable replacement

If you've tried adjusting your rear derailleur and your shifting is still reluctant, it's time for a new derailleur cable. You should also consider fitting a new one if you find yourself struggling to adjust the derailleur correctly. If the cable is sticking inside the casing, it won't retain the correct tension as you adjust.

Replace cable if it shows signs of fraying or if the outer casing is kinked or otherwise damaged. The most common places for damage are just as the casing enters the shifter or just as it enters the rear derailleur. Replace any damaged parts of casing as you go along and replace the final section of casing every time you replace the inner cable.

Sluggish shifting is a clear sign than you need a new cable as is ghost shifting when your gears take it upon themselves to change randomly, rather than waiting until you tell them what to do. The cable that connects the shifter to the derailleur needs regular attention. If it gets clogged up with dirt or is forced to make tight bends, the derailleur will get confused about which sprocket you want the chain to be in.

Inner cables are all a standard size – 1.1mm cable with a small vertical nipple on the end. They're sold in one standard length, which is long enough for rear derailleurs with a bit to spare and long enough for front derailleurs with a lot to spare.

Outer casing similarly comes in one size – 4mm. Don't forget to get enough ferrules (the plastic or metal cap that fits over the end of the casing) to put one on each end of each section of outer casing.

Casing is tough and will need to be cut with a proper pair of cable cutters. Don't try to bodge it with a pair of pliers as the end of the casing needs to be made a neat job of. It needs to be cut square and you will need to use a sharp knife to open out the inner lining. It tends to get squashed as you cut the cable and seal across the open end. Shape the ends of the casing so that they're neatly round before you try to fit the ferrules over the end. The ferrules don't need to be squashed onto the casing, they're just a press fit.

Each type of shifter is different, but removing the cable from the derailleur is the same for all of them. Start here with these three steps and then go to page 141 for triggershifters, page 143 for twistshifters and page 142 for drop bar shifters and pick up the rest of the instructions from there. Once you've finished fitting the cable, you'll have to adjust the cable tension – instructions for how to do this are on page 138. ◉

REMOVING REAR DERAILLEUR CABLE

Step 1: Shift into the smallest sprocket on the rear derailleur. Cut off the cable end on the old cable and undo the cable clamp bolt. Look carefully at how the cable fits under the cable clamp bolt so that you know where to put it back. Pull the cable out from underneath. Pull the section of outer casing that leads into the barrel-adjuster at the back of the derailleur gently backwards, releasing it from the barrel-adjuster.

Step 2: Pull the short section of outer casing off the inner cable. If there is a rubber boot that covered the barrel-adjuster, pull that off too. Leaving the rest of the outer casing in place, pull through the inner cable, working gradually back towards the shifter. When you get to the shifter, pull that section of outer casing out of the shifter so you get left with just the inner cable dangling out of the shifter.

Step 3: Inspect the outer casing. Any sections that are damaged or kinked need to be replaced and it's worth replacing the last section of casing every time. Use the lengths that are there to measure up new sections. Cut the ends clean and square. Use a sharp knife to open out the lining. Fit a 5mm ferrule on each end of each section of casing. Replace them on the bike. Now go to the appropriate page for your shifter (see text above).

Nexave-type shifters

Triggershifters are the ones with a lever on the top that your index finger fits around and a lever underneath for your thumb.

Before you remove the cable from the triggershifter, experiment to see what effect changing gear has. Pull gently on the exposed end of cable and operate first one shifter and then the other. One way pulls cable into the shifter, making it tighter, the other releases it so that it's slacker. Keep clicking until the cable is as far out of the shifter as it will go – the 'cable slack' position.

The cover of the shifter is held in place by a pair of small crosshead screws. They're clearly visible on the top of the shifter. The shifter will also have an indicator, showing you what gear you're in. The designs of some versions of these mean that a little care has to be taken when you come to replace the cover. The indicator display may be attached to the cover via a couple of small plastic pins emerging from the inside of the cover, which have to be eased into place gently so they don't snap off.

NEXAVE-TYPE SHIFTERS

Step 1: The top cover of the shifter has two crosshead screws. Wind them all the way out. They have a tendency to get stuck in the plastic of the shifter and will need to be eased gently out. Pull the top cover of the shifter off, but take care with it as the plastic is fairly brittle. You'll see the innards of the shifter with the cable emerging from the central mechanism.

Step 2: Take hold of the cable where it hangs out of the shifter, and push it gently inwards. You'll see the cable nipple push out of the little nest that it sits in. If it's a bit stuck, it may help to twist the cable slightly, so that the spiral of strands that make up the cable get tighter. Pull the cable all the way out of the shifter.

Step 3: Fit the new cable, feeding it back into the nest and then directly out of the shifter exit hole. Pull the cable all the way through and make sure that the head is neatly seated in its nest. Make sure not to allow the cable to drop onto the ground as you work or it will pick up dirt.

Step 4: Check the shifting before you go any further. Pull gently on the cable where it emerges from the shifter and then operate each of the shift levers in turn – you'll feel the cable being gently pulled through your fingers and then released in small chunks. You'll be able to see the internal parts of the shifter rotating. Shift back into 'cable slack'. Replace the shifter cover and replace the screws. They don't have to be tight, just secure.

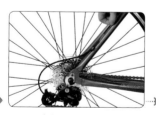

Step 5: Push the new inner cable through each section of outer casing in turn and on into the derailleur. As the cable goes through, drip a drop of oil onto sections that are going to be hidden inside the outer casing. Replace any rubber boots. Feed the last bit of the cable gently through the outer casing that connects the rear derailleur to the frame and in through the barrel-adjuster on the back of the derailleur.

Step 6: Fit the cable under the cable clamp bolt. A groove will indicate the cable route. Pull through any slack and tighten up the cable clamp bolt. Turn the pedals and shift the chain towards the larger sprockets and then back down to 'cable slack' position to shake out cable slack. Undo the cable clamp bolt, pull through slack again, retighten the clamp bolt and fit a cable end. Now adjust the cable tension, see page 138.

Fitting drop bar shifter cables

STi shifters were a revelation for road bikes, allowing you to change gear without taking your hands off the bars and reaching for a downtube shifter.

There are two types of shifter. The first has two separate parts to each brake-lever. Swinging both parts inwards towards the centre of the bike pulls cable into the shifter; pushing just the part nearest the bars sideways releases cable from the shifter. Pushing this lever repeatedly inwards slackens the cable. The second kind has a single brake-lever. Swinging this sideways towards the centreline of the bike increases cable tension. There's also a thumb button on the side of the brake-lever body. Pushing this repeatedly releases cable until you reach the 'cable slack' position. The instructions on this page start after you've released the old gear cable from the derailleur. Go to page 140 and follow the three steps there. Then you should have a bare gear cable hanging out of your shifter.

REMOVING CABLE FROM STi SHIFTERS

Step 1: Test the shifter action. Pull the gear cable gently towards the centreline of the bike. Operate the two levers in either direction – you should feel that one way pulls cable towards the shifter, the other way releases it in distinct chunks. If the cable skips about, or is reluctant to sit in some of the gear positions, the shifter is worn and will need replacing. Release it all the way by repeatedly operating the lever.

Step 2: Pull the brake-lever in towards the bars. This will reveal the exit hole for the cable. It's directly opposite the entry hole where the outer casing lodges into the shifter. There may be a black plastic cover. Pull it off. Push the exposed cable into the shifter and the nipple will emerge from the other side. Feed the new cable back through the shifter, but don't release the brake-lever until it's all the way through or it will kink the cable.

Step 3: Feed the cable back through each section of outer casing in turn and on into the derailleur. Thread it through the barrel-adjuster on the back of the derailleur. Fit the cable under the cable clamp bolt. There will be a groove on the derailleur or clamp bolt, indicating the correct cable route. Pull through any slack and tighten up the cable clamp bolt with your left. Crimp on a cable end. Now adjust cable tension, see page 138.

Derailleur angle of approach

Check the angle that the derailleur hangs at. The guide jockey needs to sit close under the sprockets, but not so close that the top of the jockey rubs on the bottom of the sprockets in any gear. There should be two clear links of chain between the bottom of the sprocket and the top of the jockey wheel. Turn the B-screw to adjust the gap. Turning clockwise increases the gap, turning anticlockwise will allow the guide jockey to move closer to the sprockets. Too close and the chain will rattle on the sprockets as you ride. Too far and shifting will be sluggish, because the chain will flex sideways when you try to change gear rather than meshing with the next sprocket.

Use the B-screw to sit the guide jockey close to the sprockets, then turn it to adjust the gap to the size you want

Fitting twistshifter cables

Twistshifters can be daunting, because you can't see what's going on inside. But don't be discouraged, there are rules to help you get the cable in and out.

Before you can get the cable out of the shifter, you'll have to release it from the rear derailleur. If you haven't done so already, follow the instructions on page 140.

You can only ever remove the cable when the shifter is in the 'cable slack' position, corresponding to the smallest sprocket position for the chain. To test this, take hold of the cable where it emerges from the shifter, and pull gently. Operate the shifter. As you shift it one way, you'll feel the cable being pulled into the shifter. Twist the shifter the other way – you'll feel the cable being released from the shifter in distinct chunks. Twist the shifter as far as it will go, to release as much cable as possible, leaving it in its slackest position so that it can be removed from the shifter.

REMOVING CABLES FROM TWISTSHIFTERS

Step 1: Look on the top of the shifter for an escape hatch. It's usually a black or grey square. Remove the escape hatch or slide it to one side and look into the shifter. You may see either the head of the nipple, the head of a 2.5mm Allen key grub screw or a black plastic cover over half the nipple. If it's a grub screw, remove it completely. If it's a plastic cover, pry it gently back with a small screwdriver.

Step 2: If you can't find an escape hatch at all, the nipple may be hidden under the rubber grip – see the toolbox below. Once you've got it, push the exposed cable that's hanging out of the barrel-adjuster into the shifter. The nipple will emerge up through the grip. Pull the cable all the way out of the shifter.

Step 3: Without moving the shifter, slide the new cable in through the shifter. It will not feed in properly if the cable is frayed so cut off any untidiness. Replace the grub screw if there is one and the escape hatch. Feed the cable back through each section of outer casing, through the derailleur barrel and under the cable clamp bolt. Pull through slack, tighten the clamp bolt. Fit a cable end. Go to page 138 to adjust cable tension.

Basic twistshifters

Some versions of twistshifters don't have a removable hatch. Instead, the nipple is concealed under the edge of the rubber grip. Shift into the highest number on the right-hand shifter and peel back the grip gently just below the row of numbers. You'll see the nipple – push the cable up through the barrel-adjuster and the nipple will emerge from the shifter. Take care not to change gear before feeding the new cable back through as you'll only be able to reach the entry point in 'cable slack' position.

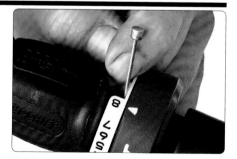

The rubber grip may have to be peeled back, or it may have a small exit hole that the nipple will emerge through

Rear derailleur: setting the 'high' end-stop screw

The end-stop screws on your derailleur – also known as the limit screws – are there to prevent the derailleur from moving so far across the cassette that it drops the chain off either side of the cassette. Luckily, in the normal course of events, this shouldn't happen anyway.

Your shifters should only allow the chain to click from one sprocket to the next and no further than either end. But the damage that could be caused by an accidental mis-shift is far too great to risk, so derailleurs also have end-stop screws as a fail-safe device.

There are often occasions when it's hard to separate the effects of cable tension and end-stop screws. For this reason, it's easiest to disengage the rear derailleur cable completely so that it has no tension and move the derailleur about by hand. This makes it easier to understand what's going on.

Each end-stop screw only affects one end of the cassette. The 'h' end-stop screw affects the derailleur movement as it approaches the smallest sprocket. If the end-stop screw is set too far out, there is a possibility that the chain will fall off the end of the cassette into the gap between the cassette and the frame. If you're riding along, this can be dangerous – your chain will jam under pressure, possibly causing you to come off the bike.

It's possible to adjust the end-stop screw too far in as well,

preventing the derailleur from dropping the chain onto the smallest sprocket. This isn't as likely to cause an accident, but it can be a bit annoying. If the chain won't reach the smallest sprocket, you'll be left without your highest gear and there will be a limit to how quickly you can go.

Even if the end-stop screw is set just slightly too far in, it can cause problems. For smooth running, the chain needs to hang vertically off each sprocket. If it runs at a slight angle, it will rattle irritatingly and your transmission will wear more quickly. It also makes it much harder to adjust your gear cable tension, because, even when you release cable tension at the barrel-adjuster, the chain still doesn't drop into the smallest sprocket, which is confusing.

Once you've got the end-stop screw positions right, they don't rattle out of place, but they may need readjusting if you crash or fall. If the bike lands on its right-hand side, it may knock the derailleur slightly inwards towards the wheel, changing the position of the derailleur relative to the cassette sprockets.

SETTING THE 'HIGH' END-STOP SCREW

Step 1: Turn the pedals and use the shifter to change into the smallest sprocket on the cassette. Then, pedal with your right hand and use your left to push the guide jockey towards your back wheel. To do this, hook your finger around the back of the derailleur and push the front part of the derailleur gently away from you with your thumb as shown in the picture. When you've got the chain into the big sprocket, stop pedalling.

Step 2: The gear cable will now be slack. Follow it back to where a section of outer casing fits into a cable stop. Pull the outer casing out of the cable stop, then wriggle the inner cable out of the slot in the cable stop. With the cable loose, you can move the derailleur freely about by hand. Turn the pedals again. You should now find that the chain will clunk back into its default position, in the smallest sprocket, automatically.

Step 3: Seen from behind, the chain should make a vertical line off the sprocket and onto the guide jockey. If the guide jockey sits too far out (right of the centre of the sprocket), turn the 'high' end-stop screw clockwise until the guide jockey sits directly underneath. If the guide jockey sits too far in, turn the end-stop screw anticlockwise until they line up. Finally, push the derailleur across so the chain sits in the largest sprocket and refit the cable.

144

Rear derailleur: setting the 'low' end-stop screw

Setting the 'low' end-stop screw is slightly trickier than the 'high' end-stop screw. For the former, you can simply release the cable tension and allow the derailleur spring to pull the mechanism outwards towards the smallest sprocket. With the 'low' end-stop screw, you have to push the derailleur across by hand.

It would be possible to do this by using the cable to pull the derailleur across, but it makes it more difficult to be sure what's going on. If you're doing it by hand and the derailleur won't reach, you know it's not a problem with the cable tension.

It's too difficult to hold the derailleur in the right place and then screw in the 'l' end-stop screw until it butts up to its tab inside the derailleur. It's much easier to push the derailleur across and test how far it will go, release it so that it falls back to its neutral position, adjust the 'l' end-stop screw, then test again until it's exactly right.

Before you start fiddling, identify the 'low' end-stop screw. If the two end-stop screws are on the back of the derailleur, it's almost always the bottom one, but it should be marked with an 'l'. The writing is usually quite small and is often in black on a black background.

It is worth getting this adjustment right, though. If the chain is allowed to move too far it will fall off over the end of the block into the gap between the cassette and the spokes. If you're

pedalling at the time, the pressure on the chain will make it into a very effective chainsaw and it will cut through any spokes it can reach. This is expensive! It may also jam, throwing you off your bike which is clearly not desirable either.

If the 'l' end-stop screw is adjusted too far in, it's mostly irritating. Either the chain won't be able to get into the largest sprocket, depriving you of an easy gear, or it will just about make it in, but will rattle constantly and may decide to change gear of its own accord.

It's worth making a quick check of your derailleur alignment while you're setting the 'low' end-stop screw. If you've not done this before, check page 146 for a full explanation. You need to pay particular attention to the clearance between the spokes and the lower part of the rear derailleur swingarm. If the derailleur has bent inwards, there is a danger it could catch on the spokes, jamming your wheel and tearing the bottom of the derailleur off. This is most likely to happen when you're putting a lot of pressure on the pedals, since this can distort the shape of the rear wheel, allowing contact.

SETTING THE 'LOW' END-STOP SCREW

Step 1: Hold the derailleur as shown in the picture (if you've already set the high end-stop screw, it's the same movement as you used before). Find a comfortable position to do this – you need to be pedalling with your right hand and operating the derailleur with your left. Tuck your index finger around the back of the derailleur and push the front part of the derailleur away from you. Keep pedalling.

Step 2: The chain should move the derailleur across the cassette towards the largest sprocket. The chain should step into it neatly, but should not be able to fall over the back of the cassette, into the gap between the cassette and the spokes – if this happens under pressure, the chain will cut through the spokes, potentially destroying your back wheel.

Step 3: If you can push the chain over the end of the largest sprocket, you need to limit the movement of the derailleur. Turn the pedals and allow the chain to drop back to the smallest sprocket. Turn the 'l' end-stop screw clockwise – try half a turn at first and retest. If the chain won't reach the largest sprocket, undo the 'l' end-stop screw anticlockwise to give the derailleur a bit more elbow room.

145

Rear derailleur: working out hanger alignment

A lot is expected of your rear derailleur. You want it to be a precise, instant-shifting piece of kit. Above all, you need to be able to rely on it in all conditions and that's why it pays to nurture it.

One of the most common problems that is routinely ignored is the alignment of the rear derailleur hanger (the part on the frame that the derailleur bolts onto). The gears are designed to work properly when the two jockey wheels hang exactly vertically underneath the sprockets. This vertical alignment is the first casualty of a crash, but it's often overlooked — you get up and brush yourself off, look at your bike and, if everything looks okay, you ride away. Bad things can happen next. If you've crashed and bent your derailleur inwards, the gears may still work, but everything has shipped inboard a little.

The next time you stamp uphill in a low gear or accelerate away from a set of traffic lights, you click the lever to find a bigger sprocket, but instead you dump the chain off the inside of the rear cassette, stuffing it into the back wheel just as you haul on the pedals. Likely results include falling off and hurting yourself with expensive damage to your back wheel.

On a less drastic level, shifting works best when the sprockets are aligned with the jockey wheels. The chain isn't being twisted as it runs off the sprocket and the jockey wheels move in the direction they were designed to, rather than being forced up into the sprockets as they move across the cassette, which is what happens if the hanger is bent.

To check your alignment, look at the derailleur from behind to get the clearest view. The sprocket, chain and jockey wheel should form a vertical line. In the most common problem, the hanger is bent so that the bottom jockey wheel hangs nearer the wheel as in the picture below right.

It's not unusual for the hanger or the derailleur to be twisted instead of, or as well as, being bent, so that as you look straight at the sprocket you can see the surface of the jockey wheels instead of just the edge. For precise shifting, the jockeys need to be flat and vertical to the sprockets. Because this is a common problem, good-quality aluminium frames feature a replaceable hanger.

There are as many different types of hanger as there are makes of bike and, even within a make and model, the hanger you need might depend on the year the bike was made. To make sure you get the right one, take the old one to your local bike shop for comparison. They are almost never interchangeable.

If you don't have a replaceable hanger the frame will have to be bent back. You can do it yourself if you are careful, but if you are unsure, then this is a job for the bike shop. You usually need to have snapped off a couple of hangers before you know how far you can go – an expensive experiment. If the bend is bad, the hanger will be weaker after you have straightened it.

If you're confident about bending the hanger back yourself, unscrew the derailleur from the frame. It can stay attached to the cable and doesn't have to be disentangled from the chain – just leave it hanging below the chainstay. Leave the wheel in the dropout to support the frame. Clamp a large adjustable spanner onto the hanger. You need about 30cm (12 in) of leverage to do the job. Get the adjustable spanner to fit as far onto the dropout as you can. This is tricky because the sprockets tend to get in the way. Ease the hanger back into place. It is very important to bend it in one movement. The last thing you want to do is work the hanger backwards and forwards to find the perfect place because it will definitely snap off. Once the hangar is straight, use the instructions from step 5 on page 148 to refit the derailleur. Once the hanger is realigned you will need to readjust the cable tension and then check the positions of the end-stop screws. The position of the derailleur relative to the frame will have changed, throwing your adjustments out.

This hanger is bent!

Servicing the rear derailleur

The rear derailleur does all the shifting work and, because it dangles down close to the ground, gets caught on twigs as well as picking up debris. It's also the part that your bike lands on first if you drop your trusty steed on the right-hand side.

If you have time to think when you're crashing, drop the bike on the left – it's far cheaper! Similarly, if you have to lie the bike down on the ground or pack it in the back of a car, lie it left side down. If your shifting is still sluggish after you've adjusted the end-stop screws and the cable tension, it's time to treat your rear derailleur to a little clean and re-lubrication. The separate sections of the derailleur need to be able to move freely so your shifting is crisp. The pivots that connect the parts work best if they're not jammed up with dirt and have a little oil to lubricate them.

◎ Remove the back wheel so you can get to everything. Hang the bike up so the rear end is off the ground or turn the bike upside down.

◎ Wipe down the outside of the derailleur. If it's really oily, pour some degreaser or bike wash into a pot and dip a cloth or brush into it. This is much better and less messy than trying to use spray degreaser. Clean off all the accumulated dirt – it might take several rinses to get it shiny.

◎ You need to move the derailleur through its range to get inside it. Not having the back wheel on makes this much easier. Operate the right-hand shifter – you'll have to reach round under the bars if your bike is upside down – so the rear derailleur moves away from you towards the centreline of the bike, as far as it will go. Clean everything you can reach. Tuck the brush down inside the body of the derailleur and clean the spring, getting all the dirt out from inside the mechanism.

◎ Clean off the jockey wheels (A). They collect oil and mud. Scrape as much as you can off with the end of a screwdriver and then scrub the wheels clean.

◎ Check how worn the derailleur is. The teeth on the jockey wheels should have flat tops, not points. Take hold of the bottom of the derailleur and wiggle it towards you. It should flex rather than knock or flap about freely. When these things happen, it's time for a new derailleur.

◎ Oil the pivot points (B). There are at least four on the derailleur body. Drop a bit of oil into the centre of the jockey wheels and on the gaps between parts of the derailleur including the knuckle where the derailleur rotates on the frame and the point where the derailleur body meets the arm (E) with the jockey wheels. Once you've oiled these parts, move them to work the oil into the gaps. Push the derailleur away as if it was changing gear and then allow

it to spring back several times. Wipe off excess oil. Refit the back wheel, not forgetting to reattach your brakes.

If you feel like giving your bike a treat, remove the rear derailleur (see page 148) and give it a thorough scrub. Undo the bolts that hold on the jockey wheels, remove them and take the back of the cage off to clean between the cage and the jockey wheels. Push the bearings (C) out of the middle of the jockey wheels, clean and oil them and then refit. Don't be tempted to swap the top and bottom jockey wheels as they're usually a different shape. There may also be a rotation direction marked on the guide jockey like the one in the picture. Set this up so that pedalling forwards makes the jockey wheel roll in the direction of the arrows. This can be achieved by bolting the jockey wheel into the derailleur so that the writing faces outward. A common mistake is to fit the back of the cage (D) on upside down. Make sure it's orientated so that the shape matches the front part of the cage that's fixed to the derailleur body.

Use a small brush to scrub dirt from inside the body of the derailleur and oil the pivot points. Refit the derailleur, again using the instructions on page 148 for fitting a new derailleur.

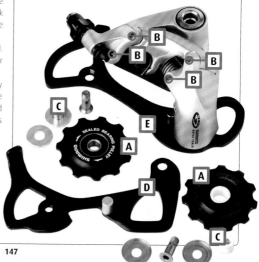

Fitting a new rear derailleur

There are many good reasons you might want to or need to change your rear derailleur. First and most pressing of all, it might have snapped in a crash.

Alternatively, it might simply have worn out after hundreds and hundreds of gear changes. Derailleur pivots will wear over time, causing sluggish shifting as the guide jockey struggles to respond to changes in cable tension.

Take hold of the bottom of the derailleur cage and rock it sideways, towards and away from the back wheel. A bit of flex is fine, but if you can feel the cage knocking, replace the derailleur.

This task is easiest when you have as much chain slack to play with as possible. That's why you should change into the smallest sprocket at the back, while at the same time dropping the chain off the smallest sprocket at the front and into the gap between the chainset and the frame.

FITTING A REAR DERAILLEUR

Step 1: Clip the end-cap off the cable. Undo the cable clamp bolt and unthread the cable from the barrel-adjuster. If you reuse the same cable, there is no need to unthread it further, although you may find that a new derailleur will have a different configuration and need a longer cable.

Step 2: It is best to split the derailleur to remove the chain from it, rather than splitting the chain, which takes longer and weakens the split link. First, undo the guide (upper) jockey wheel bolt slightly. Remove the tension (lower) jockey wheel bolt completely.

Step 3: Slide the tension jockey wheel forward. It has a washer on each side. Don't lose these – they tend to drop out as you pull the jockey wheel out.

Step 4: Rotate the back of the cage slightly so that you can slide the chain out of the cage without splitting the chain. Undo the fixing bolt that attached the derailleur to the frame. Discard the old derailleur.

Step 5: On your new derailleur, loosen the guide jockey bolt and remove the tension jockey wheel. Hold the derailleur upside down. Fit the derailleur onto the chain, laying the chain onto the guide jockey. Rotate the back plate of the derailleur cage to get the chain in under the metal tab. Trap the chain in place by inserting the tension jockey wheel from above. Ensure the chain passes inside both tabs, so the chain runs between tab and jockey wheel.

Step 6: Refit the tension jockey bolt. Tighten both jockey wheel bolts firmly. Turn the derailleur clockwise and pull it backwards, so the fitting bolt is aligned with the frame-hanger. Bolt the derailleur to the frame. As you tighten the bolt, twist the derailleur clockwise, so that the small B-tab or B-screw at the back sits behind the matching tab on the frame hanger, stopping the derailleur from swinging too far forward.

Improving your shifting

It's often difficult to know where to start with gear adjustment. Sluggish shifting can result from a combination of factors, both constant and intermittent. The rear derailleur in particular relies on everything being set up perfectly so that all the components work together.

It's also tricky to adjust gears because they behave differently under pressure. Gears that feel perfect when you're trying them out in the garage can be disappointing when you try them out for real. Occasionally, the opposite situation occurs: you can't get the gears to shift properly at all in the shop and then you go for a ride anyway and unexpectedly they feel fine.

Adjust cable tension

If you're unhappy with the shifting, the most sensible place to start is with the cable tension adjustment. Click the right-hand shifter all the way into the neutral position (high gears for standard derailleurs, low for rapid-rise) and then shift over into the neighbouring sprocket.

If the chain doesn't sit vertically under the sprocket or doesn't shift crisply you have an adjustment problem — see cable tension, page 138.

Check hanger alignment

Shift into the big sprocket and look at the chain from behind the bike. The chain should make a straight vertical line down the back of the sprocket and around the jockey wheels. If the jockey wheels are tucked in towards the back wheel, you have a hanger alignment problem — see page 146.

Replace or clean cables and casing

If your cable tension and alignment are correct, but your shifting is still sluggish, your gear cable may be dirty, kinked or corroded. Problems may also be caused by damage to the outer casing which the inner cable runs through. If this gets squashed or kinked, the inner cable won't be able to slide smoothly inside it. In particular, check the short section of outer casing between the rear derailleur to the frame. This section gets more than its fair share of abuse.

Gear cables and casing are among the least expensive parts of the bike so changing them doesn't break the bank. It's not a complicated job and the reward is instant: improved shifting.

See page 140 for instructions on how to fit a new gear cable. The cable fits into each type of shifter – rapidfire or twistshifters on bikes with flat bars, or STi shifters on drop bar bikes – in a different way, but once you've got the cable into the shifter and threaded back to the derailleur they're all adjusted in the same way.

Clean or replace your rear derailleur

Your derailleur will work much better if it's clean and lubricated. See page 147 for servicing instructions. Give it a good scrub and oil it. Wipe away excess oil afterwards as it will just attract dirt. A worn derailleur will shift sluggishly, taking its time to move from one sprocket to the next rather than skipping smartly across in response to the shifter.

If it makes no difference when you clean the derailleur, the chances are the pivots that connect the moving parts of the derailleur together are worn out. To test whether this is the case, take hold of the bottom of the derailleur where the tension jockey bolts on. Wiggle the whole of the bottom of the cage from side to side. It may flex a little – there will be a little bit of movement even in a new derailleur – but you should not be able to feel any knocking or clicking. These both indicate that the pivots are worn enough to warrant a new derailleur.

Replace shifter

If none of these methods works, check that your shifter is sending crisp signals. Shift into a large sprocket and then click the shifter as if changing into a small sprocket, but without turning the pedals. This creates slack in the cable. Pull the section of casing that joins the bars to the frame forward and up, out of its cable stop. Slide the casing toward the back of the bike. This exposes the cable as it enters the shifter. Take hold of the cable and pull gently away from the shifter. Operate the shifter, checking that as you shift in either direction the shifter pulls through little chunks of cable and then releases them neatly, one at a time. If the shifter slips or misses clicks, service or replace it — see pages 160–169. Shift back into the slackest cable position to refit the outer casing in its cable stop and then lift up the back of the bike and pedal until the chain finds a sprocket.

Check cassette and chain for wear

If you find the chain skipping from gear to gear randomly, or the chain slips under pressure, check whether your chain and cassette are worn out. See page 166 for methods of checking how much life your chain has in it. Cassettes and chains both wear at the same rate, so should be replaced at the same time. This may also be caused by a stiff link in the chain, see page 159 for suggestions for finding and curing this.

Front derailleur: adjusting your cable tension

Follow these simple steps so that your chain moves swiftly across the chainring as you change gear and doesn't rattle on the derailleur cage as you ride along. This is one of the most irritating types of rattle because it will only happen in certain gears and it will then mysteriously disappear as soon as you have the time to try and solve it.

If you're getting slow shifting or find that some gears are noisy, use the three steps below to adjust the cable tension. You'll find that this sorts out the problem nine times out of 10. However, if you're still getting changes that rattle, it's worth looking at the state of your gear cable and the derailleur itself – it may not be aligned perfectly with the chainrings. It may also be bent or just plain worn out.

Front derailleurs do tend to collect a lot of the water and road dirt that gets sprayed up off your back wheel, especially if you haven't got mudguards, so if you have trouble adjusting the cable tension, check the state of the derailleur first. If it's gummed up with grit, it will struggle to move your chain smoothly across the chainset. See page 156 for tips on how to get your derailleur clean, or replace it. Look inside the cage and check for grooves indicating where the chain has rubbed on the metal of the cage. Deep, striated ridges in the derailleur cage indicate that it's replacement time, since these catch on the chain rather than lifting it neatly from chainring to chainring.

Unlike rear derailleurs, front derailleurs don't have a barrel-adjuster on the mechanism. Instead, it's located at the shifter. In terms of altering cable tension, it doesn't actually matter how far along the cable the barrel-adjuster is – it's just that it's a little more awkward to reach when you're trying to get the derailleur cage in precisely the right place. The exception is road bikes, which don't have a shifter at either end of the cable. Instead, it's in the middle on the left-hand side of the down tube where the cable emerges from the outer casing. Turn the outside of the barrel-adjuster upwards to increase tension, downwards to reduce it.

To adjust the derailleur cable, you have to know what effect shifting has on your cable tension. Starting at the shifter, note where the outer casing emerges from the shifter and follow it backwards. At some point a section of bare inner cable will emerge from the outer casing. Take hold of the middle of this section and pull it gently away from the frame of the bicycle. Keeping tension in it, operate the gears. You'll feel the tension in the cable changing as you shift – work out what you have to do to make the cable tighter and looser.

ADJUSTING THE FRONT DERAILLEUR'S CABLE TENSION

Step 1: Shift so the cable tension is at its loosest, turn the pedals. The chain should drop down into the smallest chainring. If not, see page 151. Keep turning the pedals, change the shifter into middle gear. The chain should lift into the middle chainring. If not, the cable tension is too slack. Click the lever back to the slackest position, undo the cable clamp bolt, pull through slack cable, retighten cable clamp bolt. Repeat until chain shifts into middle ring.

Step 2: Now fine-tune the cable position. Leaving the chain in the middle chainring use the right-hand shifter to change into the largest sprocket at the back. The chain runs between the two plates of the front derailleur cage. You're looking for the gap between the chain and the back plate – the one closest to the frame. Ideally, this should be 1–2mm ($\frac{1}{24}$–$\frac{1}{12}$ in) at its closest point.

Step 3: Use the barrel-adjuster on the shifter (on road bikes, this is on the left side of the downtube) to adjust the cable tension – turning it anticlockwise increases the tension, moving the cage nearer the chain. Turning the barrel clockwise increases the gap. Once you've got the gap right, try pedalling and shifting onto the large chainring. The chain should lift up easily. If not, see p151 (front derailleur 'high' end-stop screws) or p 155 (front derailleur alignment).

Front derailleur: the end-stop screws

End-stop screws limit the movement of the front derailleur so that the chain cannot drop off either side of the chainring.

There are two separate screws: the 'l' (low) screw stops the derailleur swinging too far inwards; the 'h' (high) screw stops the chain from moving too far outwards.

You'll have to check which screw is which. They won't necessarily be the same way around as those shown in the pictures. The low will be marked with an 'l' but the marking letters are often small

and indistinct. You may have to clean up the area around the top of the derailleur to find out. Another possible marking is a set of three different-sized parallel lines. These represent the chainset so the screw nearest the shortest line adjusts the position of the derailleur over the small chainring and the screw nearest the long line adjusts the derailleur over the large chainring.

HIGH AND LOW END-STOP SCREWS

Step 1: Start with the chain in the middle chainring at the front and the largest sprocket at the back. Check the shifter is in the middle of its three positions. Look carefully at the gap between the chain and the back of the derailleur cage. It's quite tricky to see clearly, but there should be a gap of 1–2mm (¹⁄₁₆ in or less) between chain and derailleur cage.

Step 2: If the gap between chain and derailleur cage is wrong you'll need to adjust the cable tension. Find the barrel-adjuster on the left-hand shifter (this one shows a rapidfire shifter, but the same applies to other types). Turn the barrel-adjuster outwards – anticlockwise, looking along the cable into the shifter – to move the derailleur outwards, clockwise to move it inwards.

Step 3: Now that the cable tension is correct, turn the pedals and shift into the smallest sprocket at the back. Keep turning the pedals and shift into a high gear. The chain should lift onto the largest chainrings. If it won't go onto the 'h' high end-stop screw, it needs to be unwound. Check carefully which screw is which – yours may be the opposite way around to the one shown in the picture – and unscrew the 'h' (anticlockwise).

Step 4: Once you've got the chain onto the big chainring, you need to make sure it doesn't go too far. Leave the chain in the big chainring and gently roll in the 'h' end-stop screw inwards (clockwise) until you can feel it touching the body of the derailleur. Then back it out again half a turn for a little breathing space. Turn the pedals and test by shifting down into the middle chainring and back up again to the big one.

Step 5: Turn the pedals and try shifting down into the small chainring. The chain should drop in first time. If not, back off the 'low' adjusting screw. Again, look carefully for markings. The correct screw on your derailleur may be in the opposite position to the one pictured. Turn the 'l' screw clockwise. Try a half-turn at a time and test by trying to shift into the small chainring. Keep going until the chain shifts easily.

Step 6: If the chain shifts easily onto the small chainring, make sure the derailleur won't go too far. Leave the chain in the small chainring at the front and shift into the largest sprocket at the back. Look at the gap between the chain and the back plate of the front derailleur. Turn the end-stop screw inwards until the gap is around 2mm (¹⁄₁₂ in).

New cables for rapidfire shifters

Rapidfire shifters are common on flat bar bikes. They're easy to learn how to operate, and will work reliably in the rain, or in bad weather.

There are two basic types. Those that hang under the bars – like those pictured – usually have a small hatch on the outboard end of the shifter or sometimes just an exit hole for the cable. Shifters that sit up on top of the bars – for example, Shimano Nexave – work in just the same way, but the cable is easier to access as the cover of the shifter can be removed by undoing the two crosshead screws

on the top. Take care with these as they're small. Once you've got the cover off, the same principles apply as below – the shifter must be in 'cable slack' position to remove the old cable and refit the new one. Take care when refitting the shifter cover. If it has a moveable gear indicator, you may need to wriggle this into place gently so that it's snugly in place before you refit the fixing screws.

FITTING A NEW FRONT DERAILLEUR CABLE TO RAPIDFIRE SHIFTERS

Step 1: Shift into the 'cable slack' position by flicking the upper lever (or thumb button) while turning the pedals. If you're not sure you've found the slackest cable position, pull on an exposed section of the gear cable while changing gear in both directions, so that you can feel what effect shifting has on the cable tension. At the front derailleur, cut the cable end off the old cable, undo the clamp bolt and ease the cable out from underneath.

Step 2: Thread the cable back piece by piece through the outer casing. Watch how each section works so that you can see how to thread it back again. Inspect the outer casing as you go along – any bits that are damaged, kinked or too short should be replaced. You'll need to use good cable cutters to chop them to length and a ferrule on either end of each length of casing. See page 157 for more information on outer casing.

Step 3: Once you get back to the shifter, pull the outer casing away from where it disappears inside the shifter and pull the cable all the way through, so that it dangles out of the end of the shifter.

Step 4: Many rapidfire shifters simply have an exit hole, directly opposite the position where the outer casing enters the shifter. If not, remove any covers – in the example in the picture, there's a hatch with a crosshead screw that you have to remove. If your shifter sits on top of the bars, remove the top cover completely by undoing the two crosshead screws. Take care with these as they're small and often make a break for freedom.

Step 5: Push the old cable into the shifter. As long as the lever is still in 'cable slack' position, the cable nipple will emerge from the shifter. Pull the old cable all the way out and then, without changing gear, feed the new cable in the same way. When the end of the cable emerges, pull it all the way through the shifter and then give it a firm tug to settle the nipple in place in the shifter.

Step 6: Feed the cable back through the outer casing all the way back to the derailleur. Fit the cable under the cable clamp bolt. There will be a groove that indicates exactly where the cable should go. Pull up any slack with one hand and then tighten the cable clamp bolt with the other hand. Crimp on a cable end and then go to page 150 to adjust the cable tension.

New cables for STi shifters

Front gear cables on STi levers tend to last for years as they don't get forced around tight bends and aren't used as heavily as rear shifters.

The exit point for the cable is hidden beneath the cowl of the shifter. To access it, you need to pull the lever right back towards the handlebar. The exit hole will be on the outside of the lever blade, directly opposite the point where the outer casing enters the lever. The cable can only be extracted when the gear shifter is set so that the cable is slack.

There are two types of STi shifter. In the first, the brake-lever is in two parts. Swinging both inwards towards the centre of the bike makes the cable tighter; swinging just the back one towards the centreline loosens the cable. In the second, there is a single brake-lever, which you swing inwards to tighten the cable. A thumb button on the inner face of the hood loosens the cable.

FITTING A NEW FRONT DERAILLEUR TO STi SHIFTERS

Step 1: Shift into the 'cable slack' position by flicking the inner lever (or thumb button) repeatedly while turning the pedals. Confirm this has got you to the right place by pulling up on the cable where it passes along the downtube or toptube, while changing gear in both directions. Cut the cable end off the old cable, undo the clamp bolt and ease the cable out from underneath it.

Step 2: Pull the end of the outer casing away from its seat in the lever, exposing the inner cable. Pull the cable out of the outer casing, drawing the whole cable through towards the lever. Watch its route as it comes out, so you can feed it back the same way later. Inspect the outer casing as you go along since any bits that are damaged or too short should be replaced. See page 157 for more information on outer casing.

Step 3: Pull the brake-lever towards the handlebars. You can see where the cable enters the lever – it comes out directly opposite and can only be removed when the lever is in its 'cable slack' position. There will either be a little exit hole or a little black plastic cover that will have to come off. You may need pliers.

Step 4: Push the old cable through the lever until the nipple emerges from the outer side of the lever. When you can see it, take hold of it and pull it all the way out. If you can't get the cable to emerge, the most likely problem is that you're not in the correct gear. Check and shift again if necessary. If the cable has started to fray inside the shifter, it may help to turn it gently as you twist.

Step 5: Feed the new cable through the lever until the nipple is firmly bedded down. Refit any hatches etc. Check that the shifter is working properly. Take hold of the cable just as it emerges from the shifter and step through the gears with your other hand. If it doesn't index nicely now, it's not going to work with a derailleur attached to it. Shift back so that the cable tension is slack.

Step 6: Feed the cable back through the outer casing all the way back to the derailleur. Fit the cable under the cable clamp bolt. There will be a groove that indicates exactly where the cable should go. Pull up any slack with one hand and then tighten the cable clamp bolt with the other hand. Crimp on a cable end and then go to page 150 to adjust the cable tension.

New cables for twistshifters

Twistshifter cables have an undeserved reputation for being difficult to fit, though it's true the very first models were a bit of a three-dimensional jigsaw puzzle.

For current designs – all models since 2000 – it takes less time to fit a cable to a twistshifer than to a triggershifter. You'll need to shift into a particular gear to expose the head of the cable.

When you look at your gear indicators, one may be in a different colour to the others or one of the numbers may

have a circle drawn around it. If all the numbers look the same, shift into '1' on the left-hand side.

Gear cables are pretty much a standard size now – almost everybody uses a 1.1mm diameter cable. However, there are still a few of the older 1.2mm size knocking about. These are fine for most shifters, but are not quite flexible enough for the internals of twistshifters.

FITTING A NEW FRONT DERAILLEUR TO TWISTSHIFTERS

Step 1: Cut the cable end off the old cable, undo the clamp bolt and ease the cable out from underneath it. Go to the shifter and pull the outer casing away from where it enters the shifter. This exposes some of the inner cable. Pull the whole inner cable so that you're left with bare cable hanging out of the shifter. Cut off all but the last 10cm (4 in). Turn the shifter to the '1' position.

Step 2: Your next task is to find the cable hatch. It's often next to the line of numbers on top of the shifter. If you can't find a hatch, see the box below. Remove the hatch or slide it to one side and look into the shifter. You may either see the head of the nipple, the head of a 2.5mm Allen key grub screw or a black plastic cover over half the nipple. If it's a grub screw, remove it completely. If it's a plastic cover, pry it gently back.

Step 3: Push the exposed cable into the shifter. The nipple will emerge through the hatch. Pull the cable out of the shifter. Without moving the shifter, slide the new inner cable in. Pull it all the way through. Replace grub screw, covers and hatches. Feed the cable back through the outer casing and in the groove under the cable clamp bolt. Pull through any slack and tighten the bolt. Now go to page 150 to adjust cable tension.

Fitting front derailleur cables to twistshifters

Some versions of twistshifters don't have a removeable hatch. Instead, the nipple is concealed under the edge of the rubber grip. Shift into the number '1' on the left-hand shifter and peel back the grip gently just below the row of numbers. You'll see the nipple. Push the cable up through the barrel-adjuster and the nipple will emerge from the shifter. Feed the new cable back through without changing gear.

The end of the cable needs to be in good condition to pass freely through the bowels of the shifter. It's easiest with new cables, which have a blob of solder on the end. Otherwise, use a good pair of cable cutters to make a clean square end of the cable. It can also help to make a slight bend in the end of the cable about 2cm (1 in) from the end. Then twist the cable slightly as you feed it through the shifter – the bend in the cable will help it find its way through.

Look for the magic number

Front derailleur alignment

Don't be distracted by all the fiddly stuff around it. The front derailleur will only work properly if it's correctly aligned on the frame and sitting at the right height.

The derailleur position is just as important for double chainsets as it is for triple chainsets. Although they have to deal with a much narrower range of gears, front derailleurs designed for road bikes have a much narrower cage. This makes it essential that care is taken with their alignment – cages that are fitted at an angle will inevitably rub in some gear combinations.

Fitting a new front derailleur

To remove the old derailleur, follow the instructions for servicing a front derailleur on page 156 up to step 4 and pick them up again from step 5 to fit the new one. The trickiest part is making sure you get the correct replacement part. See the toolbox below for an overview of the different types.

CORRECT FRONT DERAILLEUR ALIGNMENT

Step 1: Change gear so that the chain is in the middle chainring and then pull the front derailleur away from the frame, using both hands as shown so as not to distort the cage. Hold the cage so that the front plate of the derailleur is directly over the largest chainring. There should be a 1–2mm (¹⁄₂₄–¹⁄₁₂ in) gap between the cage and the chainring.

Step 2: The angle of the derailleur is also important. Look down onto the cage and chainring from above. The outer plate (A) of the derailleur cage should be parallel to the outer chainring. Some front derailleurs have a wider section at the back – ignore this part and concentrate on the flat section of the front of the cage.

Step 3: If the derailleur isn't in the right place, shift it on the frame. Disconnect the gear cable by undoing the cable clamp bolt slightly and then loosen the bolt that holds the derailleur onto the frame. Reposition the derailleur, then retighten the bolt. Refit the cable and then adjust its tension (page 150). It may seem like a pain to undo the cable, but if you don't, it pulls the derailleur down the frame as you try to position it.

Choosing the right replacement derailleur

There are two basic types of front derailleur – 'conventional' and 'topswing'. The conventional type is the older design, where the clamp attaches to the frame higher than the derailleur cage. Topswing derailleurs have a cage that sits higher than the frame clamp. In most cases, the two are completely interchangeable. Some full-suspension designs force you to use one or the other, because the frame or the shock gets in the way of the derailleur. If in doubt, replace your derailleur with the same type.

Your frame will also dictate whether the derailleur is 'top pull' or 'down pull'. Down pull cables head down from the cable clamp towards the bottom bracket, under the bottom bracket and up the downtube. Top pull cables head straight upwards around the corner

where your seat clamps on and along the toptube. As a small concession to simplification, some front derailleurs – e.g. Shimano Deore – are made with a dual cable clamp routing so that they can be used as either top pull or down pull derailleurs.

You'll need to count the number of teeth on your outer chainring. Smaller sizes (44T and below) will need a 'compact' cage, which is shorter with a tighter curve.

The last vital piece of information you need to know is your frame diameter. The three sizes are 28.6mm, 31.8mm and 34.9mm. Shimano Deore derailleurs get even more points for simplicity because they come in a one-size-fits-all package with a clamp for 34.9mm plus shims for the smaller sizes.

Front derailleur service

Front derailleurs are right in the firing line for anything and everything that gets thrown up off the back wheel – another good reason for using mudguards.

Like V-brakes and rear derailleurs, front derailleurs work by using a cable to pull the mechanism in one direction, then a spring that returns the mechanism when the cable tension is released. The spring can never be strong enough to cope if the mechanism is gummed up with road dirt. Equally, gritty or frayed cables will prevent the mechanism moving smoothly in either direction.

As well as getting dirty, front derailleurs can also get bent. The cage part is particularly vulnerable. This can happen if you crash or if you lock a pile of bikes up together and they get tangled up. As the derailleur gets older, the inside surfaces of the cage do get worn away where the chain rubs on them as you change gear. Once the metal gets thinner, it bends easily.

SERVICING A FRONT DERAILLEUR

Step 1: Take a good look at the position of the derailleur before you remove it to make it easier to replace later. Cut off the cable end, saving as much as possible of the cable to make it easier to refit once you've finished. Turn the pedals and use the left-hand shifter to change gear into the smallest chainring at the front. If you've not got the bike up on a work stand, get a friend to lift the back wheel off the ground.

Step 2: Undo the cable clamp bolt and release the cable completely. Pull gently on the end of the cable and click the left-hand shifter all the way across its range and back to the slackest position. It's worth doing this before you start. If the cable doesn't move smoothly, cleaning up or replacing the derailleur won't solve the problem and you'll have to replace the cable as well.

Step 3: You can only clean the derailleur properly if you remove it from the bike, but the chain runs through the middle of the derailleur cage. Get it out by removing the bolt holding the back of the cage together, as shown. However, on cheaper derailleurs the cage is riveted rather than bolted. In this case, you are forced to split and rejoin the chain. This is less than appealing because splitting it always leaves a weak spot.

Step 4: Use a crosshead screwdriver to remove the bolt. Once you've got it out, keep it somewhere safe. They're very small (so easy to lose) and an odd size (so hard to replace). Ease the back of the derailleur cage apart and slide the chain out of the gap. Take care not to bend the metal of the cage as you spring it just far apart enough to get the chain out of the gap.

Step 5: Locate the bolt that straps the front derailleur to the frame. It may be on the far side of the frame or tucked up next to the cage on the chainset side. The bolt will almost always be a 4 or 5mm Allen key. Remove the bolt completely and then pull the two halves of the band that straps the derailleur to the frame apart. Remove the derailleur completely. Clean the newly exposed area of the frame.

Step 6: Clean the entire mechanism thoroughly using a toothbrush to get into all the gaps and a degreaser to shift stubborn dirt. Once it's really clean, drip a drop of oil onto all the pivots and wipe off any excess. Fold the band back around the frame, securing it loosely. Don't refit the cable yet. Use the instructions on page 155 to position the front derailleur correctly first. Tighten fixing bolt securely.

Cable care

Check casing regularly for cracks and kinks. Damaged casing should be replaced straight away before it splits and leaves you stranded miles and miles from home.

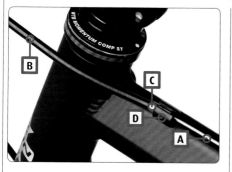

◎ **A) Cable:** the wire that connects a shifter or lever to the component. It's usually silver.

◎ **B) Casing:** the cover that supports and guides the cable.

◎ **C) Ferrule:** a metal or plastic cap on the end of the casing, which prevents the end of the casing from splaying out under pressure.

◎ **D) Cable stop:** this is the part of your frame that the outer casing slots into. A slot in the cable stop allows you to slide the cable out of the cable stop for cleaning.

◎ **Cable end:** a small metal cap that you squash over the end of the cable to prevent the cable fraying.

◎ **Nipple:** the blob on the end of the cable that fits into the lever or shifter, stopping the cable from pulling through.

The outer casing used for gears is different to the casing used for brakes:

◎ Brake casing is always made from tight spirals of square section wire.

◎ Gear casing is made from round section wire, formed into much longer spirals. It is covered in plastic (usually black), which protects the wire and keeps it in shape and lined with a second Teflon tube (usually white), so that the inner cable moves smoothly inside.

The casings differ because they perform different functions. Brake cable must be very strong, because it handles a lot of pressure. Gear cable must transmit a very accurate signal. When you shift from one gear to the next you pull only through millimetres of cable, so it is vital that the gear casing does not compress and

influence the cable as you change gear or turn the handlebars. The long spirals prevent the gear casing shortening under pressure or as the sections of casing articulate with the bike.

The advantage of the tight spiral wind-in brake casing is that, while it is strong, when it fails it does so gently. Gear casing cannot take as much pressure, but that's all right because gear levers are short so you can't exert much pressure on them anyway. When the casing does fail, it tends to be catastrophic as the casing splits open and you get no shifting at all. Were this brake casing, it would be bad news because it is likely to break under a strong braking force, i.e. when you need it most.

Getting the cable and casing right is a cheap task that greatly improves your bike. It's worth changing the last section of outer casing on your rear gear cable – the piece that takes the cable into the rear derailleur – every time you change the inner cable as it's nearest the ground. More expensive derailleurs have a boot (rubber gaiter) protecting the end of the cable, and so stay cleaner, but this piece of cable costs so little in relation to the importance of smooth changing, that changing it remains worthwhile anyway.

The casing is really tough so you need proper wire cutters to chop it to length – pliers won't do. It is important to cut the ends neatly and squarely. If you cut ragged or at an angle, the casing deforms as you change gear, making your shifting sloppy. Once you've cut the casing, check inside that the lining hasn't got squashed. If it has, open it out with the point of a sharp knife. Finish off each end of each length of casing with a ferrule. These protect the ends of the casing and stop them splaying out.

Getting exactly the right length can be tricky. If the casing is too long, it adds friction to the cable, which again means sloppy shifting. The spring in the derailleur has to pull the slack that is created when you release cable at the shifter all the way back to the derailleur, so the less friction here the better. If the casing is too short, the inner cable will be constricted as it goes around tight bends. Care needs to be taken with sections of casing that join parts that move relative to each other such as the section of casing that joins the handlebars to the frame and the frame to the derailleur. Dual suspension bikes need extra care with the sections that connect the main frame to the rear end. Make sure you have enough casing to allow suspension to move without stretching the casing. Ghost shifting is often caused by casing that is restricted or stretched. Replace these sections of casing every time you replace the inner cable. When the casing is the right length, it approaches the cable stops parallel to the frame and looks elegant.

Splitting chains

Every time you split and rejoin your chain, you risk making it weaker, so try not to split it unnecessarily. Leave it intact whenever you can.

It's best to leave your chain on the bike when cleaning it. Similarly, when fitting a new derailleur, take the derailler cage apart and reassemble it around the chain rather than breaking it and feeding it through the cage of the new derailleur.

Chains are split by pushing out the rivet that holds two adjoining links together. There's a specific tool that does this, called a chain

tool. It's designed to support two adjacent chain plates while pushing the rivet out. It is important to do this carefully so as not to create a weak point which will break later under pressure.

Shimano chains need to be treated differently; you cannot refit a rivet once you've pushed it out. See page 160 for instructions on dealing with Shimano chains.

USING A CHAIN TOOL TO SPLIT A CHAIN

Step 1: Lay the chain onto the chain tool on the set of supports furthest away from the chain tool. Screw in the handle of the chain tool. As you turn it, the stud on the chain tool approaches the chain. When it gets close, line up the stud precisely with the centre of the rivet on the chain.

Step 2 Carry on turning the handle and you'll see that the tool begins to push the rivet through the chain. It's important not to push the rivet all the way out because you'll struggle to get it back in. With a Park tool, keep turning until the handle of the tool jams on the chain tool body. With other tools, turn until the amount of rivet poking out is slightly shorter than the width of the chain – you need about 1mm left in there.

Step 3: Once you think you're there, check. Unwind the tool out of the chain. Flex the chain as shown in the picture and push away with your thumbs. Ideally, you should have to push it a little bit before you can pull the two halves of the chain apart. This means you have left a little stub of rivet poking out of the inside of the chain plate, which you can use to relocate the rivet once you come to rejoin the chain.

Powerlinks

Powerlinks allow you to split and rejoin chains without tools. Identify the Powerlink – it may be a different colour to the others and will have a key-shaped hole around the rivet. Push the links on either side of the Powerlink towards each other. You may also need to squeeze the plates of the Powerlink together from the sides. This can be a little tricky, but once you've got the angle right, the Powerlink rivets should pop back into the inner parts of the key-shaped hole, allowing you to pull the Powerlink apart sideways.

To rejoin, fit one of the pieces of Powerlink into each end of the chain, facing in opposite directions. Pull the two ends of the chain together and overlap the Powerlink pieces. Push the ends of the rivets through the hole in the opposite plate and then pull the joined halves of the chain away from each other to lock the Powerlink in place.

Powerlinks let you split and rejoin chains without tools

Rejoining chains

Rejoining is slightly more complex than splitting. One end of the chain has the rivet you're going to reuse sticking outwards.

There should be a small stub of this rivet left inside the outer chain plate. You're going to have to use this stub to relocate the chain so that the rivet fits into the rivet hole in the other end of the chain.

Once you've finished rejoining the chain, you'll usually find that it's a little bit stiff and needs flexing.

The thing is that each link needs to be able to rotate freely around the rivet that joins it to the next link. And the problem is that rejoining the chain can ofen mean that the links are squashed together.

Check a rejoined link by wiggling it. If it doesn't move as smoothly as its neighbours, see 'dealing with stiff links' below.

REJOINING CHAINS

Step 1: The two ends of the chain have to be eased back together. The end with a rivet sticking out has to be snapped over the other end. There should be a little stub of rivet sticking through the inside face of the outer chain plate, so you'll have to flex the chain slightly as shown. Once you've slid the two ends together, the stub of rivet should snap into place.

Step 2: Back the handle of the chain tool right off by unwinding it and place the chain back into the set of supports furthest from the handle. Wind the handle inwards, pushing the rivet back through the chain until an equal amount of rivet shows through either side of the chain.

Step 3: If you find you've gone slightly too far, take the chain back off the chain tool, turn the chain tool around and approach again from the other side. Once you've finished, check that the link that you've just rejoined moves as flexibly as all the others. There's a fair chance it might now be quite stiff – if so, see below from step 2.

DEALING WITH STIFF LINKS

Step 1: To locate the stiff link, lean your bike up. Pedal slowly backwards with your right hand and watch the chain as it feeds out of the bottom of the cassette around the jockey wheels and off the bottom of the bottom jockey wheel. Stiff links will skip over the jockey wheels, rather than passing smoothly around them. Once you spot one, keep pedalling and allow the chain to pass slowly through your fingers – you'll feel the stiff link.

Step 2: Once you've found the stiff link, lay the offending rivet over the chain tool on the supports nearest the handle. Wind in the handle until it lines up exactly with the centre of the rivet and touches it. Carefully wind the handle in a third of a turn and then back it off and test the link. If it's still stiff, repeat, but turn the tool around so that you approach from the other side of the chain.

Step 3: If you don't have a chain tool, hold the chain in both hands with the stiff link in the middle. Put both thumbs on the stiff link and flex the chain gently backwards and forwards. You should feel the stiff link gradually loosen off. Don't overdo it though, as you don't want to end up twisting the chain.

Shimano chains

Shimano Chains need to be treated differently to other chains. It's worth checking whether yours is a Shimano – they're often fitted as standard on new bikes. They are very tough and make your gear changes feel very smooth, but are not designed to allow the chain rivets that hold the links together to be pushed out and reused.

The original rivets are made to be exactly the same size as the holes in the chain plates, which means that they have to be installed with enormous force and accuracy – far more so than you have hope of applying with a hand-held chain tool.

This makes the chains very strong, but if you were to try to reuse an old rivet you'd find that it wouldn't press easily back through the chain plates. Usually, you'll find that, instead of reseating itself neatly in the chain plate hole, it tears the hole open, mangling the link beyond repair.

Luckily, Shimano have come up with a way of dealing with this problem: they make a special chain replacement pin. It's twice as long as you'd expect a rivet to be.

The first half is slightly narrower than the chain plate hole and acts as a guide. The second half is the full diameter of the hole and so is pushed into place with a chain tool as normal. Obviously, this leaves the guide part of the replacement rivet sticking out, which then has to be snapped off with pliers.

One of the rivets on your chain is the original joining link that was fitted when the bike was first assembled. You mustn't split the chain again at this link. You can identify it easily as most of the links have words printed around the

rivet, specifically 'Shimano'. The original joining link has no words printed around it, so you know to avoid it.

Also avoid splitting the chain in the same place twice. Any previously replaced rivets will have smoother heads than the rest, so you'll be able to pick them out fairly easily by cleaning off a few adjacent links. As long as you choose a different place every time, you can split and rejoin the chain as many times as you like.

Shimano chains are not designed to be used with Powerlinks or any other kind of split link, so, if you have a Shimano chain, it's worth obtaining and carrying around one of the special replacement pins. They weigh almost nothing, but if you need one, nothing else will do. Use gaffer tape to stick one to the underside of your saddle, so that it's always there when you need it.

Eight-, nine- and 10-speed chains are different widths and so need a different length replacement pin. Even though the difference in lengths is minimal, they're not interchangeable. New chains come with a spare replacement pin in a little plastic bag that's easy to lose as it's quite small. You can also pick them up separately from your bike shop.

REJOINING SHIMANO CHAINS

Step 1: Lay the chain on the set of supports furthest from the handle. If you have a Shimano-specific chain tool, it may only have one set of supports, so use that one. Wind the handle of the tool inwards so that the stub on the tool approaches the chain. Line the stub up precisely with the rivet and keep winding the handle in, so you push the old rivet all the way out of the chain.

Step 2: To rejoin the chain, push the two ends together so the holes in either end line up. The replacement pin is in two halves, with a groove between them. Push it all the way through the chain. Start it by hand then, using the chain tool until the groove and a sliver of the second half of the pin re-emerge from the other side of the chain.

Step 3: Use pliers to snap the guide end of the pin off at the groove. Look carefully at the link you've just installed – the same amount of rivet should stick out from either side. Use the chain tool to even up the rivet. You may now find the link you've just joined is stiff. If this is the case, go to step 2 on page 159, dealing with stiff links.

Chain length

The correct chain length is essential. Your chain needs to be long enough to reach around a large chainring at the front and a large sprocket at the back at the same time. If it's too short, disaster happens when you try to shift into this gear. The chain will not reach and will jam halfway through the process of lifting off one sprocket and on to the next, possibly throwing you off your bike and usually tearing off either your derailleur or the part of the frame it attaches to.

In an emergency, it's acceptable to shorten the chain more than you would normally do – for example, if one of the links becomes twisted and you have to remove it.

But it's not a long-term solution. Even though the gear is not one you'd normally use – there are other ratios that will give the same gear – it's too difficult to remember not to change into it accidentally. Once the potential is there, you find yourself inexorably drawn to the forbidden gear.

Chains that are too long have a similar effect. If you shift into the small sprocket/small chainring combination, there's too much slack chain hanging around. Your rear derailleur copes with excess chain by folding the tension (lower) wheel jockey backwards. Too much extra chain means that the tension jockey folds so far backwards that the chain is in danger of getting entangled in itself, once more jamming the chain and potentially breaking the rear derailleur.

Mountain bikes and hybrids tend to have a wider gear range than road bikes. The sprockets are more widely spaced and there

are usually three chainrings rather than two. This means that derailleurs designed for these types of bikes have a longer cage, so that the tension jockey can move further back, taking up more slack. Road bike derailleurs are more compact, making them lighter and neater, but won't cope with such a wide range of gears.

It's a common misconception that problems with slipping gears caused by a worn or 'stretched' chain can be solved by removing a few links from the chain.

Sadly, although this is a simple procedure, it doesn't work. Worn chains slip over worn cassettes because the distance between each rivet has become longer, so that the link no longer meshes neatly with the valleys between each link in the cassette. Taking links out of the chain will do nothing to solve this problem. The shorter chain will skip just as much as before, and the rejoined link will be weakened and so is more likely to snap. If your chain is worn, it – and most likely the cassette as well – will have to be replaced.

SORTING OUT CHAIN LENGTH

 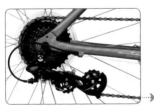 

Step 1: This chain is too long. It's easiest to see this when the chain is in the smallest sprocket and the smallest chainring. Look at the chain as it wraps around the derailleur. The cage has folded up on itself, so much so that the lowest stretch of chain almost touches the section of chain that wraps around the guide jockey. There is a risk that the two parts will snag, jamming your transmission.

Step 2: This chain is too short. It will only just reach around the largest chainring and the largest sprocket. If you need to remove a link for any reason – for example, because one of them has become twisted – you'll be left with a chain that doesn't reach.

Step 3: Just right: the chain still has a little extra bounce, even when it's in the largest chainring and largest sprocket. Even if you have to remove a link in an emergency, there will be enough length left. But there isn't any more slack than the derailleur can cope with.

Cassette overview

Cassette is the general word for the collection of sprockets that sit in the middle of your back wheel. They're also known by a handful of other terms such as sprockets, block and cluster. The way they work is straightforward: the chain meshes with the teeth on the sprockets, pulling the wheel around as you pedal.

The cassette fits into the splined freehub body

much quicker than the ratcheting mechanism, but them being one unit means that both must be replaced at once.

The other advantage of the cassette system over the older freewheel system is that the wheel bearings on the wheel sit at the outboard end of the cassette, near the frame. This makes the axle less likely to break and reduces wear on the bearings. The axles on freewheel type wheels had a tendency to bend or even break under heavier or stronger riders – something you very rarely see with the axles on cassette–type wheels.

The two systems are not compatible and a wheel made for a freewheel cannot be converted for use with a cassette wheel.

The original cassettes were seven-speed. When eight-speed transmission came along, the freehub body had to be made longer to accommodate the extra sprocket, so seven-speed cassettes won't fit on eight-speed freehubs. However, the changes to nine- and then 10-speed were made the other way, leaving the sprockets (and the gaps between them) narrower in order that they can fit into the same space.

This means that 10-speed chains are narrower than nine-speed ones, which are in turn narrower than eight-speed ones, so chains cannot be swapped between transmissions with different numbers of gears.

There is a minor triumph in the compatibility department as almost all cassettes are made to fit onto the same pattern freehub body and so are compatible between different makes. Almost all doesn't mean all, however, and the exception in this case is Campagnolo. Its cassettes and freehub bodies are of a similar design and are fitted and removed in the same way, but don't quite fit and need their own cassette-removing tool to do the job.

Cassettes will last much longer if they're kept clean. Dirt on the surface of the sprockets will get trapped under the chain and will quickly abrade the narrow profile of the teeth, changing their shape so that they no longer mesh neatly and securely with the chain.

The cassette is the set of sprockets which is connected to your back wheel via a freehub body. The freehub body is normally hidden from view and you hear it much more than you see it. The visible part – the cassette – slides over the freehub body on a series of grooves, which mean that as you pull the chain over the cassette sprockets the freehub body and the wheel turns. But there's a ratchet inside the freehub body as well so that, if you turn the cassette the other way, the cassette turns but the wheel doesn't. This allows you to freewheel. If the ratchet wasn't there and you tried to stop pedalling, the spinning wheel would mean that the cassette would keep spinning, which would mean your pedals would keep turning. When you freewheel, the clicking noise comes from the pawls of the ratchet flicking back against the inside of the freehub body.

There's an older system that you may still come across and is still used on cheaper bikes, called a 'freewheel'. These look very similar from the outside, but instead of the cassette and freehub body being separate units, they're combined into one component. This is a bit of a waste because the teeth on the sprocket wear out

Removing and refitting cassettes

Your cassette will wear with your chain, so generally they must be changed at the same time. Worn cassettes allow the chain to slip over the sprocket teeth.

Getting cassettes on and off requires a couple of specialist tools, and unfortunately they're the kind that aren't really useful for anything else at all. A chain whip is basically a metal bar, with a short length of ordinary chain riveted onto one end. This is used only when you take the cassette off and is essential to stop the cassette rotating on its own ratchet when you try to undo the lockring. The second

specialist tool is a splined driver, that meshes into the splines in the lockring, and has flats so that you can get a spanner onto it.

The type of splined cassette-remover you need depends on whether you have a solid rear axle, with nuts to bolt it onto the frame; or a quick-release axle, with a hole through the middle that your quick-release lever fits through.

REMOVING CASSETTES

Step 1: Remove your wheel from the bike. If it has a quick-release lever, hold onto the side with nuts and unwind the lever side until the nut falls off the end. Remove the whole skewer, catching and keeping the little springs as they come off. If the axle has nuts, remove the right-hand nut and any washers. Slide the splines of the remover tool into the splines in the lockring, pushing the tool firmly home.

Step 2: Stand the wheel up in front of your feet with the cassette facing away from you. Take the chain whip in your left hand and lay the section of chain over the top of the cassette, so that the handle is facing out horizontally to your left. Fit the spanner over the removing tool so that it sticks out horizontally to your right. Once you've got both secure, push down firmly on the spanner and the chain whip.

Step 3: The lockring will make a horrible crunchy noise as you free it. This is normal, so don't worry. Remove the lockring completely. You'll now be able to slide the cassette off, by pulling it outwards away from the wheel. The part that this reveals is the freehub body. Have a play with it – turn it one way, it will spin the wheel. Turn it the other – the wheel stays still and the ratchet makes that familiar clicking noise.

Refitting the cassette

Refitting is much easier than removing. Clean off the splines on the freehub body and, if you're refitting an old cassette, do the same to the splines on the inside. The cassette is usually in two parts – most of the sprockets joined together in a single block with the smallest one or two loose. Look at the cassette and the freehub body – in both cases, you'll see that one of the splines is narrower than the others. Match up the narrow spline on each, and slide the main block of sprockets over the freehub body. Follow it with the loose sprocket(s), taking care to line the narrower spline on the freehub body with that on the sprocket. There may also be a thin, spindly washer. If you have

one of these, look carefully at the loose sprockets. You'll see that one of the sprockets is slightly narrower than the others. Insert the washer onto the freehub body under the thinnest sprocket, so that the spacing between each sprocket is equal. Take particular care when fitting the final, smallest sprocket – it's a bit fiddly to align.

Screw the lockring on. Start it by hand: the threads are very fine, and it's easy to crossthread it by mistake. Finish it off by refitting the removing tool and tightening it with a spanner. You'll hear it crunch again as you tighten. Again, this is fine. Refit nuts and washers, or quick-release skewer and springs, and refit wheel.

163

Chainset removal

Chainsets have to be removed to access the bottom bracket or to replace individual chainrings. You'll need a special tool for this – a crank extractor.

The crank and chainset fit onto opposite ends of the bottom bracket axle and there are two different styles – square taper and splined (circular with ridges along it). Both styles are removed and refitted in exactly the same way, but need different-sized tools. If you're not sure which type you have, you'll have to remove the crank bolt and look into the hole where you'll see the end of the axle. If it's square – like the one in the picture below (step 2) – you'll need the smaller tool. If it's circular – like the one in step 1 on page 165 opposite – you'll need the larger-sized tool. The chainset is removed using the same procedure as the left-hand crank, but take extra care not to slip and catch your knuckles on the chainrings.

REMOVING CRANKS AND CHAINSETS

Step 1: Look at the centre of the crank. You may see an Allen key, the head of a nut or a flat plastic cover. If it's a plastic cover, lever it off. This should reveal the nut head underneath. Remove the nut with a 14mm socket. The Allen key will normally be 8mm, but may also be 7mm or 10mm. Use the appropriate tool to remove the bolt. Get rid of stray washers or dirt over the end of the axle.

Step 2: Look into the hole where the bolt came out of and check that you have the correct crank extractor (see above). Hold the outer part of the tool and turn the handle or nut end of the inner core. You'll see that, as you turn in either direction, the inner core moves in and out of the outer part of the tool.

Step 3: Back off the inner core of the tool as far as you can, so that its head is flush with the end of the outer part of the tool.

Step 4: Screw the outer part of the tool into the crank, starting by hand as the threads in the crank are very soft and fine and will be damaged if the crank tool goes in wonky. It may take a couple of goes to get it in there straight. Once it's going in straight by hand, finish it off with a spanner so that it's firmly bedded into the crank.

Step 5: Screw the inner part of the tool into the outer part. It will be easy to turn at first, but then it will come up against the end of the axle and get a lot harder to turn. As you continue to turn the inner part of the tool, it's going to push the end of the axle out of the crank. Take care here as, once it starts to move, the tool will give suddenly. Line it up so that you don't catch your knuckles on the crank or chainrings.

Step 6: Once you've started the crank moving on the axle, give the tool a couple more turns and the crank will come off easily in your hands. To get the tool off the crank, retract the inner core into the outer part first, by unwinding the handle and then unscrewing the outer part from the crank. Repeat the same procedure for the chainset.

Refitting the chainset and crank

Refitting the chainset and crank is slightly easier than removing them – or at least not quite as scary since you don't have to go through the part where you have to push really hard on the tool and hope that the axle comes off the crank, rather than the tool pulling out of the crank threads. The key here is cleaning the old parts off and checking you've got everything aligned correctly.

If you're replacing both bottom bracket axle and chainset at the same time, you won't have a cleaning issue. If you do, take a bit of time getting the interface between the two parts really clean as any grit trapped between them will prevent the two surfaces from locking together, which will mean they rock over each other as you pedal. It's amazing how quickly this can cause irreversible wear.

Compatibility between chainsets and bottom brackets can be tricky to work out. If you're replacing a chainset with one of exactly the same type, you should have no problem. However, different makes and different models within makes require a different-length bottom bracket axle, so that the chainset sits the correct distance out from the frame. If the chainset sits too far away it will cause clunky shifting across the chainrings. Too close can be even worse: when there isn't enough clearance between the chainset and the frame, the inner chainring will rub on the frame under pressure and cut through it. If you're in doubt about the compatibility between your old chainset and a replacement, get your bike shop to give you a second opinion.

Before you start refitting the crank and chainset onto the axle, clean off the outer surfaces of the axle. These often get caked in dirt, so scrub it off with degreaser and an old toothbrush. Do the same to the holes through the crank and the chainset. Inspect all surfaces closely for damage.

Square tapers should be clean and flat with no sign of distortion at the corners. Round, splined axles shouldn't have notches or tears in the splines.

Clean off the crank bolt too. If it's got an Allen key head, pick out any dirt so that the tool will fit as deep as possible into the bolt head. Check for washers as any that came out from under the bolt will need to be replaced. Square taper axle bolts don't usually need a washer, but splined axle bolts often come with one. It may be wedged onto the bolt, just under the head to stop you taking it off and losing it. If a washer came off when you removed the bolt, make sure it goes back when you refit it.

The pictures below show a splined axle – the procedure is just the same for a square taper axle.

REFITTING THE CRANK AND CHAINSET

Step 1: Start on the chainset side. Line up the axle with the chainset and push it on firmly. Take particular care with splined axles. The chainset needs to be pushed firmly onto the axle, so the splines on the axle lock securely into the grooves in the chainset.

Step 2: If it's an Allen key head, clean out the head of the bolt so that when you come to tighten it, the tool will sit all the way into the bolt. Pop some grease on the threads of the crank bolt. Grease under the head of the bolt as well. If there were washers under the bolt head when you took it off, replace them. Splined axle bolts often come with a very slender one that needs a bit of grease on either side. Screw the bolt into the axle.

Step 3: The bolt has got to be done up really tight (if you have a torque wrench it's 50 Nm). Line up the Allen key so that it's almost parallel to the crank and tighten them against each other. Take a bit of care here as it's easy to get overenthusiastic and let the Allen key slip in the bolt. Avoid this as you'll skin your knuckles on the chainrings. Repeat on the other side, taking care to line the cranks up so they face in opposite directions.

Chain and chainring wear

Your chain is under constant pressure as you pedal. New chains are exactly the right size to mesh with the teeth on your sprockets and chainrings.

Gradually, however, the chain stretches so that the gap between each link grows. Eventually, the distance between each link is enough to allow the chain to slip over each tooth instead of meshing securely with it. This is bad news. It happens when you're putting most pressure on the pedals when the last thing you want is for the chain to slip and suddenly there's no resistance.

The chain and cassette on a bike will wear at the same rate, so by the time the chain is stretched enough to slip, it will have worn the cassette out too. You'll have to replace this at the same time. If you stick a fresh chain over a worn cassette, the cassette will wear out the new chain in no time, wasting your money. You'll definitely need to replace both at the same time.

THREE WAYS TO MEASURE CHAIN WEAR

Option 1: A chain-measuring device is the quickest and most accurate way to measure chain wear. The best ones are made by Park Tools and come with an easy-to-read dial. Buy one as they save you time and money.

Option 2: Alternatively, measure 12 links of the chain. On a new chain, this length will be exactly 12 in. If it's 12⅛ in or under, you can change the chain without changing the cassette. Any more and you'll have to change both at once.

Option 3: You can still get an idea of chain stretch without using a chain-measuring device. Put the chain in the biggest chainring and the smallest sprocket. Hold the chain at the 3 o'clock position on the chainset and pull it outwards. If the bottom jockey wheel of the rear derailleur moves in response, it's time for a new chain. If you can pull the chain off enough to see a whole tooth, then it's time for a new cassette as well.

Chainring wear

Every time you stand up on the pedals and stamp up a hill, accelerate away from the lights or even try to pick up a bit of speed when you're loaded down with shopping, you're dragging the chain forward by rotating the chainrings. Each tooth on the chainring takes your full force in turn and this will eventually wear them out.

A worn chainring (B) will cause your chain to wear prematurely. When your chainring is crisp and new (A), the profile of each tooth is even and each tooth is tall enough and broad enough to support the link of chain that's wrapped around it. This means that, under pressure, the chain is supported by several teeth in a row. As the chain stretches and the gaps between each chainring tooth gets bigger, the chain will find itself being supported by just one tooth at a time, which will wear that tooth very quickly, stretch the chain further and accelerate the whole process.

Compare your chainrings to those in the picture. Shallow valleys and teeth with pointed tips are signs that the chainring is worn out. The middle ring will usually suffer most as it's used a lot and wears faster than the large one because the pedalling force is shared between fewer teeth.

A

B

Replacing chainrings

Chainrings need to be replaced if they start to look like those on page 166 or if your chain skips across the teeth under pressure.

The teeth that wear fastest are those under the most pressure — the ones at the top and bottom of the chainring when the cranks are horizontal. If your chainring teeth are worn sharp or the faces of the teeth are splayed outwards, replace the chainring.

Bent teeth will catch on your chain as you pedal, preventing the chain from dropping off the chainring at the bottom of each pedal stroke. This doesn't necessarily mean you need a new chainring.

Remove the chainring as below and clamp it flat in a vice. Support the chainring as near as possible to the bent tooth and ease it gently straight with pliers. Try to do this in one movement since sawing the bent tooth back and forward will weaken it.

REPLACING CHAINRINGS

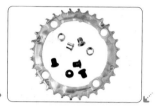

Step 1: The smallest chainring must be removed first. Rest the chainset on a workbench or the floor, protecting the teeth of the largest sprocket with cardboard. Use an Allen key to undo all the bolts on the smallest chainring a half-turn and then go around removing them completely. Look at the orientation of the small chainrings. It should have a size or make printed on it. Make a note of whether this points in or out.

Step 2: Undo the Allen keys holding the middle and outer rings a half-turn each and then go back around and remove them. Be careful undoing these bolts as they are hard to shift and then give suddenly, so mind your knuckles. An Allen key does the job, but sometimes the nut on the back of the chainring moves around. A special tool called a chainring bolt tool is made for holding this, available from bike shops.

Step 3: As you remove the chainrings, note their orientation. There will often be a tab on the middle chainring and a peg on the outer chainring. Both of these will have to line up with the crank when you refit the chainrings. Check which way the chainrings face as the middle chainring may have plates riveted to the inside face. Check also to see if there are any washers between the chainrings as you will need to replace these correctly.

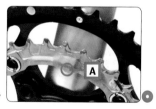

Step 4: Clean the chainrings and check them for wear. You put most force on your pedals when your cranks are horizontal, so the two areas of chainring at 90° to the crank will wear fastest. Hooked or pointed teeth like the ones in this picture will not mesh properly with your sprocket. This chainring will need replacing. Take worn chainrings with you when you go to buy new ones, so that you can match up the bolt pattern.

Step 5: Clean the crank (especially the arms that the chainrings bolt onto) and clean out the bolt holes. Clean any of the old rings that you reuse. Check them carefully for bent teeth or teeth that have splayed under pressure. Bent teeth can be carefully bent back, but the alignment is critical, so take your time about it. Splayed teeth are a sign that the ring needs to be replaced.

Step 6: Reassemble middle and outer chainrings. Get the orientation and position right by lining up chainring tabs (A) with your cranks. If your crank has a chainring bolt underneath it, orientate the chainring so the tab is directly opposite the crank. Refit any washers. Grease the bolt threads and refit one at a time. Tighten each one firmly, but don't go mad. The bolts snap if you overtighten them. Refit the smallest chainring.

Fitting rapidfire shifters

Shifters do wear out over time. The clicks become less distinct, leading your chain to wander vaguely over your cassette, rather than dropping precisely into the gear you've chosen. Shifters will also snap or bend in crashes. Luckily, they're relatively easy to replace, although you don't want to be doing it too often as the units aren't cheap.

New shifters almost always come supplied with a new cable already fitted into the shifter, which saves you some trouble. Take a little care with it to make sure the cable doesn't drag on the ground when you're fitting the shifter, picking up dirt from your floor. Take care also with the cable just as it emerges from the shifter. It's a bit vulnerable to being bent or linked until it's safely installed inside some outer casing. Keep it coiled up until you're ready to fit the casing.

Also consider fitting new outer casing whenever you fit new shifters. Sometimes it comes supplied in the box with the shifters, but if not, get a length of it so that you can cut off the sections you are going to need. For not a lot of extra cost, outer casing will make your new shifters feel much better. You'll need good-quality wire cutters to trim the casing to length. Buy a roll a couple of metres long, so that you can cut the lengths you need. It's better value than trying to buy outer casing in pre-cut lengths, which are always slightly too long or slightly too short.

Shifters come in two types. Integrated units consist of the brake-lever and shifter combined into one unit. They're slightly lighter and slightly cheaper than a separate brake-levers and shifter. Separates can be adjusted independently on the handlebar, so that you can find a comfortable position and so that they can be replaced individually if they don't magically both wear out at exactly the same time. Either way, shifters come in pairs and your chances of being able to replace just a left or a right are very slim.

The key when replacing shifters is not to scratch your handlebars, either when getting the grips off or when sliding the shifters/brake-levers about. This is not an aesthetic consideration as the parts you're working on will be covered up by the grips when you've finished anyway. It's more that cracks grow from scratches and you definitely want to avoid cracks growing invisibly under your grips.

Sticking grips back on must be done with care. The last thing you want is to get up off the saddle and find your grip comes away from the bars. Everybody has their own recommendation for this such as hairspray and Renthal grip glue (from motorbike shops). If you don't have access to these, leave the grips in a cup of hot water for a couple of minutes before you fit them, obviously taking care not to burn yourself. Don't use spray lubricant as the grips slide on easily, but they slide off easily too.

FITTING RAPIDFIRE SHIFTERS

Step 1: Start by peeling back the inside edge of the grip. Get something soft under there to lift the grip up. A chopstick is ideal, but if you don't have one, use a screwdriver with care. Ease the end of the chopstick under the grip and squirt some light oil under there. Work the chopstick deeper under and around the grip and then pull it off the bar. Resist the temptation to cut off old grips since this will definitely scratch the bar.

Step 2: Undo the bolts holding the brake-lever and shifter (or combined unit) and remove them completely. Slide a screwdriver into the gap in each clamp and twist it slightly. This should open out the clamp enough to enable you to slide the lever or shifter right off the bars. Brake-levers can be left connected to their cables but you may have to turn the bars so there's enough slack to pull them off the ends.

Step 3: Slide the new levers on in the same way, opening the clamps slightly as before. Leave them hanging loosely and then sit on your bike and find a comfortable angle. You should be able to reach the levers comfortably and quickly. Slide your grips on (see above for tips) and then replace the clamp bolts and tighten them securely. Now see page 138 for fitting rear gear cables and page 150 for front gear cables.

Fitting twistshifters

Twistshifters feel great when new and are instinctive to use: you don't have to take your hands off the bars to change gear. The problem is that they need so little thought to operate that you barely notice them becoming less distinct. Once they get sloppy, your transmission will start to wear. Instead of sitting neatly on a sprocket, your chain will start to wander over your cassette, rubbing away and changing gear randomly. Fit new shifters before this starts to happen!

Secure the shifters so they don't roll about on the bars

The majority of twistshifters are made by SRAM. They make many different models at different prices and generally shifters that cost more will give you crisper shifting for longer. There is an important compatibility issue with rear gear shifters. The shifter must pull through an exact amount of cable every time you click through a gear. The standard amount is set by Shimano and SRAM make many shifters compatible with Shimano rear derailleurs. All of these shifters have names like 'rocket' or 'MRX'. In addition, SRAM make a range of derailleurs that need more cable to pull through every time you shift – these and the matching shifters all have numbers like '7.0' and '9.0' instead of names. All named shifters can be used with all Shimano rear derailleurs and all SRAM-named rear derailleurs. Numbered SRAM shifters can only be used with numbered SRAM derailleurs. Front shifters are easier as all front shifters work with all derailleurs.

As with any of the work you do on your bars, the key is not to scratch your bars as you fit and remove grips and shifters. Scratches on the surface of the metal that the handlebar is made of create a weakness that can grow into a crack which can cause your handlebar to break. It doesn't happen very often, but it's not worth encouraging.

The stationary grip, the part on the outer end of your bars that stays still when you change gear, is shorter on bikes with twistshifters than it is on bikes with triggershifters. This means the bars have less grip length and grips will need to be replaced fairly regularly. Grips that twist around on the bars are dangerous since, if they slide off the end of the bar suddenly, you may lose control of the bike when you least need it. Sometimes a new shifter comes with a new stationary grip – if so, use it. Otherwise, you can buy new special short grips or use normal-length ones cut down with a pair of scissors or a sharp knife.

To remove the old shifters, slide something soft like a chopstick under the inboard end of the stationary grip. If you're going to discard the grip, you can spray a little light lubricant like GT85 or SuperSpray under the gap, work the chopstick around and under the grip and pull the grip off the end.

There's a flat plastic washer between the stationary grip and the shifter so pull that off too. The shifter is clamped onto the bar with a small Allen key in the thickest part of the shifter. Undo this a few turns and slide the old shifter gently off the end of the bar. Slide the new shifter on in its place.

Hold the stationary grip up to the space left on the end of the bar and check there's enough room for it. If not, undo the clamp that holds the brake-lever on to the bar. Move the brake-lever and shifter inwards to make more space.

The last thing you want is part of the grip hanging off the end of the handlebar. Replace the plastic washer and then slide the new (or reused) grip into place. Make sure it's stuck properly. Use hairspray or hot water to slide it on – never use spray lubricant. Push the shifter up to the grip so that there's no gap. Find a comfortable position for the brake-lever. You should be able to reach it comfortably and quickly while riding along. Firmly tighten the brake-lever clamp. Twist the shifter around, so that the barrel-adjuster sits just under the brake-lever, but leave enough room so that you can turn the barrel-adjuster. Tighten the Allen key that clamps the shifter to the bars. Try twisting the brake-lever, shifter body and grip to ensure they're secure. Now, you'll need to fit the derailleur cable – see page 138 for rear derailleurs and page 150 for front derailleurs.

Hub gears

Hub gears have gone through all the highs and lows of fashion during the last few decades. There was a time when they were the only sensible choice for town bikes, propelling deliveries, shoppers and tourers alike. The unquestioned favourite choice was the Sturmey Archer three-speed hub, which could be relied upon to work fine for years under a regime of neglect and would last for decades if an occasional teaspoon of 3-in-1 was poured into the oil port on the hub.

Each one was stamped with the month and year of manufacture and it's not uncommon to come across hubs from the 1930s still happily chugging along. But with mountain bikes, emerged a desire for more and more gears and suddenly bikes with only three fell out of favour. Bikes with a plethora of close ratios made the big gaps between three seem clunky. Sturmey Archer, based in Nottingham, upped and sold all its machinery to the Far East and it seemed like hub gears were history.

But all was not lost. Some aspects of hub gears are just too attractive to ignore, especially for around town. Having a single chainring at the front makes it easy to fit an effective chainguard, reducing the amount of chain oil on your clothes. The city is also a particularly harsh environment for exposed gears, which tend to pick up all the nasty chemicals that get spat out of the back of cars in traffic and use them as a grinding paste, reducing expensive derailleur components to waste within a couple of thousand miles. Derailleurs also have plenty of delicate dangly bits, which don't respond well to being tangled up in big piles with other bicycles. So there are a lot of good arguments for tucking the complicated gear mechanism away inside the hub.

There is also a spectacularly bad argument for using hub gears, which is that they don't need any maintenance. While it may be true that they need a lot less attention than derailleur bikes, it's expensive to completely ignore them. Most damage is done when they get ridden around out of adjustment. The internal gear mechanism is made up of lots of tiny cogs and pawls. When these are all correctly aligned, they wear very slowly, but slight misalignments can cause rapid wear. This is where the problems start – as they wear, the cogs generate lots of tiny flakes of metal. Since the hub is enclosed, these have nowhere to escape to, and so travel around the internal mechanism, wearing away everything they come across. However, adjusting your hub to run smoothly has been made very simple and can usually be done with no tools at all. The most important thing is to be alert to possible problems. If your gears start to feel sluggish, don't change as quickly as you're used to or start changing randomly as you're riding along, check the adjustment straight away.

There are other simple procedures that can also be carried out without special tools. Changing the sprocket is not nearly as complicated as it looks. It's a good idea to change the sprocket every time you change the chain, since they wear together and putting a new chain on an old sprocket will wear your nice new chain very quickly.

Another good reason to change the sprocket on your hub is to change your range of gears. You can't change the gap between each gear as this is determined by the internal mechanism, but you can change where the range starts and finishes. Changing your sprocket for a slightly larger one will make all the gears slightly lower. The gaps will remain the same, but each one will be easier.

Changing the size of the sprockets also affects chain length. Minor changes – say one tooth more or less – can usually be accommodated by shifting the rear wheel backwards or forwards in its dropout (since you don't have a derailleur to take up the slack, this is the only way of ensuring the correct chain tension). If you're fitting a smaller sprocket, you can shorten your chain slightly. A larger sprocket will require a longer chain. It's usually more successful to fit a complete new chain than to try to add links from another chain as the uneven amount of wear in the links means the chain will be unlikely to mesh smoothly with the sprocket or chainrings. Luckily, decent chains for hub gear bikes are around half the price of a similar-quality derailleur chain and last twice as long. They don't have to move sideways across a cassette or chainset and always run in a straight line from sprocket to chainring.

Hub gears are also an excellent choice for folding bikes with small wheels because the absence of a derailleur means there's less to get caught up when you're collapsing or reassembling your machine. Keeping all the oily messy gear parts inside the hub makes you a more popular commuter too, being less likely to leave black stripes on other people's luggage in crowded train compartments. As well as the more traditional three-speeds, seven- and eight-speed versions have a wide enough range of gearing to get you up and down most hills. A 14-speed hub, by Rohloff, gives as wide a range as you'd get with a triple chainset, with smooth, close gaps between each gear.

Adjusting hub gears

Keeping hub gears adjusted correctly is the single most important piece of maintenance you can do to them. You'll most likely feel it if the adjustment starts to drift out and your bike may even take it upon itself to start shifting randomly when you least expect it. Be alert for any changes in the quality of your shifting and re-adjust sooner rather than later. Badly adjusted hubs will wear very quickly, requiring the replacement of expensive internals.

If these simple adjustments fail, it almost always indicates that some of the internal workings of the hub are already badly worn and will need to be replaced. This is the kind of fiddly job it's worth having your bike shop do – mainly because the range of different hubs has grown to such an extent that ordering exactly the right spare parts can be a bit trial and error.

These instructions are for the 2006 Shimano eight-speed hub, but the general principles apply across all their hubs. All Shimano hubs have one common method of adjustment. The cable starts at the shifter on the handlebar and ends at a cassette joint on the right-hand side of the hub. Shifting gear pulls the cassette joint around the hub in distinct steps, corresponding to the number of gears. One of the gears is always marked differently on the shifter. The number may be written in a different colour or have a circle around it. Set the shifter in this gear to adjust the cable tension.

The cable is the correct tension in this gear when the two halves of the cassette joint – the odd-shaped collection of plates that sits in the middle of the back wheel, between the sprockets

and the frame – line up. They're made with coloured tabs, so that you can get the alignment right.

These tabs can sometimes take a little bit of finding as they're quite small and can be covered in road dirt. They may simply be short fingers of metal marked by a red stripe or they may be concealed beneath a tiny plastic window on the cassette joint. Once you've found the tabs, lining them up is simple. There will usually be a barrel-adjuster on the shifter – turn this and experiment to find out which way brings the tabs further apart and which way brings them closer. The alignment needs to be precise, with the two coloured tabs in as straight a line as possible, so you'll find yourself making quarter- and even eighth-of-a-turn adjustments to find the right place.

There are two possible locations for the barrel-adjuster. It may be on the shifter, where the cable emerges, or on the other end of the cable near the rear wheel. You may even have one at either end. It doesn't make any difference which one you use, but if you've got a choice, use the one near the rear wheel, since it's easier to see the adjustment tabs from there.

ADJUSTING SHIMANO 8-SPEED HUBS

Step 1: Here you can see the number 4 on the shifter is written in red. This indicates that the hub should be adjusted with the shifter set to this position. This is the most common way to pick out the right gear to do the adjustment in, but another possibility is that the chosen gear may have a circle around it. Twistshifters work in exactly the same way – just set the shifter so that it's lined up with the differentiated number.

Step 2: This view is looking down from above into the gap between the rear hub and the frame. In this case the tabs are underneath a clear plastic window – you'll have to wipe the window clean of road dirt before you can see the tabs clearly. Older hubs have two small exposed fingers of metal with a red stripe painted on each. You can see here that the two stripes are not in line – the right one is slightly lower.

Step 3: If you look at where the cable emerges from the shifter, you'll see the barrel-adjuster, which alters the tension in the cable. Turn the barrel-adjuster gently, while looking down into the gap and watching the tabs. You'll see them move relative to each other. It's not worth trying to remember which one has what effect – just turn so that they get closer, rather than further apart. When they're exactly lined up, stop.

Removing hub gear wheels

Hub gears often make people particularly nervous about the possibility of having a rear wheel puncture. Follow the instructions below and you needn't worry.

It's isn't always particularly obvious how to disentangle the gear cable enough to get the back wheel on, or how to reattach the gears once you've successfully repaired the puncture.

It's a little different to the procedure for derailleur gears, but luckily can be done with a minimum of tools. The main difference between hub gears and derailleur gears is that the gear cable is actually attached to the rear hub, so it has to be wriggled free before the wheel can be removed.

Be warned though, there's a slight added complication when refitting the wheel too – the position of the rear wheel in the frame needs to be set in such a way that the chain has the right amount of tension.

REMOVING THE REAR WHEEL OF A SHIMANO NEXUS HUB

Step 1: Take a moment to look into the gap between the rear wheel and the frame while you change gear. You'll be able to see the cassette joint stepping around the hub as you shift gear. Once you can see the effect that changing gear has on the cassette joint, set the shifter so that the cable is in its slackest position, where the indicator is pointing at gear 1.

Step 2: This is the most important step and the one that everybody misses out. It's essential that, when you come to refit the cable, it's correctly routed. However, once everything's come apart, it's not obvious how it goes back together. Take a moment to look at the cassette joint from behind and trace where the cable goes, so that you can put it back there later. If you haven't got a photographic memory, make a sketch.

Step 3: Look at the cassette joint from behind. You'll see a tiny hole, just below the cable clamp bolt. It's just the right size for a 2mm Allen key. Poke the key into the hole and use it as a lever, gently turning the cassette joint anticlockwise to create slack in the cable. It can be tempting to do this with your fingers, but don't as the spring inside the hub is strong and, if you slip, you'll definitely end up with sore fingers.

Step 4: Keep the Allen key in position, holding the cassette joint. This gives you enough slack in the cable to pull the gear outer casing gently to the right and out of the end of the cassette joint, as shown. There should now be enough slack to pull the inner cable out of the slot in the cassette joint. Release and remove the Allen key.

Step 5: You should now have enough slack in the cable to allow you to wriggle the cable pinch bolt completely free of the cassette joint. Note which way it sits before you release it so you can get it back into the same place afterwards. You'll have to use both hands to twist the cable, easing the pinch bolt out of its slot. Take care not to kink the cable.

Step 6: This leaves the gear cable completely free of the back wheel. With V-brakes and cantilevers, release the brake cable. If you have hub brakes, remove the bolt that holds the hub brake arm onto the frame/fork. It's essential to remember to refit these when you come to refit the wheel. Undo the wheel nuts on either side of the frame and slide the wheel forward and out of the dropouts.

Refitting the rear wheel

Refitting the back wheel simply means reversing the removal procedure. It's worth checking the gear alignment, as the cable may settle into a slightly different place.

It only takes a moment at the end of this process to reassure yourself that the adjustment is correct. In the unlikely event that the adjustment has slipped, it will save you the damage that riding on slipping gears does to them and to you.

The key to refitting the back wheel is to get the chain tension correct before you start messing around with the

gears. Chain tension is automatically sorted out for you with derailleur gears as the rear derailleur takes up any excess slack in the chain.

With a single sprocket, you have to do this as you refit the wheel. It is for this reason that hub gear bikes (and single-speed bikes) have a horizontal dropout (see toolbox on page 174).

REFITTING THE REAR WHEEL

Step 1: Hold the wheel in the back end of the frame between the chainstays and loop the chain around behind the sprocket. Pull the back wheel back into the dropouts. If you removed any nuts and washers, replace them. On many Shimano hubs, these will be left- and right-specific with a tab that sits in the dropout to hold the axle at the correct angle. Locate the washers neatly in the dropouts. Tighten the wheel nuts by hand.

Step 2: Pull the wheel back in the frame to take up frame slack. It must be straight in the frame, with equal spacing between the tyre and the chainstay on either side. The chain needs to be almost tight. Pedal backwards to find the tightest point and make sure that you can still move the middle of the chain, halfway between the sprocket and the chainring, up and down 1.5cm (½ in). Tighten both wheel nuts securely. Refit brakes.

Step 3: Before you go any further, check the condition of the gear cable. The outer casing should be free from splits or kinks and should be long enough so that you can turn the bars in both directions without stretching it. Check that the cable pinch nut is tight on the cable. You'll need two spanners: one to hold the back still, the other to tighten the nut on the front.

Step 4: Before fitting the cable back into the cable stop, take the cable pinch nut and fit it back into the cassette joint. It will only fit into its nest at one particular angle and you'll have to roll it slightly further anticlockwise than you'd expect. Seat it securely and then route the cable back around the back of the cassette joint. There will be a groove for it to sit in. It should follow a straight path down and around.

Step 5: As and when you removed the cable, pop a thin Allen key into the hole in the cassette joint and roll it around anticlockwise. This should give you enough slack to refit the outer casing back neatly into its cable stop. Shift through the whole range of gears and check that the cassette joint moves around with each click.

Step 6: Finally, check the cable tension. In theory, the hub shouldn't need adjusting, but in practice the cable often settles back out of place. This has to be done in a specific gear. Look at the shifter – one of the gear indicator numbers will be a different colour to the others. Shift into this one. Check the gear alignment tabs are lined up exactly. If they're not, use the barrel-adjuster at the shifter, turning it until the tabs are aligned.

Replacing the hub sprocket

While hub gears can get along fine with far less attention than derailleur geared versions, it's a mistake to think that this means that they can be neglected.

Just as on a bike with derailleurs, hub gears mean that you're constantly putting pressure on the chain as you pedal and that inevitably means that the chain, sprockets and, to a lesser extent, the chainrings will wear out.

If left for too long, you will reach a point where the chain will slip over the sprockets under pressure. This is irritating at the best of times and dangerous in busy traffic. Chains are relatively easy to replace, but sprockets on the most common hubs are trapped behind a handful of hub-gear specific mystery components. These need a little care to remove and it helps a lot when you come to reassembly if you concentrate on the order and orientation of the parts that come off.

Sprockets are worn when the teeth start to get very sharp or when the two sides of the teeth don't look symmetrical. You may also find that the pressure of the chain on one face of each tooth has caused the surface of the tooth to splay outwards, making sharp lips at either side. It's not worth waiting until the chain links actually starts slipping over the sprocket before you replace them. By that time the worn sprocket will already have started to damage the rest of your transmission.

You'll need a tool that you don't often come across in bicycle repair toolboxes: circlip pliers. These are only useful for one job, which makes them a bit irritating to invest in, but it's difficult to do the job without them. People do improvise with screwdrivers, but it's far too easy to slip and stab your own fingers with the end of the screwdriver. Invest in the proper tool. These come in two variations: external and internal. External circlip pliers prise a circlip off the outside of a tube whereas internal ones lift them out of a groove on the inside of a tube. The kind you need here are external circlip pliers. You can get cheap versions that are supposed to be able to do both, but they're usually fairly wobbly at either end and so quite difficult to use and, if they slip in the middle of getting a circlip off, they'll most likely take a vindictive bite out of your fingers at the same time.

A completely different reason for changing a sprocket would be to alter your gear ratio. The steps between each gear can't be changed as they're determined by the design of the internal parts of the hub. But the entire range of gears can be shifted in either direction, since this is determined by the ratio of the chainring size to the sprocket size. You can change either of these – fitting a larger chainring has the same effect as fitting a smaller sprocket, both will make all your gears a little bit higher. You'll be able to ride faster on downhill sections, but will struggle a little more getting up steep ones.

All the pictures below right show Shimano hubs. They're the most common type, but there are others. SRAM have been making internal hubs for many years, which are reliable and last for many thousands of miles.

The same sprockets fit on both types of hub. SRAM ones are held on by a similar circlip arrangement, but it's easier to get to. The SRAM hubs don't use a cassette joint, so the circlip and sprocket are revealed as soon as you remove the back wheel.

DROPOUTS – vertical and horizontal – the merits and differences

This is one of those terms that sounds more complicated than it is. The dropout is the slot in the frame that the wheel bolts onto – it's the same word for the front and back wheels. Traditionally, the slots on the rear wheel dropout were almost horizontal, allowing you to slide the rear wheel back and forward in the frame. However, this is unnecessary for derailleur gears, since the derailleur takes up the slack in the chain and so vertical dropouts became more common. They provide a very secure fitting, since you cannot pull the rear wheel out of the dropout however hard you stamp on the pedals. This is a particular problem when the wheel nuts/quick-release levers aren't done up tightly enough or break, pulling the back wheel out of its slots and jamming it on the chainstays.

Swapping hub sprockets

Ideally, you should swap the sprocket every time you replace the chain. If you put a new chain on an old sprocket, you'll wear the new chain out fairly quickly.

Sprockets are available in a range of sizes and usually have a slight dish. This means they sit slightly off to one side when you fit them onto the hub. This allows you to line up the sprocket with the chainring so the chain makes as straight a line as possible between the two, reducing the amount it wears. Take note of which way the old sprocket faces when you remove it so you can get the new one back on correctly. There's only one common fitting for the sprockets, making them simple to interchange.

You'll have to remove the gear cable and then the wheel – as on page 172 – to get access to the sprocket. Remove the nut and all washers from the right-hand side of the axle, keeping a note of the order and orientation.

SWAPPING HUB SPROCKETS

Step 1: The cassette joint sits over the centre of the sprocket and so has to come off first. It's removed in layers. Correct removal and refitting depend on lining up a series of dots and arrows on the cassette joint. The first layer is a locking ring. It comes off anticlockwise. Steady the cassette joint by holding the cable stop and turn the lockring gently. It only moves about a quarter-turn and then lifts off.

Step 2: The next layer is of yellow dots. Look carefully at the next layer of the cassette joint and you'll see it's made up of two parts. Both parts have yellow dots printed on them. If there's lots of road dirt floating about, you may have to clean it off. Hold the back of the cassette joint steady with the cable stop and then turn the top layer of the cassette joint until all the yellow dots are aligned. It will now simply lift off.

Step 3: Repeat the procedure with the red dots that are now exposed, taking off the last layer of the cassette joint. Lay the parts out in the order they came off, all facing upwards so that you know how they need to be replaced. Wipe all the parts clean as it makes them easier to get back together if there isn't any grit in between the layers.

Step 4: Next is the tricky bit where you'll need your circlip pliers. Locate the circlip – it's the ring of metal pressing onto the face of the sprocket. It may be a round section or a square section. It doesn't quite make a complete circle. Locate the gap, slip the noses of the pliers into the gap and squeeze the pliers to open out the circlip enough so that you can lift it up off the hub. Don't get in there with your fingers or it will bite you.

Step 5: Before you lift the sprocket off, check which way it faces – it's not usually flat. Now you can lift the old sprocket off and replace it with a new one, facing the same way as before. Line the three lugs on the sprocket up with the grooves on the hub and ease it into place. Lever the circlip back into place with a small screwdriver, keeping fingers well clear.

Step 6: Replace the first layer of the cassette joint, lining up the red dots and wriggling until it fits snugly. Repeat with the yellow dots. Finally, the lockring fits over the top and then twists to lock in place. It only needs a quarter of a turn or so to lock it, but if it won't move, don't force it. Instead, remove and recheck the previous layers fit snugly. Replace washers and nuts and replace the wheel (page 173).

Singlespeed

Riding singlespeed means no complications with gears. You can't ride too quickly, because you run out of faster gears straight away and there's a limit to how fast your feet can spin around. If you have gears, you're tempted to shift up a gear and go faster. But with only one, you are forced to ride round calmly and arrive at places in your own good time, rather than hot and bothered, having just beaten your own personal best time for the journey for no apparent reason whatsoever.

Light, cheap and, above all, simple

You can buy singlespeed bikes off the shelf in a bike shop. You'll probably need to find a small friendly independent dealer rather than a big chain, but there are a few available from some of the big brands, although they're not routinely stocked.

You can also make one out of your normal, geared bike. This has its advantages as a maintenance procedure – it mainly consists of taking parts off your bike and stashing them away to be recycled in a future project.

Shifters, cables, and derailleurs can all come off. Your chainset too. If it has removable chainrings, get rid of all but one of them. The chainring bolts that hold everything together will be too long to hold your now single chainring securely, but luckily they're available in a shorter size too. They're called single chainring bolts and you'll need as many as you have arms on your chainset. If your chainrings aren't removeable, you can either just continue to use the chainring you have, ignoring the chainrings you're not using, or replace it with a single chainring.

Deciding on your gear ratio can be a bit tricky. It's a case of trial and error and working out what feels good to you. You need a gear that's low enough to get you up the steepest hill you normally climb without busting a gut. It depends on a combination of how fit you are and how flat the area you live in is. Once you've got rid of all the other kit, you need to concentrate on the back end

of the bike. If you're converting from a geared bike, you have several potential solutions available to you.

- Simply leave the cassette on the bike, choose a gear that suits you and leave the chain running over that sprocket. With no shifters, the chain will stay put. This is the simplest solution and a good idea on a temporary basis, giving you a chance to experiment with gear ratios.

- Replace your cassette sprockets with a single sprocket and spacers to make up the gap. The DIY version is to use one of the sprockets you've already got and make up spacers from plastic plumbing pipe, cassette spacing washers or whatever else you can come up with. Make sure the washers take up all the available space and clamp it all on with your lockring. There are commercial versions of this such as the Gusset converter, pictured left.

- If your wheel is on its last legs, replace it with one that has a purpose-built singlespeed hub – those made by Surly are great value, but for bling, check out Phil Wood singlespeed hubs.

The shape of your rear dropout determines what you do next. Look at the dropout and work out what direction the wheel moves in when you take it off the bike. If it moves downwards, you have a vertical dropout. If the wheel moves forwards (or even backwards), you're in luck as this is the easiest to deal with.

Vertical dropouts: these mean you need a gadget to take up the chain slack, a bit like a derailleur but without the guide jockey since you don't need to move the chain sideways. These are called singulators – although you can use a normal rear derailleur if you're prepared to be a little bit inventive in getting it to hang exactly under your chosen sprocket.

Horizontal dropouts: these don't need to be precisely horizontal – sloping is fine as long as you can move the wheel back and forth in the frame. This allows you precise control over the chain tension. Pull the wheel back until the chain has about 1.5cm (½ in) of movement at its slackest point. Tighten wheel nuts firmly.

Fixed wheel

The step beyond single speed is fixed wheel. Fixed wheel bikes are similar to singlespeeds in that they only have one gear – a single sprocket at the back and a single chainring – but there is no freewheel in the back wheel. This is the ratchet that you can hear ticking along when you cruise without pedalling on a normal bike. Riding fixed wheel means you have a really direct connection between the pedals and the back wheel and can control the speed of the bike very precisely.

You can slow the bike down just by pedalling more slowly. This feels odd at first. It's very much like pedalling forwards, but you have to put pressure on the pedal when it's at the back of its stroke, rather than the front. Riding fixed takes some practice to do safely as there are a few quirks that can catch you out.

It's often said that, once you learn to ride a bicycle, you never forget. Riding fixed, you have to deliberately unlearn some of the most basic lessons. The trickiest is that you cannot stop pedalling – the wheel will keep on spinning and the pedals are directly connected to it, so they'll keep moving. If you tell your feet to stop, the pedals will catch them and drag them forwards, jerking you with them. This is unsettling – a bit like thinking you've got to the bottom of a flight of stairs and then finding that there's another step. Cornering is another problem area. Cornering at speed usually means leaning into the corner. If you're on a normal bike which freewheels, you can stop pedalling and lift the inside foot up to stop the pedal scraping on the ground. On a fixed model, you can't stop pedalling so you have to judge corners very carefully, otherwise your pedals will slam onto the ground as you lean into the corner and flip you off the bike.

As well as going along and cornering, there's another potential problem as well – stopping. Fixed wheel bikes were inherited from track racing, where fit people on sparse track bikes hurtle round banked wooden tracks at unfeasible speed in the kind of tight bunches that means it's in everybody's interests to stay upright. Brakes in this situation are a liability – as long as everybody is moving at the same speed, there's hope of keeping your place in the pack. The last thing you want is for the person in front of you to panic and haul their brakes on. The gaps between each rider can be inches and there would be no time to take evasive action. Bikes that have been built for the track may not have brakes at all or, if they do, they've just been stuck on there to make the bike legal to sell.

Transferring the bike onto the streets involves different demands. Your biggest danger is a truck turning left in front of you, not the potential for inadvertently bringing down somebody riding right up your tail, so it's essential to fit some properly working brakes. Many people make do with just a front one,

because you can use the pedals to slow the back wheel down. There are occasional fashions among couriers to have no brakes at all, relying on the back wheel alone to stop them.

This is just stupid. It does make the bike look lean and mean, until you wrap it around something you should have been able to avoid. It may then still look pretty if it was a nice colour to begin with, but it won't work very well. Fit proper brakes.

You can buy a track bike off the shelf, or make one by removing all unnecessary complications from a suitable geared bike. The one essential requirement for a conversion is horizontal dropouts for the rear wheel. You have to be able to shift the rear hub back and forth in the frame, in order to get the chain tension correct. Since most modern frames are built with vertical dropouts, this restricts you to old road frames, and newer frames that have been specifically designed for the track.

Track-specific frames will have a narrower spacing between the rear dropouts, to take a 120mm hub rather than the standard road size (130mm) or mountain bike size (135mm). The 120mm size is a much older standard than the others, dating from before the days when it was considered essential to stuff as many sprockets as possible onto the rear wheel.

It's essential to use the right kind of hub with fixed wheel. As well as a normal, right-hand thread for the fixed sprocket, it also has a slightly smaller reverse thread. This is for the lockring. The lockring must be tightened securely against the fixed sprocket, stopping it from unwinding when you put pressure on the pedals to slow down and stop.

It's essential that the threads on the fixed sprocket, the lockring and the hub are in good condition, so that there is no possibility of the sprocket working loose under the constantly reversing pressures from your pedal. Don't be tempted to make up a fixed hub out of a normal freewheel wheel and any likely-looking lockrings you may have lying around – the reverse thread on a fixed-specific hub is essential for holding everything safely together.

It may seem from this that riding fixed is anachronistic and more trouble than it's worth, but it does feel fantastically direct and makes any journey more exciting.

8 – Wheels

The quality and condition of your wheels make more difference to your bike than any other single thing. After all, you only need your gears when you want to change how fast they spin and you only need your brakes to stop, but your wheels are going around all the time you're going along. Treat them right and they'll roll along without complaining. Neglect them and they'll make every climb feel like a vertical wall and every corner feel like you're riding on jelly.

Wheels

Considering how little they weigh, bicycle wheels are incredibly strong. They are built to resist three main forces. When you sit on the bike, the wheels have to support your weight – this is a vertical force. In the same direction – but much stronger – is the force you subject your wheels to when you bump down off a kerb, fill your panniers up or pop your kid in the child seat.

Sideways forces occur if you're moving fast and decide to change direction. Your wheel has to be strong enough to persuade your bike to follow the front tyre without folding up.

The third type of force is rotational – you turn your wheels to make your bike move when it's still and you drag your brakes on rim or rotor to slow yourself down when you're going too fast.

This chapter looks at the elements that make up your wheel – hub, spokes, rims and tyres. Later in the chapter, we'll look at truing wheels and replacing spokes, but we'll start with the centre of the wheel – your hubs.

Bearings have been around since Roman times and appear in working drawings by Leonardo Da Vinci. His design for an early tank featured a device for enabling the gun turret to turn in different directions. He rested the upper part of the structure on a circle of wooden balls that allowed it to turn freely and support the weight (wood isn't the best bearing material, but is still used in cycle track racing rims). The modern ball bearing pioneer was Sven Wingquist, a visionary Swedish inventor who founded the SKF bearing company in 1907. The company still produces quality stainless steel bearings.

The bearings in the centre of your wheels take different forms, ranging from handfuls of cheap steel balls to fancy sealed units, but they all do the same job – keep the wheel securely fixed onto your bike with no side-to-side movement, while allowing it to spin as freely as possible. Well-adjusted bearings run for years without complaint. Bearings that are too loose or too tight slow you down and wear out in no time, so it pays to check them regularly.

Checking your wheel bearing adjustment

Pick up each wheel and spin it gently. It should continue rolling a couple of times on its own, even after a really gentle spin. If it slows down quickly, first check that the brake blocks or pads are not rubbing on the rim or rotor, which can have the same effect as bearings that are too tight. If that's the problem, go to the brakes chapter and sort them out first and then come back

to bearings. If the brakes aren't the problem, then your bearing is too tight and it's slowing you down. Put the wheel down again and crouch beside the bike. Hold the rim of the back wheel where it passes between the stays (seatstays or chainstays on a hardtail, otherwise whatever lies between the main frame and the back wheel). Just pinch the rim between your thumb and finger. Hold onto the nearest bit of frame with your other hand and rock your hands toward and away from each other, pulling the rim toward the frame then pushing it away.

The rim may flex slightly, but that's not what you're looking

Check for play by rocking the wheel in the frame

for. You need to check if there's a knocking feeling or even a clicking noise as you pull the rim back and forth. This indicates movement between the bearings and the surfaces supporting them and means the bearings need adjustment.

Repeat with the front wheel, holding the rim where it passes through the fork and rocking gently across the bike. Again, the rim may flex slightly, but it shouldn't knock at all. The wheel should spin freely, gradually slowing down over a couple of revolutions.

You may also be able to hear the bearings grinding around as the wheel spins, or feel the vibration in the frame. Either of these indicate that urgent bearing attention is needed.

Bearings

The most common type of hubs have cup-and-cone bearings. A cone-shaped nut on the axle traps a ring of bearings into a cup-shaped dip in the hub. The cone can be adjusted along the axle, making enough space for the bearings to spin but not enough for the wheel to move sideways.

The cones are locked into place by wedging a locknut against each one and then tightening the cone against the locknut. The advantage here is that the parts can be serviced and adjusted with a minimum of tools. The other type that you may come across is the sealed bearing type – see below.

The picture on this page shows a hub that's been completely taken apart, so that you can see all the parts.

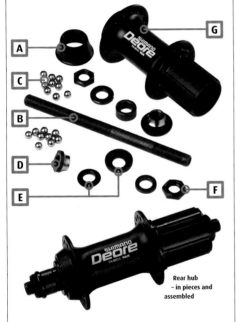

**Rear hub
– in pieces and
assembled**

◎ **A) Rubber seal**. This simply pushes over the locknut. The front hub usually has one on each side and rear hubs just have one on the left.

◎ **B) Axle**. This runs through the middle of the hub and is threaded so that, as you turn the cones and locknuts, they move along the axle, adjusting the amount of space available for the bearings to roll around in.

◎ **C) Bearings**. These are almost always ¼ inch in rear hubs and ³⁄₁₆ inch front hubs. These should be replaced every time you service hubs.

◎ **D) Cones**. These have curved surfaces, so when they're set in position on the axle, they trap the bearings against the hub-bearing surface. Because the cone is threaded onto the axle, as you turn the cone it moves the cone along the axle. This changes the amount of space the bearing has to move in. As you roll the cone inward, it reduces the amount of space the bearings have to move in, tightening the cones. Moving the cone outwards gives the bearings more space so that they can spin freely. The correct adjustment is where the bearings can spin perfectly freely without the hub being able to move sideways on the axle.

◎ **E) Washers/spacers**. The thinnest of these simply help the locknut grip the cone, stopping them from working loose. Fatter ones act as spacers, ensuring that the wheel sits centrally in the frame.

◎ **F) Locknuts**. These are tightened to wedge against the adjusted cone, so that neither can work loose. They have serrations on their outer face to help grip the inside of the frame when the wheel is bolted on.

◎ **G) Hub**. The hub body has holes to lace the spokes through and the rear hub has the freehub body attached, which is the ratcheting mechanism that allows you to freewheel and supports the cassette.

Front and rear hub adjustments

Cones on the front and rear hubs work in the same way with a locknut on either side wedged against the cones, keeping the two cones spaced precisely on the axle so that there is the right amount of space for the bearings to roll around in.

The rear hub is slightly complicated by the drivetrain. The cassette sits on the right-hand side of the hub, obscuring the cone and most of the locknut. For this reason, all adjustments are carried out from the left. Front hubs are simpler in that you can access either side, so it doesn't matter which side you approach from. Since the axle runs freely through the middle of the hub, it doesn't matter which side you adjust the cones on as the axle will settle in a position where there is an equal amount of space for the bearings on either side.

Adjusting front hub bearings

It's easy to neglect your front hub as it's one of those uncomplaining components that carries on working whether you nurture it or not. But don't forget that, whenever you're moving, your front hub is rolling around. A little attention will keep it running smoothly, which will always make you more efficient. If it's properly adjusted, it will take a lot longer to wear out and give up.

Front wheel bearing adjustment can be checked easily, without taking the wheel off the bike. Lean the bike up against a wall. Take hold of the rim with one hand and the section of fork just beside it with the other. Your two hands should now be fairly close together. Now, move your hands gently towards each other and then away from each other, rocking the wheel sideways across the frame. What you're looking for is a knocking or clicking sensation. If the wheel is really loose, you may be able to hear or even see the wheel knocking. It's completely normal to hear a little bit of flex in the wheel as the spokes stretch, but if the wheel knocks, the bearings are too loose. The bearings need to be slightly tightened so that they can spin freely but not move sideways.

As well as checking the bearings aren't too loose you need to check that they're spinning freely. Pick up the wheel and spin it gently. Look first at the brake blocks and check they're not rubbing on the rims. Then roll the wheel around. Even if you spin it gently, it should keep rolling for a couple of complete turns after you've released it. If it grinds to a premature halt, the cones need to be loosened slightly to give the bearings a little more breathing space.

Once you get more familiar with how bearings work, you'll be able to feel something is wrong as you ride along. The first sign your bearings need adjustment comes when you're cornering. The slight space between bearings and their surfaces mean you'll be able to feel a slight hesitation when cornering, as the wheel takes a tangible instant to respond to your handlebars turning.

Getting the adjustment right

The steps below aren't difficult to follow, but it can often take several goes to get the adjustment exactly right. The difference between 'too tight' and 'too loose' can sometimes be as little as a quarter-turn of the cone spanner. It's made more difficult by the need to wedge the locknut firmly against the cone once you've got the cone in place. Irritatingly, this often changes the adjustment. There's no way around this: you'll have to go back and repeat the adjustment. If you find yourself struggling to achieve the correct cone adjustment, you may need to service the hub. Broken or worn bearings will shift about in the bearing races as you roll the axle around.

ADJUSTING THE FRONT HUB BEARINGS

Step 1: Remove the front wheel and take off the skewer or the nuts and washers. Peel off any rubber seals. On either side, the locknut is nearest the end of the axle, with washers/spacers under them. The cones are almost concealed in the hub; only the ends with spanner flats are visible. Take hold of both locknuts and try to turn them by hand. If you can, the hub has been running loose, and will need servicing, not adjusting – see page 184.

Step 2: Starting at the right-hand side of the wheel, slide a cone spanner onto the cone and tighten the locknut down securely onto it as pictured. Slide the cone spanner onto the left cone and hold the cone still. Undo the left-hand locknut a couple of turns. Transfer the locknut spanner onto the far side of the wheel and use it to hold the right locknut and, therefore, the axle still.

Step 3: Make the adjustment on the loose left-hand cone. Turn the cone clockwise to move it into the hub, reducing play in bearings. Move it anticlockwise to make more space for the bearings to spin freely. Once you're happy, hold the cone still and wind the left-hand locknut back up to wedge against the cone. Start by hand, then use the spanner to tighten the cone against the locknut. Repeat adjustment if neccesary.

Adjusting rear hub bearings

Wheel bearings, once adjusted correctly and locked down tightly, should not need regular servicing. They should last for years without having to be opened up or fiddled with. However, it is worth checking them for play regularly since, once the bearings do get loose, they will wear very quickly and soon get to the stage where their movement damages the hub.

If you can catch them straight away as soon as they've developed any play or are dragging, the bearings can be adjusted from the outside without having to take the hub apart. But if they've been running loose for a while, the ball bearings will have worn unevenly and should be replaced – see page 186 for servicing instructions. A service is also needed if you find yourself struggling to get the adjustment right. If the bearings or cups are worn, the 'perfect' position will vary as you rotate the axle, so you'll think you've got the adjustment just right and then find that the axle wobbles or binds as soon as you turn it.

You'll need a special spanner for cone adjustments. The cone is mostly concealed inside the hub, leaving just a little bit poking out for you to work on. Cone spanners are very thin so they fit into this gap. They come in different sizes, but the most common are 15mm for rear hubs and 13mm for front hubs. Although there's a cone on either side, you can adjust and service your hub with just one cone spanner. Since the axle runs all the way through the hub it doesn't matter which side you work on as the axle will pull through the hub of its own accord and settle when there's an equal amount of bearing space on either side. Don't use cone spanners for anything else as they're so thin that they get damaged quickly if used to remove other things like wheel nuts. The locknuts, which hold the cones in place, are more exposed than the cones, and can usually be turned with a standard spanner. The most common size is 17mm.

These pictures below are just of the hub – without rim, spokes, or cassette so that you can see both sides of the hub at once. When you come to work on your bike, you'll have the whole wheel in front of you. Before you start adjusting the cones, remove your wheel. If you've got a quick-release hub, take the skewer off. If you have an axle with nuts, remove the nuts that clamp the wheel onto the frame and any washers that sat outside the frame. The cassette can stay on for simply adjusting bearings, although it has to come off for hub services. See page 163.

As with front hub adjustments, it can often take several tries to get the bearing position right and to get it to stay that way when you tighten the cone against it. Leave plenty of time to do the job – it does get easier with practice.

ADJUSTING THE REAR HUB BEARINGS

Step 1: If the left locknut is covered by a rubber seal, peel it off. Looking from the left end of the axle, nearest the end is the locknut, under which are any spacers, then the cone – most of which is hidden inside the hub. Get hold of the left locknut and the right locknut on the far side of the hub. Try to undo them with your fingers. If they move, the hub has been running loose and will needs servicing – see page 186.

Step 2: Use a cone spanner to hold the left cone still. The flats are narrow so a normal spanner won't fit. Undo the locknut a couple of turns. Transfer the spanner to the right-hand locknut and use it to hold the locknut and therefore the axle still. Turn the left cone to adjust play in the bearings – clockwise to move the cone into the hub and reduce play, anticlockwise to move it out of the hub and reduce resistance.

Step 3: Once you've found a place where there is no play at all, but the axle still spins freely, tighten the locknut down onto the cone. Start by hand and then use both spanners to wedge the cone firmly onto the locknut. Test the adjustment and repeat as necessary. It may take several goes to get the right place. Once you've got it right, replace seals, nuts/washer or quick-release skewer, cassette and replace wheel.

Front hub service

If you're tackling hub services for the first time, the front hub is the best place to start. It's much simpler than the rear since you haven't got the cassette to worry about.

Once you've got the hub open, it has to be cleaned and inspected for damage to the bearing surfaces. The ball bearings themselves don't need inspecting – they should be replaced routinely – but the bearing surfaces are a different matter. Both the inner surface of the hub and the cones need to be free from pits. If the cones have pits, they can be replaced. Be sure to take the old cone to the bike shop with you to match them up as there are a huge number of different sizes and shapes and they have to be an exact match. It may be cheaper to buy a whole new axle if both cones are worn. In some cases, the cones are not separately available, so this is the only option

Pits on the hub surface are a different matter. Normally, the ⊘

FRONT HUB SERVICE

Step 1: Remove the front wheel. If it's got a quick-release axle, remove the skewer and the two little springs that sit on either side of the hub. If it's got nuts, remove the nuts completely, along with any washers that sat outside the frame. The hub may have rubber seals on both sides, covering the locknuts etc. If so, peel them off carefully – try to do it with your fingers to avoid tearing them.

Step 2: Looking from the end of the axle, the first thing you see is the locknut. Under that will be any washers and under that the cone. You won't be able to see the entire cone as most of it is hidden inside the hub. Slide a cone spanner onto the left-hand cone. Use an ordinary spanner on the left-hand locknut – it's normally 15mm. Holding the cone still, undo the locknut and remove it completely. Pull off any washers.

Step 3: Transfer the locknut spanner to the right-hand side of the hub and use it to hold the right-hand locknut and therefore the axle still. Undo the left-hand cone and remove it completely. Pull the axle out completely from the right-hand side of the hub, catching any ball bearings that come out with it.

Step 4: Use a small screwdriver to extract all the bearings from both sides of the hub and count them so that you know how many to put back in there at the end. Clean the bearing surface thoroughly – cloth twisted around a screwdriver is a great way to get in there. Use degreaser for stubborn bits. Don't worry about cleaning the bearings. It's too difficult to tell if they've worn evenly, so they should simply be replaced.

Step 5: Leave the right-hand cone and locknut attached to the axle for now and clean and inspect the cone-bearing surfaces. A narrow worn track is fine as long as it's even, but pits mean the cones must be replaced. You'll have to take the old cones with you to the bike shop to match up new ones. If there are pits worn in the bearing surface of the hub, that's more serious – get it to the bike shop for a second opinion.

Step 6: Pitted cones must be replaced. If the right-hand cone is worn, it will have to come off the axle. Note how much axle pokes out beyond the locknut. Hold the cone steady and remove the locknut. Pull off any washers, wind off the old cone and replace it with a new cone. Replace washers and then wind on the locknut until the stub of axle showing is the same size as it was. Thread the cone along the axle to butt up to the locknut.

hub surface is the hardest-bearing surface and wears the least, but it's the most expensive to replace. The bearing surface is an integral part of the hub and cannot be replaced separately. Worn surfaces usually mean a new wheel. If you find any, take your bike along to the bike shop for a second opinion. It's tempting to believe that small pits don't matter, but any irregularity that you can feel on the bearing surface is cause for concern. You can't do this job without a special cone spanner – they're narrower than standard spanners to fit into the narrow gap between the locknut and the hub.

The locknut, which wedges against the cone to stop it from working loose as you ride, will usually take a standard spanner, rather than needing a special cone spanner. Common sizes are 15 and 17mm. Ball bearings for front hubs are almost always the

same size, 3⁄16 in. There are different qualities available. Standard bearings are good enough for most hubs, but if you want to add a little bit of smoothness to your bike, get some 'grade 25' bearings. They look very much like the normal ones, but are rounder, so last longer, make your hubs easier to adjust, and reduce damage to your hub bearing surfaces. They're usually about twice the price of standard bearings, but they're so cheap compared to most other parts of your bike that it always seems worthwhile. And while you're there, a tube of nice bicycle grease will last you years, since you need so little of it. As well as keeping everything running smoothly, good grease is quite sticky, making it easier to keep all the bearings under control as you assemble the hub components.

FRONT HUB SERVICE cont.

Step 7: Whether you replaced the cone or not the right-hand cone needs to be tightened against the right-hand locknut. Hold the cone steady and wedge the locknut onto it firmly. Now's a good time to wash your hands before you start playing with new clean grease and bearings.

Step 8: Dry the hub bearing surfaces and then pack clean grease in on both sides. There needs to be enough so each ball bearing will sit in grease up to its middle. Pack bearings in on top of the grease. There need to be the same number on each side and there should be a small gap at the end as bearings need breathing space. If you find they keep dropping out, reclean and dry the bearing surfaces.

Step 9: Feed the axle through from the right-hand side of the hub, taking care not to dislodge any bearings. Once it's through, trap it by winding the left-hand cone (cleaned or replaced) onto the axle. Wind it in until it just touches the bearings – you should still be able to spin the axle freely. Feed the washers onto the axle and then the locknut.

Step 10: Now, you need to adjust the position of the cone, so that the axle can spin freely, but can't wobble from side to side at all. Since the right-hand locknut is firmly wedged onto the axle you can hold the axle still with the locknut spanner on the right-hand locknut. Use the cone spanner to tighten or loosen the cone. Check for sideways play by rocking the axle from side to side. Check that it spins freely.

Step 11: As you look at the left-hand end of the axle, turning the cone clockwise will tighten the cone, eliminating excess space between the bearing surfaces and the bearings. Turning the cone anticlockwise will loosen the cone, allowing the axle to spin more freely. As you make these adjustments, remember to hold the right-hand locknut steady.

Step 12: Once you think you're close, tighten the left locknut down onto the cone and then lock the cone and locknut tightly together with both spanners. Check the axle for play again. This bit can be quite frustrating as tightening the two together often throws the adjustment off and you may have to loosen the locknut off and re-adjust several times.

Rear hub service

Rear hubs take plenty of punishment as they carry most of your bodyweight along with everything you lug about in your panniers.

In addition, you're constantly driving them forward with your pedals, and holding your wheel at an angle every time you lean into a corner. So it's not surprising that the bearings don't last for ever. You'll be able to pick up indications of a loose bearing fairly easily – the first sign of any problem is being able to pull your wheel across sideways at the rim, creating a knocking that

you can feel or hear. Your first response should be to adjust the cones which may have worked loose. But if the bearings have become damaged – broken or worn out of shape – you'll struggle to adjust the bearings correctly. This is a sign that you need to disassemble the axle, clean the bearing surfaces, and replace the ball bearings with fresh ones.

REAR HUB SERVICE

Step 1: Remove the wheel and quick-release skewer or nuts and washers. Take the cassette off – see page 163 for instructions if you've not done it before. Look at the left-hand side of the wheel – you will normally see that the locknut and cone are covered up with a rubber seal. Peel this off carefully. You may have to lever the edge up gently with a small screwdriver.

Step 2: Look carefully at the exposed left-hand end of the axle. Outermost is a locknut, which holds everything in place. Under this may be washers/spacers, then the cone – you'll only be able to see part of it, the rest is concealed by the hub. Hold the cone still with a cone spanner, then loosen and remove the locknut. Remove all washers/spacers.

Step 3: Now, swap the lockring spanner to the lockring on the right-hand side of the wheel. Use this to hold the axle still. Keep the cone spanner on the left-hand cone and use it to wind the cone off the axle. Line up the cones, spacers and locknut so that you keep them in the right order and separate from the parts that you're going to take off the other end of the axle. Draw the axle out of the hub from the right-hand side.

Step 4: Cleaning and inspection time. Clean the axle with the right-hand cone, locknut etc still attached. Clean the parts that came off the left-hand side. Remove all the bearings from the hub, counting them as they come out. Clean the bearing surfaces in the hub and the cups. Get right in there by wrapping kitchen paper round a screwdriver. Inspect all the bearing surfaces.

Step 5: If the cones have any pits, they have to be replaced. The right-hand cone must be removed from the axle. Before you take it off, note how much axle sticks out beyond the end of the locknut. Hold the cone steady on the axle with the thin cone spanner and then use the locknut spanner to wind the locknut off. Then remove any washers etc and the cone. Take old cones to your bike shop to size up replacements.

Step 6: Wind the right-hand cone onto the axle from the same end it came off and then slide on the washers and locknut. Set the locknut so that there's as much axle poking out beyond it as before. Wind the cone up to it, hold the locknut still and firmly tighten cone and locknut against each other. Grease the cups, then pop back in as many ¼ in bearings as came out – usually nine on each side.

Once you've got the hub apart and clean, you'll be able to see the bearing surfaces. The first parts to wear are normally the cones, which thread onto the axle. They need careful inspection once you've got them out and have cleaned them. The constant rotation of your wheels will wear a track in each cone as time goes by. You'll be able to see it quite clearly.

As long as the track is smooth, and not too wide, the cone can be reused. If it's wider than 2mm (1/12 in) or has any pitting at all, it will need to be replaced. Take the old one along to your bike shop so that you can get the correct replacement. There is a profusion of different shapes and sizes. Once you've checked the cones, you'll need to inspect the cups, which are the bearing surfaces inside the hubs. Pits in the cups are serious, and usually

mean a new hub or wheel. If you find any, take the wheel to your bike shop for a second opinion. Luckily, the cones are deliberately made slightly softer than the cones, so wear faster because they're easier to replace.

The pictures on this page just show the hub, without rim and spokes, for clarity – you'll be working on the whole wheel, spokes and all.

But you'll need to have removed the cassette – it's not impossible to service the hub without doing this, but it's very frustrating. See page 163. As with adjusting the cones on your rear wheel, you'll need a special, narrow spanner to adjust the cones. Rear hubs almost always need a 15mm cone spanner. The locknut is usually 17mm and a standard spanner will fit.

REAR HUB SERVICE cont.

Step 7: Slide the axle with its tightened-on locknut, washers and cone into the hub from the right-hand side. Take care not to dislodge your newly fitted bearings as they have a habit of escaping into the cavity in the middle of the hub. The cone should almost disappear into the hub, under the freehub body.

Step 8: Hold the right-hand side of the axle still by gripping the locknut with your fingers. Wind the new or cleaned left-hand cone onto the axle. Roll it right up to the bearings, so the cone traps the bearings, but not so tight that the axle can't spin freely.

Step 9: Refit the spacers in order, followed by the locknut. Tighten the locknut down by hand so that it wedges against the spacers. Then fit the cone spanner onto the cone and use that and the locknut spanner to wedge cone and locknut firmly against each other.

Step 10: Now test the adjustment – it's rarely right first time. Hold the wheel so that the left-hand end of the axle faces towards you and rock the end of the axle gently from side to side while holding the wheel still. There should be absolutely no play at all – you should not be able to move the axle from side to side. Then try spinning the axle – you should be able to roll it between your fingers with little or no resistance.

Step 11: If the adjustment is not yet perfect, hold the left cone still and undo the lockring a couple of turns. Transfer the lockring spanner over to the other end of the axle, and use it to hold the right-hand locknut – and therefore the axle – still. Adjust the left-hand cone. Turn the cone clockwise to tighten and reduce knocking, anticlockwise to loosen so that the axle spins more freely.

Step 12: Then, holding the cone still in its new adjustment, transfer the locknut spanner back from the right-hand to the left-hand locknut and tighten it against the cone. You may have to repeat the process several times and sometimes tightening the locknut against the cone changes the adjustment. Persevere as you will find the right place. If necessary, replace any rubber seals, the cassette and the quick-release skewer or nuts.

Tyres for the city

Your tyres are the only part of your bike that touches the road. When you actually start to think about it, the contact patch – like your brake blocks – is frighteningly small, in some cases only a couple of thumbprints. These tiny patches of rubber have to transmit the force of your pedal strokes to propel you along, steer you around corners in all kinds of loose and slippery conditions and bring you to a swift, controlled stop at the drop of a hat. So it's worth spending a little time thinking about them and paying them a bit of attention.

Puncture resistance

The single factor that's encouraged so many people to get back on their bikes in the last few years hasn't been fancy gears or radical frame materials/design – it's been an unseen strip of puncture-resistant material woven into the fabric of tyres, under the tread. A puncture-resistant strip will stop the majority of nasty little sharp things worming their way through to your tube. They make the tyre slightly heavier and more expensive, but it's worth it.

Quality

A good-quality tyre will be made of stickier rubber, which lasts longer and grips the road better. You should expect to get around 6,000 miles out of a good-quality tyre as long as it's kept properly inflated and never ridden around when punctured. Cheap tyres tend to wear out more quickly; they last about half as long as good ones.

Pressure

Pressure is critical. The correct amount of air in your tyres is the single thing that makes a difference to how long they will last. The correct pressure is printed on the sidewall of the tyre as it's a legal requirement to include it. There's nothing in the law that says it has to be easy to find, however, so it's normally printed in black on a black background. You'll need a pressure gauge to check the pressures at first. After a while, you get a feel for what the correct pressure feels like when you pinch the tyre, but it takes a while to learn. Many pumps come with a pressure gauge included. These are worthwhile, although the number given by gauges on cheaper mini pumps should be treated more as an indication than an exact reading.

Tread

Contrary to expectations, this is the least important aspect of a tyre designed for road use. If you're riding off road on muddy trails, it's another story since the shape, depth and layout of all the knobbles is critical. But for tarmac you generally just need to maximise the

Smoother tyres mean more grip

amount of rubber in contact with the road, so the smoother the better. On a hard surface, knobbles aren't good as they mean the tyre sits proud of the road and the only contact you'll have is the heads of three or four knobbles at a time. If you're going to be riding on towpaths and the like as well as tarmac, it helps to have a smooth raised central ridge, with knobbles at the side.

Condition

Tyres are in constant contact with the road and we ask a lot of them. It is absolutely inevitable that they will wear out. There are a few things you can do to make them last as long as possible, but don't expect miracles. Inspect regularly and often. If you take a little minute every week to just go round each tyre and pick out any bits of glass or other stuff, you'll halve the number of punctures you have. It takes a while for stuff to work its way through your tyre to the tube and, if you catch it before it gets there, you'll save yourself a tube and some hassle. This gives you an ideal opportunity to keep an eye on the condition of your tyre. Slashes and holes in the surface of your tyre are an ideal shortcut for glass. Once they've begun to accumulate, replace the tyre. The surface of the tyre will start to wear and won't grip as well – replace it as soon as the tread begins to fade.

Rims and rim tape

Rims are one of those boring parts of your bike that you ignore unless something goes obviously wrong, but there are a few points about them to be aware of. Simpler, cheaper rims are U-shaped in cross section. The tyre sits directly in the 'U'. Many new bikes come with this type of rim and they work fine.

If you're after something stronger, box section rims are stronger and more durable. These are deeper than U-section rims with a stiffening rib just under the tyre. Another sign of a good-quality rim are eyelets. Rims are made of aluminium, which is light but relatively soft. A steel eyelet pressed into each spoke hole will spread the pressure from the nipple and provide a smoother surface of the underside of the nipple to turn on. Single eyelets sit on the inner surface of box-section rims. Double eyelets are shaped to spread the pressure over both inner and outer surfaces, making the rim even stronger.

If you're using rim brakes, you need to keep an eye on the braking surfaces – especially if you live and ride in a big city, where pollution tends to cover your rims in black gunk, which is frighteningly abrasive. The surfaces of the rims are not very thick, maybe a couple of millimetres, so it doesn't actually take that long to wear through them. You need to catch this before the rim has got so thin that it is weakened. It's under pressure from the tube inside, so if it gets too thin, it will explode outwards.

Recently, it's become common to add rim wear indicators to rims. These take two forms. The most common is a hole drilled halfway through the braking surface of the rim from the inside. When the rim is new you can't see the hole from the outside, but there's a sticker with an arrow that shows you where the hole is. Keep checking the rim above the sticker. As the rim wears through, it will eventually get to the bottom of the hole and you'll be able to see a little black patch of tyre through the hole – time to replace the wheel. The second common type is a groove milled around the braking surface. The bottom of the groove is a different colour to the rest of the material. If the rim is black, the groove is silver and vice versa. This makes it easy to spot when you've worn the rim away to the level of the base of the groove, because the groove disappears. Check regularly and replace when worn. Make sure you check both sides as they won't necessarily wear out at the same rate.

When your bike or your wheel is brand new, your rim is round and flat. As time goes on, it picks up wobbles and may also get gradually get more egg-shaped. Small variations can be pulled back into shape by altering the tension in the spoke and straightening the rim. This process is called 'truing' the wheel. Bigger bends present more of a problem as if the rim has been badly distorted

the spokes around the bend need to be put under a lot of extra tension to pull the rim back into shape. This area of increased tension unbalances the rim, which will tend to creep out of adjustment ever afterwards. Rims that have been constantly ridden with a little bit of a bend also tend to refuse to straighten satisfactorily.

Rim tapes are the thin strips of material around your rims, inside the tyre and under the tube. Originally, these covered the end of the spokes, preventing them from sticking up through the inner diameter of the tube and puncturing it. Box section rims mean the end of the spoke is concealed inside the box, rather than poking up onto the tube. This doesn't make rim tape less relevant though. The concealed surface of the rim under the tyre has a hole over the end of every spoke, so you can fit and reach the nipple that holds the spoke in place. The tube will puncture if it gets forced into one of these holes, so it's important to ensure the rim tape covers and overlaps the holes. If you've had a puncture, check the rim tape as well as the tyre. Small slivers of spoke hole are the worst as the tube will work its way in there slowly as it gets inflated, so a little bubble of tube gets stuck inside the rim. It will stay there until next time you ride over a pothole, when the sudden increase in pressure will shift the tape, cutting off the bubble and leaving enough of a hole to cause instant pressure loss. The tape needs to sit evenly in the rim well. If it rides up the sides or wavers about across the rim well, the bead of the tyre won't sit evenly on the rim, making you feel like you've got a wobbly wheel, which is very disconcerting.

Box section rims are stronger and stiffer

Truing wheels

Truing wheels is quite contradictory – the concept is quite simple and it needs the bare minimum of tools, but it takes a fair bit of practice to make a decent job of it. It's worth making sure you have plenty of spare time before you try this for the first time as it takes longer than you expect and doing it slowly gives you much more chance of making an improvement. If you hurry, it's far too easy to get confused and start putting more tension in spokes that are already over-tensioned. This is not just frustrating – you can damage the rim, putting permanent bends into it.

The idea with truing your wheel is to obtain a balance in the tension of the spokes so that the wheel is perfectly round and runs in the centre of your frame and fork without the rim wobbling from side to side as it spins.

The best place to start is to spend a little bit of time trying to understand what's going on. It's very tempting just to launch in and start twiddling nipples but don't. Start with the front wheel, because it's easiest to understand. Take off your front wheel, remove the tyre, tube and rim tape. Turn your bike upside down – or put the wheel in a wheel jig if you happen to have access to one – and replace the wheel in the bike. Now, look carefully at the spokes. You'll see that, if you follow each spoke from the rim back down to the hub, neighbouring spokes are connected to opposite sides of the hub. The hub has a ridge on either side with all the spoke holes in it. This ridge is called the flange. The ends of the spokes are curled around the holes in the flange, ending in a head that stops the spoke pulling through the hole. Alternate spokes have the heads pointing in opposite directions, so that half the heads point inwards towards the middle of the hub and half away from the hub.

The bend at the end of the spoke, as well as trapping the spoke in the flange, means that the spoke cannot rotate in the hole. The reason for this becomes clear when you look at the other end of the spoke where it connects to the rim. The rim end of the spoke is screwed into a small nipple, basically a specially shaped nut with four flats instead of the more usual six. The nipple is fitted in through the rim from the outside. You should be able to see the heads of the nipples because you've removed the rim tape.

The heads of the nipples are too fat to pull all the way through the rim, but the part of the nipple with the flats is narrow enough to be accessed whether the tyre is fitted or not. The nipple acts as a nut so that, as you turn it, it screws further onto the threaded spoke. Since the spoke is trapped at the flange at one end and the rim at the other, threading the nipple onto the spoke makes the spoke effectively shorter, tightening it.

This is the key to truing your wheel. Since the spokes are laced to alternate sides of the wheel – left and then right – it gives you precise control over the position of each section of the rim.

As well as ending up round, the spokes all need to be fairly tight. It's no good just looking straight – the wheel has to stay that way, even when you're cornering under load, so the spokes shouldn't be particularly flexible.

If you take a neighbouring pair that are almost parallel and squeeze them together, they should resist. Floppy spokes will allow your wheel to flex under pressure and loads will be borne by small numbers of spokes, rather than being shared between all of them.

The most important piece of advice anyone can ever give you about truing wheels is to proceed slowly and carefully. Of all the jobs in this manual it's the one that needs fewest tools but takes most practice to get right.

A wheel jig isn't absolutely essential , but it makes truing wheels quicker and easier

True wheels: wheel words/ tensioning and truing wheels

When you're done truing the wheel, the spokes must all be tight, so the wheel is strong and perfectly balanced and the rim runs true. The balancing breaks down into four separate operations: correcting the true, the hop, the dish and the tension. Part of the reason that truing wheels has always been considered to be difficult is that adjusting a spoke to correct one of these factors affects all the others. (This can be really infuriating and will require patience on your part to get right.) Here's what these terms mean.

True

The spokes are laced alternately to left and right sides of the hub. For example, a zone of the rim that is too far to the left can be corrected by tightening the spokes that go to the right. Since every other spoke is connected to opposite sides of the hub, this can be broken down into a series of very small steps, always truing just the part of the rim with the worst bulge.

Hop

The rim must be an equal distance from the centre of the hub all the way around. If it isn't, the brake blocks will be hard to set up, you will kangaroo down the road and the wheel will fall apart in no time at all. If a section of the rim hops outwards (i.e. is too far from the hub), it can be drawn inwards by tightening two or four spokes centred around the peak of the hop. Tighten the same number of right-hand side spokes as left. Adjusting the hop always throws the wheel slightly out of true, but try to minimise the effect. It's easier to correct an outward hop where a section of the rim is too far from the hub, than a flat spot.

Dish

The rim must end up centred between the locknuts (A) so that when you put the wheel into the bicycle frame, the rim runs evenly between fork legs, between seat and chainstays or between swingarms. Tightening all the spokes on the right-hand side will move the entire rim to the right, tightening all the spokes on the left will move the entire rim to the left. The rear wheel has a cassette bolted onto the right-hand side

so that the heads of the spokes on that side are closer to the centre of the hub. This means that the right-hand spokes have to be tighter than those on the left in order to keep the rim central – that's why they're more likely to break than those on the left-hand side of the rear hub.

Front disc hubs also have to allow a little bit of extra space on the left-hand side to fit the rotor in, but the dishing required is minor.

Tension

Tension is tricky to get right. You can easily destroy a rim by over-cranking the spoke tension until the rim collapses. For the home mechanic, the easiest way to ensure the tension is correct on the wheel you're building is by comparison with another set. Take hold of a pair of almost-parallel spokes on a completed working wheel and squeeze them. Then do the same with a pair of almost-parallels on a working set. Be sure to compare like with like; front wheel spokes have lower tension than backs and the right-hand side of back wheels has higher tension than the left when the dishing is correct.

Stress relief

When you put tension in the wheel and true it, the spokes can get twisted. Instead of the nipple turning on the spoke thread, it can twist the whole spoke. The tension may look correct, but the first time you cycle down a bumpy road on your newly trued wheel, the twisted spoke will unwind as the tensions in the spokes change and the wheel will immediately drop out of true.

Tightening the spokes

As long as you set yourself up carefully and leave yourself plenty of time to do the work, there's no reason on earth why you shouldn't true your own wheels.

It's easiest if you have, or can borrow, a wheel jig. This is a metal stand that holds your wheel steady by the axle so that you can spin it.

There are two moveable indicators at rim level – one approaching the side of the rim, one approaching the outer surface of the rim where the tyre normally sits. The tyre and tube need to be removed so that you can see what you're doing.

If you haven't got access to a wheel jig, turn the bike upside down, take the tyre and tube off and put the wheel back in the frame. As a last resort, you can use the brake blocks to judge the wobble in the rim, but it makes your eyes go funny quite quickly. A better option is to wrap a ziptie around part of the frame, cut it off fairly short and twist it so that the stray end approaches the rim.

TRUING WHEELS

Step 1: Set the wheel in the jig and spin it. Pluck the spokes with a fingernail. To start the truing process, most of them need to be tight enough to get a note from. If not, start at the valve hole and tighten each spoke a quarter-turn. Repeat until the wheel has some tension. Then you can start truing it. Adjust your side indicator and set it so that, when you spin the wheel, it only touches the side of the rim in one place.

Step 2: Find the centre of the biggest bulge. Loosen the spoke leading to the outside of the bend a half-turn and tighten the spokes on either side a quarter-turn. This won't make much difference, but that's okay. This bit has potential for going horribly wrong, so we take it in very small steps to maximise our chances.

Step 3: Repeat the procedure. Spin the wheel, identify the worst bulge, loosen the spoke at the centre and tighten those at both sides until the wheel moves from side to side no more than 10mm (⅜ in). This can mean working repeatedly on the same area: don't worry as long as you are always attacking the biggest bulge.

Step 4: Once you have the wheel vaguely true, spin the wheel again and check for hops. Move the hop indicator on your wheel jig as close as it will go and watch the gap vary as the wheel turns. Concentrate on areas where the rim hops outwards. As with truing the wheel, always work on the largest hop. When you find it, tighten the two spokes at its centre a half-turn. Repeat until the total hop in the rim is less than 3mm (⅛ in).

Step 5: Dish next. Turn the wheel over in the jig or in the bike without moving the indicators. If the wheel is perfectly dished, the rim sits in the same place again. If it's off to one side, it moves over in the jig. Correct by tightening all the spokes on the outer side one quarter-turn. Repeat until the wheel sits centrally. Continue in the following order: true, check hop, true, check dish, true, etc until the wheel is round, true and central.

Step 6: Relieve the stress in the spokes. On each side of the wheel, look at the spokes – you'll see they divide into parallel pairs. Take each pair in turn and squeeze them together. If they all feel very soft, go around the wheel and tighten each spoke a quarter-turn and then repeat. You need to repeat a true/hop/true/dish/true cycle until you can make a complete circuit of stress-relieving squeezes without affecting the truth of the wheel.

Why spokes break and what to do about it when they do

Spokes usually break as the result of a crash, but they also break from being worn out. When you look at the wheel, it usually has one area with a big buckle in it. Run your fingers over the spokes and it's possible one may come away in your hand.

It's important to deal with it as soon as possible. Wheels rely on even spoke tension for strength. A broken spoke weakens the entire wheel structure, which quickly falls further out of true. Spokes usually break on the right-hand side of back wheels. The back wheel takes more of your weight than the front since you sit almost on top of it. Derailleur gears mean the cassette sits on the right-hand side of the hub, so the spokes on the right approach the rim at a steeper angle. They have to be tighter to keep the rim central in the frame, so they are the most vulnerable to breakage. They are also the most awkward to replace as the cassette has to be removed to fit a standard spoke into the holes in the flange.

The new spoke has to be pretty much exactly the same size as the old one to the nearest 2mm. If it's too short, the nipple will have too few threads to grip onto and you'll have another broken spoke before long. If you can see more than four threads emerging from the nipple when you've trued and tensioned it, your spoke is a little short. In the same way, if the spoke emerges right through the head of the nipple, it's too long – you

can file off the top, but it's annoying. Get a fresh spoke nipple at the same time, rather than reusing the old one – they often, but not always, come with the spoke.

If you find that you break spokes frequently, it's usually an indication your rim is twisted. Once the rim has picked up a permanent bend, you have to put lots of tension in the spokes nearest the bend. Because they're pre-stressed, it only takes a big pothole or extra weight in your panniers to pop a spoke. Once you get to this stage, replace the wheel or get your bike shop to rebuild it on the same hub with new, stronger spokes and rim.

If you have a broken spoke, remove the wheel and then the tyre, tube and rim tape. For rear wheels, remove the cassette (instructions on page 163). Locate the broken spoke and remove it. If it's broken near the head, pull the spoke out through the nipple hole and push the head out through the flange of the hub. If it's broken at the nipple end, push the nipple out and weave the spoke back so that you can pull it out of the hub. You may have to bend it to get it out.

REPLACING SPOKES

Step 1: Measure one of the other spokes to determine the length. Make sure you measure one from the same side of the same wheel as the broken one – lefts and rights can be different lengths. The spoke length is measured from inside the elbow where the head curves over to the very end, which will be inside the rim. Look at adjacent spokes from the outside of the rim to estimate how far they protrude through the rim.

Step 2: It's vital to weave your spokes back in the right order. Look at your hub – alternate spokes are 'heads in' and 'heads out'. Your new spoke must follow the pattern. 'Heads in' is easiest – start from the far side of the hub and post it through the hole. 'Heads out' is trickier – post through the near side of the hub and curve the spoke gently upwards so it comes out above the first spoke-cross on the opposite side of the wheel.

Step 3: Next, weave the spoke to match the pattern on the rest of the wheel. The pattern repeats every four spokes, so start at the empty nipple hole, count three spokes in either direction and look at the next one. Your spoke must match this one. Curve it gently to weave it around. Post the nipple through from the outside of the rim and onto the spoke. Take up the slack with a spoke key, go to page 192 to true the wheel.

9 – Suspension

Suspension makes your ride a lot more comfortable, ironing out both the constant small vibrations from the road surface and occasional bigger shocks as you roll through potholes or bump off kerbs. Suspension relieves strain on your muscles and can often help stop sore arms, shoulders and backs. This means you can go further without getting tired. It gets you places faster, too – the accumulated effect of gliding over many small holes and lumps, rather than climbing over or out of them, speeds you up more than you imagine.

Suspension

There are three main places where you'll find suspension – seat posts, front forks and rear suspension. Where the rear end of the bike hinges, its movement is controlled by a shock unit mounted near the middle of the frame.

The cheapest way of making your ride smoother and more comfortable is a suspension seat post. A telescoping post with a spring trapped between the two parts is simple and will last a while with a minimum of attention. It adds little weight to your bike, typically 300g (10.5 oz). They generally have no adjustment other than the chance to set the amount the post settles under your weight – the sag. Even though this is a simple procedure, nobody seems to bother to do it. Check page 202 for advice.

Next up in price, comfort and complication are suspension forks. These come as standard on many bikes designed for town. They're inspired by the forks designed for use on off-road mountain bikes, but the versions designed for city bikes are simpler with fewer adjustments and refinements. Being less complex, they won't make you a slave to a rigorous maintenance routine – but they'll appreciate occasional attention.

The most expensive is rear suspension where the shock is an integral part of the frame. The rear part of the frame needs to rotate about the front part, adding hinges and bearings that must be inspected, lubricated and occasionally replaced. While rear suspension has become much more popular for mountain bikes, it is not clear-cut whether it's worthwhile around town. Many cheap supermarket bikes have very basic shock units that tend to bounce you up and down rather than absorbing road shock in a controlled way. Generally, the cheapest rear suspension on this type is more trouble than it's worth.

There is – as always – a trade-off somewhere: you can't have the advantages of suspension without a downside. Suspension forks are slightly heavier than rigid, unsuspended ones. This doesn't make much of a difference when you're riding around. Their effect in smoothing your path more than makes up for the extra kilo, but if you live up a couple of flights of stairs and have to carry your bike, it makes a difference. Suspension forks made for the road don't generally demand an excess of attention, but they will appreciate an occasional clean. They've got extra moving parts, which have to be checked over every couple of months – a brief once-over is enough to ensure that all's well; they don't need to be disassembled routinely. They'll also need setting up when they're new to adjust the spring and, if necessary, any rebound damping to suit the load they're going to support. This has to be done individually, because people's weight varies and so does the shape of the bike, which will affect what proportion of your weight the suspension has to support.

Jargon

Spring: The point of all suspension is to absorb sudden forces that would otherwise jar your body and possibly cause a loss of control. This is done by trapping a spring between two moving parts. The spring is commonly a simple coil spring, but may also be a rod of elastomer – rather like a long, rubber cork – or (and this is usually more expensive) a trapped tube of air.

Sag: This is the most important setting on your bike. The point of suspension is to hang your bike between the two extremes of the suspension's travel. It's essential that when you sit on the bike the suspension gives a little under your weight. The purpose of this is to allow for some return movement.

The easiest way to imagine this is to think about what happens to a suspension fork when you ride through a pothole on an otherwise level road.

As you ride over it, the fork should be able to extend downwards, forcing the front wheel down into the hole and therefore keeping you and the rest of the bike travelling on a horizontal path, rather than dropping down into the hole and climbing back out of the other side. Sag is set by measuring how far the suspension compresses when you sit on the bike and is an adjustment you have to make to new parts to match the stiffness of the spring to your weight.

Damping: This is always treated as if it were a complicated word. It's not. The spring controls how far the suspension moves when a force is applied to it. Damping controls how fast the spring moves. This might seem a minor consideration but it makes the difference between a suspension that just bounces you around all over the place like a space hopper – the result of little or no damping – and suspension that slows the effects of forces down to a speed at which you can react to them. Fancy forks may allow you to control the speed of the damping and may control the rebound and compression speeds separately. However, there are many perfectly good forks where the damping is preset in the factory, saving you from fiddling with it.

Travel: The total distance that the suspension can move – all the way from stretched out to completely squashed. Generally, more travel means bigger bumps can be absorbed, but more pedalling energy gets wasted bobbing you up and down.

Setting fork sag

The essential adjustment you must make to your forks when they're new is to set them up for your weight. The stiffness of the spring in the fork must be set so that, when you sit on the saddle in your normal riding position, the fork compresses just a little bit.

Normally, for town use, the setting is about a quarter to a fifth (20-25 per cent) of its total available travel. This initial compression is called 'sag'. You can alter the sag on your forks by adjusting the 'preload' on your spring. If you can't find the preload adjustment knob, dig out your fork owner's manual, which will tell you where to find it.

It's quite normal for only one of the fork legs to have a preload adjuster as they often only have a spring in one side. You'd think that this would make the fork unbalanced, but the two lower fork legs are connected together sufficiently stiffly by the brake arch and the front axle to enable them to work as a single unit, rather than as two separate fork legs.

The optimum amount of sag is dependent on the total travel, so it varies from model to model. You can measure the travel by removing the spring altogether and seeing how far the fork will move, but there are easier ways to find out. The best is to look at your fork owner's manual. If you bought the bike new, it will have been included in the stack of paperwork that came with your bike. Otherwise, it will be listed in any specifications or advertising for your bicycle model.

Forks designed for use around town have a much smaller travel than mountain bikes. Almost all are within a range of around 50-60mm (2-2⅜ in), so if you can't find the manual, a

good estimate for optimum sag is to set it to around 10-15mm (⅜-⅝ in). A very precise measurement is unnecessary as the fork won't settle to the same level every time you sit on it. The sag should be treated as a guideline rather than a precise setting.

Forks designed for off-road use are generally more complex than those made for use around town. The general principle is the same but they'll have more knobs to fine-tune the speed and extent of fork movement. They may also use an air chamber instead of a steel coil or elastomer spring. These more complex adjustments are beyond the scope of this manual.

Fine tuning

Once you've got your sag set up and had a chance to ride your bike, you can fine-tune your forks for your personal riding style. You may want to make your forks slightly softer, so that your ride is more comfortable, or slightly stiffer, to maximise your efficiency.

You'll know if your forks are too soft, because they'll 'bottom out' on impact - this simply means that they'll reach the end of the available travel. It's usually a fairly soft landing - rather than coming to an abrupt halt, they just won't go any further. Don't worry if this only happens from time to time. But if it becomes a regular occurrence, reduce the amount of sag in your forks, so that they're stiffer.

Measuring sag and adjusting preload

If you know (from your owner's manual) how much travel your fork has, work out the sag you need - approximately ¼-⅕ of total travel. If you can't find a specification for total travel, aim for 13mm (½ in). Lean your bike up against a wall and measure the distance along one of the fork stanchions between the bottom of the fork crown and the top of the black rubber wipers on the lower legs. Note down the measurement. Then - leaving your bike leaning against the wall - climb carefully aboard your bike and sit still in your normal riding position. Don't bounce up and down. Get a friend to repeat the measurement you just made. Now you can get off the bike.

If you take the second measurement away from the first, it'll tell you how much the fork sagged when you sat on it. Compare this to the sag that you calculated.

If you find that you're sagging a bit more than you should be, the spring is too soft. The solution is to increase the preload by turning the preload adjustment clockwise. If the fork hasn't moved as much as it should, the spring is too stiff. Turn the preload adjustment knob anticlockwise to reduce the preload. Once you're done, climb back onto the bike and measure again. Repeat until you've got approximately the right amount of sag.

Fork care and maintenance

Regular, careful fork maintenance will save you money. If you keep the forks clean, there's less chance of dirt finding its way into the internal workings. This can also be a good opportunity to spot potential problems as well as worn or damaged components that need further attention.

All fork maintenance starts with a good clean. Drop the wheel out of the frame, so that you can get to the forks properly. If you have V-brakes, you'll have to disconnect them to get the tyre out past the brake blocks. For disc brakes, push a wedge of clean cardboard between the disc pads. This is in case the brake-lever gets accidentally squeezed while the wheel is out. This should be avoided as, without the rotor in between, the brake pads won't have anything to arrest their travel and will carry on moving out of the brake calliper until they squash together.

Go through the steps below. If you find worn or broken components, it's probably time for a fork service, although it may be cheaper simply to replace the forks. Take them to your bike shop to get an idea of the costs of different options. Don't ride damaged forks as they may let you down without warning.

- ⊚ Start by washing the lower legs (A), stanchions (B) and fork crown (C). Plain water is fine, although if they're really grimy, use Muc-Off or other similar bike-cleaners.
- ⊚ Inspect the dropouts (D). Check for cracks around the joint between the fork leg and the dropout, inside and out. Take a look at the condition of the surfaces that your wheels clamp onto, inside and out. These grip the axle and stop the wheel popping out of the fork. The serrations on the quick-release and axle make dents in the fork — make sure that these are clean, crisp dents, rather than worn craters that indicate the wheel has been shifting about.
- ⊚ Check each fork leg in turn. You're looking for splits, cracks or dents. Big dents will weaken the fork and prevent the stanchion from moving freely inside the lower legs. Cracks and dents both mean that it's new fork time.
- ⊚ Disc brakes: check mounts (E) for cracks and check that all calliper-fixing bolts are tight.
- ⊚ V-brakes: check that the bolts which hold the brake units on are secure.
- ⊚ Some forks are held together with bolts at the very bottom of the fork legs – they may be Allen key or nut types. Either way, check they're secure. Don't worry if you can't find any bolt to check down there as some models won't have anything external to tighten.
- ⊚ Clean muck out from behind the brake arch (F) as grit has a tendency to collect here.

- ⊚ Inspect the wipers that clean the stanchions as they enter the lower legs. Tears or cuts will allow grit into the wipers where they will scour your stanchions. The tops of the wipers are usually held in place with a fine circular spring that should sit in the lip at the top of the wiper.
- ⊚ Check the stanchions. If grit gets stuck in the wipers or seals, it will be dragged up and down as your fork cycles, wearing vertical grooves in the forks.
- ⊚ Check all the adjuster knobs. They often stick out so that you can turn them easily, but this does make them vulnerable.
- ⊚ Refit the wheel and reconnect the V-brakes. Pull the front brake on and hold one of the stanchions just above the lower leg. Rock the bike gently back and forth. You may be able to feel a little bit of flex in the forks, but you should not be able to feel the lower legs knocking. Lots of movement here means you need new bushings. This is best done by a bike shop, which has the right tools and spares.
- ⊚ Push down firmly on the bars, compressing the forks. They should spring back smoothly when you release the bars. If they stutter or hesitate about returning, it's time for a fork service.
- ⊚ Finally, finish off by polishing the lower legs. It makes the forks look better, which is important in itself, but also leaves a waxy finish that means dirt doesn't stick so well to the fork.

Cleaning and lubricating the stanchions

Although there are many makes and models of forks, the vast majority are made to a similar pattern. The crown is the part that joins the two legs together at the top.

The stanchions extend down from the crown, and slide into the lower legs – the fatter part of the fork that your brakes and front wheel are connected to. The steerer tube protrudes up from the fork crown, out of sight through the headtube of your frame and up out of the top, where your stem clamps onto it. Headset bearings at the top and bottom of the headtube support the steerer tube so that, when you turn the handlebars and stem, the forks point where you want to go.

How long should suspension forks last?

Forks that are made for off-road use are often covered in gadgets, designed for adjusting damping, spring rates and whatever. There's no reason why you shouldn't use this kind of fork around town, but it is likely to be unnecessary.

The variation in terrain isn't anything like as extreme on the road and bikes that are used for regular commuting actually put in far more hours than weekend leisure bikes. The demands are different – forks for use around town have less travel, less adjustability and are not generally made to have their innards taken out and fiddled with.

On the other hand, they're a lot cheaper than the highly specialised type found on the off-road machines that inspired them. The combination of all these factors means that the forks found on town bikes are generally designed to be replaced when they've worn out, rather than to be regularly stripped down and serviced. This isn't merely an excuse to ignore them. The three things that they do need are to be adjusted correctly for your weight when they're new, to be inspected regularly for wear or damage and to have their stanchions cleaned and oiled three or four times a year.

Your forks bob constantly up and down as you ride, a little bit on the road surface and more if you bump off a kerb or ride through a pothole. The upper, exposed part of the stanchion tends to attract road dirt. If this can work its way down into the gap where the stanchions disappear into the lower legs, it will wear out the bushings that support the stanchions. Tucked inside the top of each lower leg there's a seal, designed to keep dirt out and lubrication in. Above the seal is a wiper: this is a black rubber ring, often with a very fine spring looped around it. These wipers form the first line of defence against unwanted grit, preventing it from getting onto the seals, and need occasional lubrication.

Keeping the area around the wipers clean and free from grit will make a surprising difference to how long your forks last and requires no special tools or equipment. Pay special attention to the area between the stanchion and the brake arch – this tends to act as a dirt trap.

Wiper care

Clean dirt away from around the stanchions, the wiper and the gap between the brake arch and the stanchion. Use plain water as degreaser will seep in under the seals, stripping lubricant out. Once everything is shiny, use something slender like the point of a knife to gently lift up the edge of the wiper, but take care not to cut the rubber. Drip a little oil into the gap between the wiper and the stanchion. Release the wiper and then push down onto the bars and release them to start the oil spreading up and down the stanchion. Wipe off excess oil.

Clean the wiper regularly

Rear suspension

Front suspension has become much more common on utility bicycles, absorbing vibrations and potholes to make riding around much more comfortable. Rear suspension is still mostly the preserve of mountain bikes, where it helps the rear wheel find grip on uneven off-road terrain, cushioning the kind of shocks you get from jumping on and off things. But some people find that the smoother ride that rear suspension gives you means you're less worn out at the end of your journey.

Rear suspension means more moving parts, which in turn means more maintenance and the actual shock unit tends to get more than its fair share of this. In some ways, though, once you've got the shock unit set up for your weight and riding style (see the opposite page), it's the pivots that need most attention since they're in constant motion as you ride along.

One of the complications of having full suspension is that, in order for the back wheel to move up and down reacting to variations in terrain, the whole rear end of the bike must be able to rotate about a pivot or a series of pivots.

The movement of the back wheel about these pivots must be as smooth as possible, so the pivots are either high-quality bushings or (more expensive) bearings.

However good they are, the constant oscillation means that they'll eventually wear out. Once this starts to happen, the back end of the bike will start to slop about sideways in addition to the up-and-down movement in the vertical plane that it's supposed to have. As well as being disconcerting when cornering, this can increase the speed at which your transmission wears and will eventually damage the pivots.

There should be no lateral movement between the pivots

Check the pivots for side-to-side play by holding the main frame still and rocking the back end of the bike. There should be no lateral movement between the two parts and definitely no knocking or clunking noises.

All of these are signs that the pivots need replacing. This isn't a particularly difficult task although there are so many different designs of rear suspension and pivots that you will have to refer to your owner's manual for details.

The key is to make sure you order replacement bushings/bearings before you start since there are more variations in size and shape than it's possible for a bike shop to keep in stock, so you may have to wait for them.

You can make pivots last longer by giving them some lubrication occasionally. Identify all the hinge points on the back of your bike and clean the area around each one. It's worth getting right in there and taking a little time about it as the last thing you want is for your lubricant to drag dirt into the pivot.

Once the area around each pivot is shiny, drop a little good-quality bicycle oil – whatever you use to lubricate your chain should do the job – onto the gap between the two moving parts. Sit yourself on the bike and give it a bit of a bounce, to work the rear suspension, while dragging the oil into the gaps. Then, go back to each pivot and wipe off any excess oil. If you just leave it there, the sticky oil will attract dirt which will hang around where you need it least.

It's also worth paying attention to how your rear suspension affects other components. One issue that often gets ignored is the rear brake and derailleur cables.

Both of these have to travel across the 'hinge' in the middle of the bike. When you're fitting a new cable, it's important to leave enough slack in the cable and casing for the suspension to move. If your gear cable and casing are too short, the movement of the rear suspension will cause 'ghost shifting' – when your chain skips unexpectedly and seemingly randomly across the rear cassette. A short brake cable and casing will mean that your brakes drag as the suspension moves. In both cases, the solution when you fit a new cable is to check that the suspension can move easily through the full range of its travel.

Rear suspension: travel and sag

There are two basic types of rear suspension shock according to the material that the spring is made of. The first type are coil springs with a thick steep coil wound around a central shaft in which any damping mechanism is concealed. The other type is an air shock, where the spring is a pressurised bottle of air.

How much sag are you aiming for?

As with front forks, the optimum sag will be a proportion of the total available travel, which you will either have to find out or measure before you can calculate how much sag you're aiming for. Total available travel and the optimum proportion of this that should sag as you sit on the bike fall into a much wider range than front forks, so it's impossible to give anything more than guidelines – you have to check with the shock manual. Common recommendations are that the sag should be 20–25 per cent (⅕–¼) of the total travel.

Checking travel

The easiest way to establish the amount of travel is, as usual, to look it up in the owner's manual or on specifications for your bike. If this fails, measure the travel to calculate the optimum sag. It's not difficult. Look carefully at the shock and you'll see it's bolted onto the frame at either end. Measure the distance between these two fixing bolts and release the spring entirely. In the case of a coil spring, this means undoing the adjustment disc and releasing the spring until it sags loosely on the central shaft. With an air spring, take the cap off the valve and push the pip in the middle of the valve inwards so all the air rushes out. Lean on the bike to squash the shock as far as it will go.

Measure the distance between the two fixing bolts again. Taking the second measurement away from the first gives you your total travel.

Coil springs

Preload on coil shocks works by turning the adjustment disc that traps the coil spring on the central threaded shaft. Calculate the sag by measuring the distance between the fixing bolts on either end of the shock. Climb gently onto the bike, and get a friend to re-measure the same distance. Taking one measurement from the other will give you the sag. If there's too much sag – the shock compresses too much when you sit on the bike – increase the preload by winding the adjustment disc up the threaded central shaft, compressing the spring so that it's stiffer. If the shock doesn't move enough when you sit on the bike, undo the adjustment disc, making the spring softer.

Air springs

Sag can be controlled precisely by adding or removing air. The air valve is a normal Schraeder type, but the air pressure must be controlled precisely, so a special suspension pump is needed. These have a very thin barrel, so a single stroke just puts a little more air into the shock, and a very precise air-pressure gauge.

SETTING SAG WITH AN AIR SPRING

Step 1: You'll find a rubber o-ring on the shaft of the shock. Push this as far up as it will go, so that it rests against the body of the shock with no gap.

Step 2: Lean the bike up against a wall and get onto the bike. Sit in your normal riding position without bouncing around. Get off the bike. Your weight will have compressed the shock, pushing the o-ring along the shaft. Measure the gap between the shock body and the o-ring. This is your sag.

Step 3: If the measurement is less than you're expecting, release a little air from the shock by pushing the pip in the centre of the valve. If it's more than you expected, add a little air using a shock pump. Remove the shock pump and repeat steps one and two. Save time next time by making a note of what pressure you ended up with!

Suspension seat posts

These have become a lot more common and are now frequently fitted to new hybrids. They used to be a bit of a gimmick to comfort people who thought they were missing out on the whole suspension revolution. In the meantime, they've quietly got better and are actually quite a good idea. They work best if you have a fairly upright riding position, which puts most of your weight onto your saddle. The suspension takes the edge off the constant jolting in and out of potholes.

Suspension seat posts often help if you get a sore back and shoulders through cycling. They are even more effective in combination with a good-quality saddle.

Getting the seat height right can take a little bit of getting used to. When you sit on the saddle it squashes the post a little bit. This is called 'sag' and is supposed to happen. It has a side effect, however, since when you get off the saddle, it pops upwards a little bit, making it seem like it's set too high. You just have to get used to lifting yourself up a little higher to get up onto the saddle. The alternative is to set it to your normal height, so that it's easier to get on to but, once you're aboard, the slight sag means you're sitting too low down so your legs never get to have a proper stretch.

The standard pattern seat post – there is remarkably little variation in design – works by trapping a spring between two telescoping parts of post. The bottom part of the post that fits into the frame looks normal. The top section of the post is narrower and slides into the bottom part. This top part may be covered with a flexible rubber boot to keep the dirt out. The spring lives inside between the two parts and may either be a long metal coil spring or an elastomer rod.

Before you ride, the sag in the seat post has to be set up so that it settles into place the correct amount under your weight. The post is supposed to give a little bit so that it's got room to spring upwards, supporting you if the bike drops into a dip. It has to be able to compress as well, so that if you hit a bump the bike can ride upwards, without kicking you upwards with it. The ideal is to set the preload on the spring inside the post, so that, when you sit on the bike, the natural resting point of the saddle is some way between the two extremes.

The total travel on seat posts isn't a great deal of distance, usually around 40mm (1½ in), so you're looking for the seat to sink about a quarter of that when you sit on it – about 10mm (⅜ in).

You'll need assistance for this bit as you have to sit on the bike and then let someone else measure how much difference you've made.

ADJUSTING SAG FOR SUSPENSION SEAT POSTS

Step 1: Lean the bike against a wall and measure from the top of the seat post – where the post meets the clamp – to the bottom of the knurled nut. Take a note of the measurement. Leave the bike against the wall and climb on. Sit still in your normal riding position. Get a friend to measure again between the same two points as before. The difference between the two measurements should be around 10mm (⅜ in).

Step 2: If the sag isn't right, undo and remove the clamp holding the seat post into the frame. Turn the post upside down. You'll be able to fit an Allen key in the cap in the bottom. If you've got more than 10mm (⅜ in) sag, the spring is too soggy – turn the Allen key clockwise, adding preload. If you've got less, the spring is too firm – turn the Allen key anticlockwise, reducing preload. It's important not to undo the cap so far it protrudes out of the end of the post.

Step 3: You'll have to refit the post in the frame and repeat the measurements to check that the amount of sag is correct. It may take several goes to find the right place. Once you're confident about the sag, you'll need to reset your seat height. If you're not sure about how to work out the correct height, use the instructions on page 35.

Care of suspension seat posts

Suspension seat posts seem to be one of those things that people ignore – perhaps because they come fitted to new bikes rather than having been specifically chosen, or perhaps because their performance deteriorates so slowly that you don't really notice until the moment when they actually stop working completely.

The most common problem is that the knurled nut that holds the two parts of the post together has a tendency to work itself slowly loose. The spring that's trapped between the two parts then finds itself with plenty of elbow room.

When this happens, the spring isn't compressed at all by your weight and just rests at the bottom of its travel without supporting you in any useful way at all. If the knurled nut continues to work itself loose, the top part of the post can become completely detached from the bottom part.

Normally they don't separate of their own accord, because the top part rests inside the bottom part, but if your bike falls over or you bump off a deep kerb, they will soon part company.

You do get some warning when this starts to happen – instead of absorbing bumps smoothly as you ride, the post will sink slowly to the bottom of its travel, resting at its lowest point. You'll start to feel every bump you ride over, and you may even feel the post knocking as you go round tight corners.

The other problem that can occur is that the interface between the two telescoping parts of the post can corrode, so that they don't slide easily over each other and, however strong the spring is, the post won't respond to bumps. It doesn't happen all of a sudden. There will be a period when the movement of the post starts to feel lumpy and the saddle shifts in discrete jerks rather than with a smooth flow. If you catch it at this stage, there's hope as you can give the post a new lease of life by taking it apart, cleaning it and re-greasing it. The steps below show you how to do this. If you leave it much longer, the spring will become embedded in the post. The simplest and cheapest solution at that point is usually to replace the post.

It's worth getting the post out of the frame regularly and re-greasing the outside of the post as well as the inside of the frame. You don't need to use anything particularly fancy; ordinary bike grease will do the job just fine. If you don't do this and simply leave the post in the same place for years at a time, it will end up stuck (seized) within the frame. Parking your bike outside frequently will mean it's exposed to the weather, which will greatly increase the speed of corrosion.

A seized seat post is not an immediate problem as long as you never want to change its height, but you won't be able to access the bottom of the post to adjust the spring preload. Moreover, you'll be stuck if you ever want to lend the bike to someone who's a different height, or to sell it.

SERVICING SUSPENSION SEAT POSTS

Step 1: Ensure that the knurled nut at the top of the bottom section of the post is screwed down securely. These often work loose without anyone noticing. You'll have to lift the black rubber boot up and out of the way to turn the knurled nut. Keep turning the nut – if you stand over the saddle the nut must turn clockwise although you won't actually be able to see it because the saddle will be in the way.

Step 2: Remove the seat post from the frame. There's a cap on the bottom of the post. Note how deeply the cap is recessed and then use an Allen key to remove the cap. The spring will drop out. Clean it since it will be greasy and sticky. Once it's clean, spread a generous dollop of fresh grease all over it as the sides of the spring rub inside the post and need lubrication. Replace the end-cap, taking care that it goes in square, not cross-threaded.

Step 3: Tighten in the end-cap so it's as deeply recessed into the frame as before you removed it. The end of the cap must not protrude beyond the end of the post. Clean the outside of the post and the inside of the frame, then smear grease on the outside of the post. Refit the post. Insert it far enough into the frame so the 'min insertion' marks – a band of short parallel lines – disappear. If your saddle is too low, the seat post is too short and should be replaced.

10 – Bottom brackets & headsets

Bottom brackets and headsets are the two major bearings on your frame. The bottom bracket runs through the frame, connecting your cranks and transferring the vertical force you input through the pedals into rotational motion which drags your chain around your chainset. The headset connects your forks to your frame, keeping the front wheel securely attached while allowing you to rotate the bars to steer the bike. Well adjusted and protected from the elements, the bottom bracket and headset will both run uncomplainingly for years.

Bottom brackets

Bottom brackets and headsets both need precise adjustment. Play (side-to-side movement) in your bottom bracket causes sloppy shifting from your front derailleur, wears your chain and chainset and, in addition, gives you sore knees. Play in your headset means movement between frame and forks, leading to loss of vital control during braking and turning.

Overtight bearings are just as bad. Tight bottom brackets rob you of pedalling efficiency, making every pedal stroke that bit harder. Tight headsets make it difficult to turn the bars, forcing you to yank on them around corners.

This chapter leads you through the process of checking adjustments on both these major bearings. The bottom bracket section tells you how to fit and remove chainsets and cranks and how to replace bottom brackets. The headset section shows you how to adjust and service headsets. Bearings can be regreased without too many tools, but once the bearing surface has become worn, the headset must be replaced. It's best to take your bike to your shop for this as the job doesn't need doing very often, but it does require expensive tools. Bottom brackets used to be adjustable, but almost all of them are sealed units now, which means that, when they become worn, you must remove and replace them.

Routine maintenance of the bottom bracket

The bottom bracket is the large main bearing that passes through your frame, between the cranks. Actually, it is a pair of bearings, one on each side bolted into threads cut on both sides of the frame. As with all the sealed parts of the bicycle, water and dirt will get in with enough time and abuse. This slows you down and wears out the bearings. The length of time that they'll last is difficult to predict, but a normal lifespan might be two or three years.

In the beginning, bottom brackets were sold in their separate parts: the axle that ran through the middle, the cups that bolted into the frame and the bearings that sat in the gap between the two. The advantages of this system were that the gap between the bearings could be adjusted so that the bearings ran smoothly with no drag and that the parts could be regularly disassembled, cleaned, re-greased, reassembled and adjusted. But we were all too lazy to do this often enough, so now almost all bottom brackets are sealed-

in cartridges. They stay cleaner and, when they wear out, they have to be replaced as a unit.

Bottom brackets have a reverse thread on the right-hand side, so the cup on the chainset side of the bike has to be turned clockwise to remove it and counterclockwise to fit it. This is true of almost all bikes – mountain bikes, hybrids, folders and shoppers. The exceptions are a few fancy Italian road bikes, which have a standard tighten-clockwise thread on both sides. These bikes serve to demonstrate why the reverse thread is necessary — bottom brackets with the Italian threading are prone to unravel under pressure from the pedals and require special attention from mechanics to stop this happening.

Bottom brackests used to be adjustable but almost all of them are sealed units now. This means that they tend to stay cleaner than they used to but also means they have to be replaced as a unit when they wear out

Different types of bottom bracket

Around the late-1990s, we'd finally come to settle on a standard fitting to attach cranks to bottom-bracket axles when somebody came along with another improvement. History is now repeating itself with the appearance of a new bunch of designs. The standard for a while was called 'square taper', which worked fine. Newer bottom brackets are splined and are generally lighter than before.

Your bottom bracket type must match your crank type. There is no compatibility at all between the different types as you cannot exchange cranks or bottom brackets between systems. Luckily, both types work in the same way when it comes to getting them on and off. In all cases, a bolt pulls the crank onto the axle, using either an 8mm or 10mm Allen key or a 14mm bolt (now usually found on older bikes). You remove the crank by clamping a tool into its threads and then wind in the centre of the crank extractor tool to push off the axle wedged into it.

Square taper (A)

A square-shaped axle fits into a similar hole on the crank. Since the axle and the hole in the crank are both tapered, as you tighten the bolt on the end of the axle you push the crank farther onto the axle, wedging it firmly in place. The idea is simple, but if the crank comes just a little loose on the axle, it tends to loosen more, damaging the soft metal of the crank at the same time. This problem is particularly marked on the left-hand side. Since the crank bolts both have a standard thread, the one on the left has a tendency to loosen as you put pressure on the pedals, whereas the right-hand one generally tightens itself. Check the bolts regularly.

Shimano Octalink (C)

Below is the Shimano splined bottom bracket. It has eight splines, rather than the 10 you get on an ISIS bottom bracket. ISIS bottom brackets and chainsets are not compatible with Shimano ones. When refitting chainsets, always clean the splines on the chainset and bottom bracket carefully, otherwise the chainset will work itself loose as you pedal. Retighten the crank bolts after the first 50 miles.

ISIS (B)

ISIS stands for International Spline Interface Standard. This is the type of bottom bracket used by Bontrager, Race Face, Middelburn and others. There are 10 splines on each side. The chainset has matching splines. To fit the chainset to the bottom bracket, slide it over the splines and tighten until the back of the chainset butts up firmly onto the shoulder of the bottom bracket axle.

Take good care lining up the second crank — the cranks fit just as easily into every one of the 10 splines, so make sure your cranks point very accurately in opposite directions before you tighten down the bolts.

Removing cranks

The same method is used to remove both crank and chainset. The correct tool is a crank extractor. You can't do the job without it, but sadly it's not useful for anything else.

There are two sizes of crank extractor. The older, smaller type is for square-taper bottom brackets. The newer, larger size is for splined axles, and the same tool will work for both ISIS and Shimano Octalink cranks. If you've got a small crank extractor and a splined axle, you can convert it using a small plug that you slip into the end of the axle, called a TLFC-15. But if your crank extractor is designed for fatter, splined axles, it will not work at all with square-taper axles.

Take care with the crank threads, they're very soft and will get damaged if you try to force the tool into them crookedly. Always start the tool into the crank by hand, so that you can feel it going in smoothly. Once it's nicely threaded in, you can use a spanner to wind it in as far as it will go.

REMOVING A CRANK

Step 1: The crank bolts should be tightly fitted so you will need a long Allen key (or for older bikes a 14mm socket with a long handle) to undo the bolt. If you find the bolts come off without too much effort, tighten them more firmly next time! Check inside the crank, where the bolt came out, and remove any washers left in there.

Step 2: Check inside the hole that the bolt came out of, to see what kind of tool you need. If you can see the square end of an axle with a bolt hole in the middle, you need an older, smaller crank extractor. If you can see the end of the axle and it's round with the ends of eight or 10 splines visible, you need a fatter, new-style crank extractor.

Step 3: Hold the handle or the nut end of the inner part of the tool and turn the outer part of the tool. You will see that turning one against the other means the inner part of the tool moves in or out of the outer part. Back off the inner part of the tool so that its head disappears inside the outer part of the tool.

Step 4: Thread the outer part of the tool into the threads in the crank that you've revealed by taking off the bolt. The crank is soft in comparison with the tool, so take care not to cross-thread the tool and damage the crank, which will be expensive. Thread on the tool as far as it will go.

Step 5: Start winding in the inner part of the tool. It will move easily at first, but will then meet the end of the axle and stiffen. You need to be firm with it. Once it starts moving, turning the tool gets easier as it pushes the axle out of the crank.

Step 6: Once you've started the crank moving on the axle, the crank will come off in your hand. Pull it off the axle and remove the tool from the crank. Repeat the same procedure on the other side to remove the chainset.

Refitting the crank and chainset

Before you start refitting the crank and chainset, use the opportunity to give the area that's normally hidden behind the chainset a good clean – you'll find it much easier than normal to reach round behind and inside your front derailleur too, so if it looks a bit grubby, take the chance to give it a thorough once-over.

As stated opposite, the same procedure is used to fit both crank and chainset. Start with the chainset. Clean the end of the axle and the hole in the chainset thoroughly. Make sure there's no dirt left on the tapers or between the splines or you will get creaking. Apply anti-seize to any titanium parts.

There are two different opinions about whether the axle should be greased before you fit the cranks onto it. Opposing schools of thought are often fiercely loyal to their points of view. The advantage of greasing the axle is that the lubrication allows the crank to be pulled further onto the axle, fitting it more tightly. Those who prefer not to grease the axle say that the grease layer allows the two surfaces to move against each other, leading to potential creaking and then allowing the parts to work themselves loose. New bottom brackets often come with anti-seize already applied to the right-hand axle – this should be left on.

Inspect the surface of both the axle and the holes in the cranks. Square-taper axles should be flat with no pitting. The crank hole is the place you're most likely place to find damage – the hole needs to be perfectly square and must fit smoothly over the axle. The most common problem is where loose cranks have rounded themselves off on the axle, smearing the shape of one or more of the corners of the square. Splined cranks will also be damaged by being ridden loose. Each spline should be crisp and clean. Replace damaged cranks immediately – even if the distortion appears to be slight. Once worn, they will never hold securely and will cause expensive damage to your bottom bracket axle.

Slide the chainset over the end of the axle. Line it up with the square or splined axle and push on it firmly. Grease the threads of the fixing bolts and add a dab of grease under the head of the bolt, which may otherwise creak.

Fit the bolt and tighten firmly. If you have access to a torque wrench, you're looking for around 50Nm. For the final tighten, line the crank up with the Allen key/socket spanner, so they are almost parallel. Hold one in each hand and stand in front of the chainset. With both arms straight, use your shoulders to

tighten the crank bolts. (This makes use of the strength of your shoulders and reduces the chance of stabbing yourself with the chainring if you slip.)

Next, fit the crank onto the other end of the bottom bracket axle. Line it up so that it points in the opposite direction to the one on the other side. This is simple with square tapers but takes a little care with splined designs – the bike feels very strange if you accidentally fit the crank to a neighbouring spline. Once everything is aligned, grease the crank bolt in the same way and tighten the bolt firmly.

It's worth retightening all types of crank bolts after the first ride – you often find they work themselves a bit loose as they bed in. Both types of crank – square-taper and splined – depend on the shape of the hole in the crank being exactly right. Riding with loose cranks stretches the shape so the cranks will never fit firmly enough again, leaving replacement the only option. The material of the crank is softer than that of the axle so it wears first, but if the worn crank is not replaced, it also eventually wears down the shape of the end of the bottom bracket axle.

Hold crank steady, retighten crank bolt firmly

Removing the bottom bracket

You'll have to remove your chainset and crank to access the bottom bracket – see page 208. Page 209 will tell you how to get these two items back on again.

The key to bottom bracket jobs is remembering that the right-hand cup has a reverse thread, so undoes clockwise. The only exceptions to this rule are a few fancy Italian racing bikes.

Before starting, check what kind of fitting you have. Almost everything now uses a Shimano-pattern splined fitting with 20 narrow splines in each cup. ISIS bottom brackets use the same size and number of splines, but the hole in the middle of the tool must be bigger to fit over a fatter axle. ISIS-type tools work fine on Shimano bottom brackets.

Always fit the tool firmly into the splines before applying pressure. If it slips, you'll damage the cups and, on top of that, you may also hurt yourself.

REMOVING THE BOTTOM BRACKET

Step 1: After removing both crank and chainset, start on the left-hand side of the bottom bracket. Clean out all the splines on the bottom bracket cup so that the tool fits into them firmly. It's worth getting a little screwdriver and picking the dirt out of all the splines before you start. They're right down near the ground and tend to pick up all sorts of rubbish, which can stop the tool from engaging with the full depth of the slots.

Step 2: Insert the tool, firmly clamp on a large adjustable spanner and turn the tool anticlockwise to loosen the cup. It may be very firmly fitted. Don't let the tool slip off as it will damage the splines and it's easy to hurt yourself. If the cup won't come out easily, clamp the tool onto the bottom bracket. This calls for ingenuity as you need to fashion a washer that allows you to bolt the tool on with your original crank bolt.

Step 3: Remove the left-hand cup completely. Check the condition of the splines and the threads, especially the cheaper plastic cups. These work fine and are light, but the splines can get damaged easily.

Step 4: Shift the tool onto the right-hand side and fit it firmly into the spline. Remove the bottom bracket by turning the tool clockwise. It can be tough to turn. Clamp on the tools if necessary. Bottom brackets often seize on, so a release agent like Shimano Get-a-Grip could be handy. Spray or drip on and leave the release agent to do its chemical magic for half an hour before you try to shift the cup again.

Step 5: Remove the body of the bottom bracket. Don't throw it away straight away as you will need to measure it to get the right size for your new one. The two measurements you'll need are the axle length – right from one end to the other – and the width of the part of the frame that you removed the bottom bracket from (normally 68mm [2^{11}/$_{16}$ in] or 73mm [2^{7}/$_{8}$ in]).

Step 6: Once both sides are out, take a look at the inside of the frame. Clean it out carefully. If it holds lots of debris, work out where the dirt is getting in and block up the hole. Make sure there are bolts in all the water bottle bosses, even if they have no cage mounted to them.

Refitting the bottom bracket

The threads on your bottom bracket will either be metal on both sides, or plastic on one side and metal on the other. Grease metal threads – plastic ones don't need grease.

Generally, the cups are marked 'L' (left) and 'R' (right). Usually, the body of the bottom bracket is the right-hand side, with a loose cup that attaches from the left. This is not universal, however. If it's the other way around, reverse the fitting order. The bottom bracket threads are very fine, so take care when fitting that you don't 'cross-thread' (thread in crooked) the cups. Start each side by hand, so you can't force the threads to start unless they fit properly. Riding with a loose bottom bracket will damage the threads. New frames, and those that have been re-sprayed, may have paint stuck in the threads that prevents the new bottom bracket fitting. Unless they are too badly damaged, they can be cut again with a tap, a tool which recuts the thread.

REFITTING THE BOTTOM BRACKET

Step 1: Roll the left-hand cup a couple of turns into the thread on the left-hand side. Start fitting the right-hand side – the main body of the bottom bracket – into the right-hand side of the frame, tightening anticlockwise by hand. Once you've got it in a couple of turns, look from the left-hand end of the bottom bracket to check that the axle is coming out exactly in the middle of the hole in the cup you just fitted.

Step 2: Tighten anticlockwise. It needs to be fitted really firmly – you need about 300mm (12 in) of leverage and a good grunt home. Once the body of the bottom bracket is fitted firmly, tighten up the left-hand cup. Take care with plastic cups as they need to be fitted fairly firmly, but won't take as much force as the main body of the bottom bracket. Overdo it and you damage the plastic splines for removal next time.

Step 3: Refit the crank as on pages 209. If you're fitting a new bottom bracket, watch as you fit the chainset side. Even if you've measured carefully, it's worth checking that the chainset doesn't jam on the chainstays as you tighten the crank bolt. You need at least 2mm ($\frac{1}{12}$ in) of clearance between the chainset and the chainstay — if there's not enough, remove the bottom bracket and try one with a longer axle.

Removing stubborn bottom brackets

Sometimes bottom brackets get wedged in hard. It means they weren't fitted with enough grease or anti-seize or that they've simply been in there too long. Living by the sea in a salty atmosphere doesn't help either. Try the following measures. A good dose of release agent helps in three or four applications over a couple of days – especially if, in the middle of proceedings, you put everything back together and go for a good hard ride. A light spray such as GT85 will work although you can get something tougher at your hardware or auto shop. Brands such as PlusGas are good and there are other versions of similar stuff. You can also get bike-specific release agent from your bike shop – Shimano makes one called Get-A-Grip that is effective. All release agents contain nasty chemicals, so use sparingly in a well-ventilated space and don't get any on your skin. Always turn the tool in the correct direction as it's easy to get confused. Looking from the right-hand side of the bike, the right-hand cup is removed by turning it clockwise – a reverse thread. Looking from the left-hand side of the bike, the left-hand cup is removed by turning it anticlockwise – a normal thread. Once you've soaked the bottom bracket thoroughly, try using as long a lever as possible on the tool. Find a tube that fits over the end of your adjustable spanner and use that to increase your leverage, bracing yourself carefully so you don't slip and hurt yourself when the tool starts to move. Clamping the tool in place helps too. Use the crank bolt and find a washer that stops the crank bolt from slipping into the hole in the centre of the tool without interfering with the spanner flats. If you have assistance from a friend, take off the wheels. Drop the tool into the vice and clamp it so the bike is held horizontally over the workbench. Use the bike as a lever and turn it to undo the tool.

Bottom brackets: creaking noises

A creaking bottom bracket is annoying and needs investigating straight away – bicycles rarely complain unless something is loose, worn or about to snap.

Fat-tubed aluminium bikes amplify the smallest sound. Anything with any tube fatter than you can get your hand around is basically a soundbox and it will do its level best to ensure you hear everything that is in any way out of kilter.

The end result is that you start lusting after a narrow-tubed Italian steel racing bike, then suddenly you're visiting your mother for Christmas in full Lycra, duck shoes and aero helmets. Tighten your cranks instead.

Try these measures to stop the creaking. If nothing works, note that frames transmit noises strangely, so creaks can sound as if they come from somewhere else. Common causes include loose handlebar and stem bolts as well as worn rear-hub bearings.

SORTING OUT NOISES

Step 1: Tighten both crank bolts clockwise. They both need to be properly tight so you will need a long – at least 200mm [8 in] – Allen key, not just a multitool. The 8mm Allen key on multitools is for emergencies only. If you have access to a torque wrench, they need to be somewhere around 50Nm.

Step 2: If that doesn't work, remove both crank bolts, grease the threads and under the heads, then refit firmly.

Step 3: Tighten both pedals. Remember that the left-hand pedal has a reverse thread — see the Pedals chapter for more details.

Step 4: Remove both pedals, grease the threads and refit firmly. This sounds far-fetched, but it does the trick more often than you'd imagine. Dirt or grit on the pedal threads will also cause creaking, so clean the threads on the pedal and inside the crank.

Step 5: Take hold of each pedal and twist it. The pedal should not move on its own axle. If it does, it could well be the source of the creak and needs stripping and servicing (see the Pedals section page 233). Spray a little light oil, like GT85, on the cleat release mechanism. Don't use chain oil as it's too sticky and will pick up dirt.

Step 6: Remove the crank and chainset, loosen the left-hand bottom bracket cup, tighten the right-hand cup firmly – remember it has a reverse thread – and then tighten the left-hand cup (normal thread). Refit crank and chainset and tighten bolts firmly. See page 209 for more details.

Bottom brackets: checking for giveaway movement

Bottom brackets suffer from being invisible much of the time. They are essential bearings and are expected to turn smoothly even when you stamp on the pedals, yet, because they can't be seen, tend to be ignored. But a worn bottom bracket slows you down without you noticing and also makes your chain and chainset wear quickly.

Check regularly for play – the bottom bracket should spin freely and shouldn't rock from side to side at all. Worn ones should be replaced – otherwise, they'll accelerate wear in your transmission.

Crouch on the right-hand side of the bike. Line up the right-hand crank with part of the frame such as the chainstay, seattube or downtube. Hold the crank – not the pedal – in one hand and the frame in the other, so that your hands are as close together as possible. Rock your hands gently towards and away from each other.

You should not hear or feel any knocking or play between the crank and frame – no side-to-side movement at all. Repeat at other angles, lining the crank up each time with a part of your frame and rocking across the bike – you might get more knocking at one angle than another. Repeat on the left-hand side with the crank. Once more with feeling...

Once you've checked both sides, you can decide whether the play comes from a worn bottom bracket, from the bottom bracket moving in the frame or from the crank moving on the bottom bracket axle. If you can only feel knocking from one crank, most likely that crank is loose.

Tighten the crank with a long 8mm Allen key or, if it's an older bottom bracket, a 14mm socket. This bolt must be firmly fitted or it will work loose. Your work tool needs to be at least 200mm (8 in) long and you need to tighten hard. Extend short Allen keys by sliding them onto a longer tube. Tighten both sides while you're at it. Test again to see if the rocking has gone away. If the cranks still rock after tightening, you have a worn or loose bottom bracket.

You may be able to work out where any movement is by looking into the gap between your left-hand crank and the frame as you rock the crank.

You can only see the very end of the bottom bracket cup, since most of it is invisible inside the frame. There should be no movement at all between this sliver of bottom bracket cup and the frame. Check the right-hand side as well.

This is trickier to see because the chainset is in the way. If the bottom bracket is loose in the frame, you can usually cure the problem simply by tightening it in the frame. You'll have to remove the chainset and crank; see page 208. If the bottom bracket is worn out, you will see the axle shifting in the cup as you rock the crank. In this case, you have no option but to replace the bottom bracket – see page 210.

Next, check that the bottom bracket bearings spin freely. Change into the smallest chainring at the front and then reach around to the back of the chainset and lift the chain off the smallest chainring.

Drop it into the gap between the chainset and the frame below the front derailleur, so that the chain is not connected at all to the chainset. Spin the pedals. They should move freely and silently. Grinding or crunching noises or any other resistance mean it's time to change your bottom bracket. Lift the chain back onto the top of the smallest chainring and pedal forward slowly to re-engage the chain with the chainring.

If the crank rocks sideways, you have a problem

Headsets

Your headset is the pair of bearings that connect your frame to your forks. The bearings are held on a pair of cups, each pressed into your headtube, top and bottom. These allow the fork to rotate freely in your frame so that you can turn corners and balance. But while the bearings must have enough room to move freely, there mustn't be enough room for any rocking movement between the fork and the frame, which will make your bike feel unstable when cornering or braking.

It's useful to learn how to adjust these bearings properly as they will wear surprisingly quickly if they're wobbly or if the forks are stiff to turn. The page opposite shows you how to check your headset adjustment – the method of dealing with it will depend on what type of headset you have.

Threaded headset

There are two basic types of headset bearing. The traditional type (threaded headset) has been around for a hundred years and has a thread at the top of the steerer tube. The top cone of the headset is also threaded and screws down onto the fork. This pulls the steerer tube up through the headtube, gradually squashing both sets of bearings, top and bottom. When they've got just the right amount of space, a second nut is tightened onto the threaded cone, wedging the two together so that the headset won't rattle out of adjustment. The stem is then fitted into the hole in the steerer tube, set to the desired height and tightened in place with a wedge bolt.

The newer type of headset is, confusingly enough, called an A-headset or threadless headset. With this system the top cone of the headset isn't threaded, it's pushed straight onto the steerer tube. There will probably be some washers next and then the stem slides loosely over the top. The key to tightening the bearings is the top-cap. This covers the top of the steerer tube, overlapping the stem, and threads into a nut inside the steerer tube. Tightening the top-cap bolt pushes the stem, and thus

the washers and the top bearing cone, down the steerer tube, drawing the steerer tube up through the headtube and trapping both sets into a smaller space. Once the correct adjustment has been reached the stem bolts are tightened firmly, locking the bearing adjustment in place.

There are good points about either system. The major advantage of the threaded system is that it makes it very easy to change your handlebar height. This is useful round town as many people like to set the position of their bars so that they're nice and upright and they can see where they're going. It's not particularly aerodynamic, but generally people don't tend to attain the kinds of speed around town that make aerodynamics a major consideration.

The advantage of the threadless system is that bearing adjustments can be make easily with a couple of Allen keys. Threaded systems require a pair of special headset spanners that are generally quite pricey and useless for almost anything else.

There aren't any significant differences in terms of weight or quality between the two systems and they both respond well to being correctly adjusted and being given a clean plus some fresh grease occasionally.

Threadless A-headset

Check for play in headset bearings

A correctly adjusted and secured headset will seldom rattle itself loose, so you shouldn't need to reposition it too frequently.

With a little practice you'll also be able to feel very quickly whether something's wrong as you ride your bike. If, for example, applying your front brake makes your bike judder to a stop or you can feel or hear a knocking sound as you brake, further attention is indicated. A loose headset will also affect your cornering – if your bike hesitates when you try to make tight turns, or feels unstable changing direction when you're moving fast, it's worth taking the time to check your headset bearings. It's tempting to ignore very small amounts of play, but if you can feel any movement in the headset, it's worth dealing with straight away – precise adjustment will make the bearings last much longer.

CHECKING FOR PLAY

Step 1: Pick up the front end of your bike by the frame. Turn the handlebars. They should move easily and smoothly without resistance or grinding. If they're a little stiff, they can be adjusted. If you can feel notches, the bearing surfaces are worn out and, although adjustment will help temporarily, ultimately the headset will have to be replaced. This is a job for the bike shop.

Step 2: Drop the bike back onto the ground and turn the bars to 90°, so that the wheel points to one side. Hold the front brake on to stop the wheel rolling and rock the bike gently back and forth in the direction that the bike (not the wheel) is pointing. The wheel may flex and the tyres will give a bit, but there shouldn't be any knocking or play.

Step 3: If you can feel a knocking, but are not sure whether it is coming from the headset or from somewhere else, then hold the headset around the cups, both above then below the headtube, while you rock the bars. If the headset is fine you shouldn't be able to feel the cups moving.

Toolbox

THREADLESS HEADSETS – ADJUSTING BEARINGS:
◎ Allen key to fit stem bolts
◎ Allen key to fit top-cap
    Both of these are almost always a 5mm or 6mm Allen key, although you may occasionally come across a 4mm Allen key fitting.

ADJUSTING STEM HEIGHT:
◎ The same Allen keys as above, to fit your stem bolts and top-cap

THREADLESS HEADSETS – SERVICING:
◎ Allen keys as above
◎ Tools to disconnect your brake cable, lever or disc calliper: almost always the same Allen keys as above: 4mm, 5mm or 6mm

◎ Degreaser to clean bearing surfaces
◎ Good-quality grease: preferably a waterproof grease such as Phil Wood
◎ Fresh bearings: ball bearings for headsets are generally 5⁄32 inch, but take your old ones to your bike shop to match them up.
◎ Bearing races can be replaced by loose bearings, which are fiddlier to fit but roll more smoothly and last longer.
◎ Cartridge bearings should be taken to the shop to be matched up for fresh ones: there are a few different types in use, all of which look very similar. The most common type of cartridge bearings for Shimano headsets also fit in headsets made by other manufacturers.

Threadless headsets: adjusting bearings to eliminate play

The bearings are adjusted for no play at all, while allowing the fork and bars to rotate smoothly in the frame without resistance. Check the bearings (page 215). If they're tight or there is play, adjust them. You wear your bearings out really quickly if you ride with them either too tight or too loose.

It's vital to check that your stem bolts are tight after finishing this job. Some people will tell you to leave your stem bolt slightly loose so that, in the event of a crash, your stem will twist on the steerer tube rather than bending your handlebars. You should not do this. The consequences of your stem accidentally twisting on your steerer tube as you ride are far too serious and dangerous. Always tighten your stem bolts firmly. However, it is fine to slacken the top-cap bolt off as it's only needed for headset adjustment and can be a handy emergency bolt if something else snaps!

You may find, when you try to follow the instructions below, that you cannot eliminate the last scrap of play or that you have to crank the top-cap bolt down so hard that it risks splitting. This is quite a common problem and means that the stem has been pushed so far down that the top-cap is jammed on the top of the steerer tube, preventing you from making further adjustments. If you suspect that this is the case, remove the top-cap and have a look under it. Make sure that the top of the steerer tube sits at

least 2–3mm (1/12–1/8 in) below the top of the stem so that you have room enough to push the stem downwards. The top-cap often has a little ridge around the edge of its underside to locate it centrally in the hole in the stem. This will mean that you'll need a little extra breathing space between top-cap and steerer tube. Luckily, this problem is relatively easy to solve – you need to pop an extra washer in below the stem to bring it upwards.

They're supplied in a range of widths, so estimate how much extra lift you need. There are two different diameters, 1 in (mainly road bikes) and 1⅛ in (much more common), so take a sample from your bike with you when you get a new one. Follow the instructions on page 217 for adjusting your stem height, just adding the extra washer under the stem rather than shifting any of the others around. Dirt or corrosion on either the steerer tube or the inside of the stem means the stem won't slide easily over the steerer tube, making it hard to adjust the bearings. If so, remove the stem, clean both surfaces thoroughly and refit before adjusting.

ADJUSTING THREADLESS HEADSET BEARINGS

Step 1: Loosen the stem bolt(s) so the stem can rotate easily. This ensures that it will slide up and down on the steerer tube. It's easier to adjust a headset that's too loose – if this is the case for you, go straight to step 2. If your headset is too tight, begin by loosening it right off. Pull the front brake on and rock the bars back and forth, gradually undoing the top-cap until you can feel the bearings knocking.

Step 2: Slowly retighten the top-cap. Check constantly for play by turning the bars sideways and rocking them with the front brake on. Stop when there's no knocking movement. Pick the front of the bike up and bounce it on the floor a couple of times, to settle the bearings into place, and check again.

Step 3: Once you have the adjustment correct, align the stem with the front wheel and firmly tighten the stem bolts. Check the stem is secure by holding the front wheel between your knees and twisting it. If you can turn it, the stem bolts need to be tighter. Check the adjustment again and repeat if necessary – sometimes tightening the stem bolt shifts everything around.

Threadless headsets: stem height

If your handlebar is set at the correct height, you will be more comfortable, not to mention the fact that your bike will also be more stable and easier to steer.

However, this is more difficult to do with threadless headset stems than it was with the older threaded types – you cannot simply shift the stem on the steerer tube. Dramatic changes are best made by swapping the whole stem for a different one, since you can change both the length and the angle at the same time – see page 229.

However, it is okay to make minor changes to the stem height by swapping the positions of washers that are already on the steerer tube between the stem and the headset. Shifting these so that they sit above the stem, between the stem and the top-cap, will lower the bars slightly. You'll definitely need to readjust headset bearings afterwards – see page 216.

SWAPPING WASHERS ON THE STEM TO CHANGE BAR HEIGHT

Step 1: Remove the top-cap. You'll need to undo the top-cap bolt all the way and wiggle the cap off. This reveals a star-fanged nut inside the steerer tube. Lift off any washers that were sitting between the top-cap and the stem. Check the condition of the top-cap. If it's cracked, or the recess where the bolt head sits is distorted, replace it.

Step 2: Loosen the stem bolts so that the stem moves freely on the steerer tube. Pull the stem up and off. You may need to twist it a little to help it on its way. Tape the entire handlebar assembly to the toptube, so that hoses and cables don't get kinked under the weight of the bars.

Step 3: If you've hung the bike in a work stand, keep a hand on the forks so that they don't slide out of the headset. Add or remove washers from the stack under the stem. If you're adding washers, you can only add washers that came off above the stem.

Step 4: Replace the stem, then any leftover washers. Basically, everything that came off the steerer tube should go back on. The washers are all necessary because, as you tighten the top-cap, they push down onto the stem and then the bearings, adjusting the headset.

Step 5: Check the height of the washer stack above the top of the steerer tube. There should be a gap of 2–3mm (¹⁄₁₂–¹⁄₈ in) (A). If possible, this should be a single washer, not a stack of thinner ones as individual washers have a tendency to get caught and stop you adjusting the headset properly. Add or remove washers from the top of the stack to achieve the desired 2–3mm (¹⁄₁₂–¹⁄₈ in) gap.

Step 6: Replace the top-cap, and go to 'Threadless headsets: Adjusting bearings' on page 216. Once you've finished adjusting the bearings, make sure that the stem is securely tightened and that the bars are facing forwards.

Threadless headset servicing

Headsets are remarkably simple to service, needing no special tools at all, just one or two Allen keys, some degreaser or other cleaning agent and good-quality grease.

Headsets, like bottom brackets, are frequently ignored and gradually deteriorate without you noticing. Regular servicing will help keep them turning smoothly and will make your bike feel more responsive. Cleaning the dirt out and replacing the grease with fresh stuff will help make the bearing surfaces last as long as possible. With the ball type, it's worth replacing the bearings at every service – new ones only cost a few pounds. Cartridge bearings are more expensive and can usually be resuscitated – see page 223 for help servicing them. Always take the old cartridge bearings along to your bike shop to match up new ones. The size and shape are crucial and there can be confusion between deceptively similar types.

Check carefully for pitting once you've cleaned out the headset. Even very tiny pits are a sign that your headset needs replacing. The surface that suffers most is the crown race, the ring at the very bottom of the headset that's attached to your forks. Your bearings will quickly wear a groove in this, showing you where they run. The crown race should be completely smooth. You should be able to run a fingernail around the groove without it catching in any blemishes on the surface.

Although headsets can be serviced at home, replacement is a job for your bike shop. The new headset needs to be pressed into your frame with the top and bottom surfaces exactly parallel – otherwise the headset will wear very quickly and bind at some

handlebar angles. The cups are a tight fit, and so must be pressed in carefully to avoid damaging the shape of the headtube. Ignore anybody who tells you that it's okay to fit new headset cups by bashing them into the headtube with a block of wood.

Headset hints

Before you start remove the front wheel altogether. It's easier to do this job if you disconnect either the front brake-lever from the front brake or the front brake-lever from the handlebars. This way you won't damage the cable or hose when you remove the forks.

With cable brakes, disconnect the noodle from the brake – don't undo the fixing bolt, all you have to do is quick-release it – line up the slots on the barrel-adjuster with the slot on the lever, pull the cable gently out and wiggle the nipple free from its nest inside the brake-lever.

With disc brakes, have a look at the lever. If it's fixed on with two bolts on either side of the handlebar, simply remove them both, untangle the hose from the other cables and tape the lever to the forks to stop the hose getting snagged on anything. Otherwise, remove the handlebar grip on the front brake side, gently loosen the brake-fixing bolt and slide the brake-lever off the end of the bars.

Untangle the hose from any of the other controls that are in the way, and tape or tie to the fork leg.

SERVICING THREADLESS HEADSETS

Step 1: Undo the Allen key on the very top of the stem, the top-cap bolt. Remove the top-cap completely, revealing the star-fanged nut inside the steerer tube. Undo the bolts that secure the stem while holding onto the forks. The stem should pull off easily.

Step 2: Tape or tie the stem to the toptube out of the way (protect the frame paint with a cloth). Pull off any washers and set them aside. Pull the forks gently and slowly down out of the frame.

Step 3: The fork may not want to come out. Lots of headsets have a plastic wedge that sits above the top bearing race and that sometimes gets very firmly wedged in place. Release it by sliding a small screwdriver into the gap in the plastic wedge and twisting slightly to release the wedge. You could also try tapping the top of the fork with a plastic or rubber mallet. Don't hit it with a hammer!

Step 4: Catch the pieces as they come off and note the orientation and order of bearing races and seals.

Step 5: Once you've got the fork out, lay out all the bearing races and cups in order. Clean all the races carefully: the ones attached to the frame top and bottom, the loose one off the top chunk of bearings when the fork came out and the crown race still attached to the fork. If you have cartridge bearings, see the section on servicing the cartridges.

Step 6: Look carefully at the clean races and check for pits or rough patches. Pitted bearing races mean a new headset. This needs special tools, and so is a job for your bike shop. Otherwise, clean all the bearings and seals carefully. If you used degreaser, rinse it off and dry everything. Grease the cups in the frame sufficiently, so that the bearings sit in grease up to their middles.

Step 7: Don't grease the crown race on the fork or the loose tophead race. Fit a bearing ring into the cups at either end of the headtube and replace the seals. The direction the races face is crucial, so replace them facing in the same direction as before. Slide the fork back through the frame and slide the loose top race back down over the steerer tube. If it had a plastic wedge, put it next, followed by any washers or covers in the order they came off.

Step 8: Refit the stem and any washers from above the stem. Push the stem firmly down the steerer tube.

Step 9: Make sure there's a gap of 2–3mm (1/12–1/8 in) (A) between the top of the steerer tube and the top of the stem, adding or removing washers if necessary. Refit the top-cap, then adjust bearings (see page 216). Tighten the stem bolts securely, then refit your brake-lever or cable and your front wheel. Check your stem is tight and facing forward. Now check your front brake is working properly.

Checking the condition of the steerer tube

While you've got the forks out, it's worth checking the condition of the steerer tube. This will break if abused, so it is worth inspecting regularly. Adjustment of the bearings also depends on the stem being able to slide easily up and down the steerer tube when the top-cap is tightened or loosened.

Hold a ruler up to the steerer tube. The side of the ruler should lie flat against the length of the steerer. Any bends in the steerer will show up as gaps between it and the ruler. Gaps greater than 1mm (1/25 in) mean that the steerer is bent and should be replaced.

Feel along the surface of the steerer with your fingers. There should be no bulges, dips or irregularities in the diameter of the steerer.

Check for cracks, especially down at the bottom of the steerer tube, near the crown race.

Check that the crown race is a tight fit on the forks – you should not be able to move it with your fingers.

Check the area that the stem bolts onto. It's important that this is clean and smooth. Some stems will damage the steerer if tightened too much: replace it if it is distorted.

The top of the steerer must be smooth. If you've cut down the steerer, file the cut surface so that there are no overhanging snags of metal – these will get caught in the stem and prevent you from adjusting the bearings.

Threaded headsets: stem height

Stand in front of the bike, holding the front wheel between your knees. Try to twist the bars. If you can move them, the stem bolt is too loose. Retighten.

If the stem is tricky to tighten, it may indicate that the steerer tube (the central part of the fork extending up through the frame and onto which your stem is bolted) is damaged. Alternatively, the wedge at the bottom of the stem – which is pulled upward when you tighten the stem bolt – may have become twisted in the steerer tube. Either way, if you can't tighten your stem,

get your bike shop to have a look at it and your steerer tube and replace the forks if necessary. Also make sure that the front wheel is pointing straight forwards. If it's not, loosen the stem bolt, twist it so the wheel and bars are at 90° to each other and retighten. If you've raised the stem, check you can still turn the bars in both directions without stretching or kinking the control cables.

ADJUSTING STEM HEIGHT

Step 1: Undo the expander bolt at the top of the stem. This almost always needs a 6mm Allen key, but you might need to prise off a rubber bung first. Undo it in four complete turns.

Step 2: As you turn the bolt the head rises up out of the stem. Tap the Allen key with a rubber mallet or block of wood, so that the Allen key drops down flush with the stem again. This releases the wedge that holds the stem in place.

Step 3: Once the stem is loose, you can adjust its position. Make sure you don't raise it above the safety mark – an arrow or a row of vertical lines around the stem (A). They should not be visible, but stay hidden inside the headset. Retighten the 6mm Allen key bolt firmly.

Toolbox

The main reason for the demise of the once-ubiquitous threaded headset is that it requires a pair of expensive spanners to adjust – unlike the threadless headset, which can be adjusted with an Allen key.

TOOLS FOR THREADED HEADSETS: ADJUSTING STEM HEIGHT
◎ 6mm Allen key
   If the expander bolt is wedged firmly, a plastic hammer or a block of wood is needed to knock it down.

TOOLS FOR THREADED HEADSETS: ADJUSTING BEARINGS
◎ Ideally you need two headset spanners. The most common size is 36mm although older 1 in headsets need 32mm spanners.

It is possible to use an adjustable spanner on the top lock nut instead of a headset spanner, but take time to tighten the spanner carefully onto the nut flats, since they are soft and easily damaged.

Threaded headsets: bearings

You need two spanners to adjust the bearings. The most common size for 1⅛ in headsets is 36mm. You may also come across 1 in headsets, which need a 32mm spanner, and even the rare 1½ in headsets, which need a 40mm spanner.

The lower, adjustable nut is quite narrow so you will need a special narrow headset spanner. The top locknut is wider so use an adjustable spanner if you only have one headset spanner. To check your headset, pick the bike up by the handlebars and turn the steering. The bars should turn easily and smoothly, with no effort. You should not be able to feel any notches. Drop the bike back onto the ground again and turn the bars 90° so that the wheel points off to one side. Hold on to the front brake to stop the wheel rolling, and rock the bike gently backwards and forwards – in the direction the frame points, not the direction the wheel points. The wheel might flex and you may feel the tyre giving a bit, but you should not feel or hear any knocking or play. Sometimes it helps to get hold of the cups, above and below, while you rock – you shouldn't feel any movement.

The top of the fork steerer tube is threaded and held into the frame with two big nuts. The lower of these has a bearing surface on the bottom in which the top set of bearings runs. Tightening the nut draws the fork up into the frame, squashing the bearing surfaces closer together and eliminating play between fork and frame. Loosening this nut increases the space the bearings sit in, allowing them to turn more smoothly. The correct adjustment is found by turning this nut to a position that eliminates play, while still allowing the forks to rotate freely. Once you've found this magic position, the top nut can be locked down onto the adjusting nut, holding it firmly in position so that it doesn't rattle loose as you ride along. Once bearings have been correctly adjusted and the top nut firmly locked down, they should not work loose over time, so they will not need frequent readjustment. However, the bearings often settle a little bit after servicing, which means they will often need readjusting. If you find yourself having to readjust your bearings often, check that the threads on the forks and the headset are in good condition. The threads will suffer if the headset is ridden loose because both nuts will rub constantly over the fork threads.

Remove the stem, then the top locknut. Have a look at the threads inside the nut. They should be crisp and distinct, with sharp edges. The fork threads should be the same. Unscrew the lower adjusting nut and check the threads on it as well as the fork threads that were concealed by the adjusting nut. If the threads are slightly damaged, reassemble the headset with Loctite on the threads to prevent the nuts from working loose. A new top locking nut will also help. However, if either the fork threads have been badly worn or the nut has worn grooves in the surface of the fork, the fork should be replaced immediately.

ADJUSTING BEARINGS

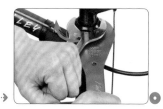

Step 1: Hold the adjusting nut still with one spanner and undo the top nut a couple of turns with the other. The two will be firmly locked together, so you have to be firm with the spanners to get them moving.

Step 2: Once the top nut is loose, use the lower spanner to sort out the position of the adjusting nut. Ideally you're looking for the place where the adjusting nut is as loose as possible without allowing the forks to rock in the frame. Turn the adjustable cup clockwise to eliminate rocking and anticlockwise to allow the headset to turn more freely. Test by holding the front brake on and rocking the bike back and forth.

Step 3: Once you've found the right place, hold the bottom nut still with the spanner to maintain the adjustment and lock the top nut firmly down onto it. Test the adjustment again as you often find that locking down the top nut changes the adjustment, meaning you have to repeat the procedure. Take care as you do this not to overtighten the adjusting cup because, if you wedge it down onto the bearing surface, you'll damage the bearings.

Threaded headsets: servicing

Headsets benefit from regular servicing. Pick up the bike by the handlebar and twist it. The bar should move freely with no crunching noises.

If the headset feels notched or gritty, or it's been ridden loose for a while, it will need servicing. You'll have to take the bars and stem off to get at the headset bearings. Release the front brake, and wiggle the brake cable loose from the front brake lever so that it hangs free. Take the front wheel off too – you'll have to take the forks out to do the job, and the wheel makes them

heavy and unwieldy. Remove the stem and loosen the expander bolt on the the top of the stem four turns. Knock the head of the bolt gently down into the stem with a block of wood or a wooden mallet – not a hammer! Pull the stem up and out of the steerer tube, and tie or tape it to the toptube of your frame to keep it out of the way. Now you're ready to service the headset.

SERVICING HEADSETS

Step 1: Remove the top nut. It is wedged tightly against the lower nut so you need two spanners of the right size – one to hold the adjusting nut still, one to loosen the top nut. Slide off any washers. Lay out everything you take off in order so you know how to put them back together again.

Step 2: Hold the fork still and undo the adjusting nut. When you've removed it, you should find that you can slide the forks out from the bottom of the frame. Make sure you catch any bearings or seals that come off and note which direction they were facing in. Be particularly careful with bearing races as they must go back together in the correct order and orientation.

Step 3: Clean cups, bearings and seals carefully with an old toothbrush and some degreaser. Rinse and dry afterwards. Inspect the bearing surfaces carefully. Any kind of pitting means replacing the headset, a bike shop job. Pay particular attention to the crown race as it's the part that usually suffers first. If the bearings are dirty, replace them since fresh bearings make your headset last longer. Make sure you get the correct size.

Step 4: Grease the cups at either end of the head tube. There should be enough grease to cover the bearings up to their middles. Cartridge bearings are the exception: you do not need to grease the cups. Grease the threads on the adjusting and top nuts and dab a little on the bottom surface of the top cup.

Step 5: Pop bearings and then seals into the cups, paying attention to the direction of the bearings. Slide the fork up through the frame and trap it in place by threading on the adjusting cup. Make sure it's flat when it goes on as it's easy to cross-thread by mistake. Tighten until the fork doesn't rattle around in the frame, but no tighter for now.

Step 6: Replace any washers. If the fork has a slot cut down through the thread, orientate any washers with a tab, so that the tab fits in the slot. Fit the top nut and tighten it down until it touches the adjusting nut. Grease and replace the stem, far enough down so that the safety mark is hidden. Tighten the Allen key bolt at the top of the stem firmly. Replace the front wheel and front brake, then adjust bearings as on page 221.

Headset bearing types

When headsets are new it makes little difference how they are made. As long as they are properly adjusted, cheap ones feel about the same as expensive ones. The difference shows up later after they've been through a bit of a battering, bouncing off kerbs, skidding over muddy trails and carrying your shopping home.

The major advantage of better headsets is usually the sealing. Cheap headsets let in snow, grit and dust and deteriorate quickly. Once a headset starts to get sticky, it retains everything that works its way in as a gloopy paste. Soon this wears pits in the bearing surfaces and then the bearings fall into these pits as you turn the bars. Not long afterwards, the pits get bigger and the

bearings become slightly less round. This is new headset time!

Cartridge headset bearings (A) are more expensive. These have a separate sealed ring that fits precisely into the headset cups. The ring encloses the bearings completely so that they rotate on its inside surface. The advantage to this system is that when you replace the cartridge you are replacing both the bearing and the bearing surfaces. It's a very good idea for headsets, since replacing the cartridges is the equivalent of a new headset without having to go to the expense of having new cups pressed into the frame. The cartridges themselves are slightly more expensive than buying loose bearings.

A variation on the loose bearing idea is the needle bearing (B). Instead of a ring of balls, these use a ring of small rods fanning out from the centre, at an angle. Some people swear by these as they're supposed to spread the bearing load out over a wider area. Others like their ball bearings round. If you have needle bearings, treat them in the same way as normal round bearings.

Basic headsets use two rings of ball bearings (C), sealed above and below with a rubber washer. If you have this type, it's worth getting into the habit of servicing your bearings at least once a year to prevent a build-up of dirt that leads to bearing pitting.

SERVICING CARTRIDGE BEARINGS

Step 1: Using a very sharp knife, carefully peel back the seal on one side of the bearing. Take care not to bend the seal or cut it. Keep the knife as parallel to the seal as possible and always take care to push the knife away from your fingers as it's easy to slip. Once you've lifted the edge of the seal, run the knife carefully around, lifting it off without bending it. Repeat on the other side.

Step 2: Soak the bearing in degreaser and scrub all the grease out. An old toothbrush is perfect for this. Dry the bearing. Hairdryers are great, but do remember to clean them thoroughly before returning to their owners. Clean the seals, too.

Step 3: Pack the bearing half-full with good-quality bicycle grease, like Finish Line or Phil Wood waterproof grease. Spin the bearing to spread the grease evenly around the bearings. Refit the seals, easing them into place with both thumbs. Wipe excess grease off the outside of the bearings.

11 – Components

This chapter is where you learn how to fit and adjust essential components. It includes a range of jobs. You might be inspired to fit new panniers in order to go off and do something exciting, whereas you might be forced into fitting a new seatpost because somebody took a shine to yours when you left your bike locked up at the train station. Either way, these are jobs that can be tackled without the need for expensive tools and they allow you to customise your bike so that it suits your riding style and needs.

Fitting a rack

Follow the steps here to ensure your rack ends up flat, level and secure. Once this is done, you can either hang panniers off it or bungee your load to the top.

If your frame doesn't have the special lugs which are needed for bolting the rack to, you'll have to take your bike to the shop and investigate brackets.

As well as the p-clips mentioned on the opposite page, there is a whole range of specially made little gadgets for bolting the rack to the frame. The most common is a monostay adapter

bracket, which allows you to bolt a rack onto the type of frame where the seat stays merge into one tube above the rear wheel. Rack-mounting seat collars can also save the day, especially on smaller frames. These replace the ring that you tighten to adjust your seat height, with a similar version that has additional threaded holes for the rack to bolt onto.

FITTING A RACK

Step 1: Work out which end is the front – more confusing than you think! The stays will bolt onto holes in the top of the rack. The holes on the back are for attaching reflectors and lights to – in this picture, you can see a separate plate on the back. You may have to spread out the legs of the rack slightly to fit over the frame – the rack stays go on the outside of the frame on either side of the back wheel.

Step 2: Bolt the legs of the rack to the outside of the frame, just above the back wheel axle. Use a washer under the head of each bolt. Take special care on the right-hand side of the bike as the bolt must not protrude through the frame, where it may interfere with the sprockets. If it does, either use a shorter bolt or take the bolt out and add extra washers directly under the bolt head. Don't tighten the bolts yet.

Step 3: Next, attach the stays loosely to the front of the rack. Two common kinds consist of a pair of thin, flexible stays or a stiffer pair of stays with a selection of different-length extra sections to be bolted on. The stays bolt into slots rather than holes, so that you can adjust the position of the rack to suit the shape of your bike. If you're using shake-proof washers, you'll need a spanner to hold them while you tighten the bolts.

Step 4: Next, fit the front of the stays loosely onto the frame. If you've got flexible stays, bend them gently so that you can get the bolts into the frame – take care not to crossthread the bolts. If you've got a selection of joining pieces, choose a length that allows the stays to reach the frame.

Step 5: With all the bolts loosely attached, you should now be able to pull the rack into place so that the top of the rack is level with the ground. Look from above too and check it's pointing straight forwards. You may have to twist it into place.

Step 6: Once it's in place, go round systematically and tighten all the bolts – on the bottoms of the legs, on the stays and where the stays join to the frame. Check again that the bolts on the bottoms of the legs don't protrude through to the insides of the frame and interfere with your sprockets.

Fitting panniers

Once you've got your rack fitted, you're ready for panniers. These need to be attached securely since, if you pack them full of stuff and it starts shifting about while you ride, it makes your bicycle feel very unstable. The worst case scenario is your pannier partially bouncing off the rack and getting caught in your wheel... or bouncing somewhere into the distance when you go over a pothole. The chances are that you won't notice this happening...

Each pannier will have a pair of hooks that loop over the tubing of the rack. Better versions have a secondary clip that hooks under the tubing, so the pannier won't come off unless you release it. You'll generally find the rack is longer than the width between the pannier hooks, so you can choose how far back along the rack the pannier should sit. Keeping the weight as far forward as possible will maximise stability. However, if the panniers sit too close to you, you'll bang your heels on them every time you pedal – this is really irritating. You should be able to shift the position of the hooks sideways on the bag, choosing a position that prevents the bag shifting. As well as keeping your load stable, this helps to prevent the pannier hooks wearing through the rack tubing by constantly shuffling back and forth.

The bottom part of the bag must also be secured to the rack. This may seem superfluous when the bike is standing still, but out in the real world it's essential. If the back of the bike bounces around, the bottoms of the panniers flap outwards and may become dislodged.

Before you ride off, ensure that you've got any straps or bungees neatly tucked away. If they dangle down, they will inevitably flap about and get tangled in the back wheel, bringing you to an unexpected halt. If you're going to be carrying a lot of weight, just take a moment to check your rear-tyre pressure. A well-inflated tyre will give your wheel a bit of extra protection.

With panniers, it may seem tempting just to get one big one and stuff everything into it. But I would suggest two smaller ones rather than one big one. Although it's slightly more expensive, it's worth it for a couple of reasons. The first is that it's a lot easier to be organised if you've got two separate panniers – put your work papers in one side, and your sandwiches in the other. It's also less tiring to ride with an evenly loaded pair of bags than a single, heavy one. You rock from side to side as you pedal, so the bike dips slightly over to one side, and then down on the other. Evenly weighted bags will bob across like a pendulum, counterbalancing each other, whereas a single bag will have to be dragged back upright with every revolution of your feet.

POSITIONING A PANNIER

Step 1: Pop the panniers on the rack and sit on the bike. Put your feet on the pedals in their normal pedalling position, with the ball of your foot directly over the pedal axle and pedal backwards. Move the pannier until your heel just clears the bag. Check your rear light is still clearly visible. Push the backs of the bags in towards the wheel and check that they won't go far enough to get caught in the spokes.

Step 2: Loosen the bolts that hold the pannier hook in place and slide the hooks so they trap the cross-struts of the rack or the rail across the back of the rack. This prevents the bag from sliding forwards and backwards on the rack. Retighten the hook bolts.

Step 3: The bottom of the pannier needs to be attached to the rack stays, so that it can't flap outwards. In this case, a plastic tab must be positioned so that it hooks behind the rack leg. Other options include a strap or loop of elastic that hooks around the bottom of the pannier leg. The pannier may come with a hook to loop the strap around. You'll have to undo the bolt that attaches the rack to the frame and refit it with the hook underneath.

Replacing your seat post

This is the most irritating job you will do on your bike. Since seat posts rarely wear out, the only time they need replacing is usually when somebody pinches them.

The important thing to note when replacing seat posts is that there are about 30 different common sizes, in increments of 0.2mm. A size too big won't fit in your frame, whereas a size too small will fit but will rock slightly at every pedal stroke, slowly but inevitably destroying your frame. It's essential to get exactly the right size. If you still have the old post, you're in luck – the right size will be

stamped on it. If it's been stolen, this option isn't open to you. The measurement needs to be more accurate than anything you can do with an ordinary tape measure. If you have a Vernier gauge or a micrometer, use that to measure the internal diameter of the seat tube. Otherwise, you'll have to drag your bike to the bike shop and get them to measure up a new post.

REPLACING A SEAT POST

Step 1: Clean out the inside of the frame, removing all the old grease and dirt that's accumulated. Re-grease the frame – the only exception to this rule is if you're fitting a carbon seat post, in which case check the manufacturer's instructions on whether to treat the post and, if so, what with. Release the seat binder bolt so it's loose.

Step 2: Slide the post into the frame without the saddle for now. Check as you do so that the post is the right size – you shouldn't have to force the post. If it won't go in easily, it won't come out at all. Push it in until the 'min insertion' lines disappear completely into the frame. Before tightening the seat post binder bolt, try rocking the top of the seat post – if there's enough room for the post to knock, it's too small.

Step 3: Tighten the seat post binder bolt just enough to hold the seat post in place. The clamp bolt is the one that holds the plates at the top of the seat post together. Loosen it off completely, so you can twist the top plate a quarter of a turn sideways. While you're there, pop a bit of grease on the clamp bolt threads and under the head of the bolt. Place the saddle on top of the grooves in the bottom clamp plate.

Step 4: Now, twist the top plate back, so that its grooves line up with the seat post rails, trapping the seat post rails between the top and bottom plates. It's a bit fiddly getting in there past the saddle, but it's worth taking time to get the alignment right.

Step 5: Leaving the clamp bolt slightly loose for now means you can change both the angle and position of the saddle by rolling the clamp plates over the top of the seat post. You can move the saddle nearer to or further from the bars, by sliding the saddle rails along in the grooves. See page 35 for tips on what kind of a position to aim for. Once you're satisfied, tighten the clamp bolt firmly.

Step 6: Set the saddle to the right height (page 35 tells you what height to aim for). If you've got an Allen key fixing, tighten it. Quick-release skewers can be a little more pesky. They should be set in a position where folding the quick-release lever secures the post. If the lever won't close easily or doesn't secure the seat post, open the lever and adjust the Allen key bolt on the opposite side and then close the lever.

Fitting a new Aheadset stem

The changeover from threaded to threadless headsets has made it possible for people to adjust their headset bearings with a couple of Allen keys.

But there's a downside too as changing the height of your handlebars has got more awkward. On the older type, you could undo the bolt at the top of the stem, haul the stem upwards and retighten. Achieving the same on bikes with an Aheadset, you remove the stem and swap it for one of a different length or one that comes off the bar at a different angle. The most common complaint is about bars that are too low and too far away. The solution is to buy and fit a shorter stem that kicks upwards quite steeply, bringing the bars up and towards you. The job's much easier with a 'front loader'-type stem, with two or four bolts clamping a plate onto the front of the bars, as shown below. Removing all the bolts allows you to lift the bars out of the stem, without having to remove the controls and the grips.

FITTING AN AHEADSET

Step 1: Loosen all the bolts that clamp the handlebars onto the stem and then remove them. This allows you to take off the plate at the front of the stem and remove the bars. Taking care not to kink the control cables, tape them onto the frame of the bike to keep them out of the way while you work.

Step 2: Remove the bolt from the top-cap – it's the one on the very top of the stem. Lift the top-cap off completely. Undo the stem binder bolts. If you've got the bike in a work stand, you'll have to support the forks at this stage, otherwise they may well drop out of the bottom of the frame.

Step 3: Pull the old stem up and off. Loosen the stem bolts on the new stem and slide it onto the steerer tube, pushing it firmly down. The top of the steerer tube should sit 2–3mm ($\frac{1}{12}$–$\frac{1}{8}$ in) below the top of the stem, as shown. If the stem sits too high, remove it and take off washers from under the stem. If the steerer approaches or protrudes above the top of the stem, add more washers below the stem to correct the gap.

Step 4: Replace the top-cap, trapping the stem in place. Fit the bars into the new stem and tighten the fixing bolts evenly. There should be an equal gap between stem and faceplate above and below the bars. Tighten four-bolt-style stems in a cross pattern, to ensure that they're equally tensioned. Point the stem straight forwards in line with the front wheel. Get on the bike and check that the bars are at a comfortable angle.

Step 5: (If you've not adjusted headsets before, use the full instructions on page 216) Adjust the top-cap so that the forks can still spin freely in the frame, but there is no play in the headset – the forks should not be able to rock in the frame. Tighten the stem fixing bolts firmly and evenly. Check the stem is tight by standing in front of the bike, front wheel between your knees. You shouldn't be able to twist the bars.

Step 6: Changing the stem altered the position of the handlebars. If they're higher or further forward, the control cables may be too short. Check by turning the bars all the way to either side, making sure this doesn't stretch any of the control cables. Cables that are too short will have to be replaced with longer ones – you will almost always have to change the inner cable as well as the outer casing.

Fitting new handlebars

This job appears much more daunting that it actually is in practice. A new set of handlebars can make a remarkable difference to how your bike feels.

A slightly curved shape or a pair of handlebars where the grips sweep backwards slightly can make a big difference to the comfort of your bicycle, giving you a more upright position from which to attend to the road ahead.

Bars must also be replaced if they get bent or if the surface becomes scratched. Either of these factors will mean that the

bar is weakened and, when they do break, they tend to do so without warning, so it's worth being proactive about it.

Getting the position of a new pair of bars right takes some trial and error. You can't really know the most comfortable angle until you've got them on the bike and have had a chance to sit on it. Don't be tempted to leave the bars loose then climb on to the

FITTING HANDLEBARS

Step 1: Remove the grips. It's easiest to slide a chopstick or a thin screwdriver under the grip and use that to lift up the grip enough to spray something slippery underneath. Hairspray works really well as it makes the grip slippery for a bit then sticky – perfect. Otherwise, use warm soapy water. Twist and pull to get the grip off. Remove light brackets, computer brackets and anything else that's bolted onto the bars.

Step 2: Unbolt and remove shifters and brake-levers without scratching the bars. If the levers and shifters won't slide off easily, remove the fixing bolts altogether and open up the clamp very slightly with a screwdriver, just enough to slide the levers off. Don't bend the clamps! If the cables are too short to get the controls off without kinking the cables, wait until after the next step when you've released the bars from the stem.

Step 3: If the stem has a separate plate on the front clamped over the bar with two or four bolts, remove the bolts completely, pull off the face of the stem and remove the bars. If the stem has a single bolt, loosen it and wiggle the bars out of the stem. If the bars have kinks in them, you may find that rotating the bars gently in the stem makes them easier to slide out.

How long do bars last?

Handlebars don't break very often, but that doesn't mean it never happens and, if it does, it's likely to be relatively unpleasant. There are three circumstances under which handlebars should be replaced.

⊚ If you have a crash or anything else happens that means the bars are visibly bent, they should be replaced straight away. Don't be tempted to ride your bike until you have new bars. Bending the bars weakens them and means that, if you go over a big bump or a pothole or drop off a kerb, there is a chance that the weak spot will give way and the bars will break. You lose the ability to steer or brake and in most circumstances the combination is bad news.

⊚ Sometimes bars get scratched or dented through careless fitting of brake-levers, gear-levers or light fittings. At other times you may have a crash that leaves the shape of the bars intact, but twists brake-levers around or into the bar. Again, this spells the end of the road for your bars.

⊚ Aluminium bars should be replaced regularly whether you've bent them or not as they don't last forever. Steel bars, although much cheaper, are much more durable and they'll last pretty much until they rust through. Replace aluminium bars every five years. If you're a heavy or aggressive rider, you might consider doing so more often.

saddle – if you lean down on them, they'll slip round underneath you. Tighten the stem bolt before you put any pressure on them. The first time you ride the bike you'll probably change your mind about the angle you've chosen, so take an Allen key with you for fine-tuning.

If you're swapping your bars for ones of a different shape, it's worth being aware before you start that this will affect your control cables. If the new bars sit higher or further forwards than the old ones, there is a chance that one or all of the cables will struggle to reach when you're turning to one side or the other. It's not easy to tell in advance if this is going to be the case, so it's worth arming yourself with the necessary extra cable and casing to do the job if you have to.

Handlebar quality

One handlebar looks much like another, so again it can be difficult to understand price differences between apparently similar products. The cheapest bars are made of steel. These are robust, but they're also heavy and are only found on the most basic machines. Next up in price, and down in weight, are aluminium bars. As well as being lighter, these flex slightly as you ride. Although the actual movement is small, it's enough to absorb vibration from the road, making them a good choice for comfort. Shaving off more weight (and adding more money) means carbon fibre bars. Carbon fibre is strong enough for the job, but needs extra care – bars that are damaged will break rather then bending, so they must be inspected frequently and replaced immediately if your bike is involved in a collision.

FITTING HANDLEBARS cont

Step 4: Clean out the internal surface of the stem, so your new bars will grip securely without creaking. Use degreaser on stubborn bits. Grease the fixing bolts – both on the threads and under the heads.

Step 5: Refit the new bars in the stem – for single-bolt stems, slide the bars through. For two- and four-bolt stems, trap the bars behind the face plate and fit all the bolts loosely.

Step 6: Slide the controls back onto the handlebars. If the cables are too short to allow the controls over the ends of the bars, slide the whole bar sideways in the stem. Align the bar centrally in the stem – you'd be surprised how many people miss out this step – and tighten the stem bolt(s). Two- and four-bolt stems need to be tightened so that there is an equal gap between the stem and the face plate above and below the bars.

Step 7: Sit on the bike, and check that the bars fit comfortably in your hands – if not, get off the bike, loosen the fixing bolts, retighten and check again. Once you're happy with the position of the bars, twist the controls around so they're easy to reach. A good place to start is with the brake-levers at an angle of 30–45° to the ground and the shifters tucked up close underneath them.

Step 8: Grips need to go on next. They should be a tight fit and it's tempting to spray lubricant in there to get them on. It's a really bad idea though as they are liable to slide around on the bars next time it rains. Use a proprietary grip glue like Renthals (from motorbike shops), hairspray or hot water. Grips that slide on very easily are worn out and should be replaced.

Step 9: Now's when you get to find out if your cables are compatible with your new bar set-up. Turn the bars all the way in both directions, and check that this doesn't pull the cables at a sharp angle at either end – even at their full extension, the cables should make a graceful curve out of the levers. Short cables – inner and outer casing – will have to be replaced.

Fitting dynamos

Many people who are otherwise quite confident about their mechanics get daunted by dynamos and all that goes with them. They're not that complicated though – there must be a unit generating the electricity, which must then have an uninterrupted route out to each light and back. The easiest way to achieve this is to use dual-core wire – the type that often connects speakers to amps. The electricity runs to each lamp unit along one of the strands of the dual-core wire and then earths back to the generator along the other.

- It always makes sense to start by fitting the dynamo body to the bike. If you're using a hub dynamo, this can be easily accomplished by fitting the front wheel. Take care with orientation – they are designed to roll in one direction, which will be printed on the hub flange. Shimano dynamo hubs also come packaged with a circle of card slotted around the axle. Align the wheel so that the arrows point forwards.

- Bottle-type dynamos, which run on the sidewall of the tyre, are a little more complex. They require a bracket to fit them to the bike, which as often as not doesn't come supplied with the dynamo body. The dynamo bottle will work equally well on front or back wheels, but the bracket needs to hold the dynamo body so it sits forward of its mounting. The bottle is sprung to hold the head in onto the tyre. If it's mounted backwards, the tyre pulls the bottle constantly closer to the wheel, causing excessive drag. There's a particularly neat dynamo bracket made by Busch and Miller that fits the brake mounting boss on the front fork and holds the bottle safely out of the way in front of the front brake.

- The angle that the bottle sits at is crucial for smooth running and minimum drag. If you look at the dynamo from the side and imagine a straight line running directly through the centre of the bottle, the bottle should be rotated on its bracket so that the straight line also passes through the wheel axle. Once you've decided on the correct position, secure the bracket. Since you're using dual-core wire with a separate earth, it's not necessary to ensure there is a bare metal connection between the dynamo body and the frame.

- Next, secure the lamp units. Set them so that they're as high as they can practicably be for maximum visibility and so that they're not obscured by any of your other baggage.

- Now, start with the front light. Measure out sufficient dual-core wire – leave enough to wrap the wire around the frame to secure it with plenty to spare as there's no harm in a little slack. Make sure there's enough slack for the handlebars to turn in both directions without stretching the wire. Secure to the frame with tape or zipties.

- Separate the last 10cm (4 in) of the dual-core wire into two separate strands – the joining web is thin and soft and will simply pull apart. Strip the last 5mm (¼ in) of plastic coating off each end of each wire.

- One of the two wires will be marked – usually with a pale line or a ridge in the insulating plastic. Connect the marked line to the live terminal on the lamp and the live terminal on the dynamo bottle. Then repeat, with the unmarked line attached to the earth terminals on the lamp and the bottle. You may find that there isn't a specific earth terminal on the lamp, the bottle or both. If this is the case, the stripped end of the wire must be trapped under a metal part of the bracket, either where two parts of the bracket clamp together or where the bracket clamps to the frame. It is essential that an electrical connection is made, so bare metal must touch bare metal.

- Repeat with the rear lamp unit, remembering, if the bottle runs off the front wheel, to leave enough slack in the cable for the front wheel to turn. Strip off the last 5mm (¼ in) of insulating plastic from each end of each wire and attach both ends of the marked wire to the live terminals and both ends of the unmarked to the earth terminals.

Now, spin the wheel to test. Both lamps should come on. If not, investigations should proceed in the following order:

- If one of the lamps works and the other doesn't, it's the bulb or the wiring. Check the wiring carefully, especially at the terminals. Then try replacing the bulb. Front and rear bulbs have different power rating so you can't just swap them – you'll have to get another one.

- If neither lamp works, try disconnecting first one then the other. If one light suddenly starts working when the other is disconnected, the other has a wiring fault – check that both earth and live wires are connected correctly. If neither lamp works, even when they're disconnected one at a time, the generator is either faulty or worn out – replace it.

Servicing clipless pedals

Clipless pedals are expensive and the shortness of the axle means that the bearings will wear out quickly once the pedal starts to develop any play.

But they're very satisfying to repair – although it's a bit fiddly, you'll be able to feel the difference straight away.

The first sign that your pedal bearings are worn often comes when the pedal starts to click under pressure. Check by holding the crank still in one hand, and the pedal body in the other. Try to twist the pedal – there should be no sideways movement, but

the pedal should roll easily on the axle and it should continue for several turns if given a bit of a spin. If the axle is wobbly or stiff, it's time for a pedal service.

It's well worth replacing the bearings once you're in there, but they're an unusual size (³⁄₃₂ in). If your bike shop doesn't have them, try a bearing shop.

SERVICING SHIMANO PD-M747 PEDALS

Step 1: Remove both pedals from the bike, remembering that the left-hand pedal has a reverse thread and so comes off clockwise. Clamp the tool in a vice and turn the pedal in the direction of the arrow printed on the tool. Wrap a cloth around the pedal for extra grip if necessary. The threads are plastic and will strip if forced backwards, so check the direction carefully.

Step 2: Pull the pedal right off the axle. Take the axle out of the vice, remove the plastic tool and clamp the pedal axle back in the vice, narrow end upwards. You'll be able to see the top row of bearings, trapped under the cone. The second set is between the steel tube and the washer below it.

Step 3: At the top end of the axle, you'll see the locknut and the cone. The locknut is on top and needs a 7mm spanner. The cone is next, and needs a 10mm spanner. Shimano manufacture a neat cone-adjusting tool which makes the job easier (like the one shown in step 6), but if you don't have one, ordinary spanners work fine – in this picture, a 7mm socket wrench. Remove both cone and locknut completely.

Step 4: Pick off all the bearings that were trapped under the cone and then pull off the steel tube. Pull the rubber spacer off the axle and then lift off the lower washer complete with bearings. Pull off the plastic sleeve and rubber seal. Clean all parts carefully and check for pitted bearing surfaces. If they're worn out, replace the axle. While you're there, clean out the inside of the pedal body.

Step 5: Refit rubber seal and plastic sleeve. Grease the curved washer, place 12 ³⁄₃₂-inch bearings on it, and slide it gently over the axle to rest on the plastic sleeve. Refit the rubber washer. Grease the bearing surface in one end of the metal tube and pack another 12 bearings onto it. Slide it carefully over the axle. Tighten the cone onto the axle by hand, curved side down. Make sure it traps all the bearings. Refit the locknut loosely.

Step 6: The cone must be tightened onto the bearings enough so that there is no play between the axle and the metal tube, but the tube can still turn freely. Then, holding the cone still, tighten the locknut onto it. This is fiddly and you'll have to repeat the adjustment several times. Refit the axle assembly back into the pedal. Tighten with the grey plastic tool, using the direction arrows printed on the tool.

Rim brakes troubleshooting

Symptom	Cause	Solution	V-brakes	Cantilever	Calliper
Brakes squeak	Brake blocks set flat to the rim, or with the back of the brake block touching first	'Toe in' brakes so that the fronts of the brake blocks touch first	110	n/a	117
	Rims dirty, especially with oil	Clean rims with degreaser	114	n/a	n/a
Brakes don't stop the bike, or don't stop the bike quickly enough	Brake blocks set too far from rim	Set brake blocks closer	110	n/a	117
	Surface of the brake blocks have become contaminated or picked up debris	Remove wheels, pick debris out of the wheels with a sharp knife, roughen surface of blocks with sandpaper, replace wheels	114		
	Rims contaminated or dirty	Clean rims with degreaser	114		
	Brake blocks worn out	Check wear on blocks – replace if necessary	110	123	117
	V-brakes – brake units too close together, head of noodle jams on cable clamp when braking	Reset units to vertical by adjusting the cable, reorder brake block washers for minimal rim clearance	108	n/a	n/a
	Cantilevers – link wires make straddle angle too wide/too narrow	Reset straddle or link wire angle, readjust brakes appropriately	n/a	125	n/a
Brake-levers take a lot of effort to pull on	Cables frayed or dirty, outer casing damaged	Replace cables, and outer casing if necessary	108	124	118
Brakes will pull on, but won't spring back from the rim when you release the brake-lever	Brake blocks have been set too low, and have worn so that a lip of brake block gets trapped under the rim	Remove wheel, cut off offending lip with a sharp knife, replace wheel, reset brake block position appropriately	110	123	117
	Dirty or frayed brake cable, damaged outer casing	Clean and oil, or replace brake cable	108	124	118
	V-brakes – noodle squashed or dirty inside	Replace noodle, check cable condition and replace that too if necessary	108	n/a	n/a
	Caliper brakes – brake pivot dirty or bent	Service calipers, inspect condition, replace if necessary	n/a	n/a	120
	Brake-levers damaged	Release cable, check lever will pull smoothly towards bars when there's no cable tension, replace levers if necessary, refit cable	102	124	118
	V-brakes – brake pivots dirty or corroded	Service brake units, oil and refit	112	n/a	n/a
Brake blocks wear out very quickly	Rim surface worn	Inspect rim surface – replace wheel/rim if there are cracks, bulges or deep ridges. If there is one, check rim wear indicators	115		

234

Disc brakes troubleshooting

Symptom	Cause	Solution	Page
Mechanical Brakes – Brake pads don't pull back smoothly after braking	Brake cable gritty, corroded or frayed inside casing	Clean and lubricate brake cable or replace it	127
	Piston heads dirty	Remove pads and clean, or replace	n/a
	Dirt has worked its way into the calliper body, jamming the mechanism	Strip and clean calliper body	126
	Pads have become contaminated with oil	Replace pads	128
	Rotors have become contaminated	Clean rotors with degreaser, isopropyl alcohol or warm soapy water	n/a
	Pads are too far from rotors	Adjust pad position	127
Mechanical Brakes – Brakes rub constantly on rotors	Rotor is warped	Bend back or replace rotor	n/a
	Calliper body is touching rotor	Adjust calliper body position	126
	Pads set too close to rotor	Adjust pad positions independently – outer pad using cable tension, inner pad using adjustment screw	127
Mechanical Brakes – Brakes not very effective – cannot lock wheels by pulling lever	Pads have become contaminated with oil	Replace pads	128
	Rotors have become contaminated	Clean rotors with degreaser, isopropyl alcohol or warm soapy water	n/a
	Pads are worn out	Check pad thickness – replace if less than 0.5mm (1/50 in)	126
Hydraulic Brakes – Brake pads rub on rotor	Calliper misaligned	Refit calliper, with rotor central between pads	n/a
	Rotor warped	Bend back or replace rotor	n/a
Hydraulic Brakes – Brake-levers feel squidgy, brakes ineffective	Air in system	Bleed brakes	130
	Leaking hose	Inspect hose carefully, especially at joints, tighten leaking joints, bleed brakes	130
Hydraulic Brakes – Brakes squeal	Contaminated brake pads or rotor	Clean rotor, replace pads	129
	Worn or roughened rotor surface	Replace rotor	n/a
	Loose fixing bolts causing vibrations	Check and tighten brake-fixing bolts and rotor-fixing bolts	n/a

Transmission troubleshooting

Symptom	Cause	Solution	Page
Chain slips, giving way suddenly under pressure	Worn cassette and chain	Measure chain for wear, replace if necessary, replace cassette at the same time	158–163
	Worn chainrings	Replace chainrings	167
	Damaged teeth on chainring	Realign bent teeth back	n/a
	Worn or damaged freehub body	Replace freehub body	n/a
	Twisted chain links	Straighten or remove twisted link	158, 159
	Dirty or dry chain	Clean and lubricate chain	85
	Badly adjusted rear indexing	Adjust cable tension	138
	Incompatible chain, cassette or chainrings	Ensure compatability, especially between chain and cassette – don't mix eight- and nine-speed components	135
Rear derailleur doesn't index correctly	Incorrect cable tension	Tighten lockring and adjust gears	138, 163
	Dirty cable	Clean and relubricate cable/replace cable and casing	156
	Split outer casing	Replace casing	157
	Bent derailleur	Replace derailleur	148
	Bent derailleur hanger	Replace or bend back hanger	146
	Shifter worn	Disconnect cable from derailleur and test operation of shifter while pulling on cable as it emerges from shifter – replace if necessary	168, 169
	Casette lockring loose, so that sprockets can move around on freehub body	Adjust cable tension	138
Rear derailleur usually indexes correctly but suffers ghost shifts when being ridden	Casing too short from handlebars to frame, or between sections of full suspension frame, so that movement of bars or frame tenses cable	Replace sections of outer casing with longer bits – you may also need to replace cable – ensure that casing cannot snag on parts of the frame	140
	Chain worn	Measure chain wear, replace chain and cassette if necessary	166
Chain won't shift into smallest or largest sprocket	End-stop screws are too far in	Undo end-stop screws so that chain can shift into the extremes of the cassette	144–145
	Incorrect cable tension	Adjust cable tension	138
	Guide jockey wheel too far from sprockets	Adjust B-tension screw	142

Transmission troubleshooting

Symptom	Cause	Solution	Page
Front derailleur doesn't index correctly	Incorrect cable tension	Adjust cable tension	150
	Incorrect front derailleur position	Adjust front derailleur so that the outer plate is parallel to the chainring, with 2–3mm ($\frac{1}{12}$–$\frac{1}{8}$ in) of clearance between chainring and derailleur	155
	Bent derailleur	Bend back or replace derailleur	156
	Dirty or corroded cable	Clean or replace cable	152–154
	Frayed cable	Replace cable	152–154
	Split or kinked outer casing	Replace outer casing and cable	152–154
	Worn or broken shifter	Disconnect shifter from derailleur, pull gently on cable as it emerges from shifter, operate shifter to check for three distinct positions – replace if necessary	168, 169
Shifting sluggish	Worn chain	Replace chain and cassette	158–163
	Worn derailleur pivots	Clean and lubricate derailleur, replace derailleur	156
	Ferrules missing from ends of sections of casing	Ensure that there's a ferrule at each end of each section of casing to help prevent the casing from shifting in the cable stops	157
	Cable in wrong position under clamp bolt	Remove cable and inspect area under clamp bolt – the correct position for the cable will be indicated by a groove in the derailleur	150
	Brake casing used instead of gear casing	Always use correct gear casing – brake casing is stronger but will compress slightly under load, causing erratic shifting	157
Front derailleur won't shift into largest sprocket	'High' end-stop screw too far in	Undo 'high' end-stop screw to allow chain to shift onto large chainring	151
	Chainset sits too far out from frame, so that derailleur cannot reach at full extension	Fit shorter bottom bracket or fit chainset that sits closer to frame	208–211
	Incorrect cable tension	Increase cable tension	150
Front derailleur won't shift into smallest sprocket	Incorrect cable tension	Reduce cable tension	150
	'Low' end-stop screw too far in	Undo 'low' end-stop screw to allow chain to drop into smallest sprocket	151
Chain drops into middle or smaller ring randomly	Worn shifter	Replace shifter	168, 169

Wheel troubleshooting

Symptom	Cause	Solution	Page
Bike feels slow, you feel tired after short rides	Cones too tight on front or rear wheels, or both	Adjust cones so that wheels spin smoothly	182, 183
Bike feels uncertain when cornering	Cones too loose – wheel will wobble from side to side on the frame	Adjust cone so that the wheel can't rock from side to side in the frame	182, 183
	Wheel is buckled	True wheel so that rim runs true and doesn't waggle from side to side as the wheel spins	190–193
	Insufficient tyre pressure	Inflate tyre to minimum pressure marked on the sidewall of the tyre	188
Rim brakes – rim rubs on V- or cantilever brake blocks	Wheel is buckled	True wheel, so that rim runs true, and doesn't waggle from side to side as the wheel spins	190–193
Brake blocks wear quickly	Rims dirty	Clean rims with degreaser	85
	Rims worn	Check rims for scours, grooves or ridges – replace rims or wheels	115
Spokes loosen repeatedly	Rim buckled	Uneven spoke tension in buckled wheels causes spokes to loosen – rebuild wheel with new rim	n/a
Frequent punctures	Tyre still has sharp things stuck in it	Check tyre carefully, feeling around the inside for protruding thorns or glass – fold the tyre inside out, so that you can see more clearly	90–93
	Spokes poking through the rim	Run your fingers around the inside of the rim, checking for sharp spoke ends – file sharp ends off	90–93
	Rim tape shifting, exposing spoke holes	Replace rim tape with wider, tighter one	189
Tyres much more worn on one side than the other	Constantly carrying pannier on the same side	Swap pannier from side to side, remove tyre and replace the other way around regularly, or (best!) spread the load out between two panniers	90–93
Rear tyre always wears much more than the front	Your weight is distributed further towards the back of the bike, putting more load on the rear tyre	This is normal! You usually have to replace the rear tyre much more frequently than the front	188

Bottom bracket troubleshooting

Symptom	Cause	Solution	Page
One crank rocks from side to side, the other is firm	Loose crank bolt	Tighten crank bolt	209
Both cranks rock from side to side	Bottom bracket unit loose in frame	Remove both cranks, tighten bottom bracket in frame, replace both cranks	208–211
	Bottom bracket worn out	Replace bottom bracket	208–211
Cranks loosen repeatedly	Crank bolt loose	Tighten firmly – use a longer wrench for more leverage	209
	Crank mating surface worn by being ridden loose	Replace crank	208–209
	New crank still loosens repeatedly	Replace bottom bracket	208–211
Creaking noises from bottom bracket area	Dry or loose interface between components	Remove cranks, clean interface between cranks and axle, replace, retighten firmly	212
	Bottom bracket loose in frame	Remove both cranks, tighten bottom bracket in frame, replace both cranks	208–211

Headsets troubleshooting

Symptom	Cause	Solution	Page Aheadset	Page Threaded
Steering sluggish, unresponsive	Headset too tight	Loosen headset	216	221
	Headset clogged	Service headset	218–219	222–223
Front of bike rocks when braking	Headset loose	Tighten headset	216	221
Bike uncertain when cornering	Headset loose	Tighten headset	216	221
Headsets don't last long, wearing out frequently	Bearing surfaces pitted	Take to bike shop for new headset	n/a	n/a
	Headset cups not parallel in frame	Take to bike shop to have headset re-pressed into frame	n/a	n/a
		Take to bike shop to have faces of headtube reamed flat	n/a	n/a
Creaking noises when bars turn	Brake and gear cables flexing in cable stops	Check that all sections of casing have ferrules and oil ferrules	157	157
	Headset dry – insufficient or contaminated grease	Service headset, repack with plenty of good quality grease	218–219	222–223

239

Glossary: the language of bikes

From Aheadset to Ziptie, this list covers most of the odd word and phrases that you are going to need in order to talk about bicycles and their mysteries. It's easy to get confused since many of the names that refer to specific parts also have more general meanings. Stick with these definitions and you should be okay.

- ◆ **Aheadset:** the bearing that clamps the fork securely to the fame, while allowing the fork to rotate freely, so you can steer. The now-standard Aheadset design works by clamping the stem directly to the steerer tube of the forks, allowing you to adjust the bearings by sliding the stem up and down the steerer tube with an Allen key.

- ◆ **Air spring:** used in both suspension forks and shocks, an air spring consists of a sealed chamber pressurised with a pump. The chamber acts as a spring, resisting compression, and springing back as soon as any compressing force is released. Air has a natural advantage as a spring medium for bicycles – it's very light.

- ◆ **Antiseize:** compound spread on the interface of two parts, preventing them sticking together – vital on titanium parts, since the metal is very reactive and will seize happily and permanently onto anything it's bolted to.

- ◆ **Axle:** the central supporting rod that passes through wheels and bottom brackets, around which they can rotate.

- ◆ **Balance screws:** these are found on V-brakes and cantilevers, and allow you to alter the preload on the spring that pulls the brake away from the rim, so that the two sides of the brake move evenly and touch the rim at the same time.

- ◆ **Barends:** handlebar extensions that give you extra leverage when climbing, and a variety of hand positions for long days out.

- ◆ **Barrel-adjuster:** a threaded end-stop for the outer casing. Turning the barrel moves the outer casing in its housing, changing the distance the inner cable has to travel from nipple to cable clamp bolt, and so altering the tension in the cable.

- ◆ **Base layer:** a closefitting vest worn in cold weather, that wicks perspiration away from your skin, keeping you warmer, drier and more comfortable.

- ◆ **Biscuit:** (1) useful things, like odd nuts and bolts, that you keep in an old biscuit tin for emergencies; (2) suitable offering to your bike shop in exchange for past and future favours.

- ◆ **Bleeding:** opening the hydraulic brake system, allowing air to escape, and refilling the resulting gap with oil. Bleeding is necessary because air is compressible, unlike brake fluid, so if there's air in your system, pulling the brakes on squashes the air, rather than forcing the brake pads onto the rotors.

- ◆ **Bottom bracket:** the main bearing that connects the cranks through your frame. Often ignored, because it's invisible, the smooth running of this part saves you valuable energy.

- ◆ **Bottom bracket cups**: the threaded cups on either side of the bottom bracket that bolt onto your frame. The right-hand cup has a reverse thread and is often integral to the main body of the bottom bracket unit.

- ◆ **Bottoming-out:** a suspension term, meaning that the fork or shock has completely compressed, to the end of its travel. Sometimes accompanied by a loud clunk, bottoming-out is not necessarily a problem – if you don't do it at least once every ride, you're not using the full extent of the travel.

◆ **Brake arch:** on suspension forks, a brace between the two lower legs, passing over the tyre and increasing the stiffness of the fork. Still called a brake arch even if your brakes are now down by your hub.

◆ **Brake blocks:** fit onto your V-brake or cantilever brakes. Pulling the brake cable forces them onto your rim, slowing you down.

◆ **Brake pads:** on disc brakes, hard slim pads fit into the disc callipers and are pushed onto the rotors by pistons inside the brake calliper, cable- or hydraulically operated. Being made of very hard material, they last longer than you'd expect for their size and, unlike V-brake blocks, do not slow you down if they rub slightly against the rotors. Contamination with brake fluid renders them instantly useless.

◆ **Brake pivot:** stud on the frame or forks onto which cantilever or V-brakes bolt, which your brakes rotate around so that the brake blocks hit the rim.

◆ **B-screw:** sits behind your derailleur hanger and adjusts its angle. Too close, and the chain rattles on the sprockets. Too far, and shifting is sluggish.

◆ **Burn-in time:** new disc brake pads need burning in; they never brake powerfully fresh from the box. Burn new pads in by braking repeatedly, getting gradually faster, until the brakes bite properly.

◆ **Cable:** the steel wire that connects brake- and gear-levers to shifters and units. Must be kept clean and lubricated for smooth shifting and braking.

◆ **Cable stop:** the part of the frame that holds the end of a section of outer casing, but allows the cable to pass though.

◆ **Calliper brakes:** found on road bikes, these are simple and light. A horseshoe-shaped brake unit holds a brake block against the rim on either side.

◆ **Callipers:** mechanical or hydraulic disc brake unit, which sits over the rotor and houses the brake pads.

◆ **Cantilever:** (1) an older rim brake type, connected to your brake cable by a second, V-shaped cable; (2) suspension design where the back wheel is connected to a swingarm, which pivots around a single point. These designs are simple and elegant.

◆ **Cantilever brake:** see cantilever.

◆ **Cartridge bearing:** a sealed bearing unit. These are more expensive than ball bearings but are usually better value – the bearing surface is part of the unit, and so is replaced at the same time.

◆ **Casing:** the (usually) black flexible tube that supports cables. Brake and gear casing are different – brake cable has a close spiral winding for maximum strength when compressed, gear casing has a long spiral winding for maximum signal accuracy.

◆ **Cassette:** the cluster of sprockets attached to your back wheel.

◆ **Cassette joint:** not to be confused with a cassette, this is a fiddly metal contraption fitting over the sprocket of Shimano hub gears. Rotating the cassette joint, using the gear cable, selects one of the internal gear ratios.

◆ **Chain-cleaning box:** clever device for making chain cleaning less of a messy chore, and so increasing the chances of you doing it. (Now you just need a chain-cleaning-box-cleaning box.)

◆ **Chainring:** one of the rings of teeth your pedals are connected to.

- **Chainset:** the chainset is made up of three chainrings that pull the chain around them when you turn the pedals.

- **Chainsuck:** a bad thing! When your chain doesn't drop neatly off the bottom of the chainring, but gets pulled up and around the back, jamming between chainring and chainstay. Usually caused by worn parts, although occasionally completely inexplicable.

- **City bars:** curving upwards and backwards towards you, these handlebars are comfortable and allow you to sit quite upright – the style of bars often seen on Dutch town bikes.

- **Clamp bolt:** these hold cables in place. There is usually a groove on the component, indicating exactly where the cable should be clamped.

- **Cleat:** a metal key-plate bolted to the bottom of your shoe that locks securely into the pedal and releases instantly when you twist your foot.

- **Clipless pedal:** a pedal built around a spring that locks onto a matching cleat on your shoe, locking you in securely and releasing you instantly when you twist your foot.

- **Coil springs:** usually steel, but occasionally titanium, these provide a durable, reliable conventional spring in forks and rear shocks.

- **Compression damping:** control of the speed at which forks or shock can be compressed.

- **Cone:** curved nut, with a smooth track that traps bearings while allowing them to move freely around the axle, yet leaving no room for side-to-side movement. The amount of space available for the bearings is adjusted by moving the cone along the axle, which is then locked into place with the locknut.

- **Crank:** your pedals bolt onto these. The left-hand one has a reverse pedal thread.

- **Crank extractor:** tool for removing cranks from axles. Two different kinds are available – one for tapered axles, one for splined axles.

- **Cup and cone bearings:** where the bearings roll around a cup on either side of the hub, trapped in place by a cone on either side. Set the distance between the cones, adjusted by turning the cones so that they move along the axle threads, so that the wheel can turn freely with no side-to-side movement.

- **Damping:** damping controls how fast a suspension unit reacts to a force.

- **Derailleur:** see Front derailleur and Rear derailleur

- **Derailleur hanger:** the part the rear derailleur bolts onto. These are usually the first casualty of a crash, bending when the rear derailleur hits the ground, and once bent make for shifting sluggish. Luckily, hangers are quick and easy to replace, but there is no standard size; take your old one when you buy a new one, and get a spare for next time too.

- **Disc brake:** these use a calliper, mounted next to the front or rear hub, braking on a rotor, or disc bolted to the hub. Hydraulic versions are very powerful. Using a separate braking surface also means the rim isn't worn out with the brake pads.

- **Dish:** rims need to be adjusted to sit directly in the centre line of your frame between the outer faces of the axle locknuts. Adding cassettes or discs to one side or the other of the hub means the rim needs to be tensioned more on one side than the other, to make room for the extra parts.

- **Dishing tool:** allows you to test the position of the rim relative to the end of the axle on either side of the hub.

- **DOT fluid:** is used in DOT hydraulic brakes. Higher numbers, eg, 5.1 rather than 4.0, have higher boiling temperatures.

◆ **Drivetrain:** a collective name for all the transmission components – chain, derailleurs, shifters, cassette and chainset.

◆ **Drop bars:** these curve forwards and downwards and are usually seen on road bikes. The brake- and gear-levers are combined into one unit for fast and instinctive shifting.

◆ **Duct tape:** like the Force, it has a dark side, a light side, and holds together the fabric of the universe.

◆ **Dynamo bottle:** small generator that runs off the sidewall of your tyre, making electricity for your lights.

◆ **Elastomers:** a simple spring medium, usually now only found in cheap forks.

◆ **End-cap (cable end-cap):** these are crushed onto the ends of cables to prevent them fraying and stabbing you when you adjust them.

◆ **End-stop screw:** these limit the travel of the derailleurs, preventing them from dropping the chain off either side of the cassette or chainset.

◆ **Eye bolt:** found on cantilever brakes. The stud of the brake block passes through the eye of the bolt. Tightening the nut on the back of the bolt wedges the stud against a curved washer, holding the brake block firmly in place.

◆ **Ferrule:** protective end-cap for outer casing, supporting it where it fits into barrel-adjusters or cable stops.

◆ **Fixed wheel:** without a ratcheting mechanism in the back wheel, the pedals must keep turning with the back wheel. Beloved of couriers worldwide, they allow you to control the speed of your back wheel precisely, and look cool parked outside the coffee shop while you wait for your next package.

◆ **Freehub:** ratcheting mechanism that allows the back wheel to freewheel when you stop pedalling. It's bolted to the back wheel and has splines the cassette slides onto. This is the part that makes the evocative 'tick tick tick' noise as you cycle along.

◆ **Freewheel:** an older version of the sprocket cluster on the back wheel, which combines the sprockets and ratcheting mechanism in one unit. Freewheels are rarely used for multi-speed bikes now – the cassette/freehub set-up is far stronger as it supports the bearings nearer the ends of the axle – but freewheels are often found on singlespeed bikes.

◆ **Front derailleur:** moves the chain between the chainrings on your chainset.

◆ **Gear ratio:** the number of times your back wheel turns with one revolution of the pedal. Calculated by dividing chainring size by sprocket size, and multiplying by wheel size in inches.

◆ **Guide jockey:** the upper of the two jockey wheels on the rear derailleur, this does the actual derailing, guiding the chain from one sprocket to the next as the derailleur cage moves across beneath the cassette.

◆ **Hop:** sections of the rim where the spokes don't have enough tension and bulge out further from the hub than the rest of the rim.

◆ **Hub gears:** also known as internal gears, these have a single sprocket and chainring, with three, four, seven, eight or 14 gears concealed within the rear hub. The added bulk of the rear hub means they're affectionately known as 'tin can gears'.

◆ **Hydraulic brakes:** usually disc brakes, these use hydraulic fluid to push pistons inside the brake calliper against a rotor on the hub. The key factor is that brake fluid compresses little under pressure, thus accurately transmitting all movement at the brake-lever to the calliper.

◆ **Indexing:** setting up the tension in gear cables so shifter click moves the chain across neatly to the next sprocket or chainring.

◆ **Instruction manuals:** often ignored or junked, these contain vital information. Keep them and refer to them!

◆ **International Standard:** refers to both rotor fitting and calliper fitting. International Standard rotors and hubs have six bolts. International Standard callipers are fixed to the bike with bolts that point across the frame, not along it.

◆ **ISIS:** a standard for bottom brackets and chainsets, with 10 evenly spaced splines.

◆ **Jockey wheels:** the small black-toothed wheels that route the chain around the derailleur.

◆ **Lacing:** weaving spokes to connect hub to rim. This part of wheel building looks difficult but is easy once you know how.

◆ **Link wire:** used in cantilever brakes, this connects the pair of brake shoes to the brake cable. It is designed to be fail-safe; if the brake cable snaps, the link wire falls off harmlessly rather than jamming in the tyre knobbles and locking your wheel. You are still left with no brake though...

◆ **Lockring:** used on bottom brackets and barrel-adjusters, these are turned to wedge against frame or brake-lever to stop the adjustment you've made rattling loose.

◆ **Lower legs:** the lower part of suspension forks which attaches to brake and wheel.

◆ **Mineral oil:** a hydraulic brake fluid, similar to DOT fluid. Must only be used with systems designed for mineral oil. Greener than DOT and less corrosive.

◆ **Modulation:** the ratio between brake-lever movement and brake pad movement, or how your brake actually feels.

◆ **Needle bearing:** similar to a ball bearing, but in the shape of a thin rod rather than a ball. There is more contact area between bearing and bearing surface than with the ball type, so they are supposed to last longer, but can be tricky to adjust. Usually found in headsets, although some very nice bottom brackets also use needle bearings.

◆ **Nest:** the hanger or stop in a brake-lever or gear shifter that holds the nipple on the end of the brake or gear cable.

◆ **Nipple:** (1) the blob of metal at the end of a cable that stops it slipping through the nest; (2) the nut on the end of a spoke that secures it to the rim and allows you to adjust the spoke tension; (3) some perfectly ordinary part of your bicycle that many women need to buy but which causes the pimply youth in the bike shop to blush furiously when asked for it.

◆ **Noodle:** short metal tube that guides the end of the brake cable into V-brake hanger.

◆ **Octalink:** Shimano eight-splined bottom bracket/chainset fitting.

◆ **One-key release:** axle bolt and special washer which fit permanently to the bike and double as a crank extractor.

◆ **Overshoes:** nylon or Gore-Tex bootees that fit over your cycling shoes to keep the weather out. They're quite bulky, so you feel slightly foolish in them, but it's better than feeling stylish with cold feet.

◆ **Pannier:** bag or bags that sit on either side of your rack.

◆ **Pawl:** sprung lever inside ratcheting mechanism in the rear hub. It's flicked out of the way when the ratchet moves one way, and catches on the ratchet teeth the other way – this allows you to freewheel.

◆ **Pinch bolt:** a version of a clamp bolt, where the cable passes through a hole in the middle of the bolt, rather than under a washer beside the bolt. Occasionally found on cantilever straddle hangers.

◆ **Pinch puncture:** when the tyre hits an edge hard enough to squash the tube on the tyre-rim and puncture it. Also known as a snakebite flat, because it makes two neat vertical holes a rim's width apart. Apparently this is what a snake bite looks like, although I've never had a problem with snakes biting my inner tubes.

◆ **Pivot:** (1) bearing on suspension frame that allows one part of the frame to move against another; (2) rod or bearing around which part of a component rotates.

◆ **Post mount:** where brake callipers are mounted with bolts that point along the frame, rather than across. These are less common than the alternative, the International Standard mount, but easier to adjust.

◆ **Preload:** initial adjustment made to suspension springs to tune forks or shock to your weight, usually made with preload adjustment knob, or by adding or removing air from air springs.

◆ **Presta valve:** also known as high pressure valve. These are more reliable than Schraeder valves, which are designed for lower-pressure car and motorbike tyres. Their only disadvantage is they cannot be inflated on garage forecourts.

◆ **Puncture-resistant tyres:** these contain a strip of tough, pliable material under the tyre tread, preventing almost all of the glass and shards on the road from getting through to your tube.

◆ **Rapidrise (low-normal):** a rear derailleur where the cable pulls the chain from larger to smaller sprockets, then when cable tension is released the spring pulls the chain back from smaller to larger sprocket.

◆ **Rear derailleur:** mechanism attached to the frame on the right-hand side of the rear wheel. Moves the chain from one sprocket to the next, changing the gear ratio, when you move the shifter on your handlebars. Makes odd grinding noises when not adjusted properly.

◆ **Rebound damping:** controlling the speed at which the fork or shock re-extends after being compressed.

◆ **Reservoir:** reserve pool of hydraulic damping fluid, in a chamber at the brake-lever. Having a reservoir of cool fluid, a distance away from the hot rotor and calliper, helps minimise fluid expansion under heavy braking.

◆ **Reverse thread:** in which the spiral of the thread runs the opposite way to normal – undoing clockwise, tightening anticlockwise.

◆ **Rotor:** bolted to the hub, this is the braking surface of a disc brake.

◆ **Sag:** the amount of travel you use sitting normally on your bike. Setting up suspension with sag gives a reserve of travel above the neutral position.

◆ **Schraeder valve:** fat, car-type valve. The inventor, Franz Schraeder, is buried in a magical spot at the Cirque de Gavarne in the French Pyrenees.

◆ **Seal:** prevents dirt, mud and dust creeping into the parts of hubs, suspension units, headsets, bottom brackets and anything else where the preferred lubricant is grease rather than mud.

◆ **Seat post clamp:** the plates and bolts that connect the seat post firmly to your saddle.

◆ **Seatstays:** part of your frame, these connect the middle of your back wheel to the junction where your seatpost is attached.

◆ **Shim:** a thin piece of metal used to make two parts fit together precisely. The washers between IS callipers and the frame are shims, because they hold the calliper precisely in position.

◆ **Shimano joining pin:** once split, Shimano chains must only be joined with the correct joining pin. Attempting to rejoin the chain using the original rivet will damage the chain plates.

◆ **Singlespeed (1x1):** a state of peace obtained through self-liberation from the complexities of modern life by throwing away your gears.

◆ **Snakebite flat:** see pinch puncture.

◆ **Socket:** spanner shaped like a cup which holds the bolt securely on all the flats.

◆ **Splines:** ridges across a tool or component, designed to mesh with a matching part, so that the two parts turn together.

◆ **Split link:** chain link that can be split and rejoined by hand without damaging the adjacent links.

◆ **Sprocket:** toothed ring that meshes with the chain to rotate the rear wheel. The cassette consists of a row of different-sized sprockets.

◆ **Stanchions:** the upper part of the suspension forks that slide into the lower legs. These contain all the suspension gubbins – springs, damping rods and oil.

◆ **Standard tube:** a normal inner tube, designed to fit into a normal tyre, for those who don't need tubelessness.

◆ **Star-fanged nut (star nut, star-fangled nut):** pressed into the top of the steerer tube. The top-cap bolt threads into it, pushing down on the stem and pulling up on the steerer tube.

◆ **Stationary pad:** for disc brakes with one piston, the piston pushes a pad against the rotor, which in turn pushes the rotor against the stationary pad trapping the rotor between moving and stationary pads.

◆ **Steerer tube:** the single tube that extends from the top of the forks through the frame, with the stem bolted on the top.

◆ **Stem:** the component that connects your handlebar to the top of your forks.

◆ **STi:** a combined brake-lever and gear-shifter.

◆ **Stiff link:** where the plates of the chain are squashed too closely together to pass smoothly over the sprockets, jumping across teeth rather than meshing into the valleys between teeth.

◆ **Straddle wire:** connects the two units of a cantilever brake, via a straddle hanger on the brake cable.

◆ **Stress relief:** squeezing the spokes to settle them into place as you build a wheel.

◆ **Swingarm:** the rear of a suspension frame, to which the back wheel attaches.

◆ **Tension jockey:** the lower of the two jockey wheels on the rear derailleur, sprung so it constantly pushes backwards, taking up slack in the chain created by the different-teeth-size combinations of sprockets and chainrings.

◆ **Toe-clip:** these survive today only in ghost form (and are the missing clip in clipless pedals). An unfortunate loss is the accompanying toe-strap, which was an occasionally priceless emergency item (see ziptie).

◆ **Toe-in:** setting up rim brakes so the front of the brake block touches momentarily earlier than the back, to prevent squeaking.

◆ **Top-cap:** the disc on the top of your stem, bolted into the star-fanged nut in the steerer tube. Provided the stem bolts are loose, adjusting the top-cap pushes the stem down the steerer tube, tightening the headset bearings. Always retighten the stem afterwards!

◆ **Trailerbike:** these have a single wheel and clamp to the back of an ordinary bike, turning it into a mini-tandem. The trailerbike part has its own pedals and sometimes gears too.

◆ **Travel:** the total amount of movement in the fork or shock. The longer the travel, the heavier and beefier the fork or shock must be.

◆ **Triggershifters:** a gear-shifter with a pair of levers, one pulling, the other releasing the cable.

◆ **Truing wheels:** adjusting the tension in each spoke so the rim doesn't wobble from side to side when the wheel spins.

◆ **Tubeless:** a weight-saving tyre design where the bead of the tyre locks into the rim, creating an airtight seal that needs no inner tube.

◆ **Twistshifters:** gear-shifters that work by twisting the handlebar grip. Turning one way pulls through cable, turning the other way releases cable.

◆ **Tyre boot:** patch stuck onto the inside of a tyre to prevent the inner tube bulging out of big gashes.

◆ **URT:** Unified Rear Triangle. A suspension frame design where bottom bracket, chainset and front derailleur are located together on the swingarm (rear end of the bike), so the movement of the swingarm never affects the length of the chain.

◆ **UST:** Universal Standard for Tubeless, an agreed standard for the exact shape of rims and tyre beads, so that tyres and rims made by different manufacturers lock together neatly for an airtight seal.

◆ **V-brake:** rim brakes where two vertical (hence 'V') units hold the blocks, connected by the brake cable.

◆ **Vernier gauge:** tool for making very accurate measurements.

◆ **Virtual pivot:** in suspension, this is when the swingarm is made of a series of linkages that combine to rotate around a position. Rather than a physical location on the frame; this position may be a point around which the frame would rotate if it was a simple swingarm.

◆ **Wheel jig:** a frame for holding a wheel during truing, with adjustable indicators that can be set close to the rim to allow you to estimate how round and straight the rim is.

◆ **Ziptie:** for whenever you need to connect one thing to another thing.

Index

Notes

Notes